Local Economic and Employment Development (LEED)

Entrepreneurship
and Higher Education

OECD

ORGANISATION FOR ECONOMIC CO-OPERATION AND DEVELOPMENT

The OECD is a unique forum where the governments of 30 democracies work together to address the economic, social and environmental challenges of globalisation. The OECD is also at the forefront of efforts to understand and to help governments respond to new developments and concerns, such as corporate governance, the information economy and the challenges of an ageing population. The Organisation provides a setting where governments can compare policy experiences, seek answers to common problems, identify good practice and work to co-ordinate domestic and international policies.

The OECD member countries are: Australia, Austria, Belgium, Canada, the Czech Republic, Denmark, Finland, France, Germany, Greece, Hungary, Iceland, Ireland, Italy, Japan, Korea, Luxembourg, Mexico, the Netherlands, New Zealand, Norway, Poland, Portugal, the Slovak Republic, Spain, Sweden, Switzerland, Turkey, the United Kingdom and the United States. The Commission of the European Communities takes part in the work of the OECD.

OECD Publishing disseminates widely the results of the Organisation's statistics gathering and research on economic, social and environmental issues, as well as the conventions, guidelines and standards agreed by its members.

Corrigenda to OECD publications may be found on line at: *www.oecd.org/publishing/corrigenda*.
© OECD 2008

Foreword

In collaboration with the International Entrepreneurship Forum, the Local Economic and Employment Development (LEED) Programme of the OECD has carried out extensive research into the role of higher education in fostering entrepreneurship. In addition to undertaking a cross-country comparison of the different approaches to entrepreneurship teaching taken by higher education institutions in North America and West and East Europe, the work has also focused on practices in the transfer of knowledge from higher education to new and small enterprises.

This book presents the results of this research, addressing the major challenges faced by policy makers to meet the developmental needs of higher education institutions so that they can continue to compete for the best students and researchers whilst fully exploiting the potential for a new revenue stream by creating structures to share knowledge with industry.

Higher education institutions can play an important role in teaching entrepreneurial skills to young people, increasing the pool of those who may go on to start and successfully grow entrepreneurial ventures. They can also foster entrepreneurship by supporting promoting university spin-offs and research collaborations with small firms. However, obtaining the benefits for society and for higher education institutions themselves requires a shift from past practices to embrace a more entrepreneurial vision of the university, one that is better suited to todays' economy and society.

The book examines how to meet this challenge, providing a a number of ideas, models and recommendations. In the area of entrepreneurship teaching, it stresses, among other issues, the importance of integrating entrepreneurship in the wider curriculum, using interactive teaching methods and profiling role models.

It also gives a wide-ranging overview of knowledge transfer mechanisms from universities and other tertiary colleges to small firms and proposes a series of recommendations to strengthen knowledge transfers and the commercialisation of research.

The book is intended for academics, policy makers and practitioners and all those in the business community who want to learn how to introduce successful entrepreneurship promotion into university teaching and research activities.

Sergio Arzeni
Director, OECD Centre for Entrepreneurship, SMEs
& Local Development

ACKNOWLEDGEMENTS

The Local Economic and Employment Development (LEED) Programme of the OECD would like to acknowledge the contribution of the Autonomous Province of Trento in Italy to this publication, through its financial and logistical support to the OECD LEED Trento Centre for Local Development, which participated in the development of this publication.

We would also like to acknowledge the valuable input of the University of Essex, School of Entrepreneurship and Business, and the International Entrepreneurship Foundation in the preparation of this publication. Special thanks are extended to Professor Jay Mitra of the University of Essex for his intellectual input as President of the Scientific Committee on Entrepreneurship to the OECD LEED Trento Centre, and representative of the University of Essex and International Entrepreneurship Foundation.

The publication was managed and edited by Jonathan Potter, Senior Economist in the Local Economic and Employment Development (LEED) Programme of the Organisation for Economic Co-operation and Development (OECD). Very helpful support was provided by Alessandra Proto and Roberto Chizzali of the OECD LEED Trento Centre for Local Development, and Lucy Clarke and Damian Garnys of the OECD LEED Programme in Paris.

Table of Contents

Foreword 3

Executive Summary.. 11

Chapter 1 Towards an Analytical Framework for Policy Development............ 17

   Introduction.. 18
   Strategies, mechanisms and instruments.. 20
   The learning context.. 28
   The local context.. 33
   Conclusion 39
   Bibliography 41

Chapter 2 Higher Education's Role in Entrepreneurship and Economic
Development.. 45

   Introduction.. 46
   The policy context: new ventures in the economy................................. 46
   Higher education and economic development 47
   The scope and value of entrepreneurship education at universities 50
   Conclusion 60
   Bibliography 63

Chapter 3 Entrepreneurship Education in an Age of Chaos, Complexity
and Disruptive Change.. 65

   Introduction.. 66
   The four fundamental themes... 67
   What content should make up the entrepreneurship curriculum? 78
   What should be the nature of the environment for teaching and learning about,
   for and through enterprise? 84
   Who should teach entrepreneurship? 87
   What learning methodologies and processes should be utilised during teaching
   and learning about, for and through enterprise?..................................... 88
   Conclusion 90
   Bibliography 92

Chapter 4   Entrepreneurship Education in the United States **95**

Introduction 96
Entrepreneurship education 96
Education methodologies 100
Methodology 103
Analysis 104
Conclusion 110
Bibliography 114

Chapter 5   Entrepreneurship Education in Europe **119**

Introduction 120
Current entrepreneurship policy challenges in Europe 120
Analysis of trends 122
Opportunities and challenges for entrepreneurship education in Europe 126
Policy recommendations 132
Conclusion 136
Bibliography 137

Chapter 6   Benchmarking Entrepreneurship Education across US, Canadian and Danish Universities **139**

Introduction 140
The importance of entrepreneurship education 140
Approaches to entrepreneurship education 142
Methodology 143
Share of students attending courses in entrepreneurship 147
Scope of entrepreneurship activities at the universities 148
Insights and policy implications 158
Conclusion 162
Bibliography 163

Chapter 7   Entrepreneurship Education for Central, Eastern and Southeastern Europe **165**

Introduction 166
The United States vs. other OECD countries: A continental divide? 167
Undergraduate vs. graduate entrepreneurship education 169
Entrepreneurship education in Central, Eastern and Southeastern Europe 177
Assessing the impact of entrepreneurship training in higher education 182
Lessons learned 187
Conclusion 189
Bibliography 190

Chapter 8   Developments in the Teaching of Entrepreneurship in European Transition Economies 193

Introduction 194
Entrepreneurship in the European transition countries 194
Previous analyses of the entrepreneurship education 197
Entrepreneurship-oriented teaching in Central and Eastern Europe 198
Discussion of results 201
Best practices of entrepreneurship teaching in transition economies 205
Conclusion 208
Bibliography 211

Chapter 9   Higher Education, Knowledge Transfer Mechanisms and the Promotion of SME Innovation 213

Introduction 214
Higher education institutions as infrastructure 217
Small and medium-sized enterprises 217
Policies for higher education institutions 219
Policies for small and medium-sized enterprises 222
Policies for technology transfer and knowledge transfer 223
Gatekeepers 223
Conclusion 224
Bibliography 226

Chapter 10   University Knowledge Transfer and the Role of Academic Spin-offs 235

Introduction 236
Scope and coverage 236
Current policy issues 237
The spin-off route: The Swedish example 242
The licensing route: The US example 246
Conclusion 248
Bibliography 251

Chapter 11   Technology Commercialisation and Universities in Canada 255

Introduction 256
The context of Canadian universities 256
Funding of university research, science and technology 257
The "new" mandate of universities: Technology commercialisation 259
Case Study: University technology transfer in Canada's Technology Triangle 260
Supporting, encouraging and teaching entrepreneurship at universities ... 261
Case Study: Master of Business, Entrepreneurship and Technology programme 263
University technology transfer challenges in Canada 265

Conclusion 266
Bibliography 267

**Chapter 12 Promoting Innovation in Slovenia Through Knowledge
Transfer to SMEs... 271**

Introduction.. 272
The policy framework for knowledge transfer... 273
Outcomes of knowledge transfer policies 275
Conclusion 284
Bibliography 287

**Chapter 13 Knowledge Transfer Mechanisms in the European Transition
Economies.. 289**

Introduction.. 290
Defining knowledge and technology transfer 291
Theoretical foundations of the field survey... 292
Case studies of university-business linkages 297
Policy implications... 303
Conclusion 308
Bibliography 310

**Chapter 14 Entrepreneurship and Higher Education: Future Policy
Directions... 313**

Introduction.. 314
HEI missions and public policy 318
Forms of HEI entrepreneurship engagement 321
Policy recommendations 328

Executive Summary

Higher education institutions (HEIs) support enterprise creation through their three key missions of research, teaching, and interaction with the wider community. Despite the traditional "ivory tower" image of higher education, many universities and colleges have long collaborated with business – a form of interaction that has lately acquired greater urgency. Increased national and international competition among HEIs for students and researchers, limits to the capacity of public funding to meet HEI development needs, and a changing, more innovation-driven economy have had a profound impact on higher education and its role in supporting entrepreneurship and entrepreneurs. The HEIs' engagement in entrepreneurship is both a new, potentially lucrative revenue stream and a new tool for them to compete for other resources. A growing number of institutions are providing entrepreneurship education and creating structures for sharing knowledge with industry – and the success of that trend will determine the ability of the public sector, businesses and HEIs to meet their complementary objectives.

This book introduces the reader to the major challenges and international experiences in higher education's promotion of entrepreneurship. It attempts to uncover insights into how that promotion can take place, and what HEIs, businesses and public policy makers can do to facilitate the process. The United States has led the way, and the lessons from its experience are closely examined along with important developments in Canada, Europe and elsewhere.

The main messages to emerge are as follows:

- A transformation in the activities of HEIs is required if they are to play their full part in stimulating economic growth and competitiveness in the modern knowledge economy. Greater weight needs to be accorded activities that support entrepreneurship and innovation, in particular through entrepreneurship education and knowledge transfers to enterprises.

- Leading universities and colleges have focused attention on developing new and innovative approaches to teaching entrepreneurship as well as

ENTREPRENEURSHIP AND HIGHER EDUCATION – ISBN- 9789264044098 © OECD 2008

new frameworks to support knowledge transfers to enterprises. Some are helping to commercialise the results of university research by teachers and graduates. Other institutions need to learn about what works in this domain, and to introduce appropriate activities in their own contexts.

- HEIs, governments and businesses all have a role to play in encouraging greater support for entrepreneurship in the HEI sector. Indeed, efforts may be particularly successful when they involve co-ordinated actions by these three categories of players.

- Differences in the environments in which various HEIs operate need to be recognised. Taking account of the specialisation of establishments and adaptation to local conditions is preferable to seeking uniform provision. Experimentation is to be encouraged, as the experiences outlined here will demonstrate.

The book begins with an analytical framework for investigating entrepreneurship in higher education from a policy development perspective. The emphasis is placed firmly on the importance of appreciating the specific situations and environments in which activities are undertaken. The content following this introduction examines in turn the two critical functions of HEI activities that support entrepreneurship and innovation.

The first of these is entrepreneurship teaching. The reader is given an overview of higher education institutions and how their interaction with industry has matured over time to address more directly issues of training for small and medium-sized enterprises (SMEs) and new business creation. Drawing on experiences in several countries, the chapter explores how differences in the vocabulary of enterprise and management can act as barriers to productive partnerships between universities and businesses. The important distinction is made between *entrepreneurial* education and training, which could apply to all forms of education, and *entrepreneurship* education and training, which is specifically concerned with new venture creation and innovation. The supply of entrepreneurship teaching in HEIs needs to be better aligned with small firms' expectations and their training needs at different points in their development.

It may seem ironic that a complex, chaotic and disruptive environment is often described as providing a necessary background for entrepreneurial activity; yet the focus on traditional competencies and skills in various forms of business and entrepreneurship education prevents the development of creative approaches to generating new learning methods. While there is a lack of consensus over what constitutes entrepreneurship education, learning methods based in the flow of experiences, experiments, ideas and realisation are central to the pedagogy of entrepreneurship.

It is argued that Europe has much to learn from US entrepreneurship education approaches. Comparing the two, the book draws a number of key messages for all those seeking to improve entrepreneurship education in HEIs. The discussion stresses the importance of segmenting programmes, evaluating programme impacts, integrating entrepreneurship in the wider curriculum, setting high quality standards, building a strong pipeline of entrepreneurship teachers, using interactive teaching methods, ensuring appropriate funding, encouraging cross-border collaborations, facilitating spin-offs and profiling role models.

In fact, the early start in the United States has resulted in a shift of emphasis – from entrepreneurial characteristics to the functional aspects of business, such as marketing, human resources and (more recently) new forms of teaching structured round challenges to strategy development. A survey reported finds that traditional methods of business plan writing coexist with teaching the "nuts and bolts" of small business management, although there is evidence of diverse empirical teaching and evaluation pedagogies. Technology plays an increasingly important role, as does the growing interest in different forms of provision in and out of the classroom, often involving different providers.

Entrepreneurship education is benchmarked across 27 universities in the United States, Canada and Denmark. The US universities have a wider variety of entrepreneurship programmes and classes, and the largest proportion of students attending them. The Canadian universities are more advanced than their Danish counterparts in the breadth and depth of their courses. This tends to confirm the assessment that US universities are currently leading the way in entrepreneurship education. Two types of entrepreneurship education models are identified: the magnet model, where a single entity facilitates entrepreneurship classes for all departments; and the radiant model, where individual departments develop their own offers. It is important for each HEI to select one of these models.

What follows is a critique of entrepreneurship education in Central and Eastern European countries, starting with a comparison with provision in the United States and other OECD countries. A difference is identified between the more pragmatic approaches to entrepreneurship education in the United States and the more academically orientated programmes in Europe. Certain institutional deficiencies are highlighted in many Central and Eastern European countries, including the lack of qualified teachers. There is also strong variation in the study and practice of entrepreneurship, with certain countries, such as the new European Union states, funding private foundations for such study. Early mechanisms to evaluate programmes should be developed as the latter evolve in these countries.

Provision of entrepreneurship education is then mapped for 22 European transition economies. Approximately half of the institutions surveyed offered this education. Recommendations are made for improving provision, including enlarging the number of HEIs offering courses; facilitating the sharing of good practice in teaching; developing courses to build entrepreneurial attitudes; and relaxing the regulations allowing entrepreneurs to teach.

The book then goes on to develop its second main theme: knowledge transfer from higher education institutions to business. Five chapters cover conceptual issues regarding transfer mechanisms, while the others examine specific experiences in Canada, Slovenia and the Central and Eastern European region.

The discussion begins by addressing the role of HEIs in promoting innovation in small and medium-sized enterprises within their regions, through a variety of knowledge transfer mechanisms. While public policies such as cluster policies have been successful in bringing universities into a number of formal knowledge transfer programmes, much of the knowledge transferred or shared by universities is unintended, unplanned and informal in character. This subtle and apparently invisible form of interaction does not attract as much attention as do alliances with larger firms and the tangible forms of technology transfer that bring prestige, revenue and contacts to students and staff. In terms of public policy, it is argued that generating social capital through networking is critical to strengthening knowledge transfer and seizing the opportunity for close interaction offered by geographical proximity – especially in places where a lower density of firms makes networking more of an effort.

The focus then shifts to academic spin-offs; these represent a critical vector of knowledge transfer in technology-intensive industries, because of the role of the spin-offs as mediators between HEIs and industry, and as research boutiques. The frequency, growth patterns and innovativeness of these spin-offs are examined, along with their function as "innovation providers" and contributors to the commercialisation of university research. Spin-off activity is strongly influenced by the academic and cultural profiles of the institutions involved, as illustrated in the case of Sweden. There is a warning that policy may be tempted to focus on high-growth firms at the expense of spin-offs, solely on the basis of evidence of direct job creation and without analysing the indirect effects on the economy more generally. Clear policies are needed to create either a high number of small entrepreneurial academic spin-offs or the generation of a smaller number of high-growth firms.

In Canada, the importance of commercialising university research for the sake of both the economy and university finances is a frequent theme in discussions among university administrators, communities, business and government. Many Canadian HEIs are renewing and expanding their commitment to commercialisation, with various initiatives to foster entrepreneurial attitudes and skills among both students and staff. Studies in Canada have identified a linear relationship between the technology transferred and research expenditure. Local conditions, especially for resources such as support for staff dedicated to technology transfer, are a major determinant of the effectiveness of technology transfer; there is no correlation between intellectual property ownership and better technology transfer. The three constituent parts of policy – an innovation strategy, suitable mechanisms of technology transfer and effective entrepreneurship education – are essential ingredients of the university-industry interface.

Slovenia is relatively successful in innovation by many measures, but the SME sector lags behind. Three significant barriers to greater HEI contributions to SME innovation are identified: artificial demarcation between pure and applied research in the HEI sector; the absence of targeted incentives for academics; and the relatively easy returns on investment in technology transfer to large firms. A series of recommendations is proposed to strengthen HEI-SME knowledge transfer; among them are the suggestions that universities alter their structures for academic and applied research, boost incubating activities, and establish technology transfer offices and spin-off centres.

Following discussion of Canada and Slovenia, there is a wide-ranging overview of knowledge transfer mechanisms from universities and other HEIs to SMEs, with particular reference to Central and Eastern European countries. The overview covers considerable ground and provides a theoretical framework for the study of what is described as knowledge integration and collaboration. Attention is drawn to a long list of mechanisms and instruments, including traineeships and internships, continuing professional development, collaborative research, one-stop centres, business incubation, spin-offs and spin-ins (of new ideas from business to be developed in collaboration with the university), and licensing. The reader is then given the results of a field survey of eight universities in different Central and Eastern European countries; each case study surveys the links between these universities and the business community.

The book's final chapter sets out the principal conclusions and main recommendations from the volume as a whole.

Chapter 1

Towards an Analytical Framework for Policy Development

by
Jay Mitra
University of Essex, United Kingdom

This introductory chapter provides an analytical framework for developing policies to promote entrepreneurship in higher education. It addresses two themes essential to the role of higher education institutions (HEIs): "knowledge transfer" and "entrepreneurship education and training". The chapter offers key reasons for fostering entrepreneurship in HEIs, and the nature, type and scope of entrepreneurship that can help to add value to both HEIs and the wider economy. There is a detailed and analytical account of some of the underpinning philosophies that have influenced current thinking on entrepreneurship education and its direct and indirect manifestations, such as technology transfer mechanisms and academic spin-offs. The chapter also considers the crucial issue of the context in which various developments take shape. This analysis forms the basis for developing a framework within which policy can be created to help foster entrepreneurship in universities.

Introduction

Entrepreneurship has entered the realm of "higher" learning – and as protectors of that realm, higher education institutions (HEIs) across the world have taken up the challenge of entrepreneurship. They support entrepreneurship education and training and engage in a variety of knowledge transfer activities that promote entrepreneurship, either directly (as in academic spin-offs) or indirectly (through research, training and education). Increasingly, this occurs at the regional level where HEIs enter into different relationships with other stakeholders pursuing economic growth and competitiveness.

The much praised and well-publicised roles of HEIs in new venture creation and the evolution of an entrepreneurial and learning environment – especially in the United States, and with a growing tradition in Western Europe and other OECD countries – suggest that certain antecedents are worth consideration. Since education and especially universities play a vital role in the transformation of economies and societies, the specific role of HEIs in fostering entrepreneurship was considered to be an appropriate topic of investigation, discourse and dissemination.

What lessons can be learned from good or best practice in other OECD countries? To what extent do OECD member countries and other countries whose economies are characterised by entrepreneurial growth benefit from the contribution of HEIs? What forms of involvement by HEIs would allow for optimal or maximum levels of impact on the economy? What were the driving factors for university involvement in entrepreneurial activity? Two themes or strands of higher education's role in fostering entrepreneurship inform this book's enquiry:

Theme 1: Higher education and entrepreneurship training – addresses the provision of entrepreneurship education and training and how they contribute to the promotion of successful new firm starts and small business management.

Theme 2: Knowledge transfer from higher education to SMEs – covers the mechanisms used by HEIs to enable the transfer of knowledge to SMEs in the regions in which they are located.

The two principal themes embrace a number of sub-themes reflecting the complexity of university-industry, university-SME and university-regional economy linkages. First, the locations of certain universities, and indeed of firms in particular regions, have a bearing on the nature, scope and outcome of such linkages. Secondly, the nexus of relationships are often a function of the state of the economy, the propensity of firms to absorb knowledge from universities, and the capability of universities to meet the needs of firms in the region. Thus context is a key consideration. Thirdly, while universities may often engage, formally or informally, with firms in a variety of ways, the specific impact on new firm creation is a peculiar and difficult outcome to measure. The issue is a contentious one since other factors, from individual or team motivation to venture finance and public policy, also influence the phenomenon. New firm creation follows unstructured paths, and universities are often not well placed to work in such chaotic environments. The randomness of events and activities that prevails in such uncertain environments challenges the typical need for the codification of information and knowledge by universities.

Finally, not all universities with similar capabilities have the same impact on their region, thus suggesting the varied culture of different regions and the strategic role and function of separate universities.

Different countries offer different contexts for discussion on the topic of entrepreneurship, and especially the role of HEIs in encouraging entrepreneurship. For example, the transition to market economies from a variety of command structures present Central and South Eastern European (CESE) countries with specific problems and opportunities. The economies and societies of these countries have witnessed variegated statist hegemony over economic activity; that has resulted in some states being in a better position to make the transition than other economies (Formica *et al.*, chapter 13 of this volume). Add to this complex set of circumstances the purpose and state of higher education and the role of universities in those countries. It is not difficult to infer from this description that any focus on entrepreneurship and higher education needs to take account of the environment, the institutional factors that provide the necessary rules and constraints for entrepreneurial activity and higher education involvement, and the organisational capabilities of both firms and universities to be part of an entrepreneurial network.

The rest of this chapter discusses three strands that should form the basis of an analytical framework:

- Recognition of the strategies, mechanisms and instruments used by HEIs to promote entrepreneurship, with a particular focus on entrepreneurship education and training (including vocational training) and knowledge transfer (including technology transfer and academic spin-offs).

- Understanding of the learning context and antecedents of HEIs, which inform both policies relating to higher education and the organisation of HEIs, and of how they influence the way HEIs foster entrepreneurship.

- Appreciation of the importance of the local or regional context.

Strategies, mechanisms and instruments

Numerous studies of HEI-industry links have identified support measures designed to create, develop and establish the ways HEIs interact with industry and the local community. Much of the direct impact can be measured by investigating the distribution of university employment, and local purchasing of goods and services. These are direct but static measures; they do not help to gain an understanding of the role of HEIs in fostering entrepreneurship. Promotion of entrepreneurship is better gauged by considering some of the indirect relationships that convey the dynamic environment of change in different economies.

As Goddard *et al.* (1994) and Howells, Nedeva and Greorghiou (1998) have illustrated in their studies, typical support measures include the transfer of technology based on research, the creation of new firms from university research activities or academic spin-offs, work-related training, business training, economic policy development support, and certain non-educational services.

Technology and knowledge transfer and entrepreneurship

Technology transfer plays a central role in any university's external linkages with industry. Some of the reasons attributed to the increasing importance of technology transfer as the third mission of universities include (Goddard *et al.*, 1994):

- The transformation of industry's technology base to complex and diverse forms requiring access to external sources of knowledge and technology.

- The growing importance of SMEs [since Birch's (1979) seminal study on SMEs] – especially in high technology industries – as against the decline in employment in branch plants of large firms.

- Increasing interest in seeing enhanced industrial appropriation of knowledge produced by universities using public funds.

To this list can be added the need for HEIs to seek revenues from diverse funding sources, as public funding for both research and teaching has shrunk over the years.

In fact, the term "technology transfer" has been overtaken by the notion of "knowledge transfer" in the modern HEI-industry lexicography, because of the growing recognition of forms of knowledge that are both explicit (*i.e.* codified forms in manuals and texts) and tacit (*i.e.* uncodified forms residing only in an individual or a homogeneous collective of people in a given environment). Technology's association with "solid", codifiable processes or products implies that the transfer process is linear and that knowledge is produced first within HEIs before it is transferred to industry. This linear approach does not allow for the recognition of dual forms of knowledge. Kline and Rosenberg (1986) best articulate the multiple sources and the interactive model of the innovation process. Technology transfer also does not provide any room for the realisation of opportunities for new business creation, either in the form of academic spin-offs or in terms of providing appropriate knowledge-based resources for entrepreneurs outside the HEI.

Indeed the main process by which scientific and technological knowledge is exchanged with knowledge from different agents (entrepreneurs, large firms and the government) – namely, research collaboration, information and knowledge transfer, and spin-outs (new ventures created and floated by large firms or through the commercialisation of university-based research) – all contain ingredients critical to new venture creation in, and the competitiveness of, modern economies.

The best HEIs are global players, in that their knowledge-producing functions are at the cutting edge of research and valued, respected and sought after by industry across the world. That being the case, a regional agenda may appear to circumscribe their activities. However, because of the very reasons for the importance of technology transfer cited above, and the capacity of local firms to retain their competitive advantage, it is crucial that regions boasting the presence of innovative firms take advantage of premier league research and training expertise available locally. This nexus of interactions is more likely to take place in modern industrial clusters, where there is a presence of both innovative firms and industries. But there is no reason to believe that innovative firms in all regions will necessarily work in conjunction with local HEIs – especially where there is either a deficit of HEIs or a shortfall in the type of knowledge production demanded by industry. As Mitra and Abubakar (2005) show in their comparative study of two sub-regions in the United Kingdom, entrepreneurship is more likely to be sustainable where 1) there is a correlation between university research activity and local enterprise development; and 2) because of that correlation, higher levels of social capital are generated to further boost effective linkages between firms and HEIs.

There is a lack of empirical evidence showing a causal link between knowledge transfer activities and entrepreneurship. Perhaps it is difficult to demonstrate such links, as there are other factors – not least the availability of suitable forms of new venture finance influencing new business creation. However, there is some evidence to suggest that venture finance flows to regions that provide fertile ground for high-technology ventures. As stated earlier, much of the knowledge necessary for creating and sustaining these ventures is generated at the intersections of HEI-industry links. What can be demonstrated is the kind of relationship based more on associations, rather than cause and effect; this leads to the creation of associational economies (Cooke and Morgan, 1998).

Different forms of knowledge transfer in regions that promote entrepreneurship are socially embedded. This means that local institutions are themselves entrepreneurial in nature, and are able to respond flexibly to the specific needs of local environments (Gibb, 1996). They need to have absorptive capacity to take advantage of the opportunities for new venture creation that are on offer through knowledge transfer activities. In some cases they need to set up training programmes to help their staff acquire specialist skills with which to derive best value from those activities.

Entrepreneurship education and training

A distinction should be made at the outset between *skills training in relation to entrepreneurship*, and *entrepreneurship education and training*.

The fostering of entrepreneurship is not necessarily a function of the HEIs' direct intervention in new venture creation. It can also be a function of *skills training* – the training of people who could contribute to the development of entrepreneurial organisations through their employment. The focus on certain skills and competencies, especially those of problem solving, creativity, and interpersonal and cognitive skills, can lead to the development of entrepreneurial capabilities and mindsets necessary for entrepreneurial activity.

Both HEIs and business need to articulate, recognise and promote the type of skills that enable and enhance such capabilities. This aspect of training to support entrepreneurship is often ignored by HEIs, industry and policy makers. Such skills training can be embedded in the provision of HEIs.

Skills training in HEIs is also concerned with the employability of students. HEI effort has thus been directed at offering a range of skills and competencies, embedding them in the curriculum. Employer involvement in training and mentoring, both in the HEIs' provision and in the workplace, also feature prominently in various programmes. The nature of employee/employer involvement and questions of employability are a function of both the subjects studied at HEIs and different sectoral interests. Certain subjects (for example business studies or computer science) increasingly demand novel, innovative forms of or approaches to learning. These approaches involve the sharing of resources and differentiated pedagogic platforms. Entrepreneurship and business education, especially in the United States, makes wide use of entrepreneurs and industry practitioners in the teaching of programmes (Zahra and Welter, chapter 7 of this volume), thus adopting ideas similar to those related to work-based or workplace learning. These forms of entrepreneurial learning can better prepare employees and students for work in innovative organisations. They also contribute to independent forms of learning that allow for self-sufficiency in knowledge and skills acquisition.

Alongside the growth in indirect forms of promoting entrepreneurship, there is actual *entrepreneurship education and training*, a field to which HEIs in both OECD and non-OECD countries have begun to devote serious attention. The growing value of entrepreneurship as a subject of study is based on the following key factors (Mitra, 2002):

- The growing importance of SMEs and the evolution of large firms as distributed and semi-autonomous units of activity.

- The challenge to HEIs of meeting the demands of economic and social change, and the consequent attention to entrepreneurship in business education (Porter and McKibbin, 1988).

- The large volume of academic research and empirical evidence differentiating start-up venture activity and that of mature organisations (Hills and Morris, 1998).

- The need for graduates to acquire a wide array of entrepreneurial skills.

- The increasing cross-disciplinary and cross-functional activity in both education and industry, coupled with the idea that the qualitative, applied and subjective elements of study are as important as the quantitative, conceptual and analytical forms (Ivancevich, 1991).

The equation of entrepreneurship with SME development partly has to do with the role of SMEs in job creation and innovation, and their disproportionately larger presence among all firms in most economies. They are involved in new, pan-organisational forms of economic development, such as clusters, and they offer a competitive advantage through flexible specialisation, economies of scale and scope, and agglomeration. That has engendered interest in the type of people who engage in these activities (entrepreneurial people); the types of organisations created by these people or ones in which they thrive (entrepreneurial organisations); and the wider environment in which enterprising people and entrepreneurial organisations evolve (entrepreneurial environment).

Size is not, however, the key to appreciating entrepreneurship – which is, after all, a leaky concept (Mitra, 2002). The notions of "smallness", flexibility, innovation, new opportunity identification and realisation can also be said to apply to organisations that are non-SMEs. Larger, entrepreneurial firms increasingly demand entrepreneurial people and seek to operate in entrepreneurial environments. Community-based organisations seek creative, entrepreneurial people as they identify opportunities for self-sufficiency and innovative solutions to problems in creative environments. A wider application of the concept of entrepreneurship puts less emphasis on types and traits of entrepreneurs for particular forms of economic activity, and other static features. Rather, entrepreneurship is increasingly defined as the process of creating value by bringing together a unique package of resources to exploit an opportunity (Sahlman *et al.*, 1999). The people and organisations creating value are those whose behaviour and skills are applied individually or collectively to help individuals and organisations of various kinds to cope with uncertainty and complexity (Gibb, 1996).

How do HEIs in both OECD and other countries make provision for entrepreneurship education and training? Zahra and Welter (chapter 7) refer to the extensive and varied forms of entrepreneurship in the United States, from high school through to doctoral training. In US HEIs, most entrepreneurship education takes place at the graduate level, quite often allowing for a combination of the skills of traditional academics and those of entrepreneurs. The two groups co-teach a broad set of courses that use intellectual capital within universities and human capital in industry. Undergraduate training tends to focus on skills training and the functional aspects of new business creation (see Solomon, chapter 4 of this volume, for a detailed analysis of the content, forms and methods of study in the United States).

OECD countries tend to equate entrepreneurship more with the successful management of small business. Some of the new EU countries, such as Poland and Slovenia, have developed initiatives that reflect the tradition of vocational education centred round small business creation and ownership (Zahra and Welter, chapter 7 of this volume). Entrepreneurship education remains limited despite the creation of new chairs of entrepreneurship and centres for entrepreneurship research. Unlike the United States, European OECD countries tend to give their programmes a distinctive academic flavour, grounding the study of entrepreneurship in some of the traditional disciplines of economics, sociology, and psychology. There is a growing trend in science-based entrepreneurship, with science and technology curricula offering electives in entrepreneurship.

Varied modes and methods

A variety of methods – ranging from hands-on training, creativity techniques, case studies and communication training to interpersonal skills development, team working, the use of entrepreneurs, role playing and business plan development – inform the empirical thrust of entrepreneurship programmes (Zahra and Welter, chapter 7 of this volume; Mitra, 2002). The late entry of, for example, CESE countries, and in some cases their preoccupation with forms of governance and legal frameworks to facilitate greater risk taking (Zahra and Welter, chapter 7) have slowed progress in these countries. Estonia is one of the few exceptions (Varblane *et al*, chapter 8 of this volume; Zahra and Welter, chapter 7), having introduced entrepreneurship education in the 1990s. Donor-led initiatives with a strong vocational underpinning are sometimes the most important means of educating entrepreneurs in Southeast European countries (OECD, 2003). The multiple and diverse forms of these initiatives reflect the various stages of development of different economies; it will take some time before a pattern of activities can be found in such provision.

Owing to the differences in approach to entrepreneurship education and training among OECD and other countries, it is unclear whether HEIs should adopt specific or pre-defined forms of learning and teaching entrepreneurship. These different approaches reflect the economic status of countries and their overall approach to education. To some extent, the differences are also due to the lack of consensus on the value of entrepreneurship education and whether or how it can be taught. Lack of uniform content or pedagogy adds to the confusion (Solomon, chapter 4 of this volume).

The confusion also stems from the conflation of entrepreneurship education with business education; the equation of entrepreneurship with SME management is a good example. The need for a quicker response to exploit business opportunity and the equivocal nature of the business entry require a focus on the integrated nature, specific skills and business life cycle issues inherent in new ventures (Solomon, chapter 4). Such a focus helps to differentiate entrepreneurship education from business education or SME management training.

Some of the balance can, however, be restored through various means: a movement towards a commonly accepted definition of entrepreneurship; the division of entrepreneurship into individual and corporate entrepreneurship; a move away from exploratory to causal research; and the availability of sophisticated research designs, methods and techniques (Solomon, chapter 4).

Curriculum design and the form of delivery of entrepreneurship education are influenced by its location within the field of management education. The prevailing view is that the form and content will help the learner (the start-up entrepreneur or the innovative manager to find answers to problems, which they will then apply to practice). The locus of such thinking is the positivist epistemology of practice or the model of 'technical rationality' (Schon, 1999) which states that professional activity consists of instrumental problem solving made rigorous by the application of scientific theory and practice" (Mitra, 2002).

In making concessions to "practical pedagogy", entrepreneurship programmes only address part of the challenge of entrepreneurship education. The determinants of rigour and relevance prompt avoidance of the messy bits that fall outside the scope of technical solution to problems. Value creation and the study of behaviour to cope with issues of uncertainty and complexity in different new venture creating situations require locally mediated forms of learning that are characterised by "reflection", "reflecting in action", "knowing in action" and "reflecting in practice" (Schon, 1999). True entrepreneurship education offers management education a new lease of life. It goes beyond the limitations of management education, because unlike the latter it is concerned more with the cycle of discovery and the expansive horizons of opportunity identification and realisation than with reductionist approaches to the management of organisational routines and structures. As Noteboom (2000) observes:

There must be a relation between entrepreneurship and the cycle of discovery. There is a variety of notions of entrepreneurship...and different types of entrepreneurship may be seen as belonging to different stages in the cycles of discovery...different notions of entrepreneurship emphasise different things in different combinations...

- Innovation (Bentham, Thuen, Schumpeter and perhaps Say).

- Creative destruction through novel combinations (Schumpeter).

- The identification and utilisation of possibilities for consumption and production (Cantillon, Smith, Menger, Mises, Hayek, Kirzner).

- The configuration and management of production factors for efficient production (Say, Marshall, Mises).

- The provision of capital. (Noteboom, 2000).

Recognising the diversity in entrepreneurship – taking on board the varied economic and social environments and the corresponding appropriateness of different forms of education provision in different locales of opportunity – is key to formulating the basic principles of entrepreneurship education and training. It also allows for greater appreciation of different *forms* of entrepreneurship, from new start-up ventures through to corporate and social entrepreneurship.

Another form of diversity can be introduced through international collaboration in entrepreneurship education programmes. New and emerging market economies can avoid reinventing the wheel by collaborating on certain programmes, adapting courses to meet local needs, making joint provision by different institutions possible, honouring the Bologna protocol for recognition of credits, arranging staff and student exchanges with entrepreneurs, case study development and other means.

Direct outcomes of entrepreneurship skills training (such as creating a new business venture) can be measured more effectively than indirect ones of attitudinal change and raised awareness. But even direct outcomes cannot be attributed simply to training and education. Policy makers typically look at job creation as an overriding measure for most programmes, together with other outputs such as the representation of women, or new product development. These measures can help to achieve some social and economic objectives, especially where there is under-representation or a need for economic regeneration. Such "performance indicators" can have both national and local dimensions, but their main limitation is that they only measure outputs.

What needs to be measured – especially at the regional level – are outcomes of practice, exemplified by the nature and relevance of entrepreneurship education provision, the network-based approach to education and training, and shared pedagogic platforms among different providers. Of equal value is a measure to evaluate the generation of an entrepreneurial culture in institutions and in regions as evinced in the attitudes of people towards entrepreneurship before and after training. HEIs should be able to track enrolment on entrepreneurship courses over time, the type and mix of students on these courses, the number of business created (perhaps more than the number of examinations passed), the type of jobs created and the levels of sophistication of products created (Zahra and Welter, chapter 7 of this volume). HEIs could also track the levels of involvement of staff, staff training in entrepreneurship, the development of institutional frameworks for entrepreneurship activity, and the proportionate investment of resources in entrepreneurship education in relation to income derived from entrepreneurial activities in HEIs.

Academic spin-offs and entrepreneurship

Where HEIs are directly engaged in entrepreneurship from knowledge transfer is through the mechanism of academic spin-offs. The creation and development of academic spin-offs are not recorded systematically across OECD countries, and this creates problems of definition. Given this constraint, the actual number of recorded spin-offs is around 2% of all new firm creations in any OECD country (Callan, 2001, cited in Lindholm

Dahlstrand, chapter 10 of this volume). The United States leads with the highest rates of, on average, two new firms per research institution per year. Definition does not appear to be the only problem; the low levels of such activity, the long gestation period and slow growth rates (Callan, 2001) suggest that spin-off activities may actually be quite marginal in the scheme of entrepreneurial activities. Furthermore, the close association between research-intensive HEIs and the formation of spin-off firms in their backyard, especially in clusters, indicates two things: first, there is likely to be uneven spatial distribution of these activities, and second, any pronounced effort at supporting such activity can exacerbate economic disparity between regions. Spin-offs do, however, reinforce the location-specific nature of entrepreneurship.

From a policy perspective, support for academic spin-off activities can be a costly exercise. Rather than direct forms of support, the value of spin-off activities can be realised indirectly through their role as intermediaries between industry and HEIs or as research boutiques (Lindholm Dahlstrand, chapter 10 of this volume). Countries wishing to encourage spin-off activities will need to tread carefully when developing strategies for HEIs and local entrepreneurship development. A blanket policy decision is unlikely to have an impact on economic growth. Nor are differentiated policies for regions likely to have any early impact, unless a clear assessment is made of the nature and scope of such development in different territories. If academic spin-off activities have better prospects in playing intermediary or niche roles as part of an established set of policies and activities, such as those for clusters, their promotion becomes secondary to the development of clusters and other primary activities.

The learning context

At the heart of any attempt by HEIs to promote entrepreneurship is the question of universities and their relationship to the wider world outside those institutions. Cultivating these relationships requires balancing the three key elements of the mission of universities:

- Generating new knowledge (research and intellectual capital).

- Passing of this knowledge to future generations (teaching and the generation of human capital).

- Serving the needs of industry, commerce (Goddard, *et al.,* 1994) and the wider social community (the triple helix network and the generation of social capital).

Over the past twenty years or so universities and other HEIs have not been exonerated from the rapid technological and structural changes in most economies. A range of factors (funding and resources, forms of learning, institutional relationships, etc.) have influenced the way HEIs contribute to the production and dissemination of knowledge, and their roles and responsibilities in the creation and sustainability of national systems of innovation (Gibbons *et al.,* 1994; Howells, Nedeva and Georghiou, 1998). How do HEIs interact with the wider community of learning? How do they establish institutions of good practice that identify different forms of learning and knowledge production, both within HEIs and in communication with other organisations, as part of a lifelong learning system? How do such interactions generate innovation and new enterprises? These questions gave rise to the idea of a "triple helix" of relationships between HEIs, industry and government (Leydesdorff and Etzkowitz, 1996). All three aspects of the archetypal mission of an HEI are enmeshed in these interactions. The resulting frameworks and mechanisms for HEI-industry relationships include research and consultancy links, commercialisation of research, intellectual property management, spin-off activities, and property-led developments such as science parks, links to teaching, and staff support and funding. Central to measuring the effectiveness of these links is the generation of intellectual, human and social capital.

Antecedents

A cursory review of the antecedents of university-industry relationships indicates that industry-academic links go back to the late 19th century. Industry's interest in research manifested itself through the development of in-house research laboratories and sponsorship of research in universities. Whether this link underlines any specific or direct connection between HEI research and education and economic competitiveness is, however, a debatable matter.

During the decades preceding and following the First World War, very few French firms possessed any research capacity. Nor was there any real scope for applied research within the educational system. Immediately after the Second World War the USSR boasted a significant fundamental and applied research community, bigger even than that in the United States. But while French industry made advances despite restrictive innovation acquisition practices during the First World War, postwar Soviet industry hardly grew at all (Shinn, 1998).

To understand the true value of HEI-industry links, we need to turn to Germany and the emergence of the *Technische Hochschulen* in the late 19th century. Education in Germany evolved from the classical humanist tradition of *Bildung* in the *Gymnasium* and the university to accommodation of pragmatic/utilitarian curricula such as science, technology and modern languages in the *Realgymnasium*. The *Technische Hochschulen* recruited students from the latter, and together with the *Technische Mittelschulen* they offered diverse, "pliable, transverse structures" of technical education and learning, enabling industry to recruit new employees in response to changing technology and economic opportunities (Shinn, 1998). As Shinn also points out, indirect research contributions from the *Physikalisch-Technische Reichsanstalts* (specialising in technology) also helped to establish German-based technological standards in industry and carry out significant work in the field of instrumentation.

What is apparent when considering the evolution of industry-academia links in general is the development of human capital through creation of the qualities of motivation, loyalty, flexibility, training and skills. Also demonstrated is the value of different forms of education (in this case technical education), and how diverse and flexible forms of learning must be taken into account.

What is not apparent is any direct link between academia-industry connections and entrepreneurship, defined here as the identification and realisation of opportunity for value creation through innovation and new enterprise development. History, however, offers interesting examples of certain forms of education contributing to economic development. Timing is often a key factor, as in the case of German industrial development. Innovation paved the way for growth; it took various forms: new product development, new technology standards, new supply side measures (as in education and training), and the creation of new forms of intellectual and human capital. This outcome could be taken as a reasonable proxy for entrepreneurship development. What is distinctive here is the direct involvement of diverse forms of higher education in promoting industrial development and economic competitiveness.

Diversity of systems and practises

The absence of diversity in education systems and provision has thwarted the formation of effective and entrepreneurial partnerships. Saddled by notions of high-minded science and anti-utilitarian values, academics have long rebelled against connections with industry. Despite the existence of the third dimension to the mission of HEIs, collaboration with industry was considered to be inimical to the central ethos of universities. An early OECD report (1970) also pointed to the tensions that arise from the perception that staff may be distracted from their main academic functions by industry-directed work. However, as Howells, Nedeva and Georghiou (1998, p. 7) have noted, the strongest and most productive relationships with industry are founded upon HEIs doing what they are best established to do –

that is, "pursuing excellence in research and teaching, rather than attempting to duplicate the functions of industry. The necessary cultural shift comes in terms of being able to understand the needs of industry and provide an interface which allows the swift and effective flow of knowledge and people to their most productive use."

Entrepreneurship is directly concerned with the flows of intellectual, human and social capital to their most productive use, especially in the form of new venture creation. But entrepreneurship goes beyond routine forms of industry-academia collaboration; it engages both parties and indeed government to derive competitive economic value from innovation and a cultural shift in the process of learning that results from innovation.

The cultural shift that has enabled both policy makers and HEIs to recognise this significant role of HEIs in fostering entrepreneurship has five components (Goddard *et al.,* 1994):

- Mass higher education and changes in the government's definition of the mission of HEIs.

- A related increase in the demand for skills and knowledge in all aspects of work, in response to increasing competition in the global economy.

- Increasing rates of technological change and new ways of organising the production and distribution of goods and services, including changing relationships between large and small firms.

- Changes in the structure of government and a greater diversity of bodies having a stake in the governance of local territories.

- New patterns of urban and regional development arising from the greater mobility of capital and labour, the decline of old sectors and the emergence of new ones as in the creative and cultural industries.

The five components also reflect the need for diverse approaches to education and learning. Different forms of education are necessary to generate varied capabilities, as is the need to develop forms of learning, both in traditional educational institutions and in other "centres of learning" outside HEIs. The idea of "learning organisations" indeed stems from this notion of diversity, which recognises the need for accelerated learning and innovation that cuts across traditional disciplinary lines. Gibbons *et al.* (1994) refer to this form of learning as "Mode 2 science", where scientists, engineers, technicians and managers seize on the benefits of this form of learning to solve industrial and social problems associated with their work. In this world, researchers establish an intellectually and institutionally flexible group transferring from one problem domain to another as and when opportunities arise, independently of their organisations.

The Gibbons Mode 2 model does recognise the way entrepreneurship and innovation work – namely, in a disorganised and non-linear fashion and across disciplines and profession-bound institutions. Current thinking on convergence of technologies and organisations also supports the idea of interactive, cross-institutional forms of learning.

Following recognition of the industrial and policy significance of HEI-industry links – especially in the United States in the 1970s – many universities have engaged not only in commercialisation of knowledge but also in helping to foster entrepreneurial attitudes and skills in faculty, staff and students; to identify different sources of funds for applied research and prototype development; to bring together technology and business resources in incubators; and to offer new degrees in entrepreneurship and innovation (McNaughton, chapter 11 of this volume). The development of entrepreneurial attitudes in HEIs is symptomatic of attitudes to entrepreneurship in wider society. While it may be argued that positive attitudes are higher in environments where total entrepreneurial activity (the Total Entrepreneurial Activity Index or TEA of the Global Entrepreneurship Monitor) itself is high, encouragement of accepting attitudes may be more necessary in environments where the TEA is not strong.

Numerous countries and their universities have adopted many of the measures and tools that various OECD nations and their HEIs have used over the years, with varying degrees of success (Varblane *et al*, chapter 8 of this volume). It is not clear whether the paths followed by these countries replicate the basis of knowledge production and dissemination process of most Western economies since the Second World War – namely mass production, economies of scale, integration of existing technologies, and an industrial infrastructure dominated by large firms. Luczkiw (chapter 3 of this volume) refers to the report "An Agenda for a Growing Europe", which states that economic globalisation and strong external competition demands increased movement internally and externally among firms, increased flexibility of labour markets, increased investments in research and development and education, and diversity in the innovation process. Preparing the labour market of tomorrow to acquire more entrepreneurial skills and producing knowledge that can help to manage these demands is central to the policy agenda for HEIs, industry and government.

Much of the production of knowledge in the modern economy is decentralised and distributed widely across regions and countries, and across different types of organisations. This spatial and organisational distribution of knowledge has complex outcomes for learning in both HEIs and industry. The emerging learning system mirrors this complexity, in that the most relevant forms of learning and knowledge creation now call for:

- Adaptive networks of HEIs and industry, where learning can take place in either environment and that duality can be accommodated by policies for education and research.

- Adaptive networks that continually build and make use of intellectual, human and social capital for new products, services and organisations.

- Adaptive networks of knowledge production and dissemination that are global in operational terms.

Entrepreneurship provides for contexts for learning, in that the continuous process of accelerated innovation and the creation of new forms compel us to explore learning from a variety of institutional perspectives. Possible chaos and disequilibrium are avoided through recognition of the specific and respective roles of multiple agents in generating new knowledge. Similarly, learning itself takes on an entrepreneurial character in that there is a greater recognition of each agent's unique and related contributions, which can be aligned with activities that lead to commitment from different players in a particular context.

The global character of entrepreneurship and the role of HEIs in fostering entrepreneurship can be observed in the demonstration of varied strengths of HEIs across the world. Excellence today is measured in global terms; ipso facto, knowledge is best shared among global players. However, much of the strength of HEIs in the global arena of knowledge production, dissemination and transfer is mediated at the local or regional level. It is this local/regional context of HEIs that enables them to direct intellectual, human and social capital towards entrepreneurial outcomes.

The local context

A key element of government policy for entrepreneurship, innovation and economic regeneration has been the increased role of regional governments and decision making at the local level. Part of this role stems from the notion that decisions about economic prosperity and quality of life are best made at the regional level. This has often resulted in a patchwork of institutions and arrangements to accommodate (*e.g.*) the enhanced role of business leaders in regional strategic and investment decision making (as in the creation of the regional development agencies in the United Kingdom). Universities that have always had a regional, physical presence (and, in the best of them, an international research and student profile) have been drawn into this regional agenda because of (Adams and Smith, 2004):

- The historical roots of their regional presence.

- Changes in policies for funding, and the consequent need to seek money explicitly from varied sources.

- The perceived direct and indirect impact of their work on regional economic performance.

- The profile of university research strengths and the presence of regional agglomerations of industrialised specialisms.

- Strategic policy objectives for innovation and business development at the sub-national levels.

As Malecki (chapter 9 of this volume) points out, HEIs bring long-term benefits to a region because they are seen as an important element in a region's knowledge infrastructure, and the knowledge infrastructure, to a large extent, decides the success of a region in today's knowledge-based economy. Regions increasingly organise themselves as "learning regions", and it is important to realise that as part of this organisation, HEIs are important drivers of economic growth but only as one producer of knowledge among others. This role of HEIs in the web of knowledge-producing economic actors reinforces the point about HEIs working in conjunction with other learning organisations referred to earlier in this chapter.

Spillovers

In common with the problem of HEIs being a point in the linear mode of knowledge creation and transfer, the recognition of them as drivers of economic growth suffers from the restrictive view that relies on their capacity to produce explicit and tangible forms of knowledge. What tend to get ignored are the unintended, informal spillovers of knowledge that occur from HEIs to SMEs. They do not carry the weight of prestige, money and contacts that alliances with larger firms bring. Their informal character poses problems for formal procedures-oriented institutions and their administrators. It is well recognised that much of the knowledge and technologies are embedded in academics, non-academic staff members and students. Among knowledge-intensive firms it is the personnel who hold much of the knowledge. These forms of tacit knowledge combine with more explicit ones in a process of iterative exchange and relationship among academics and SME owner-managers and their employees. It is argued that such relationships generate larger benefits for both HEIs and the firms in a given region. Furthermore, the fruitful cultivation of such relationships and the appropriate valorisation of tacit forms of knowledge and the use of social capital distinguish one region from another.

Tacit knowledge and spillovers

The literature on spatial agglomeration ("geography and knowledge spillovers") has woven together concepts of tacit knowledge and localised spillovers (Agrawal, 2001) to explain why regions post different rates of technology-based entrepreneurship (Mitra and Abubakar, 2005) and how knowledge spillovers impact on innovative capacity and technology-based entrepreneurship in regions (Jaffe, 1989; Acs, 2002). Central to the argument over geographically mediated spillovers is the distinction between tacit and explicit knowledge, introduced by Polanyi (1962), which is considered to be of fundamental importance to the geographical concentration of technological activity (Jaffe, 1989; Acs, 2002).

In a seminal work, Jaffe (1989) explored the existence of geographically mediated "knowledge spillovers" in the United States from university research to commercial innovation. Building on the tacit-explicit knowledge distinction, Jaffe agues that "it is certainly plausible that the pool of talented graduates, the ideas generated by faculty, and the high quality libraries and other facilities of research universities facilitate the commercial process of innovation in their neighbourhood" (p. 957). Technological spillovers from R&D means a) that firms can acquire information created by others without paying for that information in a market transaction, and b) that the creators or current owners of the information have no recourse, under prevailing laws, if other firms utilise the information so acquired.

Thus, university knowledge spillover refers to the non-pecuniary and untraded form of knowledge.

Jaffe's study highlighted the "public good" nature of university research as his analysis provided evidence that a corporate patent responds positively to commercial spillovers from university research. Zucker, Darby and Brewer (1998) linked the increasing number of American biotechnology firms – which grew from a nonexistent base to over 700 in less than two decades – with university research activities by arguing that the commercialisation of biotechnology is actively intertwined with the development of underlying science in local research universities. Acs (2002) concluded that university spillover plays an important role in certain industries, such as electronics and instruments, and no significant role in others, like drugs and chemical.

Research on high-technology firms seems to support the findings referred to above. It suggests that research universities serve as important origins of regional technology-based firms through mechanisms of collective learning (Lindholm Dahlstrand, chapter 10 of this volume), university knowledge spillovers (Zucker, Darby and Brewer, 1998), and university spin-offs. Universities are one of the two major sources of new-technology firm entrepreneurs (Oakey, 1995).

Yet not all research-intensive HEIs have contributed to technology-intensive economic development (Feller, 1990; Feldman, 1994). What appear to underpin successful generation of a local culture of innovation are critical notions of "untraded interdependencies" between institutions and people (Storper, 1995), collective learning in innovative milieus (Keeble and Wilkinson, 1999; Capello, 1999), and networking (Saxenian, 1994). Others have argued that the mechanisms for the transfer of knowledge in spatial terms are socially embedded due to the common technological and institutional routines in a region (Capello, 1999). Sociological insights into new venture creation support this perspective of knowledge transfer (Yli-Renko, Autio and Sapienza, 2001) – as does the literature on "firm characteristics", which argues that the main ingredient for utilisation of externally generated scientific knowledge such as that transferred from universities is "connectedness" between universities and the firms (Lim, 2000, Mitra, 2000). Lim identified three different mechanisms for fostering connectedness:

- Cultivating university relationships by way of sponsoring research, collaborating with faculty and recruiting graduate students.

- Partnering with other companies that do related scientific research.

- Participating in research consortia.

Despite the theories and the availability of some empirical observations, it is still problematic to demonstrate a clear connection between HEI activity (especially research) and the creation of technology-based ventures at an interregional level. As Zucker, Darby and Brewer (1998) have observed, "Localised spillovers may play fundamental roles in both economic agglomeration and endogenous growth (Grossman and Helpman, 1994). However, our evidence, specifically indicates localised effects without demonstrating that they can be characterised as spillovers (or externalities) (Zucker et al., 1998, p. 290)".

Social capital

The difficulties in finding causal relationships between HEI knowledge spillovers and new venture creation do not preclude an association between the two, which in turn informs a number of overlapping sets of interactions between different players in a local system. Causality notwithstanding, these relationships create institutions of learning that foster a culture of entrepreneurship in the region. Central to this culture is the creation and use of social capital, which includes structural and psychological elements in the networks of personal relationships and the sense of mutual understanding that enables people to live and work together effectively. Social capital can enhance the rapid diffusion of knowledge between individuals and communities as well as within and between firms. In essence, social capital helps harness intellectual and human capital and generates synergistic returns for the network in regions. How effectively that is done is a matter for the custodians of regional innovation systems. Regions are best able to demonstrate their competitive edge through the implementation of their innovation systems. As Bartlett and Bukvic (2005) and Audretsch (2005) have noted, research on innovation systems suggests that differences in innovative capacities between countries and regions are linked to the institutions that promote learning and technology transfer, activities that in turn depend upon the existence of institutions, and firms that permit exchange of knowledge and other resources.

HEIs, industry and government need to work to establish institutional structures that will enable networks of relationships generating social capital to be safeguarded and nurtured. These structures also need to recognise that the most successful forms of relationships transcend local geographical boundaries, as knowledge, skills and financial capital are sourced globally. Those flows of resources help establish international networks. At the same time they reinforce regional capabilities, apparently confirming the paradox of modern times: the more international the scope of economic activities in a region, the stronger the region's own economic identity. Links between HEIs, firms and policy makers in different countries tend to follow complementary areas of expertise, which helps units of explicit knowledge to be traded across geographical boundaries. This in turn strengthens local expertise. The greater the production of local expertise, the more there is an opportunity for spillovers or "untraded interdependencies" that attracts investment, technologies and skills to the area.

HEIs can help foster this culture of innovation by concentrating on mechanisms that facilitate personal interactions between firms and academics, and by creating banks of social capital. They can augment this resource by making more effective use of international connections with other leading institutions. A good example is the Internationalisation of Clusters project at the University of Essex (in the School of Entrepreneurship and Business), which brings together complementary regions in China, India and the United Kingdom and their HEIs, SMEs, trade representative bodies and policy makers (see www.essex.ac.uk/seb).

Entrepreneurship research, education and training are enriched by the study of ideas, processes, means and methods relating to the special regional dimensions. Such studies help to obtain a better understanding of the phenomenon of entrepreneurship and its various manifestations across different environments, and help to develop tools for the better practice of new venture creation and innovative growth. Different approaches make such learning useful and effective. Some courses can be embedded within various social sciences programmes generally, while others can be designed to offer distinctive qualifications in the field of entrepreneurship.

Regional variation and differentiation

Another distinction needs to be made – between regions that have a well-established profile in entrepreneurship and those that do not. It is often argued that well-developed regions benefit mainly from high levels of innovation within the surrounding area and do not depend on HEI activities fostering entrepreneurship (*e.g.* academic spin-offs), while less developed regions benefit from a proactive role of HEIs (Clarysse *et al.*, 2005). This distinction provides an interesting analytical construct but does not necessarily reflect reality. It tends to ignore the self-reinforcing nature of successful regions, such as Cambridge in the United Kingdom, where existing social capital continues to feed higher levels of HEI-business activity. Secondly, the majority of academic spin-offs tend to establish themselves in new or novel sectors, such as life sciences and information technologies (Lindholm Dahlstrand, chapter 10 of this volume). In some of these sectors the knowledge production base is often found to be stronger in business than in the universities. The creation of academic spin-offs is therefore more a necessity, in the sense that it is through industry-oriented activity that new knowledge can be generated and commercialised faster.

While HEIs in successful regions can build on the richness of social capital in their patch, it may not be appropriate for government policy to continue to support development in these regions as no additionality may be secured. A few high-growth firms may be supported at the expense of establishing a phenomenon (Lindholm Dahlstrand, chapter 10 of this volume).

Bartlett and Bukvic (chapter 12 of this volume) and Formica et al (chapter 13 of this volume) identify various measures and policy instruments that suggest that current policy considerations support multiple levels of HEI activity aimed at entrepreneurship and innovation. Many of these activities take place at the regional level and there is a clear appreciation of systems of innovation or clusters of economic activity, which bring together HEIs, business and government.

It is therefore incumbent upon policy makers both at the level of HEIs and government to develop policies to encourage entrepreneurship that can make best use of core, existing capabilities while obtaining a better appreciation of mechanisms for new forms of learning.

Conclusion

Developing an analytical framework for the proper study of HEIs and their role in fostering entrepreneurship has two purposes:

• It provides a guide to the thematic aspects of this monograph.

• It provides a basis for policy considerations relating to the role of both HEIs and governments in fostering entrepreneurship.

HEIs fostering entrepreneurship generate and use intellectual, human and social capital and various institutional norms and practices to engage with different stakeholders towards that end.

One of the key issues to emerge from the analysis of HEI roles and functions in OECD and other countries is the varied and differentiated nature of activities promoting entrepreneurship. The attraction of resources and alterative sources of income is as significant as the strategies adopted by HEIs to better inform and educate people in an era of technological, structural, organisational and social change. Entrepreneurship is a well-recognised process for dealing with those changes. As HEIs are not exempt from such change and as they affect forms and methods of higher learning, their involvement in entrepreneurial activities is a legitimate response. Equally, growth in the body of knowledge that addresses issues of change and opportunities for new venture creation that arise from such change provides for its serious and concentrated study and investigation.

A second key issue, one related to entrepreneurship education, is the regional character of HEIs. This regional character does not cancel the international aspirations of excellence of universities; the latter reinforces the former, together with the growing recognition of endogenous forms of economic growth. HEI research, education, training and knowledge transfer activities often support the concentration of global economic activity in regions. In this role HEIs are one of several players in a web of knowledge-producing actors in a region. Their value and their particular contributions are often best realised when research and education provision is linked to the work of other organisations. In this network of organisations learning takes different forms, and the greater the involvement of HEIs in these networks, the greater is the wider impact of learning for economic growth. This network approach challenges traditional HEI orthodoxy and demands alternative policies for its realisation.

The regional aspects of entrepreneurship and HEI involvement are best understood through an appreciation of the nature and effect of knowledge spillovers from both HEI research and business activities. The use of tacit forms of knowledge to derive appropriate benefits from spillovers creates opportunities for the better use of human, intellectual and social capital. Although they vary across environments, it is through the spillovers and the use of different forms of capital that HEIs and business promote entrepreneurship in specific regions.

A typical policy framework could, therefore, benefit from embracing the issues of:

- Critical underpinning philosophies affecting the provision of higher education – in particular, entrepreneurship education – and their evolution over time.

- The positioning and convergence of different instruments and mechanisms, together with their integrated evaluation within different types of institutions.

- The wider learning contexts – local, regional, national and international – in which different HEIs operate.

HEIs have a considerable opportunity to move out of mechanistic and reactive approaches to education and entrepreneurship development, and instead foster entrepreneurship through dedicated education, research and knowledge transfer activity. This involvement can help change mindsets among both the beneficiaries and providers, and generate opportunities for value creation.

Countries emerging from the shadows of a command economy to embrace the peculiarities of the marketplace need to both organise themselves and obtain support for their institutions to promote entrepreneurship. Their HEIs could play an important role, in driving some of the change processes; enabling the adoption of policies for the early introduction of entrepreneurship in society; encouraging entrepreneurial attitudes among students; and guiding existing professionals to entrepreneurial careers. Much of this needs be done both at the regional level and with local institutions. A great deal more needs to be achieved through international collaboration with partners across Europe and elsewhere. Such partnerships should be less about emulation and more about the desire to carve out distinctive entrepreneurial futures for their economy and their institutions.

Bibliography

Acs, Z. J. (2002), *Innovation and the Growth of Cities,* Cheltenham: Edward Elgar Publishing.

Adams, J. and D. Smith, (2004), *Research and regions: An overview of the distribution of research in UK regions, regional research capacity and links between strategic research partners,* Higher Education Policy Institute, Oxford.

Agrawal, A. (2001), "University-to-industry knowledge transfer: literature review and unanswered questions", *International Journal of Management Reviews*, Vol. 3, No. 4, Blackwell Publishers Ltd 2001, pp. 285-302.

Audretsch, D.B. (1995), *Innovation and Industry Evolution*, MIT Press, Cambridge, MA.

Birch, D. (1979), *The job generation process*, MIT Programme on Neighbourhood and Regional Change, MIT Press, Cambridge, MA.

Callan, B. (2001), "Generating Spin-Offs: Evidence from across OECD", *STI Review,* No. 26, OECD, Paris, pp 14-54.

Capello, R. (1999), "Spatial transfer of knowledge in high technology milieux: Learning versus collective learning processes", *Regional Studies,* Vol. 33, pp. 353-365.

Clarysse, B., *et al.* (2005), "Spinning out new ventures: A typology of incubation strategies from European Research Institutions", *Journal of Business Venturing,* Vol. 20, Elsevier, pp.183-216.

Cooke, P., and K. Morgan, (1998), *The Associational Economy: Firms, Regions and Innovation*, Oxford University Press, Oxford.

Feldman, M.P. (1994), "The University and high technology start-ups: The case of Johns Hopkins University and Baltimore", *Economic Development Quarterly*, Vol. 8, Sage, pp. 67-77.

Feller, I. (1990), "Universities as engines of R&D based economic growth: They think they can", *Research Policy,* Vol. 19, Elsevier, pp. 335-348.

Gibb, A. (1996), "Entrepreneurship and small business management: can we afford to neglect them in the twenty first century business school?", *British Journal of Management,* Vol.7, Blackwell Publishing Ltd., pp 309-321.

Gibbons, M., *et al.* (1994), *The New Production of Knowledge*: *The Dynamics of Science and Research in Contemporary Societies*, Sage, London

Goddard, J., *et al.* (1994), *Universities and Communities*, Committee of Vice Chancellors and Principals, London.

Grossman, G. and E. Helpman, (1994), "Endogenous Innovation in the theory of growth", *Journal of Economic Perspectives*, Vol.8, AEA, pp. 23-44.

Hills G. and M.H. Morris, (1998), "Entrepreneurship education: a conceptual model and review", in *M.G. Scott, P. Rosa and H. Klandt* (eds), Ashgate, Aldershot.

Howells, J., M. Nedeva and L. Georghiou (1998), "Industry-Academic Links in the UK", *Final Report to the Higher Education Funding Council for England (HEFCE)*, Bristol.

Ivancevich, J.M., (1991), "A traditional faculty member's perspective on entrepreneurship", *Journal of Business Venturing'*, Vol.6, Elsevier, pp. 1-7.

Jaffe, A.B. (1989), "Real effects of academic research", *American Economic Review*, Vol. 79, No. 5, AEA, pp. 957-970.

Jones Evans, D. (1998), "Universities, technology transfer and spin-off activities: academic entrepreneurship in different European regions" *TSER Report 1042*, University of Glamorgan, Cardiff.

Keeble, D. and F. Wilkinson (1999), "Collective learning and knowledge development in the evolution of regional clusters of high technology SMEs in Europe", *Regional Studies*, Vol. 33, Routledge, pp. 295-303.

Kline, S. and N. Rosenberg (1986), "An Overview of Innovation" in R. Lasndau and N. Rosenberg (eds.), *The Positive Sum Strategy: Harnessing Technology for Economic Growth*, National Academy Press, Washington DC, pp. 275-305.

Lambert, R. (2003), *Lambert Review of Business-Industry Collaboration*, HM Treasury, London.

Leydesdorff, L. and H. Etzkowitz, (1996), "Emergence of a Triple Helix of industry – university - government relations", *Science and Public Policy,* Vol 23, No.5, Beech Tree Publishing, pp. 279-286.

Liebenau, U. (1993), "Higher education, industry and the two souls of the British system", in Lindner, U., *et al.* (eds) *Interaction between Industry and Higher Education in the British Experience,* Franco Angeli, Milano, pp. 35-77.

Lim, K. (2000), "The many faces of absorptive capacity: spillovers of copper interconnect technology for semi conductor chips", *Working Paper 4110,* MIT Sloan School of Management, Mimeo, MIT.

Mitra, J. (2000), "Making Connections: innovation and collective learning in small businesses", *Education + Training,* Vol. 42, No 45, Emerald, pp 228-236.

Mitra, J. (2002), "Consider Velasquez: reflections on the development of entrepreneurship programmes", *Industry and Higher Education Journal,* Vol 16, No. 3, IP Publishing, pp 191-2002.

Mitra, J. and Y. A. Abubakar (2005), "Fostering Entrepreneurship ands the Role of Higher Education: Spatial perspectives on human and social networks and high technology firms", paper presented at *Institute of Small Business and Entrepreneurship, 2005 Small Firms Policy and Research Conference,* Blackpool.

Mitra, J and P. Formica (1997), *Innovation and Economic Development: University-Enterprise Partnerships in Action,* Oak Tree Press, Dublin.

Noteboom, B. (2000), *Learning and Innovation in Organisations and Economies,* Oxford University Press, Oxford.

Oakey R. (1995), *High-technology New Firms: Variable Barriers to Growth,* Paul Chapman, London.

OECD (1970), *Innovation in Higher Education: Three German Universities,* OECD, Paris.

OECD (2003), *South-East Europe region –Enterprise policy performance assessment,* OECD, Paris.

Polanyi, M. (1962), *Personal knowledge: Towards a Post Critical Philosophy,* Routledge, London.

Porter L.W. and L.E. McKibbin, (1988), *Management Education and Development: Drift or Thrust into the 21st Century?,* McGraw-Hill, New York.

Sahlman, W.A, H.E. Stevenson, M.J. Roberts and A. Bhide (1999), 2nd ed. 'The Entrepreneurial Venture' Boston, HBS Press.

Sanderson, M. (1972), *The Universities and British Industry, 1850-1970,* Routledge and Kegan Paul, London.

Saxenian A. (1994), *Regional Advantage: Culture and Competition in Silicon Valley and Route 128,* Harvard University Press, Cambridge, MA.

Schon, D.A. (1999), *The Reflective Practitioner: How Professionals Think in Action,* Ashgate, Aldershot.

Shinn, T. (1998), "The impact of research and education on industry: a comparative analysis of the relationship of education and research systems to industrial progress in six countries", *Industry and Higher Education Journal,* Vol. 12, No. 5, IP Publishing, pp. 270-289.

Storey, D. (2003), "Entrepreneurship, small and medium sized enterprises and public policies", in Z.J. Acs, and D.B. Audrestsch, (eds.), *Handbook of Entrepreneurship Research*, Kluwer, Boston, pp.473-511.

Storper, M. (1995), "The resurgence of regional economies, ten years later: the region as a nexus of untraded interdependencies", *European Urban and Regional Studies*, Vol. 2, No. 3, Sage, pp.191-221.

Swann, P. (1989), *'Academic Scientists and the Pharmaceutical Industry: Co-operative Research in Twentieth Century America,* Boston, MA, John Hopkins University Press.

Yli-Renko, H., E. Autio and H.J. Sapienza (2001), "Social capital, knowledge acquisition and knowledge exploitation in young technology-based firms", *Strategic Management Journal,* Vol. 22, pp. 587-613.

Zucker, L., M. Darby, and M. Brewer (1998), "Intellectual capital and the birth of U.S. biotechnology enterprises", *American Economic Review*, Vol. 88, No. 1, AEA, pp. 290-306.

Chapter 2

Higher Education's Role in Entrepreneurship and Economic Development

by
Jay Mitra
University of Essex, United Kingdom

Mathew J. Manimala
Indian Institute of Management, India

This chapter provides an overview of the type of role that higher education plays in promoting entrepreneurship in the economy. The authors place this role within the context of social and economic change and a growing recognition of the value of entrepreneurship in influencing and absorbing the outcomes of such change. Equating entrepreneurship with new venture creation, the authors reflect on the different ways knowledge is transferred, particularly through education and training offered by higher education institutions.

Introduction

Numerous studies on the relationship between higher education institutions and industry have examined the economic value of university activity, the contribution of staff and students to the economy, university spin-offs, the spillover effects of knowledge, and the development of entrepreneurship education (for a summary see Mitra and Formica, 1997). Central to all these studies is an appreciation of the role of institutions and organisations in the economy, especially the ways in which they facilitate and augment human interaction through knowledge creation, dissemination and spillover effects. It is the systematic practice of innovation through these institutions and organisations that engenders entrepreneurship.

This chapter concentrates on the particular issue of knowledge creation and dissemination through education – especially entrepreneurship education in higher education institutions (HEIs) and its association with new venture creation.

The policy context: new ventures in the economy

Statistics on new ventures in vibrant economies illustrate the vital role of start-ups in keeping the economy dynamic and growing. In the United States, for example, small businesses contribute 90% of all new jobs and 70% of all new products and services. In absolute terms, there are about 2 million business start-ups every year in that country, of which 50% are micro-businesses employing not more than two people (Hisrich and O'Cinneide, 1996).

Even though such systematic data on new ventures may not be available for all countries, the available indicators show that the picture is not very different elsewhere. The findings of the multi-country research project Global Entrepreneurship Monitor (GEM) reveal that entrepreneurial activity in all parts of the world has a very large component of small start-ups. On average worldwide (that is, for 37 countries), about 96% of the new start-ups have less than five employees. But growth in entrepreneurial activity does not follow a linear logic, in that there is no apparent correlation between economic advancement and the level of entrepreneurial activity. In the year 2002 the level of entrepreneurial activity in India was the second highest among 37 countries (Manimala, 2002); however, the progressive increase of entrepreneurial activity in the country could be attributable, at least in part, to the vibrancy that is being observed in that economy in recent years.

While a thriving economy will have a large number of new start-ups that demonstrate its vitality, the future of all these new ventures does not appear all that bright. Statistics show that even in a strong economy like that of the United States, two-thirds of all new ventures perish within the first five years of their existence. The story is similar with UK start-ups. In attempting to define the entrepreneurial phase in the life of a new venture, the international research team of the GEM project decided that it is in the first 42 months that the new venture needs the "entrepreneurial" care, beyond which the managerial phase begins. All this special emphasis on the initial period in the life of a venture is obviously based on an understanding of the special vulnerabilities associated with this phase.

Another new development is the growing interest in the practice of social entrepreneurship, the result of disillusionment with institutional politics and the failure of governments to address wider social problems. This new interest recognises the value of economic self-sufficiency, new market opportunities, and social well-being evinced in the practices of different communities of interest across the world. It also recognises that starting new businesses is a minority activity, and that in a world where job opportunities are uncertain even in growing economies, entrepreneurial endeavour or new venture creation – on both the economic and social fronts – is essential to shaping people's lives.

While new ventures are the source of vigour and vitality in the economy, they are also truly vulnerable and so deserve special assistance from the society. But what form should such assistance take? Is there a particular role for education and especially higher education institutions, through knowledge transfer and teaching?

The rest of the chapter tries to answer these questions by discussing the special role of HEIs, firstly by referring to the evolution of this role in the context of economic development. It is assumed that the knowledge transfer, teaching and training provided by universities are vital to the growth of an economy, and that these provisions from higher education acquire a specific significance for entrepreneurship, which has its special place in any consideration of economic growth today. Entrepreneurship's role in development has evolved; we can trace how at different points in time the association between higher education, industry and government has impacted on new venture creation and socioeconomic change.

Higher education and economic development

As organisations in society, universities provide a structure for human interaction with the wider environment. This structure is afforded through the education of students for, primarily, the future workplace, pure and applied research, skills training and, increasingly, the "third way" of outreach with industry and the wider community of people and organisations. In this attempt to generate higher levels of human interaction and act as agents of change, universities adopt particular governance structures, sets of skills and strategies; they use these to implement the rules or constraints that shape the different forms of human interaction meant to make a contribution to the economy.

In a competitive economy, much of that interaction takes place with industry – each form of interaction opens up opportunities for change. Often these translate into the formation of new ventures. Institutions (the rules of the game in society) "determine the opportunities in society. Organisations (*such as universities and industry*) are created to take advantage of those opportunities, and, as the organisations evolve, they alter the institutions. The resultant path of the institutional change is shaped by (1) the lock-in that comes from the symbiotic relationship between institutions and the organizations (*and between organizations*) that have evolved as a consequence of the incentive structure provided by those institutions and (2) the feedback process by which human beings perceive and react to changes in the opportunity set" (North, 2002, p. 7; italics added).

Using the construct for human interaction suggested by North, we could argue that the incentives provided by the economic activities of work, industry and business creation, and the institutional constraints that evolve to enable human interaction within and between those activities, are a matter of serious concern for higher education and industry. Some examples from two contrasting countries, from the West and from Asia – one the major powerhouse of modern economies, and the other a symbol of unique possibilities heralding the early re-emergence of Asian economic strength – provide for a better understanding of the relationships between institutions and entrepreneurial outcomes.

Some historical antecedents of knowledge transfer – the United States and Japan

The Renaissance and subsequent developments in Europe brought about a revolutionary change in its educational system, shifting the emphasis from philosophical pursuits to positive and applied sciences. The Meiji restoration in Japan was followed by an emphasis on technical education (as propagated in the 1872 law on modern education), which laid the foundations for that country's current economic development. Reforms in the education system have been a continuous process in Japan. The Board of Education Law of 1948 placed more emphasis on elementary and lower secondary education, and delegated powers to the local authority in an attempt to deregulate and decentralise education in line with the patterns existing in the United States.

"Universities are by tradition – one might say by intellectual necessity – open to participation by scholars from all over the world. Yet their sources of funding are almost entirely domestic, and in most countries primarily governmental" (Branscomb and Kodama, 1999). However, the true realisation of such a public good often lies in the application of knowledge and skills with the support of industry.

The links between universities and industry in the United States and Japan (for example) have a long and cherished history in both countries. Before the development of the modern corporate laboratory, inventions (mainly in chemistry) "came directly from university faculty. Since technology was largely tacit and embedded, the researchers needed a critical assembly of experience and skill, so educational institutions tended to specialise in the needs of the local economy. Thus the University of Akron (Akron, Ohio) became a main source of expertise in polymers and elastomers, supporting the Akron tire industry. Cornell pioneered the first American electrical engineering department; with Tesla as a faculty member they collaborated with George Westinghouse and built the first municipal electric power service for the mining town of Telluride, Colorado. Cornell students went to Telluride for a year to install and operate the system for Westinghouse" (Branscomb and Kodama, 1999, pp. 5-6). The growth of Bell Labs, GE and DuPont as research centres was a primary source of demand for research outputs for universities, until the Second World War. Technology and the military were the main drivers of these relationships.

The Japanese experience was similar. Strong links between large firms and imperial universities are understood to have continued from as far back as 1872 to the 1920s and 1930s. However, in both Japan and the United States this cosy relationship was broken up with the decline in the military-industry nexus, the greater emphasis on science as opposed to technology, the advent of a "social contract", and the formation of a triple helix of university science, government and industry. While US universities were more concerned with research autonomy, Japanese national policy turned its attention to accelerating market incentives for firms. In essence we can track the evolution of the relationship between universities and industry, from addressing corporate and local needs to military interests through to the abstraction of science and the development of a social contract and the realisation of competitive advantage.

The competitiveness agenda changed the way that each country allowed for new relationships to be developed. Since the HE sector is not the responsibility of the national government in the United States but rather of the states and of private institutions, the main source of federal support for universities came from the research agendas of a broad variety of government agencies, each of which had concerns about the economic impact of the research it funded. Moreover, because specific government sectors (defence, space, and energy) had involved the research universities in driving their innovation-based strategies in the 1950s and 1960s, it was seen as natural for Congress to seek to the diffusion of this knowledge to the commercial sector in the 1980s. The Japanese in turn looked at restructuring their organisations to ensure that there was greater emphasis on the "big sciences" of energy, space, research and high-energy physics (Branscomb and Kodama, 1999).

The innovation agenda

Industry dependence on innovation has been accelerating dramatically since the Second World War for a variety of reasons. The first is the creation of a scientific base for engineering; this allowed for a proper quantification of behaviour of matter and materials, which also enabled the ability to predict achievements. In addition, the economic sectors with the most rapid growth are those closest to the science base: microelectronics, software, biotech and new materials. These industries also have the most sought after "social qualities" – high wages, good environmental characteristics, low barriers to market entry for small firms, freedom from geographic constraints on the firm's location (Branscomb and Kodama, 1999; Mitra and Formica, 1997).

The scope and value of entrepreneurship education at universities

Liberalisation and privatisation of education, leading to freedom of thought and action and responsiveness to the emerging environment, are seen as a precondition for entrepreneurship and economic development. Education plays a twofold role in the development of entrepreneurship. One of these is to create the right attitudes in individuals, and the other is to develop knowledge and skills relevant for entrepreneurship.

In a study of the influence of environmental factors on the emergence of innovative entrepreneurs (Manimala, 2005), it was found that the *task environment* of business did not have any statistically significant impact on the emergence of innovative entrepreneurs. The elements of the task environment are those factors that facilitate the performance of the immediate tasks of a business enterprise. These include, *inter alia,* technical and managerial know-how, sources of finance, trained manpower, supply of raw materials, readiness of the markets and facilitating institutions. Facilitating the task environment further would be more useful in channelling the entrepreneurial initiatives into certain areas than in developing such initiatives in the first place. What helps create entrepreneurial attitudes in individuals are the factors related to the *general environment*, namely the legal-political, economic, socio-cultural and educational systems of a country. Thus education has a dual role in promoting entrepreneurship. While educators of primary and secondary levels have an opportunity to foster entrepreneurial attitudes that could lead to individuals taking up an entrepreneurial career later, the quality of entrepreneurship could be substantially improved by the technical, entrepreneurial and/or managerial knowledge and skills imparted at the higher education level (Figure 2.1). Such knowledge and skills can help the fledgling new venture survive and grow against all odds, particularly those created by its "liability of newness as well as smallness".

Figure 2.1. A model for entrepreneurship education

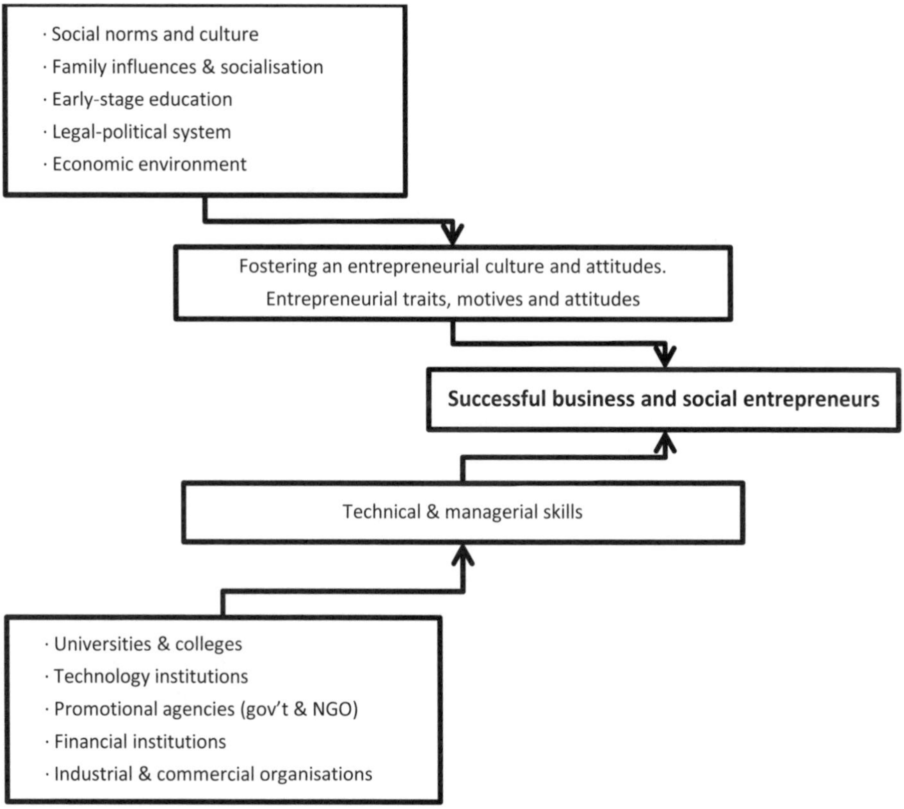

- Social norms and culture
- Family influences & socialisation
- Early-stage education
- Legal-political system
- Economic environment

Fostering an entrepreneurial culture and attitudes.
Entrepreneurial traits, motives and attitudes

Successful business and social entrepreneurs

Technical & managerial skills

- Universities & colleges
- Technology institutions
- Promotional agencies (gov't & NGO)
- Financial institutions
- Industrial & commercial organisations

Higher education and entrepreneurship: mistrust and mismatch

Only in recent times has higher education begun to be perceived as an instrument of entrepreneurship promotion; for a long time, the two kept a distance. Universities rarely considered entrepreneurship to be a discipline with a body of knowledge worthy of being taught and learned. This was to be expected, as the word "entrepreneurship" is of fairly recent origin. It was only in 1803 that the French economist J.B. Say coined the word "entrepreneur" to distinguish him from the "investor" on the one hand and the "manager" on the other. It took a fairly long time for the word to be fully accepted into the English language.

If acceptance of the word and concept was slow, research on the "subject" was necessarily slower, resulting in the development of a rather tardy body of knowledge on entrepreneurship. Naturally, universities and other HEIs cannot launch any academic programme without the support of a body of knowledge on the subject. It was only in the middle of the 20th century that entrepreneurship research picked up momentum. The first academic programme in entrepreneurship was started by Harvard University. The year was 1945, and several industrial enterprises created to serve war needs were being liquidated. The Harvard programme was intended to stimulate the economy, offering returning war veterans opportunities for self-employment. Since then, many HEIs have recognised that entrepreneurship courses could indeed be an effective tool for them to stimulate the economy through their graduates, who would start up new ventures and thereby create wealth and provide employment.

Such hopes have not always been realised, as shown by a number of studies comparing the entrepreneurial performance of entrepreneurship graduates with that of other graduates. The disappointment is not just with the educational programmes of the universities: academic institutions generally find it difficult to attract SME entrepreneurs to its dedicated training programmes. The prevailing view is that the lack of co-operation between academics and entrepreneurs is due to the latter's basic mistrust of the former. This sentiment is voiced rather strongly in the 1971 Bolton Committee report from the United Kingdom, which states that "Academic institutions of most kinds arouse in most entrepreneurs a degree of mistrust second only to that accorded to government" (Bolton, 1971).

There are indications that things have improved in the United Kingdom. However, attitudes in the developing world have not. One example relates to ownership disputes among the second-generation owners of India's largest private sector company, Reliance Industries Limited. Recently an anonymous statement made the rounds on the email system. It said: "A poor, ill-educated man created the billion-dollar Reliance Industries. Two business graduates from Stanford and Wharton are busy trying to break it up. That is education!" Obviously, the mistrust continues.

Among the reasons for SME entrepreneurs' lack of interest in university programmes are their cost, their perceived ineffectiveness, and the entrepreneurs' inability to leave their businesses to attend them. Of these, it is the perceived ineffectiveness that should cause some concern among the HEIs, as it might be due to a fundamental mismatch between what is offered by higher education institutions and what is actually needed by SME entrepreneurs. In a comprehensive analysis of the learning orientations in university education as compared to the learning needs of entrepreneurs, Gibb has identified a series of mismatches; an adapted version of his list is reproduced in Table 2.1.

Table 2.1 University offerings versus entrepreneurs' learning needs

University / Business School learning focus	Entrepreneurs' learning needs
Critical judgement after analysing large amounts of information	Gut-feel decision making with limited information
Understanding and recalling the information itself	Understanding the values of those who transmit/filter information
Assuming commonality of goals	Recognising the widely varied goals of different stakeholders
Seeking (impersonally) to verify the absolute truth by study of information	Making decisions on the basis of judgement of trust & competence of people
Understanding the basic principles of the society in the metaphysical sense	Seeking to apply and adjust in practice to the basic principles of society
Seeking the correct answer, with (enough) time to do it	Developing the most appropriate solution (often) under time pressure
Learning in the classroom	Learning while & through doing
Gleaning information from experts and authoritative sources for the sake of its genuineness	Gleaning information from any and everywhere & assessing its practical usefulness
Evaluation through written assessment	Evaluation through judgement of people and events through direct feedback
Success in learning measured by passing of knowledge-based examinations	Success in learning measured by solving problems, learning from failures and providing useful products and services to society

Source: Adapted from Gibb, 1993.

The basic difference is that universities focus on imparting knowledge and information as against entrepreneurs' need for developing implementation skills. The long traditions of imparting knowledge-oriented education through higher education institutions has come in the way of faculty developing any competence in imparting skill-oriented education. Consequently, it is natural for entrepreneurs not to trust such institutions or the programmes they offer. Time and cost constraints also get in the way of entrepreneurs making use of the programmes offered by universities and other HEIs.

Innovations in entrepreneurship education

University programmes for entrepreneurship can be classified into two categories:

- Academic degree programmes in entrepreneurship offered to first-year students aspiring to be entrepreneurs.

- Training programmes offered to active entrepreneurs with a view to improving their effectiveness.

The experience of universities offering degree programmes in entrepreneurship has not been very encouraging. Graduation in entrepreneurship has not yet become an attractive proposition for young students, partly because a degree of this kind will not guarantee entrepreneurial success. Though such a guarantee is not available for typical management degrees either, the failure of a management graduate in an established organisation is not as disastrous as the failure of an entrepreneur in his or her own venture. This is a cultural issue. Certain societies are better able to accommodate failure than others, and where there is no such accommodation, the social and economic cost of failure is higher than the cost of settling for the meagre rewards of an ordinary job. Universities in such risk-averse cultures are hardly likely to educate their students to consider failure an option – even in its most abstract form.

Entrepreneurship arises out of a fortuitous combination of factors that include knowledge and skills. Several research studies show that the performance of entrepreneurship graduates is not significantly different from that of the "non-graduate" entrepreneurs, except that the former get into the business a few years earlier than the latter. This may be because the non-graduates would work for a few years in other organisations and take the plunge only after developing confidence and competencies – and, more importantly, after perceiving the right opportunities in the market.

The importance of work experience in competency and confidence development and opportunity perception cannot be overemphasised. Ronstadt (1988) has described what he calls the "corridor principle", according to which the encounter with the real-life business situations as they happen in the course of working with such organisations opens a large corridor for the individual; he can perceive many more opportunities than he would if he were not there. It would be beneficial even for the entrepreneurship graduates to work for some time with other organisations. That would be a relatively less expensive way of gaining on-the-job training for oneself and thereby developing implementation skills, an area in which universities apparently provide very little help. It is observed that universities have greater success with training programmes for entrepreneurs who have already crossed the start-up threshold, when the need is for knowledge of management functions and an orientation for strategic thinking. The difficulty at this stage, however, is in bringing the entrepreneur into the classroom, as he/she would be increasingly worried about the time and cost constraints.

The psychological, social and cultural constraints, coupled with questions of timing and the very nature of skills or competency development, make the teaching of entrepreneurship a rather different proposition when compared to other subjects/disciplines. There is clearly a need to devise new strategies and methods for improving the effectiveness of entrepreneurship education. Many universities and HEIs have in fact already done so. One of the most comprehensive listings of best practices in this field is provided by Sandercock (2001) in a survey of the entrepreneurship education programmes of US universities. The more prominent among these practices are listed under the six major sub-headings below.

External association and assistance

Universities seek external support for entrepreneurship education mainly to fill the competence and resource gaps. As observed above, the mismatches between the traditional competencies and orientations of the universities and the needs of entrepreneurship education necessitate a constant effort to reorient the universities towards entrepreneurship education, and to developing the appropriate competencies within the university. The measures taken in this regard include: a) creation of entrepreneurship centres with financial assistance and/or advisory participation from external agencies; b) constituting advisory boards with eminent experts from various fields, including entrepreneurs; c) training of faculty especially in the technical departments by entrepreneurship experts; d) facilitating students' interaction with practicing entrepreneurs through schemes such as "entrepreneurship residence hall", student mentoring by entrepreneurs, collaborative teaching with entrepreneurs, students doing consulting work for entrepreneurial firms, etc., and e) securing external funding support for entrepreneurship outreach activities, in the form of subsidised programmes, tuition support, seed funding, and so on. Collaborations of these kinds with external agencies are intended to transfer the tacit knowledge available with entrepreneurs and other experts to the university system, and thus make the latter's programmes more effective.

They also help to change the orientation of the university faculty and reduce the cost of programmes for the clients.

Interdisciplinary programmes

Programmes for developing entrepreneurship for technology and professional disciplines are organised on the assumption that there is a greater chance for those with technical and professional skills to become entrepreneurs. Such programmes are mainly in two areas: 1) science and technology disciplines, where the programmes include a) integrated science, technology and entrepreneurship programmes, b) entrepreneurship courses for engineers and technologists, c) commercialisation courses for inventors, and the like; 2) professional careers and disciplines, where there are targeted courses for artists, musicians, entertainers, film and TV personnel, designers, architects, lawyers, chartered accountants, and so on. A third kind of programme in this category is in the reverse direction: the principles of other disciplines are applied to entrepreneurship in programmes like "The Psychology of Entrepreneurship", "Creativity for Entrepreneurship", "Marketing for SMEs", "Accounting and Financial Knowledge for Entrepreneurs", and so on.

Specialised offerings in entrepreneurship

Specialisation packages on entrepreneurship and related topics in other courses and programmes are offered by many universities in order to stimulate entrepreneurship among the participants. Such packages are made available within MBA programmes, healthcare related programmes, social work and community development programmes, technology management programmes, and so on. In these packages special emphasis is placed on topics such as business plan preparation, family business management, business and commercial law, healthcare management, entrepreneurship opportunities for the disabled and underprivileged groups, programmes on women's enterprise, programmes on technology-based entrepreneurship, and apprenticeship and mentoring schemes with established entrepreneurs.

Entrepreneurship skill development

Skill development is a component in almost all types of programmes for entrepreneurs. However, some programmes have an exclusive focus on skill development. Identifying and developing real business opportunities are two major aspects. Another initiative in this regard is the preparation of business plans by the students, which can be entered for a competition or be critiqued and evaluated by experts, including the faculty. There are also built-in skill development modules as part of entrepreneurship courses; students are asked to take up "live" projects, often with seed money assistance. Internships with entrepreneurs and other experts are also encouraged as part of the courses.

Real-life entrepreneurial opportunities

The programmes classified under this group are very similar to the ones listed under "skill development" above. Students are supported for engagement in real-life businesses, which they would carry on beyond their course. The support provided is similar to that offered in skill development programmes – namely, seed money assistance, internship with entrepreneurs and other experts, incubation, technology commercialisation, investment and fund management activities, and so on.

Distance education programmes through the electronic media

The latest trend in entrepreneurship education is to use the electronic media to increase the reach and flexibility of these programmes. Three main types of technologies are used in such programmes; singly or their combination:

- Web-based programmes, which are totally asynchronous and, which therefore offer the learner complete flexibility in terms of time and place.

- Interactive CDs in combination with web-based as well as physical contact sessions, which might reduce the flexibility to some extent but minimise the problems of web access, if any.

- Video-based transmission of lectures and synchronous interaction as an extension of the classroom, which offers practically no flexibility as to timing and limited flexibility as to place, but eliminates the need for travel and promotes more effective (quasi-face-to-face) interaction than on the web.

Such technologies can be used for delivering lectures, organising discussions, developing and discussing (live) case studies, interacting with entrepreneurs and other experts, accessing the shared databases, and so on. The main advantage of such technologies is that they would offer the entrepreneur much-needed flexibility and reduce the cost of accessing the learning inputs.

The innovations that universities and HEIs are carrying out in their attempt to teach entrepreneurship more effectively are a response to a felt need from the client group.

Measuring effectiveness

Regrettably, there is insufficient evidence on the value of entrepreneurship education programmes, measured either in terms of their effectiveness in fostering an entrepreneurial culture or in terms of generating new ventures. The difficulty lies in:

- The lack of accepted paradigms or theories of entrepreneurship education, and recognised shortcomings in the definition of entrepreneurship and small business, which leads to confusion in training provision (Hills, 1998; Gibb, 1993).

- Implicit and ill-judged assumptions that training leads to improved business performance, especially at the start-up stage (Storey and Westhead, 1994).

- The failure to link different rings in the chain of success (from knowledge and skills to forms of delivery, absorptive capacity of learners, behavioural change through learning and changes in business performance.

- The generic nature of training for small-scale entrepreneurship.

In identifying only three training programmes dealing with "purely entrepreneurial factors" that have been properly evaluated, Friedrich *et al.* (2006) point to issues of achievement motivation and achievement-associated networking (McClelland, 1961), guided self-analysis; the stimulation of enterprise behaviour, building up of business competencies, and ownership of the process of training acquired through the investment of time and energy, and behavioural competencies and indicators of successful entrepreneurs.

Based on their own work in South Africa, Friedrich *et al.* (2006) propose an action-based model that is cognitive in character and applies principles of action theory, which include heuristics, learning by doing and differentiated feedback. Taking entrepreneurs through a training programme built on elements of goal setting, continuous planning, innovation through the transformation of questions, personal initiative (as in being proactive and a self-starter) and time management, the authors found that the training group (in comparison with the control group, which did not participate in the training) had improved its business performance. Such results do not, however, lead to any conclusion about any causal relationship between training and performance outcomes.

This difficulty in measuring the value of specific entrepreneurship training for new ventures is complemented by the added difficulty in making general training programmes work for the benefit of existing owner-managers of SMEs. In a survey of 300 randomly selected SME units conducted by the NS Raghavan Centre for Entrepreneurial Learning (NSRCEL) at the Indian Institute of Management Bangalore, it was found that SMEs' interest in training and their ability to afford it are fairly low. This is probably because the respondents could have been thinking primarily about the academic programmes offered in schools and colleges rather than those tailor-made for the specific requirements of SME enterprises, which in any case are far too few in the country to get noticed and remain at the top of their minds. Among the more important findings in that survey:

- 38% of the sample felt that SMEs do not need any training at all, while 47% admitted that they need training in some areas. Only 15% acknowledged the need for training without any reservations. Among these, it was the medium-sized firms who felt the need strongly, which supports the obvious argument that the number of employees has a direct influence on the perceived need for training.

- The priority areas for training for the directors are: marketing (38%), finance (27%), quality assurance (18%), technology management (17%), venture capital and funds management (16%), leadership skills (18%), networking skills (16%), selling skills (16%) and negotiation skills (15%). For the managers they are: finance (24%), quality assurance (12%), marketing (10%) and team-skills (18%). And for the employees, they are: quality assurance (19%), production management (8%), team-skills (21%) and interpersonal skills (10%).

- SMEs are not interested in long-duration training programmes conducted away from their premises. The most preferred duration is 2-4 hours, preferably on weekends. There is a clear preference for short on-campus training programmes.

- The most preferred training providers are individual trainers and consultants (30%), followed by training institutes (28%), consultant organisations (17%), universities (7%) and industry associations (7%). It may be noted that universities are among the least preferred training providers, reinforcing the perception of mistrust or mismatch.

- Although the SMEs in the sample have expressed preferences for certain types of programmes and training providers, their actual behaviour is illustrative of the gap between their "espoused theory" and "theory-in-use". For example, the actual training providers are the accountants, family members, colleagues in the industry, technology associates, and the like. There is hardly any use of professional training providers or educational institutions. As for the participation in external programmes, only 6% of the directors, 3% of the managers and 1% of the employees have ever undergone any such training.

The picture that emerges from the survey is not very different from current stereotypes. Though there is some acceptance of the need for training at the conceptual level, the behaviour of SMEs does not support their words. Some of them were candid on this, as they clarified that their statement about SMEs' need for training was with reference to the SME sector in general, not their own enterprises. Several reasons were stated for the SMEs' disinclination towards training:

- Self-confidence arising from past successes and the belief that what could be accomplished in the past can be continued without any additional learning inputs.

- Perceived irrelevance of the offerings from some of the educational/training institutions.

- Lack of tangible effects of training in the short term, and the priority given to the tangible and immediate needs of day-to-day management.

- Inability or unwillingness to pay for the programmes (reinforced also by an erstwhile culture, particularly in developing countries, of government-subsidised SME training).

- Inability to leave one's business to attend long-duration programmes conducted during office hours on working days.

- Apprehension that the trained employees might leave the firm for better opportunities.

While all these constraints and apprehensions are genuine, there are enlightened entrepreneurs who recognise the need for training, especially in the growth phase of their ventures. The need arises both from the internal exigencies of growth and from the external dynamism of the environment. It should not necessarily be perceived as resulting from the personal inadequacy of the entrepreneur. With the development of economies, there will be more demand from SME entrepreneurs for appropriate training programmes. The demand for appropriately designed programmes for SMEs is on the increase and the participants' feedback on such programmes is very positive.

Conclusion

It is an increasingly complex world: small firms are buffeted by globalisation in a variety of ways, and the challenge for innovative business outcomes is as important for small, entrepreneurial firms as they are for large, innovative organisations. Given that complexity, there is a greater call for institutions to identify the points at which they could make genuinely differentiated interventions. Each stage should offer its own form of learning, and it is critical that education and training provision acknowledge this stage-specific differentiation and the involvement of different stakeholders. The study of entrepreneurship at each of these stages does not simply adumbrate issues pertaining to the creation or growth of a business. It also allows for the investigation of policy implications for growing such businesses in particular environments – the need to develop a relevant skills base, the facilitation of technology transfer, and the iteration and spread of knowledge among the wider community.

As the reference to historical antecedents demonstrates, entrepreneurship and economic change can be facilitated through a focused, skills-based agenda that has a spatial and temporal context. Recognition of the value of such programmes enables policy makers and providers to identify specific forms of education and training that have favourable entrepreneurial outcomes. These outcomes do not necessarily manifest themselves in terms of new business creation; they are often in the form of industrial change that affords increased prospects for new product development and innovation. As they provide an enabling function, HEIs need to take stock of their own institutional and governance structures; how such structures need to adapt to reflect different environments; and the way to maintain a balance between the production of public goods and utilitarian, economic services. Institutions should be allowed to deconstruct and build new structures and to set new or revised objectives. Moreover, they should be able to do so without being penalised by different metrics measuring static situations, and without being limited by restricted pedagogic forms. Policies allowing for such entrepreneurial changes within HEIs could help those institutions develop new cultures for entrepreneurship education.

It could be argued that the difficulties HEIs face in adapting results is the mismatch between their provision and the real needs of entrepreneurs. Programmes follow disparate paths, with institutions carving out varied routes to try and meet those needs. In doing so, universities also confront the structural constraints of analytical debate and discourse, of competency building courses that become routine and allow for relatively safe career-based outcomes. HEIs cannot be expected to change the modalities of provision for entrepreneurship education simply because it is expedient to do so, without intellectual and economic fallout. Therefore, from a policy perspective, the need to accommodate ambidextrous institutions (either separate, or in terms of different forms within the same institution) would be a useful approach to supporting HEIs.

Evaluation, rather than simple measurement of inputs and outputs, should also be an important policy imperative. Educators should be able to experiment with, develop and offer critical learning environments for entrepreneurs. To do so they need evaluation methodologies that allow for both *ex ante* and post-initiative tools; institutions can integrate these methodologies and tools into their own learning experience as they work in the field of entrepreneurship. It is difficult to argue that any one measure, such as entrepreneurship education, leads to a successful outcome, since there are many other variables influencing the entrepreneur's ability to succeed. Thus policy measures that are focused on learning outputs and that are validated by both the university and the beneficiary can have far-reaching results in allowing HEIs to work better with entrepreneurs.

Furthermore, reflecting on the critical need for both entrepreneurship in education *and* entrepreneurship education, there is a need to infuse different disciplines of study with the "spirit of enterprise". This calls for the development of a framework for entrepreneurship education that supports the study of entrepreneurship and business growth; investigation of the link between the study of technology and science and innovation; the lending of substance to recent interest in the arts; creative industries and enterprise creation; and, critically, the creation of different mindsets among learners to help them reduce uncertainties and better understand the complexities of the phenomenon of change. The challenges for the universities and HEIs are to:

- Identify these "seismic" points of innovation in the different stages of development of a business (at the start-up stage, the early-growth stage and the renewal stage), where appropriate forms of intervention could be made.

- Establish a framework for the study of entrepreneurship across the curriculum.

- Design flexible, short-duration and modular programmes offered at realistic timings and affordable costs for the SME entrepreneurs.

It is hoped that the experiences and experiments of the pioneering institutions in educating the entrepreneur will light our paths and show us the way forward.

Bibliography

Bolton Committee Report (1971), *Report of the Committee of Inquiry on Small Firms*, Cmnd 4811, HMSO, London.

Branscomb, L. and F. Kodama (1999), 'University Research as an Engine for Growth: How Realistic is this Vision?, in L.M. Branscomb et al. (eds.), *Industrialising Knowledge: University-Industry Linkages in Japan and the United States*, MIT Press, Cambridge, MA.

Friedrich, C., *et al.* (2006), "Does Training improve the business performance of small-scale entrepreneurs? An evaluative study", *Industry and Higher Education*, Vol. 20, No. 2, IP Publishing, pp. 75-84.

Gibb, A. (1993), "The enterprise culture and education: Understanding enterprise education and its links with small business entrepreneurs and wider educational goals", *International Small Business Journal*, Vol. 11, No. 3, Sage, pp. 11-34.

Harper, M. (1984), *Entrepreneurship for the Poor*, Intermediate Technology, in association with GTZ, London.

Hills, G. (1988), "Variations in university entrepreneurship education: an empirical study of an evolving field", *Journal of Business Venturing*, Vol. 3, No.2, Elsevier, pp 109-122.

Hisrich, R.D., and B. O'Cinneide (1996), "Entrepreneurial activities in Europe-oriented institutions", *Journal of Managerial Psychology*, Vol. 11, No. 2, Emerald, pp. 45-64.

Manimala, M. J. (2002), *Global Entrepreneurship Monitor: India Report 2002*, NS Raghavan Centre for Entrepreneurial Learning, Indian Institute of Management Bangalore.

Manimala, J M (2005), "Innovative entrepreneurship: Testing the theory of environmental determinism", in M.J. Manimala (eds.), *Entrepreneurship Theory at the Cross-roads: Paradigms and Praxis* (2nd edition), Wiley-Dreamtech, New Delhi, Chapter 2.

Manimala, M. J. (forthcoming), "Entrepreneurship Education in India: An Assessment of SME Training Needs Against Current Practices", *International Journal of Entrepreneurship and Innovation Management*.

McClelland, D.C. (1987), *Human Motivation*, Cambridge University Press, Cambridge, MA.

McClelland, D. C. (1961), *The Achieving Society*, Van Nostarnd, Princeton, N.J.

Mitra, J and P. Formica (1997), *Innovation and Economic Development: University-Enterprise Partnerships in Action*, Oak Tree Press, Dublin.

Muta, H. (2000), "Deregulation and decentralization of education in Japan", *Journal of Educational Administration*, Vol. 38, No. 5, Emerald, pp. 455-67.

North, D. (2002), *Institutions, Institutional Change and Economic Performance*, Cambridge University Press, Cambridge, MA.

Reynolds, P.D., *et al.* (2002), *Global Entrepreneurship Monitor: 2002 Executive Report*, Babson College, London Business School, and Ewing Marion Kauffman Foundation.

Ronstadt, R. (1988), "The corridor principle", *Journal of Business Venturing*, Vol. 3, No. 11, Elsevier, pp. 31-40.

Sandercock, P. (2001), "Innovations in Entrepreneurship Education: Strategy and Tactics for Joining the Ranks of Innovative Entrepreneurship Programs in Higher Education", Paper Prepared for the CEAE Coleman, March 2001.

Storey, D. and P. Westhead, (1994), "Management training and small firm performance: a critical review", *Working Paper No.18*, SME Centre, Warwick University, Coventry.

Chapter 3

Entrepreneurship Education in an Age of Chaos, Complexity and Disruptive Change

by
Eugene Luczkiw
Institute for Enterprise Education and Brock University, Canada

The first part of this chapter seeks to identify four fundamental themes that underline a need for leaders and policy makers to venture outside existing industrial age worldviews in order to develop a new framework with its own distinct sets of rules and regulations. These call for a new paradigm for teaching and learning about entrepreneurship.

The second part of this chapter examines the conditions and cultures needed to nurture and sustain enterprising behaviours. It provides global case studies and materials related to development of entrepreneurial ecologies and their networks.

The conclusion calls for adaptation of this emerging ecological paradigm by means of collaborations among government policy makers, entrepreneurs and educational leaders. This collaboration requires a strong sense of trust, a diversity of ideas, adaptability, flexibility, and a compelling vision of achievement, improvisation, communication and inspiration.

Introduction

We are living in a postmodern age that Vaclav Havel, the former president of the Czech Republic, described as an era where everything is possible and nothing is certain. In fact, the only way to succeed in today's global environment is to internalise a whole new set of rules that will allow us to navigate through all the turbulence.

The rules and regulations that served Western democratic societies well in the past – the stable industrial era – no longer serve us well today. The metaphor of the machine has been replaced by that of the organic network.

The scientific method, dominant in what was called the modern age, is now being challenged by the emerging scientific paradigm of the 21st century: the new Science of Complexity.

The practice of entrepreneurship holds a great deal of promise for navigating the chaos, complexity and disruptions. But the discipline of entrepreneurship needs to reflect the Science of Complexity, while the university culture continues to be the repository of the scientific method. This clash of cultures must remain a critical consideration as to what, how, why, when and where entrepreneurship should be taught, and by whom. It is clear from extensive research of entrepreneurs around the globe that certain patterns of navigation can increase the chances of entrepreneurial success. Even more importantly, it is clear that the entrepreneur's network, and how it is nurtured, holds even greater promise in the birth and growth of successful enterprises (Luczkiw, 2002).

In a number of Western democracies, entrepreneurship and small business are responsible for over 50% of employment. When the indirect benefits of these start-ups are included, the number escalates to over 60%.

The purpose of this chapter is to provide a framework for delivery of entrepreneurship education and training to those individuals seeking to create and grow small enterprises into medium and large enterprises. The discussion should also interest those who seek to internalise entrepreneurial behaviour in other fields of endeavour.

The chapter is structured as follows. Firstly, before examining strategies for teaching and learning about entrepreneurship, we explore four fundamental themes informing these strategies:

- An understanding of emerging global forces and trends and their impact upon communities.

- The need for a new science to provide a theoretical framework for interacting in today's global environment.

- A shared understanding of the meaning of entrepreneurship.

- Identification of conditions and cultures that nurture the creation, development and growth of entrepreneurship.

The discussion then turns to programme content – what should the basis be? How can we create effective programmes related to teaching and learning about enterprise and through enterprise?

The past few decades have shown that the largest rewards in the economic sphere go to those individuals or teams who rapidly deploy their genius by going in directions no one has ventured into before. The founders of Apple, Dell, Federal Express, Google, Intel, Microsoft and Virgin, to name a few, created their own realities that could only be valued once the concept was proved in the marketplace. Indeed, most of the so-called "experts" could not predict the success of any of these ventures.

Entrepreneurship, as a field, is holistic in nature; it goes beyond the walls of the business school. Psychology and neuroscience are now the fields that offer the greatest insights into the mind of the entrepreneur. It is how entrepreneurs use knowledge, emotion and instinct in concert with one another to venture in new directions – in order to uncover new landscapes of opportunity – that provides the basis of a teaching and learning methodology.

Enabling learners to discover their essence of being, and how they best perform, and then exposing them to rapid-fire trial and error improvisations, will give them much more of a sense of what entrepreneurship is really all about.

The four fundamental themes

An understanding of emerging global forces and trends and their impact upon communities

We live in an era of complexity, chaos and discontinuous change. Several major demographic, economic, social, environmental and technological forces are creating disruptions and instability as new engines of economic growth begin to emerge. Today, an interdependent culture is rapidly emerging and a new global paradigm taking shape – a paradigm that is transforming the culture of individual nation-states and exhibiting more shared values among nation states than ever before.

This emerging external environment has its own complex and divergent structures, systems and behaviour. Traditional rules and regulations that governed boundaries in space and time during the industrial age have all but disappeared. Changes brought about by the information technologies age are rapid, structural and systemic. Geographic boundaries have been stripped of their significance as bits of information are transported by electronic means across borders. The challenge is to understand how this new borderless worldview will impact upon the beliefs, behaviours and systems we develop to create our future within this environment.

Globalisation is first and foremost an economic force that deals with the creation of worldwide strategies by organisations seeking expansion and operations on a global level. To understand globalisation, it must be seen from an evolutionary perspective. Friedman (2005) discerns three stages.

The first stage lasted from the 15th to the 19th century. This was globalisation for the purposes of resources and the conquest of countries. Europe was the centre of the universe. Its competition was among states vying to possess the greatest number of colonies and their rich resources. The second stage took place from the 19th to the end of the 20th century. This stage saw the globalisation of markets, as large corporations began to leave the safety of home and compete in foreign markets around the globe. During this period, the power of the state was replaced by the power of global conglomerates. As we enter the third stage of globalisation we see the world shrinking further, as new economies from India, China and Asia emerge as the third force to compete with Europe and North America. Bangalore, India has now become the global centre for software development and tax preparation, while China is rapidly becoming a global manufacturing centre. What is most interesting in this third era, however, is that it is driven by a much more diverse form of macro capitalism that is non-western in content and form. We have reached an era where we no longer know where the next new disruptive technology is coming from.

Florida (2005) argues that we are now in the fourth era of globalisation, one he calls the new global competition for talent. The mobility of people, perhaps the single greatest feature of today's global economy, is even more powerful than the emergence of new technologies or mobility of capital. Within this environment, many places will gain specific advantages based on the diversity of their particular ecology. The global economy becomes more complex; its participants, each with their own distinct capabilities, seek out specialised niches for their ideas, forming a rich mosaic. Florida describes these participants as the "creative class", a mobile group of diverse talent that provides the substance from which new sources of value emerge to meet the ever changing needs of the marketplace. Roughly 30% of the US workforce today makes up this creative class.

Immigrants have played a significant role in US economic growth. According to Florida, foreign-born CEOs ran 72 of America's top

500 entrepreneurial firms in the late 90s. In addition, immigrant entrepreneurs accounted for 30% of all Silicon Valley start-ups during the 90s, accounting for nearly USD 20 billion in sales and more than 70 000 jobs (Florida, 2005, p. 7).

According to the "Green Paper – Entrepreneurship in Europe" (Commission of the European Communities, 2003), "Europe needs to foster entrepreneurial drive more effectively. It needs more new and thriving firms willing to reap the benefits of market openings and to embark on creative and innovative ventures for commercial exploitation on a larger scale". In that paper, the European Council sets out an ambitious agenda, through which it seeks "to become the most competitive and dynamic knowledge-based economy in the world, capable of sustainable economic growth with more and better jobs and greater social cohesion". While the European Council is aware of the need for a radical transformation of the economy, it does not include the need for transformation of the European society.

In a recent report for the European Commission entitled "An Agenda For a Growing Europe", economists propose that Europe's course since the Second World War was based on integration of existing technologies. There was a reliance on mass production to generate the necessary economies of scale, and on an industrial infrastructure dominated by large firms with stable markets and long-term employment patterns. The authors argue that this system no longer delivers in today's world, characterised by economic globalisation and strong external competition. They point out that what is needed is less vertically integrated firms, increased movement internally and externally among firms, increased flexibility of labour markets, greater availability of finance, and increased investments in research and development and education.

The impact of economic globalisation on Europe currently leads to an acceleration of the commoditisation of products and services, increasing price wars, cost reductions, job losses and shrinking profit margins. Another trend relates to consumers discovering similarities between brand name products, leading to price as the determinant in their buying decisions.

The bottom line today is that anyone with intelligence, access to Google and a cheap, wireless laptop can join the entrepreneurship game – innovating without emigrating.

Globalisation also challenges our environment's capacity to renew and regenerate itself for our survival in the midst of diseases and terrorism around the globe. In this age of seamless boundaries among nation-states, it is next to impossible to insulate oneself from these destructive forces at play.

The common denominator in the economic sphere is the emergence of the entrepreneur as the heir apparent to the large corporation, and in places other than Western democracies. Already, the necessary technologies and tools exist to create the future, and the entrepreneur will be the executor of these innovations. Unless countries take a proactive stance to create the right conditions and programmes to nurture the growth of entrepreneurs, they will fall off the ledge of future economic and social growth.

The world needs to be seen with a new set of eyes, and the turbulent waters of change navigated with a new set of rules and regulations. A new science needs to shift our existing paradigms and offer a new formula for success. That science already exists: it is the Science of Complexity.

The need for a new science to provide a theoretical framework for interacting in today's global environment

The science of the industrial age relied on the scientific method in order to establish objective truth. This method of questioning viewed systems in isolation, both from one another and from their environment. Two factors became critical in conducting research:

- One needed to separate the observer from what was being observed.

- Every physical element had to be reduced to its lowest common denominator; the parts were used to predict future behaviour.

The Newtonian mechanistic and reductionist system became the basis of scientific thought. The key components of this system included determinism, linearity, predictability and simplicity. By embodying these principles, Fredrick Taylor (in Kelly and Allison, 1998) was able to create the Scientific Management Model that continues to influence individuals, leaders and organisations around the globe as they attempt to adapt to the realities of globalisation.

What we are now facing is a major economic and social paradigm shift, and the exponential growth of information technologies and knowledge has created an ever widening gap in human understanding of the impact and nature of this change.

Paradigms are fundamental beliefs about the world (Kuhn, 1962). They provide the necessary rules and regulations, establish boundaries, and indicate the behaviours needed to succeed. Paradigms also suggest metaphors that are helpful in framing problems and arriving at their ultimate solutions. However, on the flip side, paradigms can blind individuals to facts, data and challenges that are not consistent with their thinking. Conflict between exponents of different paradigms can also lead to irrational debate.

Such debate is currently taking place at all levels of the scientific, political, economic and social spectrums as the traditional Newtonian mechanistic paradigm is replaced by the emerging complexity sciences and the entrepreneurial metaphor.

While our human mind is the new source of capital, a greater need exists to develop our imagination to the point of discovering emerging opportunities within this rapidly changing and unstable global environment. Innovation has already outpaced the rate of human evolution in ever growing quantum leaps, creating a large gap. We need to bridge this gap if we are to move to a higher order as individuals, organisations, economies and societies.

The classical model of economics, based on scarcity of resources, no longer serves as a complete source of explanation, let alone predictor of future direction. Instead of looking at a *fixed pie* approach, we need to focus on an *expanding pie* as integral to the new network economy.

Brian Arthur (Kurtzman, 1998) indicates that when we deal with scarce natural resources such as ore, after a certain point each additional ton of new ore extracted increases in cost (the law of diminishing returns). In the case of knowledge products, such as software, the cost of the first unit will be very high, reflecting the high cost of research and development. However, each additional unit will be produced at a fraction of the cost (the law of increasing returns). Together with the principle of "lock-in", software companies like Microsoft can offer its Windows format at a price sufficiently low to capture the market, thus "locking in" customers to its network. It is this network of Microsoft users, as well as other software developers, that gains the benefit of increased interaction with potential stakeholders, leading to increased possibilities and opportunities in their differentiated roles.

Kevin Kelly (1997) describes the power of this network. As networks have permeated our world, the economy has come to resemble an ecology of organisms, interlinked and co-evolving, constantly in flux, deeply tangled, and ever expanding at its edges. As we know from recent ecological studies, no balance exists in nature. Rather, as evolution proceeds, there is perpetual disruption as new species displace old, as natural biomes shift in their makeup, and as organisms and environments transform each other.

The Science of Complexity

Our world is a complex system (like our body) that consists of a series of organisational structures (economic, political, social) that interact with one another nationally and internationally. With that in mind we began to focus on the emerging Science of Complexity. That science could provide an understanding of the similarities between physical, biological and human systems, and so help develop a better understanding of our relationship with the global environment.

The Science of Complexity was developed by Nobel Prize scientists from diverse fields of study. It studies what is described as "complex adaptive systems" that include cells, embryos, brains, ecologies, economies and political and social systems. These systems consist of diverse parts that are organically related. Complexity is also a central principle of evolution that effectively demonstrates how, through a process of differentiation and integration, humans can transcend their evolutionary path. It helps explain how organisms, with more integrated physiology or behavioural repertoires, tend to gain a competitive advantage over others.

Whereas Newtonian science sought to reduce everything to its smallest component, the emerging Science of Complexity focuses on interactions and emergent behaviours where the whole becomes greater than the sum of its parts. The universe is full of differentiated agents following set patterns of distinct rules, leading to relationships that seek to uncover a hidden order.

To understand the workings of these complex adaptive systems, we need to understand their constituent parts and how they interact with one another. Let us begin with the components:

- *Agents* are known as decision-making units, and include individuals who make up an ecosystem for an enterprise.

- *Rules* determine how agents make choices. Each individual agent has his/her own rules of behaviour. People are distinct beings based on their genes, culture and gender.

- *Emergent properties* are the result of individual agents interacting with one another, each following their own sets of behavioural rules, creating a whole that is greater than the sum of their individual interactions.

The meaning of self-organisation

Self-organisation refers to how a system of agents organises itself into a higher order.

There are three distinct characteristics of such a system:

- Complex behaviours result from individual unit (agents).

- From a diversity of these individual inputs, a new solution emerges.

- The robustness of the system is greater than the sum of its individual inputs.

The Internet is such an example. It integrates a wide breadth of knowledge, captures and displays a depth of information, processes information correctly, organises information into a knowledge base, and expands the reach across the globe. When you connect millions of people from around the globe, you enhance the creative process by a power of thousands.

As a result, a complex adaptive system is a network of many individual agents (individuals) all acting in parallel and interacting with one another. The critical variable that makes the system both complex and adaptive is the idea that agents (cells, ants, neurons, or individuals) in the system accumulate experience by interacting with other agents, and then change themselves to adapt to a changing environment. If a complex system is continuously adapting, it is impossible for any such system, including the consumer market, ever to reach a state of perfect equilibrium. The complexity view is that a market that is not rational is organic, not mechanistic, and is imperfectly inefficient.

Economic, political and social systems are all complex (a large number of individual units) and adaptive (individual units adapting their behaviours on the basis of interaction with other units as well as with the systems as a whole). These systems have "self-organising properties"; once organised, they generate emergent behaviours. Finally, the systems are constantly unstable and periodically reach a crisis.

There exist two powerful tools for successful navigation within today's global environment – the networks and symbiotic relationships. The two are practical applications of complexity theory, and the critical determinants of those conditions and cultures that nurture innovation and entrepreneurship.

A network consists of individuals or groups that work to achieve their individual goals within a community of common interest. The purpose of a network is twofold:

- To enable individuals to pursue their mission.

- To share their accomplishments with others.

A network consists of people who are so closely and directly affected by each other's actions that all parties ought to consider these actions before taking an initiative. For instance, in a business environment, these include customers, suppliers, financiers and competitors.

The most effective networks are those where each person seeks to assist other members of the network without any expectation that he/she will ever be so served. However, the more you help others, the greater dependence you create on yourself. When you or your enterprise faces a crisis, members of your network are obliged to assist you. This was clearly demonstrated in the Institute for Enterprise Education's research related to the growth of over 2 700 entrepreneurial ventures.

Apple Computer is a good business case that demonstrates the power of networks. It continues to exist in spite of a number of critical strategic blunders, because of its network of stakeholders, which includes customers, distributors, suppliers, financiers and competitors. The company's recent successful reinvention and regeneration has been the result of their successful launch of the iPod MP3 player with a library of downloadable music. As a result, Apple's recent market capitalisation has rivalled that of the Sony Corporation.

Symbiosis is a biological term that describes how different organisms, living in intimate and interdependent associations, seek to co-create new possibilities that are mutually beneficial to all involved. It is about both competition and collaboration (co-opetition) in building strategic alliances.

There are two reasons for building strategic alliances:

• The need to accelerate the growth trajectory.

• The need to gain access to external core capabilities.

As the number of nodes in the network increases incrementally, the value of the network increases exponentially. For instance, if you have four friends, you have ten distinct one-to-one friendships among them. Add a fifth friend and the friendships increase to 15; add a sixth and you make 21 connections. As the number of friends increases, the total number of relationships escalates as well.

The power of the network is not gauged solely by the number of its members. Also involved is the diversity of members' talents, contributions and creativity. Together, this collective wisdom provides the critical mass required to support the successful start-up and growth of both new and existing enterprises.

A shared understanding of the meaning of entrepreneurship

Two critical factors influence today's exponential growth of new enterprises:

• An increased need for entrepreneurial talent to deal with today's emerging global realities.

• The individual's conscious awareness of the need to discover one's meaning in a world of rapidly increasing discontinuities.

For the foreseeable future, we will continue to see a growing need for entrepreneurs to develop structures, systems, processes and strategies that can deal with the emerging complexities. This has tremendous implications, not only for those seeking to begin and grow an enterprise, but also for large monolithic organisations stuck in their existing paradigms and unable to take advantage of today's global opportunities.

The "Green Paper – Entrepreneurship in Europe" (Commission of the European Communities, 2003) points out that entrepreneurship is first and foremost a mindset. "Entrepreneurship is about people, their choices and actions in starting, taking over or running a business, or their involvement in a firm's strategic decision-making. It covers an individual's motivation and capacity, independently or within an organisation, to identify an opportunity and to pursue it, in order to produce new value or economic success."

The successful growth of an enterprise hinges on an individual's ability to exploit emerging opportunities creatively, while constantly adapting and implementing the new products and/or services. The overall success of any enterprise is not based on the completion of a successful business plan, but on the interrelationships between the intrinsic motivation of the entrepreneurs, their teams and the supportive extrinsic motivation in the community that enables entrepreneurs to grow their enterprises effectively.

Before embarking on a more detailed analysis of entrepreneurs, it is critical to differentiate terms. A study entitled "Differentiating Entrepreneurs from Small Business Owners: A Conceptualization" (Carland, Hay and Bolton, 1984) distinguishes between an entrepreneur, a small business owner and a self-employed person. This study is consistent with the research findings by the Institute for Enterprise Education of over 2 700 small and medium-sized enterprises over the past decade. The findings:

- Entrepreneurs practice disruptive forms of innovation, as in the case of and Richard Branson of Virgin.

- Small business owners practice management skills as the principle activity of their enterprise. Examples include retail store owners and franchises, such as McDonalds.

- Self-employed individuals practice their skills or trades as part of their enterprise. Examples include carpenters, electricians and artists.

Both the small business owner and the self-employed person practice incremental forms of innovation, as opposed to the entrepreneur, who practices disruptive forms of innovation. Based on these terminologies, entrepreneurs make up a very small sector of the economy; most are found in the latter two bulleted categories. The needs of each of these start-up enterprises are distinct. The key is to ensure that governments, educational institutions and society as a whole understand the nature and quality of these distinct activities.

As practitioners of disruptive innovation however, entrepreneurs serve as models for every member of society. They do so because they are effective in engaging their distinct creativity and turning it into action through innovation. While entrepreneurs themselves are a rare commodity, their practice holds promise for all. We can all learn how to become enterprising in our specific fields by learning the new rules of navigation.

According to Miller (1999), creativity is an expression of who we are and not what we do. Miller further points out that it is not the strongest species that survive, nor the most intelligent, but the ones most responsive to change. This is the key for enabling every member of society to engage his or her distinct creativity, whatever the nature of work.

A study of entrepreneurial behaviour by OECD (1989) provides lessons as to how each individual in society can become 'enterprising' by connecting their distinct talents, meaning and motivation to create new opportunities and possibilities for themselves. "In short, people will need to be creative, rather than passive; capable of self-initiated action, rather than dependent; they will need to know how to learn, rather than expect to be taught; they will need to be enterprising in their outlook, not think and act like an employee or client. The organisations in which they work, communities in which they live and societies in which they belong, will in turn, also need to possess all these qualities."

A journey into the mind of the entrepreneur reveals a number of insights that societies can incorporate into creating the conditions and cultures necessary for enterprise. Csikszentmihalyi (1990) suggests that extremely high levels of intrinsic motivation are marked by such strong interest and involvement in their work, and by such a perfect match of task difficulty with the skill level, that people experience a kind of psychological "flow", a sense of merging with the activity they are doing. Amabile (1997) concludes that intrinsic motivation is conducive to an individual's creativity. Entrepreneurs generate and implement novel ideas in order to establish new ventures. All these efforts transpire in the mind of the entrepreneur, according to the study of entrepreneurial behaviour by OECD (1989).

The next question that should be asked is, how is the influence of the external environment represented in the entrepreneur's experience? As Mitton (1989) states: "Entrepreneurs see ways to put resources and information together in new combinations. They not only see the system (environment) as it is, but as it might be. They have a knack for looking at the usual and seeing the unusual; at the ordinary and seeing the extraordinary." The key, according to Shaver (1991), is to concentrate on the person in his/her situational context. Situational variables can determine the degree of motivational synergy experienced. If external incentives and supports are presented in a manner that enhances the entrepreneur's vision, it is likely to support motivation and creativity. For instance, an onerous venture capital process may weaken the entrepreneurial creativity, as may stringent controls and lack of available government programmes, regulations and taxation.

By focusing on their mindset, we begin to see how entrepreneurs – as agents of change – break from their culture and genetic determinants to create what has not been created before.

Identification of conditions and cultures that nurture the creation, development and growth of entrepreneurship

Two issues need to be considered:

- How do you create conditions and cultures that nurture each person's distinct contributions?

- How do we enable each person to engage their distinct talents in order to align them with activities that lead to commitment and involvement in the workplace?

Developing an effective framework for analysis of a local entrepreneurial culture requires a synthesis of critical factors. Entrepreneurship is one of the principal sources of economic development in local economies. Enabling people to create their own work and have a degree of control over the nature of the work itself, allows the unleashing of energies needed to get past the challenges and obstacles that are generally in the way of opportunity. While the challenges are the responsibility of the entrepreneur, the obstacles tend to be bureaucratic and structural in nature and fall under the control of governments. Defining culture and entrepreneurship is the natural starting point.

The Oxford Desk Dictionary and Thesaurus definition of *culture* is as follows: "The customs, civilisation and achievement of a particular time or people, including the improvement by mental or physical training." A culture involves group-wide practices that are passed on from generation to generation. Historically, culture evolved from a convergence of individual beliefs and values communicated by language – communication became the critical element in passing on vital information. This enabled our ancestors to create societies that took in division of labour, entry into long-term obligations and extension of co-operation beyond the bonds of kinship, while accumulating systemic knowledge, expertise and historical record (Quartz and Sejnowski, 2002).

Any analysis of the creation of an entrepreneurial culture begins with an implicit understanding of the individual himself or herself and how they can engage their distinct contribution (talents) and creativity by aligning them with the expressed needs of the community. That, first and foremost, is an obligation of society: to ensure that each person becomes all they are capable of being. To this end, we need to differentiate entrepreneurship from enterprise. Enterprise is defined as the taking of initiative to achieve a self-determined goal that is part of a future vision enabling one to pursue their meaning in life, while sharing it with others in the community (Luczkiw, 2002). This definition supports the argument stated earlier that everyone needs to become enterprising. It is also becoming clear that entrepreneurship, as a practice, transcends culture. It thus requires an ecological support system to ensure its continued birth, growth and development.

What content should make up the entrepreneurship curriculum?

The entrepreneurship curriculum needs to be multidisciplinary in nature. It needs to reflect the rules of the Science of Complexity. As individuals we are complex beings, each with our own distinct set of talents and motivation.

Csikszentmihalyi (1990), as mentioned above, points out that an individual's drive and determination emerges from a strong sense of intrinsic motivation. Intrinsic motivation stems from our internal needs for achieving competence, meaning and self-determination. Intrinsic motivation enables people to energise their behaviours in order to satisfy their desires as they seek out personal challenges. As these challenges require a leap into the unknown, one needs to stretch one's abilities and interests. Enjoyment is derived from participating in those activities that lead to increased creativity and spontaneity. By pursuing these self-determined goals, people achieve what Csikszentmihalyi calls "flow".

Csikszentmihalyi further argues that self-determined people are motivated by the activity rather than being ego-driven. Timmons (1989) noted that a common element running through research of successful entrepreneurs is the journey rather than the destination as the key motivator.

While entrepreneurs clearly demonstrate a passion for their distinct journeys, each person has the same opportunity to become self-determining, by discovering those activities that engage their inner essence of being, talent and motivation. By making this connection with external opportunities, people have the potential to become intrinsically motivated.

After an extensive research into the fields of human dynamics and enterprising behaviours, we share the conclusion of Shaver (1991): economic circumstances are important; social networks are important; finance is important; even public agency assistance is important. But none of these alone creates a venture. For that we need a person in whose mind all of the possibilities come together, a person who believes that innovation is possible, and who has the motivation to persist until the job is done.

New enterprises, according to Shaver, emerge and take the form they do because of deliberate choices made by individuals – thus the focus on choice. From the perspective of an entrepreneur, two questions are critical: can I make a difference? Do I want to make a difference?

The first question focuses on the perception of control, while the second requires the needed motivation. The answer to the first can only be affirmative if the person a) considers the choice theirs to make; b) has some initial success attributed to the self; and c) maintains an intrinsic interest in the project.

The proposed curriculum has been utilised at the undergraduate level in the business faculty as an introductory course at the teacher education level, and in the community as an introductory course in entrepreneurship. The enterprise curriculum focuses on the following five E's of learning:

- *Environment* – First a context for the learner is created, by enabling each teacher candidate to become conscious of the emergent global environment and its resultant impact on the community and individuals who inhabit it. Through the series of interactive activities that follow, participants co-create the elements that make up this environment under the title *Global Scan*. As part of this activity, we reflect upon the why, how, when, and what of these significant events.

- *Economy* – Once the context is developed, teacher candidates reflect upon potential strategies for success in this environment. Through a process of self-directed learning, participants seek out literature and research to gain a more ecological understanding. Participants also discover the nature of today's network economy and the resultant new rules of interaction, by means of experiential and highly interactive activities.

- *Entrepreneurs* – The study of entrepreneurs begins with each teacher candidate performing a personal interview with an entrepreneur in their community. By gaining insights into the workings of an entrepreneurial mind, teacher candidates observe first-hand their intrinsic motivation, the entrepreneurial process and their interaction with the environment. It is this contextual approach that provides insights into the need to have a

ENTREPRENEURSHIP AND HIGHER EDUCATION – ISBN- 9789264044098 © OECD 2008

strong sense of self prior to embarking on a journey into the unpredictable external environment.

- *Enterprise* – The environment, economy, and entrepreneur provide the underlying framework for the enterprise unit. The enterprise unit is the heart, mind and soul of the programme. It is here that the teacher candidate becomes immersed in a comprehensive process of self-discovery by means of a series of validated assessment tools and reflections dealing with one's thoughts, emotions, perceptions and instincts (our four human faculties).

The purpose of this extensive experiential process is to:

- Become conscious of one's distinct essence of being.

- Discover individual needs, strengths, talents, and values.

- Discover one's meaning and purpose.

- Define one's mission.

- Connect one's distinct characteristics with others in a diverse team environment.

- Develop one's context for learning and teaching.

Upon completion of this unit, each participant is able to develop a composite personal profile that begins the first leg of their journey into enterprise. These experiences will also become the foundation for assisting their own learners to begin the process of discovering their essence of being within the context of the classroom and the community.

- *Entreplexity* – The final 'E' is entreplexity. The purpose of this unit is to unite all five E's around the underlying Science of Complexity and the practice of entrepreneurship. The metaphor used to describe the nature of an organic, humane organisation is that of a jamming jazz band: each person's talents are nurtured, along with that person's distinct contribution to the musical repertoire created by the band.

In Collin's studies of over 1 400 Fortune 500 companies over a 30-year period (2001), he concluded that no innovation of any kind is possible without a humane organisation; further, innovation needs to begin (and continue) with the practice of management.

In addition to delivering programmes at the tertiary level of education, Intotalo – an academy based in Kajaani, Finland – has developed an entrepreneurship programme that provides a context for learning *about, for* and *through* enterprise. Intotalo is a community-based learning environment that enhances the entrepreneurial skills of both secondary school and university students. It resembles an innovative working environment rather than a school. The basis of learning is by doing.

The main foundation of Intotalo is communality. Its aim is to make entrepreneurship fun by creating opportunities to network with practicing entrepreneurs and professionals in the community. Teaching and learning involves coaches as facilitators of team entrepreneurial activities. The role of Intotalo's coaches is distinct from traditional teaching methods. Learning becomes highly interactive in nature as everyone learns together.

The philosophy of the programme is that entrepreneurship arises from within the person and not the business idea. The development of an entrepreneurial personality requires a personal approach. It is essential that people discover the nature of their entrepreneurship activity, be it innovation, self-employment, or small business ownership.

Intotalo recognises that networks are critical in the life of an entrepreneur. New entrepreneurs need to help other similar individuals. The network attempts to ensure the success of their company. Succeeding as a team creates a powerful network leading to a strong mental support net.

Table 3.1. Intotalo's two training stages

Stage 1	Entrepreneurial Characteristics and Project Skills	(8 credits)
	Project management	2 credits
	Inner entrepreneurship	2 credits
	Innovating	1 credit
	Marketing	2 credits
	Communication	1 credit
Stage 2	**Entrepreneurship and Business Skills**	**(7 credits)**
	Leadership	2 credits
	Networking	1 credit
	Economic planning	1 credit
	Company's strategic planning	3 credits

The learning method of entrepreneurship is experientially based (Figure 3.1).

The teaching-learning interactions are led in team sessions by facilitators who demonstrate proficiency in the field of practice. Learners are led through an interactive learning process based on both constructivism and humanism.

During these sessions a free flow of ideas takes place. Learners reflect on what they have learned in dialogue and discuss different issues arising from these interactions.

Intotalo's community of 35 000 appear to be truly engaged – connected nationally and generally in order to identify potential opportunities for new business start-ups.

Figure 3.1. Intotalo's learning method of entrepreneurship

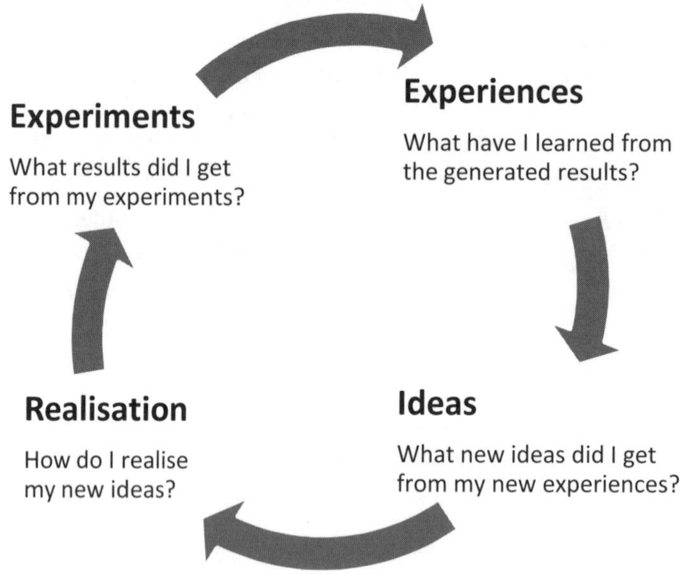

Experiments

What results did I get from my experiments?

Experiences

What have I learned from the generated results?

Realisation

How do I realise my new ideas?

Ideas

What new ideas did I get from my new experiences?

At what levels of education should these programmes be delivered?

An introductory course in entrepreneurship should be available to every student at the tertiary level of education. There is already a precedent for this.

The Entrepreneurship Program of the Istituto Tecnologico y Estudios Superiores de Monterrey (ITESM) began as a professional school for careers in engineering and administration in the 1940s in Monterrey, Mexico. ITESM has been recognised as one of the most prestigious academic universities in Mexico and Latin America.

In the 1980s the university offered professionals and postgraduates courses to develop their entrepreneurial attitudes and capabilities. The purpose was to generate new ideas and identify opportunities for students to become creators of a new culture as change agents. Later, this programme was extended to those individuals seeking to become entrepreneurs. They created an actual business environment that encompassed all the relevant business practices in society. The programme was designed by a committee of academics and practitioners. In 1979, the business became a legal entity and production operations began in March of 1980.

The classes were structured on the basis of lectures from academics, management workshops, conferences, case studies, and investigation of specific areas based on the interest of the learner. These efforts were guided by practical experiences in conceiving and creating a business that both academics and businesspersons shared with students. The original course of study evolved into a full entrepreneurship programme in 1985.

The vision was now to create the entrepreneurial person. The programme stressed the importance of a clear understanding of the emerging global environment as a setting for the development of each person's creative entrepreneurial spirit and abilities. The major focus was the generation of innovative ideas, with an emphasis on technology and organisational leadership.

Once in place in 1985, the programme was extended to fields of career studies in the ITESM system. It began to fulfil its main objective to promote and develop the innovative and entrepreneurial spirit in all students at ITESM.

In 1999 the programme brought together a number of experts who modified the content so that it could be replicated beyond the walls of the ITEMS system. Today all undergraduates are required to take the redesigned programme, entitled Development of Entrepreneurs. Academics and professionals co-ordinated the programme with entrepreneurs within the communities where these courses are offered.

Following an extensive review of literature and research, and interviews with entrepreneurs, the proposed curriculum has undergone a number of alterations at the undergraduate university level. It now consists of three courses, the first of which is available to all undergraduates. The student's journey of learning includes conception, creation, implementation, operation and development of a business project or student activity.

The training of academics involves the participation of national and global experts specialising in the different topics included in the curriculum. Academics are provided guidance and expertise as to how to make entrepreneurship an integral part of their teaching curriculum.

In addition to the required curriculum, small courses and open workshops are offered to help students reinforce knowledge and learning related to their field of interest.

The model has been transferred to many universities in Latin America. It shows how a university can play a critical role in development of the entrepreneur.

What should be the nature of the environment for teaching and learning about, for and through enterprise?

One of the most interdependent models of community enterprise and economic development was the Burgoyne Centre for Entrepreneurship (BCE) at Brock University in Canada. The Centre was founded in 1988, as a partnership between Brock University and the City of St. Catharines, Ontario, Canada. The rational for its formation was to enable communities to become effective players in today's global environment, helping them to develop an international competitive advantage by nurturing and supporting innovation and entrepreneurship. The education system needed to be a partner in this enterprise.

In January 1989, Brock University entered into a partnership with the Burgoyne Family, proprietors of the St. Catharines Standard Limited, a community newspaper. Together, they established the BCE, a unique and innovative centre for entrepreneurship in Canada supported exclusively by business and university funding. The Centre's Advisory Committee, comprising of some of the most prominent businesspeople in the Niagara community, was chaired by Henry Burgoyne, Chief Executive Officer of the St. Catharines Standard. The BCE's sustainability was ensured by means of generous support from the Burgoyne family, owners of the St. Catharines Standard. The centre was located at Taro Hall, a facility supported by a capital donation from the four partners of Taro Properties Inc. The appointment of Director Kenneth E. Loucks, PhD, an internationally recognised leader in the field of entrepreneurship and business education, ensured sustained leadership and the growth of the centre.

The BCE recognised that to successfully achieve its mission, it would have to form a broad-based community network of partnerships throughout the Niagara Peninsula of Ontario. Within three short years the BCE did just that, forging strategic partnerships with the Lincoln County Board of Education and the Niagara Regional Development Corporation. These partnerships yielded important community collaborative innovations – a broad community-based network of entrepreneur and professional advisors, the New Enterprise Store and the Niagara Enterprise Agency.

With these core partnerships firmly established, the BCE became a focal point and linkage for academic, private and government interests and activities in entrepreneurial development in the Niagara Region community. Notably, it has achieved this status without duplicating or competing with services offered by existing agencies and enterprises.

The synergy generated gained the BCE and its partners recognition. It was named the National Centre for Entrepreneurship Education by the National Entrepreneurship Development Institute – a joint business-government organisation dedicated to leadership in entrepreneurship education – and was a finalist for the Conference Board of Canada National Excellence in Business-Education Partnerships Award.

The strategies of the BCE consisted of:

- Providing a focal point in Niagara Region for academic, private and public sector interests in the entrepreneurial development of existing businesses, new entrepreneurs, and the facilitation of new venture creation.

- Promoting teaching of entrepreneurship in the secondary and post-secondary educational systems as well as to professionals, business advisors and entrepreneurs beyond the campus.

- In the teaching arena, developing and implementing high-calibre entrepreneurship curricula at secondary and post-secondary educational institutions in the region.

- Developing the research agenda with the assistance of visiting entrepreneurs, academics and facilitators. The research itself and its dissemination would take place through seminars, conferences and publications.

Innovativeness of partnership

The BCE was designed to operate as a community-based partner rather than as an institution unto itself. As an entrepreneurial institutional partner, it operated by adapting to the community environment, networking and linking with a growing number of established or new community organisations – rather than building competitive institutions – to promote its goals. In spite of the scope of the BCE and the partnerships, it purposely avoided developing any burdensome administrative organisations.

The BCE assumed an active consulting role with its partners, adding value to their missions with the injection of "intellectual capital". This consultation process led to the community's key economic development agency, the Niagara Regional Development Corporation, developing and proposing the Niagara Enterprise Agency. The latter was created to test a new concept in community-based economic development: it sought to intervene in large employer restructuring and recessionary job displacements by facilitating the development of new enterprises that would create new jobs in the region.

The creation of the New Enterprise Store, housed in an actual retail store, helped serve as a community laboratory for curriculum research, development and teacher training. It became a community-accessible incubator where individuals can test the viability of a new idea or enterprise in the marketplace before financially launching a new enterprise. The developer Landcorp Group developed the space for the New Enterprise Store.

With respect to entrepreneurial education and training, the BCE placed its educational emphasis on self-assessment, personal development and creativity rather than simply teaching participants how to develop a business plan. The same educational model was used to train teachers how to instruct entrepreneurial subjects, and the instructional concept was supplemented by pooling and focusing the educational and entrepreneurship resources of community partners.

With respect to the community, successful entrepreneurs willingly and actively served on advisory committees of the BCE and the New Enterprise Store, and frequently made guest presentations to students. In additional, many lawyers, accountants and management consultants in the community have pledged professional time at no charge to provide counsel to students evaluating new venture concepts and business plans.

The BCE and the partnerships it fostered had a profoundly positive effect on the community from the cultural, personal and strategic viewpoints. Their innovativeness cannot be overstated. The ecology that emerged developed a life of its own in the community. The initiatives undertaken by the BCE required that the centre's leadership be in a position to make instantaneous decisions. The centre was, however, accountable to the mechanistic, bureaucratic and hierarchical structures that underlie the university's infrastructure. As one member of the university pointed out, "For the university, entrepreneurship means anything other than glacial speed." This entrepreneurial worldview created a chasm within BCE itself, and eventually the ecology succumbed to the machine, leading towards it breakdown.

The university chose to focus on academic research and its undergraduate course. The rest of the programmes were left to the community partners to do with as they wished. In the end, two initiatives remained. The Enterprise Education unit became the Institute for Enterprise

Education, an independent centre for research and programme design in entrepreneurship, entrepreneurial leadership and enterprise education. This centre became a partner with the university's Faculty of Education in designing, developing and delivering a Bachelor of Education, Enterprise Education programme for pre-service secondary teachers in all subject fields. The Institute for Enterprise Education works very closely with young people in delivering entrepreneurship programmes, with leaders of large organisations seeking to create entrepreneurial cultures, and with advising agencies around the globe seeking to instil the entrepreneurial spirit.

Who should teach entrepreneurship?

Entrepreneurship cannot be taught – it can only be facilitated. In order for individuals to discover their contribution to the economy and society as a whole, they first need to learn *about* entrepreneurship – but also about themselves. That is the necessary first step to discovery.

This first step requires a facilitator who understands the person and the environment within which they interact. It requires someone who understands how people learn – not a sage on a stage, but a guide on the side. The Bachelor of Education, Enterprise Education programme aims to mould such people for teacher education. Graduates will have learned how to engage each learner's distinct talents in order to connect their creativity with opportunities in the community.

The second step deals with learning *for* enterprise. That requires a skilled facilitator who demonstrates pedagogical capability along with an able practice of entrepreneurship. The Intotalo model and the BCE model offer examples of community initiatives. The ITESM model is also an excellent teaching and learning model at the tertiary level of education.

The third step in the journey is learning *through* enterprise. This step is the practice of entrepreneurship itself. It needs to be a community-based model, best demonstrated by the BCE. This model incorporates the business practices of the community along with the theory of entrepreneurship, small business management and growth practices.

In the end, learning about, for and through enterprise requires an ecology of partners, each sharing their distinct expertise to start up and grow enterprises in their respective communities.

What learning methodologies and processes should be utilised during teaching and learning about, for and through enterprise?

Universities can play a critical role in research and evaluation of the entrepreneurial journey; however, the networked community ecology is the natural first choice for successful start-up and growth.

The entrepreneur's modus operandi and networks for success are antithetical to the organisation of business departments in university, where entrepreneurship is currently housed. The scientific method, the organisation of university cultures, and structures based on a middle-aged model of teaching and learning constrain the mental models of the entrepreneur. Whether we look at the experiences of William Gates of Microsoft, Michael Dell of Dell Computers, or Fred Smith's C+ business plan at Yale, the university model is a deterrent to successful entrepreneurship development. This may not be the case when we focus on owner-managed enterprises or self-employment initiatives.

Investment of resources needs to be made in community centres of entrepreneurship that act as ecologies rather than hierarchies and bureaucracies. Machine principles cannot be imposed on ecologies that develop lives of their own within a nurturing and supportive network of community partners.

It is best to select the enterprise model as an alternate to business plans in cases of entrepreneurship development. A model is not mechanistic, it is organic. It is a living entity that connects the entrepreneur and his/her team with the right idea for a defined opportunity. Once these three determinants are synchronised, a need to garner the needed resources arises, linking the people, ideas and opportunities into a synergistic force for dealing with the marketplace.

The enterprise model can also be used by those individuals seeking to start owner-managed firms or self-employment opportunities. In both cases, however, financial and marketing strategies will emerge based on the nature of the opportunity and resources required as a result of the findings of the Enterprise Diamond (Figure 3.2).

The Diamond is a model that seeks to connect the person, idea, opportunity and resources as a concentrated process for determining an idea's viability. The starting point is the person and their distinct talents and motivation that determine their mental models and vision of their future.

The second aspect deals with the identification of potential opportunities and development of ideas that connect the person, idea and opportunity. It is this alignment and convergence of Enterprise Diamond that determines not only the capability but also the viability of the enterprise.

By assisting and nurturing individuals in their efforts to build the necessary resources that consist of connection, they are prepared for the building of effective networks of stakeholders in their respective communities and beyond. It is through effectively serving these networks that entrepreneurs ultimately achieve success. The nature of methodologies, meanwhile, should be experiential and highly interactive.

Figure 3.2. The Enterprise Diamond

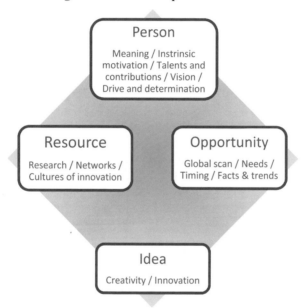

The Intotalo model's learning method is formed by constructivism and humanism (Figure 3.3).The main focus is learning from one another. Constructivism emphasised the learner's active role in the learning process. Each person constructs a picture of the current reality in the environment and, with the help of feedback, places him - or herself within it. This painting of the landscape incorporates their previous learning and the meanings they attach to the existing new knowledge. As learning is connected to the needs of the person, motivation begins to play a more critical role in the process.

In humanist philosophy, the person's self-awareness plays a critical role. Humanism emphasises the individual's unique and creative need to fulfil themselves as well as giving meaning to their personal experiences.

The methodologies practiced by Intotalo are consistent with the teaching and learning for, about and through enterprise at the Institute for Enterprise Education, the teacher education partnership with Brock University.

Figure 3.3. Learning Effectiveness Model

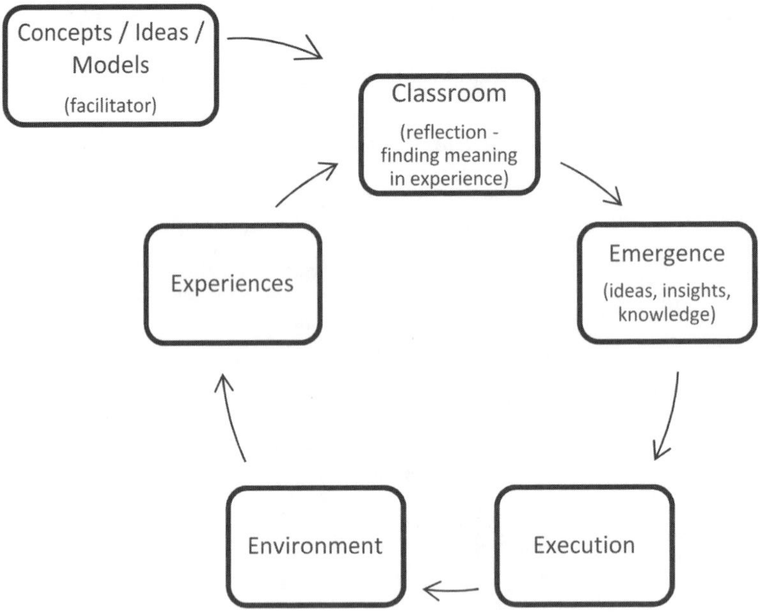

Source: The Institute for Enterprise Education.

The Learning Effectiveness Model consists of the following rules for interaction. Learners and facilitators interact with one another by sharing experiences and their reflections on the meaning of these experiences. Facilitators bring concepts and theories to develop insights and understanding of experience. Through experiential activities, learners and facilitators identify new ideas, insights and knowledge. These emergent properties are applied to the external environment, leading to discoveries that lead to new experiences – which lead to further reflection.

Conclusion

This discussion has attempted to build a case for teaching and learning about entrepreneurship by aligning its principles and practices with similar organic teaching and learning methodologies.

In order to deliver effective programmes in entrepreneurship, educators and community partners will need to recognise the changing dynamics of the global landscape and the major impact of that change on teaching, learning, and constructing communities that nurture innovation and entrepreneurship.

Any effective programme in entrepreneurship will need to begin with each person's distinct gifts, talents, contribution and creativity. By connecting each person with the emerging global realities, opportunities for births of new enterprises will increase, leading to further increased potential opportunities.

Those opportunities can be realised only if the community itself resembles an ecology of partners dedicated to nurturing and supporting a culture of entrepreneurship. It is within these types of conditions and cultures that the ecology of entrepreneurship will prosper and grow.

The spirit of partnership between universities, professionals, entrepreneurs, government agencies and community stakeholders will create the diversity required for organic networks to develop and grow, leading to exposure to similar networks around the globe.

As indicated throughout this chapter, the nature of today's global environment is that we break with the past and envision a compelling future that energises every one of us to become more enterprising as we journey along the path of the entrepreneur or that of his/her enabler.

Bibliography

Amabile, T.M. (1997), "Entrepreneurial Creativity through Motivational Synergy", *The Journal of Creative Behaviour*, Vol. 31, No. 1, Creative Education Foundation, pp. 18-26.

Carland J. W., *et al.* (1984), "Differentiating Entrepreneurs from Small Business Owners: A Conceptualization", *The Academy of Management Review*, Vol. 9, No. 2, Academy of Management, pp. 354-359.

Collins, J. (2001), *From Good to Great: Why Some Companies Make the Leap...and Other's Don't*, Harper Collins, New York.

Commission of the European Communities (2003), *Green Paper: Entrepreneurship in Europe* COM (2003) 27 final, Commission of the European Communities, Brussels, pp. 4-5.

Csikszentmihalyi, M. (1990), *Flow: The Psychology of Optimal Experience*, Harper and Row, New York.

Florida, R. (2005), *The Flight of the Creative Class: The New Global Competition for Talent*, Harper Business, New York, p. 7.

Friedman, T. L. (2005), "It's a Flat World, After All", *The New York Times Magazine*, www.nytimes.com/2005/04/03/magazine/03DOMINANCE.html, published: 3 April.

The Institute for Enterprise Education (1995), *Profit 100 Study*, St. Catharines, Ontario.

Kelly, S. and M. A. Allison (1998), *The Complexity Advantage*, McGraw Hill, New York, p. 50.

Kuhn, T.S. (1962), *The Structure of Scientific Revolutions*, University of Chicago Press, Chicago/London.

Kurtzman, J. (1998), "An Interview With W. Brian Arthur", *Strategy + Business*, Vol. 11, 2nd quarter, p. 95.

Luczkiw, E. (2002), "Instilling the Spirit – Learning Strategies for the New Millennium: The Bachelor of Education in Enterprise Education Program", *Citizenship, Social and Economics Education: An International Journal*, Vol. 5, No. 1, pp. 29-43.

Miller, W.C. (1999), *Flash of Brilliance: Inspiring Creativity Where You Work*, Perseus Books, New York, p. 12.

Mitton, D.G. (1989), "The Compleat Entrepreneur", *Entrepreneurship: Theory and Practice*, vol. 13, No. 3, Blackwell, pp. 9-20

OECD (1989), "Towards an Enterprising Culture: A challenge for education and training", *Educational Monograph No. 4*, OECD, Paris, p. 30.

The Oxford Desk Dictionary and Thesaurus (1997), Berkley Books, Oxford University Press.

Quartz, S.R. and T.J. Sejnowski (2002), *Liars, Lovers and Heroes*, Harper Collins, New York.

Shaver, K. (1991), "Person, Process, Choice: The psychology of new venture creation", *Entrepreneurial, Theory and Practice Journal*, Vol. 16, No. 2, Blackwell, p. 37.

Timmons, J. (1989), *The Entrepreneurial Mind*, Prima, Boston.

Chapter 4

Entrepreneurship Education in the United States

by
George Solomon
George Washington University, United States

The offering of small business management and entrepreneurship courses at both the two- and four-year college and university levels has grown in the United States in both number and diversity of content. This expansion of educational offerings has been fuelled in part by dissatisfaction, voiced by students and accreditation bodies, with the traditional Fortune 500 focus of business education (Solomon and Fernald, 1991). The issue is not that demand is high but that the pedagogy selected should meet the new innovative and creative mindset of students. The challenge to educators will be to craft courses, programmes and major fields of study that meet the rigors of academia while keeping a reality-based focus and entrepreneurial climate in the learning environment. Entrepreneurship is an ongoing process requiring a myriad of talents, skills and knowledge that lead to unique pedagogies capable of stimulating and imparting knowledge simultaneously.

Introduction

The past 15 years (1990-2005) have witnessed the growth of small business management and entrepreneurship courses offered at both the two - and four-year college and university levels in the United States. This expansion of educational offerings has been partly fuelled by dissatisfaction, voiced by students and accreditation bodies, with the traditional Fortune 500 focus on business education (Solomon and Fernald, 1991). The issue is not that demand is high but that the pedagogy selected must meet the innovative and creative mindset of entrepreneurially-oriented students. Plaschka and Welsch (1990) recommend an increased focus on entrepreneurial education and more reality- and experientially-based pedagogies such as those suggested by Porter and McKibbin (1988).

If entrepreneurship education is to produce real entrepreneurs capable of generating real enterprise growth and wealth, the challenge to educators will be to craft courses, programmes and major fields of study that meet the rigors of academia while keeping a reality-based focus and entrepreneurial climate in the learning environment. This chapter reports on selected data from the 2004-2005 George Washington University/Kauffman Centre for Entrepreneurial Leadership nationwide survey on entrepreneurship education.

The entrepreneurial experience can be characterised as chaotic and ill-defined, and our entrepreneurship education pedagogies should reflect this characterisation. In addition, we often make the assumption that it is relatively easy for entrepreneurship students to develop new ideas for their business start-ups. Quite a number of researchers have written about entrepreneurial competencies; however, the competencies that are required for new business start-ups are often addressed by educators in an *ad hoc* manner. There is little consensus on just what exactly entrepreneurship students should be taught. For entrepreneurship educators, the challenge is to provide the subject matter, resources and experiences that will prepare students for the myriad expectations and demands they will face as they start their new ventures.

Entrepreneurship education

As we delve into the literature, it would be helpful to define what is meant by "entrepreneurship education." Shepherd and Douglas propose this definition:

> *The essence of entrepreneurship is the ability to envision and chart a course for a new business venture by combining information from*

the functional disciplines and from the external environment in the context of the extraordinary uncertainty and ambiguity which faces a new business venture. It manifests itself in creative strategies, innovative tactics, uncanny perception of trends and market mood changes, courageous leadership when the way forward is not obvious and so on. What we teach in our entrepreneurship classes should serve to instil and enhance these abilities. (Shepherd and Douglas, 1997)

Historical perspective

Entrepreneurship education has experienced remarkable growth over the past 50 years (1955-2005), from a single course offering to a diverse range of educational opportunities available at more than 1 500 colleges and universities around the world (Charney and Libecap, 2000). The early prediction that "…the number of course offerings should increase at an expanding rate over the next few years" (Vesper, 1985) held true. In 1985, 253 colleges or universities offered courses in small business management or entrepreneurship; in 1993, 441 entrepreneurship courses were available to interested students (Gartner and Vesper, 1994). Fourteen years later, Foote (1999) reported that student enrolment in entrepreneurship classes at five top American business schools increased 92% from 1996 to 1999 (from a total of 3 078 to 5 913), and the number of entrepreneurship classes offered increased 74%. A recent estimate suggests that entrepreneurship and small business education may now be offered in as many as 1 200 post-secondary institutions in the United States alone (Solomon, 2001). Educational experiences range from traditional coursework to integrative curricula that include marketing, finance, new product development and technology (Charney and Libecap, 2000).

Differentiating entrepreneurship education from business education

Even with this remarkable growth, there is general consensus that the field is far from mature (Robinson and Hayes, 1991). As the field evolves, discussion continues regarding course content, the use of technology-driven pedagogy, and effectiveness measures. Early discussions focused on the need for entrepreneurship education and questioned whether entrepreneurship courses were not simply traditional management courses with a new label (King, 2001). While there is general agreement that the core management courses offered in traditional business programmes are essential for success in any business career (Vesper and McMullan, 1987; Block and Stumpf, 1992), there are fundamental differences between business principles applied to new ventures and those applied to large corporations (Davis, Hills and LaForge, 1985).

A core objective of entrepreneurship education that differentiates it from typical business education is the challenge "to generate more quickly a greater variety of different ideas for how to exploit a business opportunity, and the ability to project a more extensive sequence of actions for entering business" (Vesper and McMullen, 1988). Business entry is a fundamentally different activity from managing a business (Gartner and Vesper, 1994); entrepreneurial education must address the equivocal nature of business entry (Gartner, Bird and Starr, 1992). To that end, it must include skill-building courses in negotiation, leadership, new product development, creative thinking and exposure to technological innovation (McMullen and Long, 1987; Vesper and McMullen, 1988). Other areas identified as important for entrepreneurial education include awareness of entrepreneurial career options (Hills, 1988; Donckels, 1991); sources of venture capital (Vesper and McMullan, 1988; Zeithaml and Rice, 1987); idea protection (Vesper and McMullan, 1988); ambiguity tolerance (Ronstadt, 1987); the characteristics that define the entrepreneurial personality (Hills, 1988; Scott and Twomey, 1998; Hood and Young, 1993); and the challenges associated with each stage of venture development (McMullen and Long, 1987; Plaschka and Welsch, 1990).

The integrated nature, specific skills and business life cycle issues inherent in new ventures differentiate entrepreneurial education from a traditional business education. An additional comparison can be made between small business management courses and entrepreneurship courses – a distinction not always addressed in the literature (Zeithaml and Rice, 1987).

Can entrepreneurship be taught?

A most fundamental issue is whether entrepreneurship can be taught at all. Charharbaghi and Willis (cited in Adcroft, Willis and Dhaliwal, 2004) are sceptical, arguing that "entrepreneurs cannot be manufactured; only recognized." Adcroft, Willis and Dhaliwal (2004) go on to argue that management education can contribute to the provision of technical skills of entrepreneurs, but what it cannot contribute to is the "geographic chronology" – the element of serendipity – that is central to entrepreneurial events. Curran and Stanworth (1989) suggest that teaching entrepreneurship may not be cost-effective. Uncertainty of the attributes and behaviours that characterise an entrepreneur, plus the evidence that entrepreneurs may be "antipathetic towards education in most forms, all tell against entrepreneurial education being resource-effective" (p. 11). Garavan and O'Cinneide (1994) partially agree with these doubts when they state: "One has to ask – what can be taught that is specific to entrepreneurship per se? There is no body of well researched and developed knowledge which might form the basis of such programs, a fact which has been consistently emphasized in the literature" (p. 6).

On the other hand, after a review of empirical studies, Gorman, Hanlon and King (1997) report that there is evidence that entrepreneurship can be taught, or at least encouraged, through entrepreneurship education. Anselm (1993) also suggests that entrepreneurship can be learned. According to her, individuals may indeed be born with propensities toward entrepreneurship, but the level of entrepreneurship activity will be higher if entry-level entrepreneurial skills are taught. Kuratko (2003) put it even more succinctly: "The question of whether entrepreneurship can be taught is obsolete!" (p. 8).

The lack of rigorous research on the topic of entrepreneurship education has more than a few writers concerned. For example, Brockhaus (1993) notes that few "have done empirical research and very few have compared a group that is receiving the entrepreneurship education to another similarly matched group that is not receiving the education" (p. 12). Much of the research has "tended to be fragmented and [have] an explanatory, descriptive orientation" (Garavan and O'Cinneide 1994, p. 7).

Nevertheless, we have seen an increase in entrepreneurship education programs and research will likely continue as the field matures. Wortman (as cited in Plaschka & Welsch, 1990) summarized the 1980s in entrepreneurship, and the state of entrepreneurship today seems just as apt:

- A positive movement toward a commonly accepted definition of entrepreneurship and the definition of the field of entrepreneurship.

- A division of entrepreneurship into individual (or independent) entrepreneurship and corporate entrepreneurship (intrapreneurship).

- A movement toward more sophisticated research designs, research methods and statistical techniques.

- A shift toward larger research designs, research methods and statistical techniques.

- A slight movement away from exploratory research toward causal research.

Unfortunately, as reported by Gorman, Hanlon and King (1997), "there is little uniformity in the programs offered, especially if one considers the relative similarity of other business programs" (p. 61). This topic will be explored in the next sections.

Education methodologies

Course content

Despite general agreement that entrepreneurship can be taught, there is little uniformity in programme offerings or pedagogy (Gorman, Hanlon and King, 1997). This may be only natural in a relatively new field with a limited but growing body of knowledge. As researchers and scholars develop frameworks and sets of hypotheses for the study of emerging business successes and failures, the content of courses will evolve based on what is needed and can be taught for successful development (Block and Stumpf, 1992). According to Ronstadt (1990), the programme focus of "the old school" was on action, the business plan and exposure to experienced visitors who inspired students through stories and practical advice. This era of entrepreneurship education was "one venture"-centered and essentially based on the premise that entrepreneurial success was a function of the "right human traits and characteristics". The new school, while still action oriented, builds and relies on some level of personal, technical or industry experience. It requires critical thinking and ethical assessment and is based on the premise that successful entrepreneurial activities are a function of not just human, but also venture and environmental conditions. It also focuses on entrepreneurship as a career process composed of multiple new ventures and the essential skills of networking or "entrepreneurial know-who" (Ronstadt, 1990).

Another view from McMullan, Long and Wilson (1985) calls for courses to be structured around a series of strategic development challenges, including opportunity identification and feasibility analysis; new venture planning, financing and operating; new market development and expansion strategies; and institutionalising innovation. Real-time entrepreneurial activities include "projecting new technological developments, strategically planning, assisting in attracting necessary resources and arranging for joint ventures" (Vesper and McMullen, 1988, p. 10). Ideally, students should create multiple venture plans, practice identification of opportunities, and have extensive exposure to entrepreneur role models. Student interaction with these role models may occur in several important ways, including having entrepreneurs serve as coaches and mentors (Hills and Welsch, 1986; Mitchell and Chesteen, 1995); classroom speakers (Hills, 1988); and interview subjects (Hills, 1988; Solomon, Weaver and Fernald, 1994; Truell, Webster and Davidson, 1998). Effective entrepreneurial education requires that students have substantial hands-on experience working with community ventures so that they can learn to add value to real ventures and thus be prepared to add value to their own ventures (McMullan and Long, 1987).

Pedagogy

In addition to course content, educators are challenged with designing effective learning opportunities for entrepreneurship students. Sexton and Upton (1984) suggested that programmes for entrepreneurship students should emphasise individual activities over group activities, be relatively unstructured, and present problems that require a "novel solution under conditions of ambiguity and risk" (p. 12). Students must be prepared to thrive in the "unstructured and uncertain nature of entrepreneurial environments" (Ronstadt, 1990, p. 72). Offering students opportunities to "experience" entrepreneurship and small business management is a theme of many entrepreneurial education programmes.

The most common elements in entrepreneurship courses continue to be venture plan writing, case studies, and readings and lectures by guest speakers and faculty (Vesper, 1985; Klatt, 1988; Kent, 1990; Gartner and Vesper, 1994). The typical elements of small business management courses include classroom work, tests and a major project that is usually a consulting project (Carroll, 1993). Project-based, experiential learning is widespread in entrepreneurial education and takes many forms, such as the development of business plans (Hills, 1988; Vesper and McMullan, 1988; Gartner and Vesper, 1994; Gorman, Hanlon and King, 1997); student business start-ups (Hills, 1988; Truell, Webster and Davidson, 1998); consultation with practicing entrepreneurs (Klatt, 1988; Solomon, Weaver and Fernald, 1994); computer simulations (Brawer, 1997); and behavioural simulations (Stumpf, Dunbar and Mullen, 1991). Other popular activities include interviews with entrepreneurs (Solomon, Weaver and Fernald, 1994); environmental scans (Solomon, Weaver and Fernald, 1994); "live" cases (Gartner and Vesper, 1994); and field trips and the use of video and films (Klatt, 1988). Student entrepreneurship clubs are also widespread (Gartner and Vesper and, 1994).

Anticipated changes in course pedagogy include a greater use of various types of cases; increased international considerations; a more intense focus on strategy formation and implementation; and an increase in the use of technology for various purposes (Ahiarah, 1989). Computer simulations provide entrepreneurial students "with multiple experiences of simulated new venture decision making" (Van Clouse, 1990). The use of computer simulations described by Brewer, Anyansi-Archibong and Ugboro (1993) affords students realistic entrepreneurship experiences that develop skills in complex decision making and offer instant feedback.

Pedagogy is also changing due to a broadening market interest in entrepreneurial education. New interdisciplinary programmes use faculty teams to develop programmes for non-business students, and there is a growing trend in courses specifically designed for art, engineering and science students. Non-business students may require basic technology laboratories that focus on Internet-based feasibility research, so as to develop effective audiovisual pitch presentations and create professionally formatted business plans. In addition to courses designed to prepare the future entrepreneur and small business manager, instructional methodologies should also be developed for those who manage entrepreneurs in organisations; potential resource people (accountants, lawyers, consultants, etc.) used by entrepreneurs; and top managers who must provide vision and leadership for corporations that must innovate in order to survive (Block and Stumpf, 1992).

Pedagogy: teaching for competencies

Competency can be defined as an underlying characteristic of a person that results in effective and/or superior performance in a job (Boyatzis, Spencer and Spencer, cited in Bird, 2002). As to the question of which competencies or capabilities are most valuable for aspiring entrepreneurs to learn, here again there is little agreement in the field. Entrepreneurial educators impart competencies; their syllabuses reflect their beliefs and academic disciplines. Fiet (2000), for example, examined the syllabuses of 18 entrepreneurship courses and found they covered 116 different topics; however, topics did not always reflect competencies (*e.g.* family business). Plaschka and Welsch (1990) note that many programmes are evolving on a trial and error or as-needed basis, depending on the types of entrepreneurial projects undertaken and on the feedback of students experiencing deficiencies, gaps and difficulties in their courses.

Overall "essence" of entrepreneurship education

Entrepreneurship education programmes exist most generally within established university business schools; this presents a paradox that helps explain the above-mentioned lack of uniformity in curriculum and pedagogies. Traditional business programmes have come under increased criticism for failing to be relevant to the needs of today's changing business environment. One common complaint is that business education has become too functionally oriented – that it does not stress the cross-functional complexity of business problems. Other criticism focuses on the "lack of creativity and individual thinking required at both undergraduate and graduate levels" (Solomon, Weaver and Fernald, 1994). Sexton and Upton (1984) note that most business school courses are highly structured and do not often pose problems that require novel solutions.

Even entrepreneurship courses fall into this trap. Bird (2002) describes many core entrepreneurship courses as those that:

Require students to write and present a business plan and often students (in teams limited to fellow classmates who may not be rationally chosen as partners) choose the business concepts to pursue....Problems are presented and time frames for solving them given. There is often the illusion or reality of right" answers (p. 210).

It is also quite common for entrepreneurship classroom situations to focus heavily on theory – either management theory, adjusted to advise entrepreneurship and small business – or entrepreneurship theory explaining the emergence of entrepreneurs and their personal traits. Those voicing this concern note that entrepreneurship programmes often educate "about" entrepreneurship rather than educate "for" entrepreneurship (Kirby, 2003). The essence of entrepreneurship education, then, must reflect reality.

Garavan and O'Cinneide (1994) suggest that the methods best suited to an entrepreneurial learning style are active-applied and active-experimentation; these would include concrete experience, reflective observation and abstract conceptualisation (Davies and Gibb, cited in Garavan and O'Cinneide, 1994). In short, "educational programmes and systems should be geared toward creativity, multidisciplinary and process-oriented approaches and theory-based practical applications. What is needed is a more proactive, problem-solving and flexible approach rather than the rigid, passive-reactive concept and theory-emphasized functional approach" (Plaschka and Welsch, 1990, p. 62).

Methodology

Researchers at The George Washington University developed a mail survey to examine the current state of entrepreneurial education in the United States and internationally, and to evaluate the extent and breadth of methods and course offerings during the 2004-05 academic year. The study also sought to examine pedagogical developments and trends, as well as any relations between and among students, course offerings and pedagogy. A final aim was to examine what creative teaching innovations were being introduced into the classroom –use of the Internet, educational technologies, etc.

The survey's content was organised as follows:

- Identify institutional academic entities -- two-year community and junior colleges, four-year colleges and universities, and international universities and colleges offering small business and entrepreneurial educational programmes.

- Explore teaching pedagogies employed both inside and outside the class setting.

- Identify the traditional and non-traditional pedagogies employed, given the non-traditional focuses of the field.

Initially, I mailed over 4 000 questionnaires to two- and four-year colleges and universities, both in the United States and internationally. After a month, I sent a follow-up postcard, including an incentive offer to stimulate response rate. Ultimately, I received 279 qualified responses both through the mail and online submissions.

The data were analysed using the Statistical Package for the Social Sciences Personal Computer Plus software (SPSS PC+). My research team recoded the data, breaking it down into three discrete groupings (two-year community and junior colleges; four-year colleges and universities; and international universities and colleges). The questions regarding trends in entrepreneurial education were coded using the multiple response technique of SPSS PC+. The results of that analysis and the survey findings follow.

Analysis

As shown in Figure 4.1, the survey asked which courses were offered and which were the most popular at two - and four-year colleges and universities. They include: the following choices: (1) entrepreneurship; (2) small business management; (3) new venture creation; (4) technology/innovation; (5) venture capital; (6) small business consulting; (7) small business strategy seminar; (8) franchising; (9) new product development; (10) entrepreneurship marketing; (11) small business finance; and (12) creativity.

The results in Figure 4.1 indicate that the most popular course offered by two- and four-year colleges and universities in the 2004-05 academic year was in entrepreneurship (53%), followed by small business management (36%), and new venture creation (30%).

For Figure 4.2, the survey asked what types of teaching methods were used in entrepreneurship courses/curricula in two - and four-year colleges and universities, and the level of frequency. They include the following choices: (1) Case Studies; (2) Creation of Business Plans; (3) Lectures by business owners; (4) Discussions; (5) Computer Simulations; (6) Guest Speakers; (7) Small Business Institute (SBI); (8) Research Projects; (9) Feasibility Studies; (10) Internships; (11) On-site visits with small business owner/new venture; and (12) In-class exercises.

Figure 4.1. Types of courses offered 2004-05 academic year

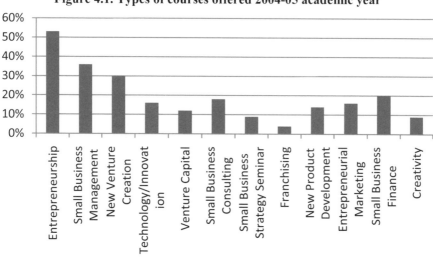

Note: Total respondents: 279.
Source: 2004-2005 Survey of Entrepreneurship Education.

Figure 4.2. Most popular teaching methods

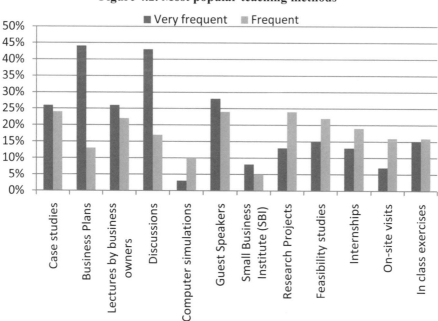

Note: Total respondents: 279.
Source: 2004-2005 Survey of Entrepreneurship Education.

The results in Figure 4.2 indicate that the most popular type of teaching method in entrepreneurship courses/curricula offered by two - and four-year colleges and universities was creation of business plans (44% very frequent), followed by class discussion (43% very frequent), and guest speakers (28% very frequent). Also, in regard to Question 3 (mentioned above), the data indicate that 60% of the instructors developed their own sets of readings and text materials.

For Figure 4.3, the question asked was whether the college or university has a: entrepreneurship centre, chair in entrepreneurship or professorship in entrepreneurship as well as a small business centre, chair in small business or professorship in small business.

Figure 4.3. Centers, chairs & professorships

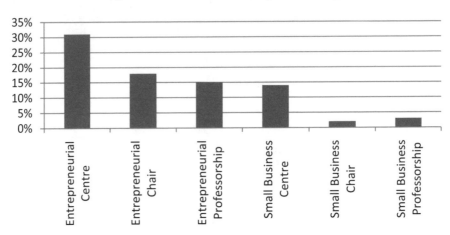

Total respondents: 279.

Source: 2004-2005 Survey of Entrepreneurship Education.

The results in Figure 4.3 indicate that the most colleges and universities had an entrepreneurship centre (31%), chair in entrepreneurship (18%) or professorship in entrepreneurship (15%), followed by a centre in small business (14%), chair in small business (2%) or professorship in small business (3%). Clearly funded chairs, centres and professorships are more likely in the field of entrepreneurship than in small business, indicating the popularity of entrepreneurship as a field of inquiry over the more traditional small business management field.

For Figure 4.4, the question asked was where the management of the entrepreneurship courses and curriculum were housed – in existing academic departments, entrepreneurial centres, a department of small business and entrepreneurship, a college or school of business, or other location.

Figure 4.4. Where the entrepreneurial curriculum is managed

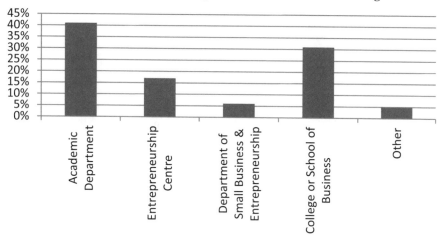

Total respondents: 279.

Source: 2004-2005 Survey of Entrepreneurship Education.

For Figure 4.4, the data for these options were: existing academic departments (41%), entrepreneurial centres (17%), a department of small business and entrepreneurship (6%), a college or school of business (31%), and other (5%). The traditional academic departments and schools and colleges are where most entrepreneurship curricula are housed and managed.

For Figure 4.5 the question asked which periodicals (if any) were used in entrepreneurship classes (required or recommended) and which were most popular. These include: (1) *Business Week*; (2) *Entrepreneur*; (3) *Fast Company*; (4) *Fortune*; (5) *Fortune Small Business*; (6) *Inc.*; (7) *The Wall Street Journal*.

The results for Figure 4.5 indicate that the most popular periodicals if any) were used in the entrepreneurship classes (required or recommended) by two- and four-year colleges and universities were *Entrepreneur* magazine (36%), followed by *The Wall Street Journal* (28%), *Business Week* (24%) and *Inc.* magazine (24%).

For Figure 4.6 the question asked which academic periodicals (if any) were used in the entrepreneurship classes (required or recommended), and which ones were most popular. They include: (1) *Journal of Small Business Management*; (2) *Entrepreneurship Theory and Practice (ET&P)*; (3)

Journal of Business Venturing; (4) *Entrepreneurship & Small Business*; (5) *Journal of Small Business Strategy.*

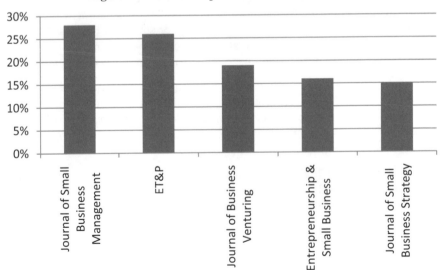

Figure 4.5. Periodical(s) used in class

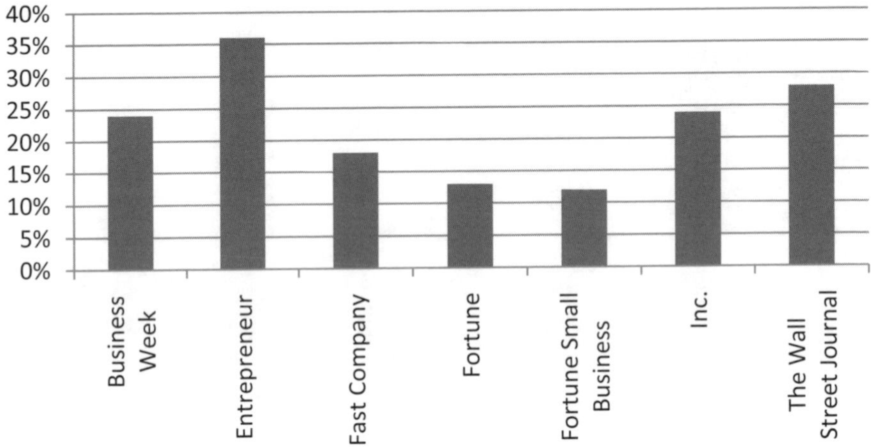

Total respondents: 279.

Source: 2004-2005 Survey of Entrepreneurship Education.

Figure 4.6. Academic periodicals used In course

Total respondents: 279.

Source: 2004-2005 Survey of Entrepreneurship Education.

The results for Figure 4.6 indicate that the most popular were *Journal of Small Business Management*; (28%) *Entrepreneurship Theory and Practice (ET&P)* (26%); *Journal of Business Venturing* (19%); *Entrepreneurship & Small Business*; (16%) and the *Journal of Small Business Strategy (15%)*.

Figure 4.7 provides answers to the following questions: (A) Did two- and four-year colleges and universities require their students to complete web-based assignments on the web (Question 5); (B) Did two - and four-year colleges and universities offer entrepreneurship course(s) on the web (Question 6); (C) Did two - and four-year colleges and universities offer information on the web regarding entrepreneurship, new venture creation and small business to both students and entrepreneurs (Question 7); and (D) Did two-and four-year colleges and universities offer management and technical assistance online for students and entrepreneurs (Question 8)?

Figure 4.7. Use of the Internet

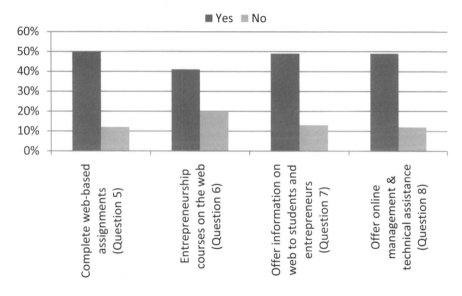

Total respondents: 279.

Source: 2004-2005 Survey of Entrepreneurship Education.

The data in Figure 4.7 indicate the following: (A) 50% of two - and four-year colleges and universities require their students to complete web-based assignments on the web; (B) 41% of two- and four-year colleges and universities offer entrepreneurship course(s) on the web; (C) 49% of two-and four-year colleges and universities offer information on the web regarding entrepreneurship, new venture creation and small businesses to both students and entrepreneurs; and (D) 49% of two- and four-year colleges and universities offer management and technical assistance online for students and entrepreneurs.

Conclusion

The 2004-05 survey indicated that the trends discovered in national surveys of entrepreneurship previously conducted (from 1977 to 2000) have continued in a similar direction, and in some areas – such as the use of technology – they have increased. The traditional teaching method of requiring students to create business plans still exists as a foundation for teaching the nuts and bolts of entrepreneurship and small business management. Yet, the data also show that educational institutions are moving towards a more knowledge sharing ecology, and the integration of theory and practice through various experiential exercises and activities are becoming more popular.

The data presented in this chapter also show that there has been movement away from more traditional non-technology-based forms of teaching and evaluation methods to greater use of educational technologies, such as the Internet-based assignments and work with knowledge portals. This opens the door to new methods of both teaching and learning. Not all technologies and educational methods using the Internet might be the correct or best-suited tool and approach. Early experiences with distance learning have not proved successful for some colleges and universities. The point, though, is to start integrating use of the Internet into the entrepreneurial education process. According to noted management expert Peter Drucker, "Technology will force the educators to restructure what they are teaching" (BizEd, November/December 2001). For example, video conferencing and the streaming of video case studies show promise as viable tools in educational technology. The ability to bring new "live" perspectives from different geographic locations and schools adds to the richness of the content and educational experience.

Clearly, for entrepreneurship to embrace the 21st century, educators must become more competent in the use of academic technology, and also expand their pedagogies to include new and innovative approaches to the teaching of entrepreneurship. Cyberspace has virtually erased time and distance; the Internet is transforming the theory of education into the practice of implementation. Professors are beginning to use this medium for communicating with other educators to learn how to improve and expand their courses. Entrepreneurship educators are also experiencing this phenomenon.

As educators move away from tests in favour of self-directed "project"-centred educational techniques such as personalised business plans, it makes sense to create a class structure that facilitates this form of learning. Also, given the nature of learning and knowledge acquisition, educators need to explore ways that they can virtually provide knowledge to students 24/7. They should also look to the full range of educational technologies as tools that will expand their reach to other schools and more students. The quantity and quality of information available on the Internet can help students and faculty develop feasibility and business plans, gain access to market data, and research industry and economic trends.

In 2001, *Newsweek* published a special article entitled "The Classroom of the Future" (*Newsweek*, 29 October 2001), in which leading teachers, inventors and entrepreneurs shared their vision for what schools will be in 2025. Among the viewpoints expressed by Steve Jobs, "One of the issues facing a society as it goes forward is to teach in the medium of the generation. The medium of our times is video and photography. We see things changing. We are doing more and more with movies and DVDs. The drive over the next twenty years is to integrate multimedia tools into the medium of the day." Peter Drucker describes this interactive frontier of education in BizEd (November/December 2001): "A good deal of teaching will still be done in the classroom, but much of it will take place off campus and in groups. Much will occur online, and much will be accomplished through self-study. Perhaps the single most important medium will be special tools that are adapted for use at home, with built-in visual and audio feedback mechanisms."

For example, rather than offering students a few traditional options to research new venture feasibility, educators can invite the institution's resource librarian to hold a tutorial on written, electronic and multimedia resources now easily accessible in most libraries. With some basic instruction, students in a matter of hours can mine data that were once the time-intensive domain of only the most advanced researchers. A final viewpoint expressed by US Senator Maria Cantwell: "The real issue is not the technology – the hardware is going to change – but the interactive nature of the education. People who interact with information retain more of that information. But most important, perhaps, education will become part of a larger more robust community" (*Newsweek,* 10 October 2001).

The field of entrepreneurial education has experienced tremendous growth in the United States. The results of this study represent a stream of research than began in 1978 with the examination of the current *state of entrepreneurship education.* In the last 27 years a great many changes have occurred, including gains in academic acceptance and credibility for the field of entrepreneurship education. The American dream is to start your own business, not work for someone else. American colleges and universities, as well as their international counterparts, are responding to this growing interest and realising that major public policy makers now believe that small and medium enterprises will continue to be the economic generators capable of propelling their economies into the next millennium.

How one evolves into an entrepreneur is unclear to most scholars. Some indicate that entrepreneurs are born or it is in their DNA (nature); others indicate that it is in their upbringing and environment (nurture). Some believe that everyone has an ember of entrepreneurial energy (spark) in them and some significant emotional event, as defined by the individual, triggers that ember to grow and become what many entrepreneurs have stated in interviews as having "fire in the belly". That is the phrase often used by entrepreneurs to convey their motivation to start a business, as Wally "Famous" Amos said to an assembled body of scholars at the 1990 International Council for Small Business World Conference. Thus the imparting of entrepreneurial knowledge through unconventional methods will foster the foundation for the 21st century entrepreneurial climate.

Growth issues, interfacing with external forces and developing a management team are all significant factors in understanding the entrepreneurial process. The closer the entrepreneurship classroom can approximate the realities of the actual environments of either a small business or an entrepreneurship operation, the better the students will learn the realities of such entities. The "living laboratory for entrepreneurship" is a meaningful tagline for entrepreneurship education in the best programmes now functioning. In addition, entrepreneurship educators should take a cue from both the Coleman and Kauffman Foundations' recent support of "cross-campus" initiatives. They should integrate the subject matter with a discussion of technology. Entrepreneurship programmes should no longer be the province of business schools only.

In 2001, US Vice President Richard Cheney delivered some remarks at the swearing in of the US Small Business Administration's new Administrator. He said, "Americans are, by nature, an entrepreneurial people – and we have filled a continental nation with small firms that create the majority of our economy's new jobs and export their products to the world. The incredible strength, vibrancy, and flexibility of our economy spring from the creative gifts of men and women striving in freedom. So every step that government takes to encourage free enterprise adds not just to the wealth of our society, but also to its character." He went on to say, "You're helping to make possible the investment and enterprise that generates jobs, strengthens communities, and improves the lives of your fellow citizens. Whether it's aiding an inventor as he turns out a new idea, or coming up to help a shop owner rebuild after a natural disaster."

Clearly small businesses and entrepreneurial ventures are important not only for the US economy, but also for all global economies. Educators have a responsibility to ensure that germane knowledge is developed and delivered in properly articulated but distinctive courses in small business and entrepreneurship.

Finally, policy makers, educators and scholars must realise that both small businesses and entrepreneurial ventures are part of the economic army of any society and that the *foot soldiers* (small businesses) are interdependent with the *tank corps* (entrepreneurial ventures) in the economic battlefront to secure a vibrant economy. The study and the teaching of small business and entrepreneurship are vital to the economic growth and stability of any free market system and the cornerstone of democracy. Learning how to properly start, manage and, in some cases, grow entrepreneurial ventures provides the next generation of small business owner-managers and entrepreneurs with the knowledge, skills and tools needed to succeed.

Bibliography

Adcroft, A., *et al.* (2004), "Missing the point? Management education and entrepreneurship", *Management Decision*, Vol. 42, No. 3-4, Emerald, pp. 512-521.

Ahiarah, S. (1989), "Strategic management and entrepreneurship courses at the undergraduate level: Can one inform the other?", *Proceedings of the 1989 Small Business Institute Director's Association National Conference*, Arlington, VA, pp. 60-66.

Anselm, M. (1993), "Entrepreneurship education in the community college", *Proceedings 38th International Council for Small Business (ICSB)*, Las Vegas, NV, pp.177-192.

Bird, B. J. (2002), "Learning entrepreneurship competencies: The self-directed learning approach", *International Journal of Entrepreneurship Education,* Vol. 1, No. 2, Senate Hall, pp. 203-227.

BizEd (2001), "What Peter Drucker Has to Say About Business Schools and Management Education As Original, Provocative As All His Observations Have Been for the Past 50 Years", November/December, pp. 13-17.

Block, Z. and S. A. Stumpf, (1992), "Entrepreneurship education research: Experience and challenge", in D. L. Sexton and J. D. Kasarda, (eds.) *The state of the art of entrepreneurship*, PWS-Kent Publishing, Boston, MA, pp. 17-45.

Brawer, F. B. (1997), "Simulation as a vehicle in entrepreneurship education" *ERIC Digest,* No. 97-1, ED, pp 433-468.

Brewer, B., C. Anyansi-Archibong and I.O. Ugboro (1993), "Using computer simulation technology in entrepreneurship and small business education", *Proceedings of the International Council for Small Business*, Las Vegas, NV, pp. 217-229.

Brockhaus, R. (1993), "Entrepreneurship education: A research agenda", in F. Hoy and T. G. Monroy and J. Reichert (eds.), *The Art & Science of Entrepreneurship Education*, Monroy Educational Systems, Berea, CA.

Carroll, J. J. (1993), "Course and curriculum design in developing and changing nations: Problems following the U.S. model", *Proceedings of the International Council for Small Business*, Las Vegas, NV, pp. 254-263.

Charney, A. and G Libecap. (2000). Impact of Entrepreneurship Education. *Insights: A Kauffman Research Series.* Kauffman Center for Entrepreneurial Leadership.

Clark. B. W., C. H. Davis and V. C. Harnish (1984), "Do courses in entrepreneurship aid in new venture creation?", *Journal of Small Business Management*, Vol. 22, No. 2, Blackwell, pp. 26-31.

Curran, J. and J. Stanworth (1989), "Education and training for enterprise: Problems of classification, evaluation, policy and research", *International Small Business Journal*, Vol. 7, No. 2, Sage, pp. 11-22.

Davis, C., G. E. Hills and R. W LaForge (1985), "The marketing/small enterprise paradox: A research agenda", *International Small Business Journal*, Vol. 3, No. 3, Sage, pp. 31-42.

Donckels, R. (1991), "Education and entrepreneurship experiences from secondary and university education in Belgium", *Journal of Small Business and Entrepreneurship*, Vol. 9, No. 1, Inderscience, pp. 35-42.

Fiet, J. O. (2000), "The theoretical side of teaching entrepreneurship", *Journal of Business Venturing*, Vol. 16, No. 1, Elsevier, pp. 1-24.

Foote, D. (1999). "Show us the money!", *Newsweek*, 19 April, pp. 43-44.

Garavan, T. N. and B. O'Cinneide (1994), "Entrepreneurship education and training programmes: A review and evaluation - part 1", *Journal of European Industrial Training,* Vol. 18, No. 8, Emerald, pp.3-12.

Gartner, W. B., B. J. Bird and J. A. Starr (1992), "Acting as if: Differentiating entrepreneurial from organizational behaviour", *Entrepreneurship Theory and Practice*, Vol. 16, No. 3, pp. 13-32.

Gartner, W. B. and K. H. Vesper (1994), "Executive Forum: Experiments in entrepreneurship education: Successes and failures", *Journal of Business Venturing*, Vol. 9, No. 3, Elsevier, pp. 179-187.

Gorman, G., D. Hanlon and W. King (1997), "Some research perspectives on entrepreneurship education, enterprise education, and education for small business management: A ten-year literature review", *International Small Business Journal*, Vol. 15, No. 3, Sage, pp. 56-77.

Hills, G. E. (1988), "Variations in university entrepreneurship education: An empirical study of an evolving field" *Journal of Business Venturing*, Vol. 3, No. 2, Elsevier, pp. 109-122.

Hills, G. E. and H.P. Welsch (1986), "Entrepreneurship behavioral intentions and student independence characteristics and experiences", in

R. Ronstadt, *et al.* (eds.), *Frontiers of entrepreneurship research*, Babson College, Wellesley, MA, pp. 73-186.

Hood, J. N. and J. E. Young (1993) "Entrepreneurship's requisite areas of development: A survey of top executives in successful entrepreneurial firms", *Journal of Business Venturing*, Vol. 8, No. 2, Elsevier, pp. 115-135.

Katz, J.A. (1994), "Growth of endowments, chairs and programs in entrepreneurship on the college campus", in F. Hoy, T. G. Monroy and J. Reichert (eds.), *The Art and Science of Entrepreneurship Education, Volume 1*, Baldwin-Wallace College, Cleveland, pp. 127-149.

Kent, C. A. (1990), "Entrepreneurship education at the collegiate level: A synopsis and evaluation", in C.A. Kent (ed.), *Entrepreneurship Education*, Quorum Books, New York.

King, S. W. (2001), "Entrepreneurship Education: What the Customer values", *Proceedings of the 46th International Council for Small Business*, Taipei, Taiwan, pp. 123-137.

Kirby, D. A. (2003), "Entrepreneurship education: Can business schools meet the challenge?", paper presented at the Internationalizing Entrepreneurship Education and Training Conference, Grenoble, 7-10 September.

Klatt, L. A. (1988), "A study of small business/entrepreneurial education in colleges and universities", *The Journal of Private Enterprise*, Vol. 4, No. Fall, pp. 103-108.

Kuratko, D. F. (2003), "Coleman White Paper: Entrepreneurship education: Emerging trends and challenges for the 21st Century", proceedings of the 17th United States Association of Small Business & Entrepreneurship Conference, Hilto Head Island, SC, 23-25 January, pp. 3-20.

McMullan, W. E. and W.A. Long (1987), "Entrepreneurship education in the nineties", *Journal of Business Venturing*, Vol. 2, No. 3, Elsevier, pp. 261-275.

McMullan, W. E., W. A. Long and A. Wilson (1985), "MBA concentration on entrepreneurship", *Journal of Small Business and Entrepreneurship*, Vol. 3, No. 1, pp. 18-22.

Mitchell, R. K. and S. A. Chesteen (1995), "Enhancing entrepreneurial expertise: Experiential pedagogy and the new venture expert script", *Simulation and Gaming*, Vol. 26, No. 3, Sage, pp. 288-306.

Newsweek (2001), "The Classroom of the Future", 29 October, pp.60-68.

Plaschka, G.R. and H. P. Welsch (1990), "Emerging structures in entrepreneurship education: Curricula designs and strategies", *Entrepreneurship Theory and Practice*, Vol. 14, No. 3, Blackwell, pp. 55-71.

Porter, L. W. and L. E. McKibbin (1988), *Management Education: Drift or Thrust into the 21st Century?*, McGraw-Hill, New York.

Robinson, P. and Hayes, M. (1991), Entrepreneurship education in America's major universities. *Entrepreneurship Theory and Practice*, 15(3), 41-52.

Ronstadt, R. (1987), "The educated entrepreneurs: A new era of entrepreneurial education is beginning", *American Journal of Small Business*, Vol. 11, No. 4, pp. 37-53.

Ronstadt, R. (1990), "The educated entrepreneurs: A new era of entrepreneurial education evolves", in C.A. Kent (ed.), *Entrepreneurship Education*, Quorum Books, New York, pp. 69-88.

Scott, M. G. and D. F. Twomey (1998), "The long term supply of entrepreneurs: Student's career aspirations in relation to entrepreneurship", *Journal of Small Business Management*, Vol. 26, No. 4, Blackwell, pp. 5-13.

Sexton, D. L. and N. E. Upton (1984), "Entrepreneurship education: Suggestions for increasing effectiveness", *Journal of Small Business Management*, Vol. 22, No. 4, Blackwell, pp. 18-25.

Shepherd, D. A., and E. J. Douglas (1997), "Is management education developing, or killing, the entrepreneurial spirit?", paper presented at the 42nd International Council for Small Business Conference, San Francisco, CA, June.

Solomon, G. T. (1988). "Small Business Management and Entrepreneurial Education in America: A National Survey Overview", *Journal of Private Enterprise*, Vol. 4, No. Fall, pp.109-118

Solomon, G. T. and L. W. Fernald (1991), "Trends in small business management and entrepreneurship education in the United States", *Entrepreneurship Theory and Practice,* Vol. 15, No. 3, pp. 25-40.

Solomon, G. T. and L. W. Fernald, (1993), "Assessing the need for small business management/entrepreneurship courses at the university level", proceedings of the 17th National Small Business Consulting Conference - Small Business Institute Director's Association, pp. 102-107.

Solomon, G. T. K. M. Weaver and L. W. Fernald, (1994), "Pedagogical Methods of Teaching Entrepreneurship: An Historical Perspective", *Gaming and Simulation*, Vol. 25, No. 3, Sage, pp. 67-79.

Solomon, G. T. (2001), "Interview at The George Washington University School of Business and Public Management".

Solomon, G. T., S. Duffy and A. Tarabishy (2002), "The state of entrepreneurship education in the United States: A nationwide survey and analysis", *International Journal of Entrepreneurship Education*, Vol. 1, No. 1, Senate Hall, pp. 65-86.

Stumpf, S., L. Dunbar and T. P. Mullen (1991), "Simulations in entrepreneurship education: Oxymoron or untapped opportunity?", in W. D. Bygrave *et al.*(eds.), *Frontiers of Entrepreneurship Research*, Babson College, Wellesley, MA, pp. 681-694.

Truell, A. D., L. Webster and C. Davidson (1998), "Fostering entrepreneurial spirit: Integrating the business community into the classroom", *Business Education Forum*, Vol. 53, No. 2, NBEA, pp. 28-29, 40.

Van Clouse, G. H. (1990), "A controlled experiment relating entrepreneurial education to student's start-up decisions", *Journal of Small Business Management*, Vol. 28, No. 2, Blackwell, pp. 45-53.

Vesper, K. H. (1985), *Entrepreneurship education 1985*, Babson College, Wellesley, MA.

Vesper, K. H. and W. E. McMullan (1987), "Entrepreneurship education in the nineties", *Journal of Business Venturing*, Vol. 2, No. 3, Elsevier, pp. 261-275.

Vesper, K.H. and W.E. McMullan (1988), "Entrepreneurship: Today courses, tomorrow degrees?", *Entrepreneurship Theory and Practice*, Vol. 13, No. 1, Blackwell, pp. 7-13.

Zeithaml, C. P. and G. H. Rice (1987), "Entrepreneurship/small business education in American universities", *Journal of Small Business Management*, Vol. 25, No. 1, Blackwell, pp. 44-50.

Chapter 5

Entrepreneurship Education in Europe

by
Karen Wilson
European Foundation for Entrepreneurship Research

This chapter assesses the state of entrepreneurship education in higher education institutions (HEIs) in Europe, comparing it to developments in the United States and outlining a set of recommendations for universities and policy makers. Comparisons include the differences in definition between entrepreneurship and SMEs, multidisciplinary learning, academic and business links, quality entrepreneurship curricula, and the role of entrepreneurship within the university. Europe has the opportunity to learn from models around the world and focus on integrating the most relevant and high-quality practices into higher education institutions. Europe's competitiveness, innovation and economic growth depend on being able to produce future leaders with the skills and attitudes to be entrepreneurial in their professional lives, whether by creating their own companies or innovating in larger organisations. Entrepreneurship education is the first and arguably the most important step for embedding an innovative culture in Europe.

Introduction

Can entrepreneurship be taught? It's an age-old debate. The answer is both yes and no. Education plays an essential role in shaping attitudes, skills and culture – from the primary level up. Entrepreneurship education provides a mix of experiential learning, skill building and, most importantly, mindset shift. Certainly the earlier and more widespread the exposure to entrepreneurship and innovation, the more likely it is that students will consider entrepreneurial careers at some point in the future.

What do we mean by entrepreneurship? There are many working definitions but for the purposes of this chapter, entrepreneurship is defined as "the pursuit of opportunities beyond the resources you currently control" (Stevenson, 1983, 1985; Stevenson and Jarillo, 1991). Entrepreneurship is about growth, creativity and innovation. Innovative entrepreneurs come in all shapes and forms. They start companies; they spin out companies from universities or corporations; they restructure companies in need of refocusing; they innovate within larger organisations. Usually they share a primary objective – growth.

Europe has an opportunity to learn from experiences in the United States, Canada and other countries around the world and to set up appropriate models, rather than importing models that might not apply to the European context. When assessing entrepreneurship education practices around the world, it is important to understand not only what works but also why. It is not simply a matter of building the infrastructure. The programmes must be market-driven and adapted to the local ecosystem.

This chapter assesses the state of entrepreneurship education in higher education institutions (HEIs) in Europe in comparison with developments in the United States, and outlines a set of recommendations for universities and policy makers. The analysis is based on the work conducted by the European Foundation for Entrepreneurship Research (EFER) over many years, as well as other recently published papers on the topic.

Current entrepreneurship policy challenges in Europe

In the United States, entrepreneurship has historically been a key driver of economic growth. In the past several decades, entrepreneurial dynamism has been evident both in the number of new enterprises created each year and in the fact that, of the leading 100 United States firms, the majority did not exist 20-30 years ago. The process of renewal, in which old companies evolve or go out of business and are replaced by more dynamic firms, is important for the vitality of economies (Birch, 2002). In Europe, many of the leading companies have existed for almost a century.

Europe needs a greater focus on entrepreneurship and innovation to help spur competitiveness, growth and job creation, and to achieve the goals set out in the Lisbon Agenda (European Commission, 2000). Despite numerous initiatives and programmes, Europe is still lagging behind these goals (Kok, 2004). Underlying issues include the mindset and skills of young people (European Commission, 2002). The low exposure to entrepreneurship combined with the lack of role models and the repercussions for failure, makes the barriers to entry in Europe significantly higher than in North America. On the other hand, there is too much focus in Europe on SMEs instead of growth entrepreneurship. Companies are not encouraged to expand internationally, and administrative and financial complexity still burdens cross-border activity within Europe.

How can Europe reinvigorate dynamism through entrepreneurship?

Entrepreneurship education can help promote an entrepreneurial and innovative culture in Europe by changing mindsets and providing the necessary skills. With the security of Europe's welfare system, people are less willing to take risks. This attitude is reinforced at the university, which traditionally has been focused on ensuring students can secure future jobs – not become entrepreneurs. Meanwhile globalisation, the rapid development of technology and the lower cost of travel have completely changed the nature of work. It is no longer enough to train students for a career. Universities must prepare students to work in a dynamic, rapidly changing entrepreneurial and global environment.

For entrepreneurship to thrive, it must operate in a well-functioning business and regulatory environment. Without the proper framework conditions, even potential entrepreneurs wanting to start companies will not do so. In the United States, business innovation is fuelled by highly competitive markets, advanced financial and university infrastructure, property rights, labour flexibility, and government support of R&D, directly and through procurement (Dennis, 2006). Carl Schramm, President and CEO of the Kauffman Foundation, has written extensively about the unique multifaceted system for nurturing high-impact entrepreneurship in the United States and provides many valuable insights for other countries (Schramm, 2004).

Entrepreneurship is viewed as a major driver of innovation, competitiveness and growth. National governments and international organizations such as the OECD, the European Commission and others have increased focus on entrepreneurship education. The OECD recently conducted a major survey of entrepreneurship education, and the European Commission is about to embark on a major study as well. These initiatives bode well for ensuring sustained momentum to encourage universities to make commitments in this area and for policy makers to help facilitate the process.

Analysis of trends

Entrepreneurship has been part of the curricula in higher education institutions in North America for over fifty years. The first graduate course in entrepreneurship was offered at Harvard University in 1948 (Katz, 2003) by Professor Miles Mace. Soon after, legendary Harvard Business School Professor Georges Doriot originated the concept of venture capital. Today, entrepreneurship courses are offered at most universities across the United States. The demand has been driven by the students themselves, who are eager to take courses ranging from business planning and start-up to entrepreneurial finance and technology management.

In Europe, entrepreneurship only substantially began to enter the curriculum in the last ten years, although a handful of institutions started earlier (Twaalfhoven and Wilson, 2004). This is in line with other trends, most notably the growth of the venture capital industry to finance innovative, growth-oriented companies. In the United States, the venture capital industry started more than forty years ago and began to take off in the 1980s. In Europe, significant growth in venture capital began only about a decade ago, in the mid-1990s.

Entrepreneurship versus SMEs

One of the main differences between entrepreneurship education in the United States and Europe is the definition and focus of "entrepreneurship". In the United States, entrepreneurship generally refers to growth-oriented ventures or companies, while in Europe it is often equated with SMEs. Just because a firm is small, that does not make it more entrepreneurial than a large company. Europe has a legacy of small and medium-sized business, many of them family-owned. These companies play a large and important role in the European economy. However, study after study has demonstrated that the majority of SMEs in Europe are not growth-oriented at all. Only a very small percent, 3% according to Professor David Birch, are high-growth-oriented – or, as he calls them, "gazelles" (Birch, 2002). While all companies should be encouraged, it is the growth-oriented ones that will have the most impact on economic dynamism.

This definitional difference means that in Europe, many "entrepreneurship" programmes are actually SME training programmes that focus on functional management skills for small business (Zahra, 2005) rather than skills for building, financing and nurturing high-growth companies.

Entrepreneurship within the university

Another key difference is the place of entrepreneurship within the university and academia more broadly. While entrepreneurship is still not fully accepted as an academic discipline, in the United States many business and technology schools have created a niche in this area and growing numbers of US schools are offering "concentrations" or "majors" in entrepreneurship (Twaalfhoven and Prats, 2000). Many US universities have academic entrepreneurship departments and a large percentage of schools offer entrepreneurship courses.

In Europe, entrepreneurship is still trying to find its home. Activities are in place across Europe but efforts are fragmented and often driven by external actors instead of by the education system itself (European Commission, 2002). Faculty champions of entrepreneurship often have to fight internal battles for support and funding of their activities. Fewer universities in Europe have academic entrepreneurship departments. Professors often teach from traditional disciplines such as economics or business administration. Also, the majority of the entrepreneurship professors in Europe are traditional academics, reflecting long-standing policies and practices.

Institutional culture, practice and policies often get in the way of developing an entrepreneurial spirit and environment within universities. Entrepreneurship champions play critical roles within the universities but there must also be strong commitment from the university leadership (provosts, rectors and vice chancellors). This requires a complete paradigm shift for the entire university, including changing the fundamentals of how the university operates and its role in society.

Multidisciplinary learning

Another key difference between Europe and the United States is the way universities view education. The world is not divided into functional silos, so the educational process should not be either. In a number of US universities, entrepreneurship is treated as an integral part of a multidisciplinary education process. Students are encouraged to take courses and engage in projects with students from other disciplines, enabling them to draw upon expertise from across the university – engineering, science, design, liberal arts and business. The universities strive to minimise the institutional barriers to this cross-fertilisation to provide the most creative and innovation learning process possible. The result is a dynamic team- and project-based learning environment.

The Kauffman Foundation, which with an asset base of USD 2 billion is the largest foundation in the world focused on entrepreneurship, is encouraging the integration of entrepreneurship across entire campuses. The Foundation has selected "Kauffman campuses" in the United States and is supporting those schools' efforts to create cross-campus, cross-disciplinary entrepreneurship programmes to instil entrepreneurial thinking in all disciplines.

Even on campuses with less of an interdisciplinary approach, US entrepreneurship programmes often connect traditional business courses with those offered in science and technology programmes. This allows for the sharing of expertise and knowledge between the business and technical students, sparking greater innovation and facilitating technology transfer. Increasingly this approach is spreading across Europe, with great examples provided by the University of Cambridge as well as a number of other institutions across Europe.

Academic-business links

Other differences lie in the attitude and approach to teaching. In the United States, entrepreneurship education is very closely linked with business practice. Professors often have experience working with start-ups. Entrepreneurs, many of them alumni of the university, are both brought into the classroom to speak to students as well as to teach courses. These courses are structured to be as experiential as possible, incorporating real-life cases, projects, internships and business plan competitions. Case studies also provide role models for students considering an entrepreneurial career path. This is an important part of creating entrepreneurial drive: if students see that people "like themselves" were able to successfully create companies, it helps to demystify the process and make that option more feasible.

While interactive approaches, usually project-based, are also used in Europe, most entrepreneurship courses are still taught by the lecture method. Case studies are sometimes utilised but they are rarely focused on European entrepreneurs as potential role models. More European case studies, featuring successful entrepreneurs, need to be developed and shared broadly through schools across Europe. More could also be done to profile these entrepreneurs in the media to create a broader exposure to such role models.

In the United States, the university is seen as playing a key role in the local ecosystem, in which links between academia and business operate both formally and informally. US universities foster networks with entrepreneurs, business practitioners, venture capital firms and business angels as part of a mutually reinforcing learning and sharing process. In Europe, most universities are government funded and, in many cases, they lack the experience and incentives to initiate proactive outreach with the private sector. Government-funded universities tend to have very traditional structures making it more difficult to integrate new approaches. In addition, they tend to be more nationally focused than internationally minded by nature of their funding base.

However, there is a change afoot in Europe, with a number of institutions, particularly in the United Kingdom, Ireland, Spain and other countries playing a more active role with the local business community and engaging entrepreneurs as well as alumni.

Quality entrepreneurship curricula

The proliferation of entrepreneurship programmes in the United States and increasingly in Europe has been positive in terms of validating interest in the field, but more depth and rigor is needed to ensure that entrepreneurship courses, materials and research are of high quality. Research and curriculum development are of particular importance in helping to ensure entrepreneurship's rightful place among the academic disciplines. The Kauffman Foundation has been focusing on this issue and recently set up a multidisciplinary panel of distinguished scholars to provide recommendations on the core elements necessary for a high-quality, university-level entrepreneurship programme.

Universities in Europe are undergoing tremendous change through the implementation of the Bologna agreement, which aims to create more standards among institutions of higher education by 2008. During this process, curriculum content must be rapidly overhauled as well and geared towards developing problem-solving skills, which are greatly needed in today's knowledge-based society. Educational systems and teaching methods must move from traditional to more creative, interactive, student-centred learning methods (EUA, 2005).

The Bologna process is an opportunity for European universities to leverage the reform process to make their institutions more innovative and entrepreneurial. Perhaps it can also open the door for more radical changes, including the way in which they manage the institution the faculty they hire, the programmes they teach, the flexibility with which they incorporate new topics and the way they teach them, and the students they attract.

Opportunities and challenges for entrepreneurship education in Europe

European universities and business schools must play a key role in promoting entrepreneurship and innovation, helping students learn not only how to start but also how to grow enterprises, including across borders. In particular, technical and scientific universities provide potential breeding grounds for high-technology/high-growth companies or "gazelles".

The European Foundation for Entrepreneurship (EFER) has conducted many surveys and research on entrepreneurship education and research in Europe. In 2004, EFER conducted a joint survey with the European Foundation for Management Development (EFMD). The goals of the survey were to gain a perspective on the level and growth of entrepreneurship education in Europe, identify trends, and understand the training and development needs of faculty teaching entrepreneurship. The results were used as a basis of comparison with other recent surveys and research conducted in Europe and the United States. EFER's conclusions are outlined below.

Box 5.1 The European Foundation for Entrepreneurship Research

The European Foundation for Entrepreneurship Research (EFER) fosters and promotes research and teaching in the field of entrepreneurship at institutions of higher education across Western and Eastern Europe. EFER was founded by Harvard Business School alumnus Dr. Bert Twaalfhoven, experienced entrepreneur and long-time promoter of entrepreneurship in Europe, and has received support from numerous other HBS alumni, banks, venture capital firms, universities, entrepreneurs and international organisations over the years.

Since it was founded in 1987 EFER has conducted research studies comparing entrepreneurship in the United States and Europe, and generated support for 50 European case studies. EFER initiated "Teach-The-Teachers" programme in the early 1990s. The first programmes were in Western Europe; they were followed by a series of programmes in Central and Eastern Europe. Most recently, EFER has partnered with Harvard Business School in creating an intensive training programme for European professors of entrepreneurship. Through these programmes, EFER has focused on building linkages between academia and students in Eastern and Western Europe.

Entrepreneurship education in Europe has grown significantly in the past 5-10 years, and strong growth is expected to continue. More needs to be done however, particularly in the following areas: curriculum development, creation of a critical mass of entrepreneurship teachers, funding of entrepreneurship, cross-border faculty and research collaborations, and facilitation of spin-outs from technical and scientific institutions.

Curriculum development

Greater clarity is needed regarding the purpose and goals of entrepreneurship education. These should be based on a broadly defined set of outcomes, not just on a narrow measurement of the number of start-ups created from universities. Entrepreneurship education is about developing attitudes, behaviours and capacities at the individual level. It is also about the application of those skills and attitudes that can take many forms during an individual's career, creating a range of long-term benefits to society and the economy. Measuring intangible outcomes is difficult. However, applying only simple measures of the potentially wrong things can result in falling far short of the intended outcomes and impact.

Entrepreneurship and innovation must be deeply embedded into the curriculum to ingrain a new entrepreneurial spirit and mindset among students. In Europe, entrepreneurship tends to be offered in stand-alone courses rather than being integrated in the content of courses in other departments or disciplines. The main exceptions are within institutions that have been teaching for longer periods. This indicates that until there is enough focus and critical mass of entrepreneurship knowledge and material within an institution, it will be difficult to leverage that content into other courses. Entrepreneurship also remains primarily elective at European universities.

Entrepreneurship education is important in all disciplines. In Europe, the majority of entrepreneurship courses are offered in business schools. Entrepreneurship needs to be expanded across the campus – particularly to the technology and science departments, where many innovative ideas and companies originate. While most business students do not start or join a new business upon graduation, statistics show that the majority in countries such as the United States do so during later stages of their careers. Therefore, exposure to entrepreneurship as well as practical training in starting and growing companies is important. Technical and scientific universities, on the other hand, are potential sources of start-ups and spin-offs. Increasingly, business and technical faculties are linking efforts to encourage the exchange of skills and ideas among students.

A range of entrepreneurship research and teaching topic areas are being addressed in Europe, including start-up/business planning, SME management, family business, business strategy, innovation (both technology and science), policy, gender/minority issues, and socially responsible entrepreneurship. At the same time, there has been a proliferation of business plan competitions and other initiatives and programmes focused on the start-up phase. Students need to learn how to manage and grow enterprises, not just how to start them. Many respondents to the 2004 EFER/EFMD survey commented that the heavy focus on the start-up phase may be overshadowing the more important trends in entrepreneurship.

In Europe, case studies and other interactive pedagogy are underutilised, as is the inclusion of business people and entrepreneurs in the classroom. Almost half of all materials used in the entrepreneurship courses in Europe are generated locally, as faculty teach with a mix of lectures as well as formats that do not use conventional course materials. Greater emphasis needs to be placed on experiential and action learning. There are numerous pedagogies that can be utilised, including case studies, team projects, and activities with entrepreneurs. Using active learning methods is more complex than traditional teaching methods. It requires engaging students more deeply in the learning process. Educators therefore must be able to create an open environment of trust, in which students develop the necessary confidence to take risks.

Creating a critical mass of entrepreneurship teachers

There are increasing numbers of entrepreneurship faculty at institutions across Europe; however, the numbers are still far below that at US institutions. As demand from students in Europe continues to grow, the demand for universities to provide quality entrepreneurship programmes will also increase, requiring more professors dedicated to the field.

According to the EFER/EFMD survey, there was an average of approximately five professors involved in entrepreneurship activities at each institution with entrepreneurship programmes in 2004, up from the reported average of 2.5 in an EFER survey conducted in 2000 (Twaalfhoven and Prats, 2000). Many of those professors also teach in other disciplines, not just entrepreneurship. In addition, in many European faculties entrepreneurship teaching is on the shoulders of part-time or visiting lecturers. This means that there is still a lack of critical mass of entrepreneurship professors at many universities across Europe. That makes it difficult not only to sustain entrepreneurship efforts over the long term, but also to allow time for entrepreneurship research and course development.

Europe lags behind the United States by a factor of four in terms of entrepreneurship chairs. By 2004 there were more than 400 chairs of entrepreneurship in the United States (Katz, 2004). In Europe, the figure was closer to 100. When comparing the total number of entrepreneurship professors, the gap widens significantly further.

It is evident that Europe needs to invest in the training and development of entrepreneurship professors and researchers. Survey respondents indicated a need for training programmes and workshops in areas such as case method teaching and other action-oriented innovative approaches. A European Commission expert group on education and training for entrepreneurship also found that the "provision of specific training for teachers on entrepreneurship is insufficient" (European Commission, 2002).

Currently, there are very few entrepreneurship doctoral programmes in Europe. Short-term training programmes and workshops are valuable but long-term solutions are also needed to enable Europe to build a pipeline of high-quality, well-trained entrepreneurship professors. A recent European Commission communication on "Fostering Entrepreneurial Mindsets through Education and Learning" (European Commission, 2006) highlighted the need to tackle the shortage of entrepreneurship professors by making entrepreneurship more broadly recognised as a specialisation for doctoral programmes.

The current pool of entrepreneurship teachers should be expanded. Entrepreneurs and others with entrepreneurial experience should be allowed, encouraged and trained to teach. It is vital to create a critical mass of entrepreneurship educators able to create the right learning experiences for students. Growing the base of experienced educators not only means providing the necessary training and education; it also requires expanding the definition of "educators" beyond professors to include entrepreneurs and other practitioners. These individuals also serve as role models, particularly if they are alumni of the school, as well as coaches and mentors. They also enhance entrepreneurial spirit within the university, and create stronger links between the university and the local community.

Funding entrepreneurship

In the United States, many universities have entrepreneurship centres and chaired professorships of entrepreneurship funded by external sources. In Europe, this is a relatively new phenomenon. Most of the funding for the centres and chairs in the United States is provided by successful entrepreneurs who graduated from those institutions. According to research conducted for the Kauffman Foundation, the 400 chairs of entrepreneurship in the United States amount to approximately USD 1 billion (Katz, 2004).

In Europe the bulk of the funding still comes from governments, although this is beginning to change as companies and foundations have begun to contribute. There are a few examples of entrepreneurs funding centres or chairs but this is still relatively rare in Europe. In general, Europeans do not feel strong ties to their own universities, which are still seen as the realm of governments; and certainly there have not yet been enough successful entrepreneurs capable of giving back at that level. In addition, very few European universities track their alumni, making it more difficult to know which ones have become entrepreneurs, let alone engage them in the work of the school.

In 2004, there were well over 100 centres of entrepreneurship in Europe; however, they differ in size and scope. Most are connected to universities, but some are stand-alone centres collaborating with universities and businesses in the local area. Many centres were preceded by units or departments focused on entrepreneurship, While most of the entrepreneurship centres started in the past five years, some have existed for 20-30 years or more.

The main issue with government funding for entrepreneurship chairs and centres is sustainability. Most government funding programmes start well after the need presents itself and stop before the programmes can have the necessary impact. Unfortunately, it seems to be a common feature in Europe.

Cross-border faculty and research collaborations

More must also be done to facilitate faculty collaboration, exchanges and research across borders within Europe. While collaboration may be strong between universities within a given country, there is a large gap in cross-border activities among European countries. Currently, networks and working relationships between faculty teaching entrepreneurs across Europe are limited and there is little sharing of good practice.

Most of the 2004 EFER/EFMD survey respondents – 90% – indicated that they work at academic institutions in their home country and less than 20% spend time teaching outside of the country. Meanwhile, the student body is increasingly becoming international. Survey respondents indicated an international student average of 21% – more than double the percentage of "non-national" professors. If faculty themselves do not have international experience, it makes it difficult for them to encourage students to take a pan-European or global perspective in starting and growing companies.

Greater mobility and exchange of experience is needed in Europe, not only between universities but also between academia and the business world. University exchanges could be both of short and longer-term duration. Short exchanges are easier to implement and provide much-needed international exposure and experience for the professors involved, often leading to longer-term engagement abroad. Longer-term exchanges allow educators to spend a significant amount of time at other institutions and/or in the private sector to truly engage, learn and develop, but these are more expensive and more difficult to implement. Europe needs more entrepreneurial learning models and greater sharing of knowledge and good practice across sectors and national borders.

At the undergraduate level, most entrepreneurship courses are conducted in the local language. At the postgraduate (MBA/masters) level, most of these courses are conducted both in the local language and English. At the executive education and doctoral levels, English predominates.

Certainly there are huge differences in university structures across countries in Europe, which makes both the sharing of best practices and cross-border collaboration more difficult. These difficulties are deepened by language and cultural differences. The Bologna reform process will be helpful but will not solve the difficulties of working across borders, cultures and languages. Increasing networks and working relationships between professors can help. What might start as an informal meeting or shared course could later turn into a research project or other academic and teaching collaborations.

An example is the programme offered by Harvard Business School called the European Entrepreneurship Colloquium for Participant-Centred Learning (EECPCL). Following a successful EFER pilot programme in 2001 that attracted 41 professors from 22 countries, EECPCL was launched in 2005, attracting 173 professors from 36 countries across Europe over the past three years. Since the first programme, a number of professors have worked on joint projects and research. EFER is supporting those efforts by holding working meetings in Europe, for those who attended past programmes to encourage continued collaboration, faculty exchange and practice sharing. EFER is also planning to launch a faculty exchange programme to provide professors with exposure to teaching in other countries as well as to students with different backgrounds.

Spin-outs from technical & scientific institutions

Innovation and R&D spur economic growth, competitiveness and employment, notably in high-tech, high-skilled and high-value areas of the economy. Europe has a tremendous asset in the strength of its technical and scientific universities. European universities provide some of the finest engineering, technology and science training in the world; however, the commercialisation of R&D is still in its infancy in Europe. While a number of European institutions have been proactive in this area, more needs to be done to encourage links between academia and the private sector, as well as the sharing of best technology transfer practices across Europe.

To foster technology transfer, scientific and technical universities should include modules on entrepreneurship; these would enhance awareness within the research community of the opportunities and modalities that exist to commercialise innovative R&D. Links with business school students and faculty as well as with the business community should also be encouraged. Venture capital firms can and are beginning to play a more important role in working with technical universities to structure and fund spin-outs.

Nurturing centres of R&D excellence in Europe is important as well. This includes attracting and retaining the most talented PhDs from around the world. The EU produces more science and technology graduates than the United States but does not leverage these potential resources. Many of the best and brightest move to the United States, where research budgets are larger and researchers are likely to get substantially higher pay.

For Europe to realise its global competitive potential, it will need to create a full ecosystem revolving around attracting and retaining the most talented researchers; encouraging links between universities and the private sector; enlarging the flow of technology transfers supported by efficient and effective intellectual property rights; and creating schemes to specifically support young innovative companies at the cutting edge of development (EVCA, 2005).

Policy recommendations

The role of higher education in society is changing. No longer are universities expected to stay within their ivory towers. Today academia is expected to be equal partners to the private and public sectors alike. European university leadership should see this new role as an opportunity and leverage the Bologna reform process to make their universities more innovative and dynamic, in line with the goals of the Lisbon agenda.

A number of actions are necessary at the European, national, regional and local levels. Universities, policy makers and the business community need to work together to seize this opportunity to fuel the engine of the Europe's future growth by preparing young people to compete in a globally competitive and dynamic world.

Below are a series of recommendations following from the analysis of the opportunities and challenges in entrepreneurship education laid out in this chapter.

- Differentiate between programmes focused on growth entrepreneurship as opposed to SME management.

As long as the two concepts are mixed, progress will be difficult and well-intended public funds will spent inappropriately. For maximum results, different initiatives should be targeted to:

– General exposure to entrepreneurship, to change mindset and attitudes.

– Functionally oriented courses (SME management, etc.).

– High-growth-oriented entrepreneurship: how to build, finance and grow companies.

• Develop appropriate measurement and evaluation of the impact, not just outputs, of entrepreneurship programmes:

– Currently there is little evaluation of entrepreneurship education programmes and almost no statistical evidence, outside of some output indicators that may or may not be the right measures.

– Without clear objectives and measurement, support for programmes may be difficult to sustain.

– As we have seen in the United States, entrepreneurship is a result of a long-developed cultural and education environment.

– Europe has already had many "starts and stops", and needs to take a much more sustained and long-term approach.

– Measures should focus on the local market needs and context.

• Integrate entrepreneurship into the curriculum and build towards a multidisciplinary learning environment:

– Increase the number of schools offering entrepreneurship courses.

– Augment the number entrepreneurship courses and make them available to a broader group of students.

– Make entrepreneurship a required course.

– Integrate entrepreneurship across other courses.

– Encourage cross-registration across disciplines.

– Build projects and programmes across disciplines.

• Set high-quality standards for entrepreneurship curricula and research:

- Ensure entrepreneurship courses meet an international quality standard.

- Encourage the development of research-oriented entrepreneurship centres at universities across Europe.

- Focus research and teaching on all of the entrepreneurial growth phases, not just the start-up phase.

- Develop high-quality local content, case studies and course materials that can also be shared at the international level.

- Create degree programmes, consistent with those at an international level.

- Promote entrepreneurship as a legitimate academic discipline.

- Build a strong pipeline of European Entrepreneurship professors and teachers:

  - Hire more professors and teachers fully dedicated to entrepreneurship.

  - Look to recruit professors who also have entrepreneurship experience.

  - Support workshops and training programmes for teachers of entrepreneurship.

  - Provide training for entrepreneurs and other practitioners to become effective educators.

  - Review regulations on the participation of entrepreneurs in teaching activities.

  - Encourage the development of specialised entrepreneurship doctoral programmes.

- Encourage the use of interactive teaching methods in the classroom:

  - Promote the application of "learning by doing" through project-based learning, internships and consulting.

  - Leverage the uses of case studies for discussion-based learning.

  - Develop the proper incentives, assessment, rewards and recognition to encourage educators to try these approaches.

  - Involve entrepreneurs and local companies in entrepreneurship courses and activities.

- Ensure a consistent and adequate level of funding for entrepreneurship education programmes:

    – Provide tax incentives to encourage donations to universities to support entrepreneurship programmes.

    – Seek private sector resources to help fund and provide expertise to entrepreneurship teaching and research.

    – Ensure that the initiatives funded are sustainable and provide the necessary funding to reach sustainability.

    – Encourage the development of local angel and venture capital funds.

- Encourage cross-border entrepreneurship faculty and research collaborations:

    – Facilitate the sharing of good practice across borders, both within Europe and internationally.

    – Create opportunities for professors and researchers from various countries to work together on projects.

    – Provide support for European-wide and international mobility and exchanges of educators and researchers.

- Facilitate spin-outs from technical and scientific institutions:

    – Advance core research and innovation in European universities and research centres.

    – Accelerate the application of science and technology to market through well-developed technology transfer offices.

    – Connect entrepreneurship and innovation programmes.

    – Establish stronger links between academia, business and entrepreneurs.

    – Provide the necessary fiscal incentives to encourage entrepreneurship.

    – Facilitate the provision of direct training and/or support programmes for entrepreneurs in the process of starting companies.

    – Ensure the time (sabbaticals, if necessary) for faculty to engage in entrepreneurial activities.

- Profile European role models:

- Create more public recognition vehicles for high-growth entrepreneurs through the media, awards, etc.

- Support the development of more case studies profiling successful European entrepreneurs.

Conclusion

The moment is right for a significant evolution of entrepreneurship education in Europe – between the growth of new private universities, the reform of existing universities as a result of the Bologna process, and the high level of interest in entrepreneurship by students, faculty, university administrators and policy makers.

Europe has the unique opportunity to learn from models around the world and focus on integrating the most relevant and high-quality practices into its higher education institutions. This should be a long-term commitment, however, not one that starts and then stops a few years later. Sustainability is a key issue. That means the objectives of these programmes should be clear from the start and outcomes should be measured to ensure that the intended results are being delivered.

Europe's competitiveness, innovation and economic growth depend on being able to produce future leaders with the skills and attitudes to be entrepreneurial in their professional lives, whether by creating their own companies or innovating in larger organisations. Entrepreneurship education is the first and arguably the most important step for embedding an innovative culture in Europe.

Bibliography

Birch, D., (2002), "Slump, What Slump", *Fortune Magazine, Small Business*, December.

Dennis, W. Jr., (2006), "Innovation – Its Creation in American Small Business", presented at IPREG meeting in Brussels, Belgium, May

European Commission (2000), Commitment by the EU Heads of States and Governments to make the EU "the most competitive and dynamic knowledge-driven economy by 2010", March

European Commission (2002), *Final Report of the Expert Group "Best Procedure"*, Project on Education and Training for Entrepreneurship, European Commission, Brussels, November.

European Commission (2006), Communication from the Commission to the Council, the European Parliament, the European Economic and Social Committee and the Committee of the Regions, "Implementing the Community Lisbon Programme: Fostering entrepreneurial mindsets through education and learning", European Commission, Brussels, February

EUA (European University Association), (2005), "Trends IV: European Universities Implementing Bologna", presented to European Ministers of Education at the Ministerial Conference in Bergen, 19-20 May

EVCA (European Private Equity and Venture Capital Association), (2005) *Private Equity and Venture Capital: An Engine for Economic Growth, Competitiveness and Sustainability*, EVCA Public Policy Priorities, February.

Katz, J.A. (2003), "The Chronology and Intellectual Trajectory of American Entrepreneurship Education 1876-1999", *Journal of Business Venturing*, Vol. 18, No. 2, Elsevier, pp. 283-300.

Katz, J.A. (2004), *Survey of Endowed Positions in Entrepreneurship and Related Fields in the United States*, Ewing Marion Kauffman Foundation, Kansas City, MO.

Kok, W. (2004), "Kok Report" report of an independent high-level expert group, headed by formed Dutch Prime Minister Wim Kok, presented to European Commission and the European Council, November.

Schramm, C.J. (2004), "Building Entrepreneurial Economies", Foreign Affairs, July/August, Council of Foreign Relations, pp. 104-115.

138 – CHAPTER FIVE

Stevenson, H. (1983), "A Perspective On Entrepreneurship", Harvard Business School Working Paper 9-384-131.

Stevenson, H. (1985), "The Heart of Entrepreneurship", *Harvard Business Review,* March-April, pp. 85-94.

Stevenson, H. and J. Jarillo (1991), "A New Entrepreneurial Paradigm", in A. Etzioni and P. R. Lawrence (eds.), *Socioeconomics: Toward a New Synthesis*, M.E. Sharpe, Inc., New York.

Twaalfhoven, B., and Prats, J., (2000), "Entrepreneurship Education and its Funding", EFER, June

Twaalfhoven, B. and K. Wilson (2004), "Breeding More Gazelles: The Role of European Universities", EFER, October.

Wilson, K., (2004), "Entrepreneurship Education at European Universities and Business Schools: Results of a Joint Pilot Survey", presented at the EISB/EFMD conference in Turku Finland, September.

ENTREPRENEURSHIP AND HIGHER EDUCATION – ISBN- 9789264044098 © OECD 2008

Chapter 6

Benchmarking Entrepreneurship Education across US, Canadian and Danish Universities

by
Anders Hoffmann, Niels May Vibholt, Morten Larsen
FORA, Danish Agency for Enterprise and Construction, Denmark

Mette Lindholt Moffett
University of Colorado at Boulder, United States

This chapter presents a benchmark study of entrepreneurship education at 27 universities – ten in the United States, ten in Canada, and seven in Denmark – that was conducted in 2003-04. A general method for benchmarking entrepreneurship education activities at university level has been constructed and applied in the study. The method allows for a quantification of the scope of entrepreneurship education. The study illustrates significant differences in both the breadth and depth of entrepreneurship education in Denmark versus the United States and Canada. US universities have a wider variety of entrepreneurship programmes and classes, and they have by far the largest proportion of students attending them.

Given a clear dearth of entrepreneurship education at Danish universities relative to their US and Canadian counterparts, the chapter points to lessons for policy makers and universities.

Introduction

Entrepreneurship is one of the main drivers of economic growth, and is becoming increasingly important in order to compete in the global economy.

Denmark's ability to rely on entrepreneurship to sustain economic growth has been limited, and as such the Danish government is actively engaged in promoting an entrepreneurial and innovative culture. In the last couple of years this issue has attracted much attention in the country. While Denmark does not appear to be short of people who would like to start their own business, Danes lack entrepreneurial competencies to make these new ventures grow. Studies indicate several reasons for this and suggest a number of possible policy responses. One is an increased focus on entrepreneurship education at all levels (EBST, 2004a).

This chapter, which addresses entrepreneurship education in higher education, is based on a benchmark study conducted in 2003-04 by FORA – the Danish Enterprise and Construction Authorities' Division for Research and Analysis. Entrepreneurship activity at the university level is quantified according to a number of fact-based questions. The main purpose of the benchmark study was to identify areas within entrepreneurship education where policy makers, universities and other educational institutions in Denmark could learn from the experiences of their US and Canadian counterparts.

The study finds significant differences between the US and Canadian universities and the Danish universities. The share of students attending courses in entrepreneurship as well as the range of entrepreneurship activities offered by the universities is significantly higher in the United States and Canada than in Denmark.

Danish policy makers and universities should accord higher priority to entrepreneurship education in the future. The education of teacher-entrepreneurs and the development of alumni networks are among the areas where action is needed.

The importance of entrepreneurship education

Benchmark studies of entrepreneurship activity show that the most entrepreneurial countries have well-developed and extensive university-level education programmes in entrepreneurship (EBST, 2004a; Kjeldsen, Rosted and Bertelsen, 2003).

Measuring the effects of entrepreneurship education at university level is, however, a difficult and complicated endeavour. In doing so it is important not to think of universities solely as breeding grounds for new entrepreneurs, but rather as a place where entrepreneurial competencies are developed. Such competencies are not needed only when someone wants to start a new business. They must also be an integrated part of the entire knowledge infrastructure (lawyers, accountants, consultants, etc.) supporting entrepreneurs and new high-growth ventures. Existing corporations will also benefit from the availability of entrepreneurial employees and business advisors with entrepreneurial skills as they attempt to sustain competitiveness through strategic innovation and entrepreneurial thinking.

Universities may serve several roles in the development of regional and national innovation and entrepreneurship (Betts and Lee, 2004). By providing entrepreneurship education they can cultivate entrepreneurial awareness; develop entrepreneurial competencies; facilitate industry ties; and assist the development of regional economies.

Cultivating entrepreneurial awareness

In deciding which career direction to embark upon, young people are influenced by the environment surrounding them. If the environment does not provide awareness and positive attitudes towards entrepreneurship, it is unlikely to be considered a career choice. Universities can do much to support and promote an entrepreneurial awareness among students (Lundström and Stevenson, 2002; OECD, 2004).

Developing entrepreneurial competencies

Entrepreneurship involves an extensive array of disciplines, some of them unique to the concept being developed. Examples include market analysis, new product development, project management, accounting and payroll system set-up, valuation and term sheet development, and strategic innovation. It is imperative that universities offer the opportunity to develop entrepreneurial competencies, as highly educated "book smarts" will enable ventures to successfully scale and sustain high growth. Charney and Libecap (2000) show that entrepreneurship graduates are more inclined to be involved in product innovation. Universities can also help develop a general knowledge of entrepreneurial environments and promote entrepreneurial thinking, which is valuable to new as well as existing firms and organisations.

Facilitating industry ties

The involvement of experienced entrepreneurs, business leaders, venture capitalists and other key persons in the entrepreneurial community – as guest lecturers, project sponsors or internship hosts – is indeed beneficial for entrepreneurship students. It exposes them to people who have hands-on experience in entrepreneurial environments. However, the involvement of the entrepreneurial community in education is also beneficial to the entrepreneurship community itself. Universities can act as a crucial network facilitator, bringing together regional actors involved in entrepreneurship thereby facilitating stronger ties within that community (Betts and Lee, 2004).

Assisting development of regional economies

If those ties are likely to have a positive effect on the regional economy, students themselves add value by helping local entrepreneurs grow their businesses. Furthermore their involvement with local entrepreneurs often leads to job opportunities after graduation, whereas they otherwise might seek employment outside the region and not contribute to job growth.

Approaches to entrepreneurship education

There are various approaches to integrating entrepreneurship education at the university level. In their conceptual framework, Streeter, Jaquette Jr. and Hovis (2002) distinguish between two: the *focused* approach and the *unified* approach (also termed the university-wide approach).

In the focused approach, faculty, students and staff are situated exclusively in the academic area of business. Harvard is an example of the focused model; its entrepreneurial programmes are targeted exclusively to Harvard Business School students. Students from other faculties may apply, but only a limited number will be admitted.

The focus in the unified approach is broader, targeting students outside the realms of business schools as well. Over the past ten years the trend toward university-wide entrepreneurship education in the United States has been strong and is gaining momentum. Examining 38 ranked entrepreneurship programmes, Streeter, Jaquette Jr. and Hovis (2002) found that approximately 75% offered university-wide programmes. There are two versions of the unified approach: the magnet model and the radiant model.

In the magnet model, students are drawn from a broad range of majors. Entrepreneurial activities are offered by a single academic entity, but attended by students from all over the university. All resources and skills are united into a single "platform" that helps facilitate the co-ordination and planning of entrepreneurial activities. This approach has been applied at MIT, where entrepreneurship programmes are administered by the Sloan School of Management.

In the radiant model, individual institutes and faculties are responsible for facilitating the integration and visibility of entrepreneurship activities; entrepreneurial activities can therefore be adjusted to the specific structure of individual faculties. Cornell University has applied this model; there, the teaching of entrepreneurship education takes place in nine schools and colleges.

Methodology

Introduction

A benchmark method has been developed and applied to compare the breadth and depth of entrepreneurship education in Denmark versus the United States and Canada.

The benchmark analysis involves a series of steps. The first is to clarify how the performance of the units (universities in this case) can be measured. The units are then ranked according to their performance (activities, processes, internal conditions) with regard to the chosen indicator(s). Activities that lead to good performance are termed "good practice". For lower-ranked units, good practice can serve to inspire improvement, and thus become a benchmark.

The underlying assumption is that countries and universities can learn from each other. That assumption is often dismissed on the grounds of differences in cultural and institutional structures. It is claimed here, however, that in a number of areas countries may be inspired by initiatives carried out in best-practice countries, although it is important to stress that learning does not equal simply copying good-practice initiatives. Good practice needs to be adapted to the special characteristics of a given society and economy as well as to the culture and traditions of a specific university.

Selection of good practice

Ideally, the selection of good-practice universities is based on entrepreneurial activity levels among university graduates. However, no comparable data are available to measure the effects of entrepreneurial activity, such as start-up activity rates among entrepreneurial graduates. An alternative approach has therefore been used.

First of all, the good-practice *countries* and universities are identified. GEM data suggest that the United States and Canada are good-practice countries concerning entrepreneurship education at university level (GEM, 2003). The data are, however, based on subjective measures and do therefore make more detailed analysis necessary.

Secondly, the good-practice *universities* within the United States, Canada and Denmark were selected. The US and Canadian universities were selected by consulting various ranking systems. While it is difficult to pinpoint the indisputably "best-practice universities", those selected have generally received high marks in various national and international entrepreneurship rankings.

Ten US universities were selected by consulting entrepreneurship rankings from the *Financial Times*, *US News*, *Business Week*, *Entrepreneur Magazine*, *Success Magazine* and *entrepreneur.com*.

Canada does not have the same tradition for ranking entrepreneurial programmes. However, a Canadian report has identified a number of programmes that are particularly interesting or unique in the way they are set up (Menzies and Gasse, 1999). The report was used in selecting the ten Canadian universities to be included in this study.

Finally, seven Danish universities were selected based on the scope of entrepreneurial programmes prevalent (EBST, 2004c; DVCA, 2004). The criterion for including Danish universities in this sample is that the institution offers at least one entrepreneurial course.

Table 6.1. Selected universities in the United States, Canada and Denmark

United States	Canada	Denmark
• Babson College	• Saint Mary's University	• Aarhus Business School
• University of Texas at Austin	• Université Laval	• The IT University
• Stanford University	• École Des Hautes Études Commerciales (HEC)	• The University of Southern Denmark
• University of Pennsylvania	• McGill University	• Copenhagen Business School
• Harvard University	• York University	• Aalborg University
• Massachusetts Institute of Technology (MIT)	• Brock University	• The Danish Technical University
• University of California, Los Angeles (UCLA)	• University of Calgary	• The University of Aarhus
• University of California, Berkeley	• University of British Colombia	
• University of Southern California	• University of Victoria	
• Cornell University	• Université de Sherbrooke	

Source: EBST, 2004b.

A model for measuring entrepreneurship education at university level

Entrepreneurship education goes far beyond basic educational programmes. To capture the breadth of entrepreneurship education, the authors have developed a model that contains a number of entrepreneurship activities. These are divided into five groups, each of which covers an important dimension of entrepreneurship education. The five dimensions are: educational set-up; educational scope; institutional characteristics; outreach, and; evaluation (Figure 6.1).

Figure 6.1. The five dimensions of entrepreneurship education

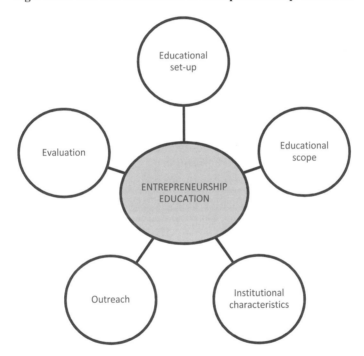

Source: EBST, 2004b.

Educational scope focuses on the breadth of programmes offered, how courses are spread across the undergraduate, graduate and postgraduate levels, and the extent to which bachelor and graduate programmes are available. The dimension also covers entrepreneurial research and lifelong learning.

Educational set-up details the extent to which guest lecturers/practitioners are involved in entrepreneurship programmes, if internships or practical experience are integral parts of the education, and the extent of private business involvement. The dimension also covers experimental teaching and culture-affecting activities, including among other things the use of role models and the extent to which the programmes seek to influence the personality of the students.

Institutional characteristics covers areas related to the interaction between faculties, the university, the student body and the business community. Institutional characteristics relate to how entrepreneurship is prioritised, how funds are allocated, rules pertaining to the transfer of credits and the presence of built-in incentives that encourage teachers to participate in entrepreneurial activities.

Outreach deals with the involvement of parties outside university boundaries that may provide counselling and aid to entrepreneurial students. The scope of university networks thus becomes a benchmark for the quality of university services offered to the student body. Counselling may include legal aid (patents), financial support for product development, professional guidance in marketing-related areas and experience-based guidance. Among other things the level and quality of outreach activities include access to a tech transfer office, university co-operation with an incubator, alumni networks, access to experienced practitioners, access to venture capital, and participation in business plan competitions.

Evaluation is vital in adjusting entrepreneurship education to the needs of students and other parties. Apart from assessing basic entrepreneurial programmes, evaluation also deals with monitoring graduate career paths and the extent to which university activities are being replicated by other institutions.

To shed light on these five dimensions of entrepreneurship education, a questionnaire containing 37 items was developed; leading national and international experts in entrepreneurship education were consulted in its drafting. All questions could be answered "yes" or "no" – a positive response was credited with one point. On the basis of the questionnaire, universities were ranked on an index ranging from 0 to 37. Qualitative data have been used in verifying and supplementing the survey data. A high score reflects strong entrepreneurial activity. The core element of the index is not the actual score, but rather detectable differences in university scores, and in how universities are grouped.

The approach used in developing the questionnaire entails treating the results with some caution. Minor discrepancies in university performance do not imply that one programme is vastly superior to other programmes. However, it is the authors' belief that solid performances across all five dimensions imply a higher quality in entrepreneurial programmes as compared to lower-ranked universities.

Share of students attending courses in entrepreneurship

Measuring and comparing the number of students in entrepreneurship programmes are very complicated tasks. First of all, entrepreneurship courses will often be spread across multiple faculties and students may attend classes at more than one faculty. As a result it is difficult to locate accurate information on the share of students attending entrepreneurship programmes, and there is a risk of double-counting.

Second, entrepreneurship programmes are defined in various ways, and any given definition will influence the level of entrepreneurial activity measured. The approach applied in this study requires entrepreneurship to be the principal element in courses offered. However, one cannot rule out the possibility that university statements regarding the scope of entrepreneurial programmes are flawed.

Third, universities are structured differently. The study distinguishes between three types: *multi-dimensional universities, business schools* and *technical universities.* While available data should be treated with some caution, comparing universities with similar structures could provide a valid image of student participation rates.

The overall picture is that the United States has the highest participation rate in entrepreneurship programmes, especially among business schools students. Universities are actively pushing entrepreneurship education beyond the boundaries of business schools. Participation rates in Canada are lower than in the United States, but still higher compared to Denmark.

Across traditional *multi-dimensional universities,* available data indicate that the share of students participating in entrepreneurship courses at universities in the United States exceed student participation at Canadian and Danish universities. At Stanford University and Cornell University, for example, student participation in entrepreneurship programmes is 15% and 20%, respectively. In comparison, the participation rate at the Canadian universities is estimated at between 5% and 7% and the multi-dimensional universities in Denmark rank even lower. None of the Danish universities reports participation rates above 2.5%.

Comparing the participation rate across *business schools* reveals the same pattern. US business schools report a significantly higher number of students participating in entrepreneurship programmes than their Canadian and Danish counterparts. Thus, the majority of students at the US business schools attend entrepreneurship courses. At Babson College, a "pure" business school, all MBA students and 35% of undergraduate students attend entrepreneurial courses. The total participation rate is approximately 70%. In Canada, the business schools report participation rates of between 20% and 50%, while their counterparts in Denmark report a much lower participation rate (3%).

Given the strength of entrepreneurship education in the United States and Canada, this should come as no major surprise. What is surprising is that all Danish universities are so far behind their US and Canadian colleagues when it comes to addressing entrepreneurship education.

Scope of entrepreneurship activities at the universities

Turning to the differences in the approaches, structures and activities of entrepreneurship education, the same overall patterns emerge. US universities report a higher number of entrepreneurship activities compared to their Canadian and Danish counterparts.

The universities fall into three distinctive groups (Figure 6.2). US universities are ranked in the top part of the index, Canadian universities in the middle section, and Danish universities in the bottom section.

Figure 6.2. Entrepreneurship activities – Total scores

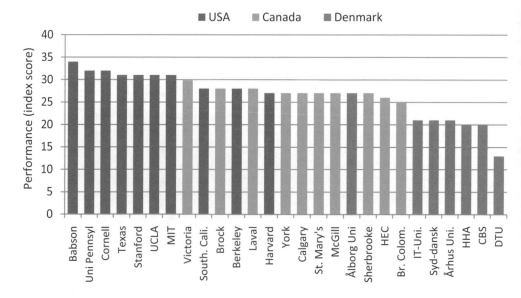

Source: EBST, 2004b.

Rankings elsewhere appear to confirm the validity of the method used here. In the study, Babson College achieved the highest marks among all selected universities, and is widely regarded as one of the premier universities in its field. *US News, Entrepreneur Magazine* and *Business Week* have named Babson as the number one entrepreneur programme in the United States. Furthermore, *Business Week* ranked Pennsylvania second and Stanford fourth.

Average scores of the performance index highlight the strong showing of US and Canadian universities, as illustrated in Table 6.2.

Table 6.2. Comparing universities in the United States, Canada and Denmark

	United States	Canada	Denmark
Share of "yes" answers	82 %	74 %	54 %
Average score (maximum = 37)	30.5	27.2	20.1

Source: EBST, 2004b.

By breaking down university scores into five dimensions, one can identify differences in the way entrepreneurship programmes have been designed. Figure 6.3 reveals a number of differences in the level of entrepreneurial activity across the three countries.

Figure 6.3. Average ranking on the five dimensions in the United States, Canada and Denmark

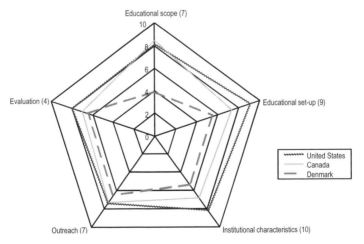

Note: The brackets show the number of questions for each category. For comparison purposes, the five dimensions have been converted into a scale of 1 to 10.

Source: EBST, 2004b.

ENTREPRENEURSHIP AND HIGHER EDUCATION – ISBN- 9789264044098 © OECD 2008

In most areas the United States outperforms Danish universities. Canada also outperforms Denmark on several dimensions.

In educational scope, universities in the United States and Canada show similar ranking, while the Danish universities lag significantly behind. The picture is roughly the same in educational set-up. The United States performs marginally better than Canada, while Denmark's performance is average. On institutional characteristics the United States is also ahead, with Canada and Denmark further behind. In outreach and evaluation the three countries are almost at the same level.

The study revealed a number of different approaches to entrepreneurship education. Universities are subject to various limitations, and each offers various opportunities. Thus the specific approach will be determined by the institutional context. The following section is devoted to identifying country differences in each of the five dimensions and to presenting good practice examples that can serve as inspiration to institutions that wish to embark on entrepreneurial ventures or aim at improving the quality of entrepreneurship programmes.

Educational scope

The dimension of educational scope covers the supply of diversified courses, the availability of BA degrees and graduate/MBA degrees in entrepreneurship, access to lifelong learning, and the scope of entrepreneurial research conducted at the university.

Strong commitment to entrepreneurship education goes beyond the immediate scope of available programmes: a wide range of academic activities is essential in building strong entrepreneurship education.

Figure 6.4 illustrates the average performance for the US, Canadian and Danish universities on educational scope, and the findings are interesting. The US universities receive high marks on issues related to graduate and postgraduate education, research and lifelong learning, whereas the US ranking in supply of entrepreneurship education (undergraduate level) is average. The Canadian universities also perform well in the area of educational scope, especially in the supply of courses at undergraduate level. Canada trails the United States in supply of graduate and postgraduate courses, research and lifelong learning.

Figure 6.4. Average ranking for the United States, Canada and Denmark – Educational scope

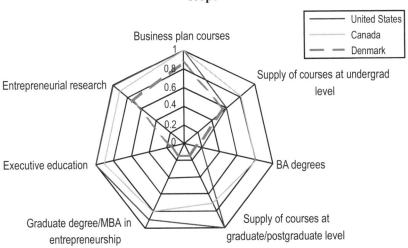

Source: EBST, 2004b.

The Danish universities are on a level with the United States and Canada in the areas of business plan courses, supply of courses at undergraduate level, and research. However, the Danish performance in other areas of educational scope is significantly lower compared to the United States and Canada.

In view of these differences in educational scope, the authors have identified a number of good practice cases that can serve as inspiration to policy makers, universities and other institutions wishing to improve the quality of entrepreneurship programmes (see EBST, 2004b for more cases).

One good-practice example is a bachelor programme offered at the University of Victoria, Canada. Business students at the university can choose a concentration in entrepreneurship. The concentration is not limited to teaching entrepreneurship – students are taught to become successful entrepreneurs. Applying an integrated design to entrepreneurship education, Victoria offers a five-course concentration that goes through the different stages of the entrepreneurial "life cycle" chronologically. The goal is not for everyone to be involved in start-up of a company. Students are taught the principles of sustainable growth, which will be useful to them either as entrepreneurs or in providing guidance and counselling to other entrepreneurs.

A second example is an executive education offered at Babson College, Boston, United States. Entrepreneurial Strategies for Innovation and Growth is a three-day interactive learning programme that helps organisations and their leaders revitalise the engines of innovation that enabled them to grow and flourish in a competitive marketplace. As organisations mature, creative, adventurous, open-minded thinking often gives way to increasingly bureaucratic systems, shareholder demand for bottom-line focus, and the growth of a risk-averse culture. The course offers a blend of learning techniques that includes case studies, guest lecturers, group problem solving, and role playing.

Educational set-up

Educational set-up covers a wide range of issues pertaining to the structure of entrepreneurship education, including: building an entrepreneurial mindset; the use of guest lecturers; education training of teacher-entrepreneurs; the availability of internships or practical experience; ongoing relations with the business community; the use of role models; the development of student personalities; experimental approaches to education; and the extent to which teachers have an entrepreneurial background.

The dimension has been included in the analysis to capture and illustrate that entrepreneurship education goes beyond traditional lectures. Educational set-up implies that universities apply a creative and innovative approach to teaching. By combining a theoretical, practical and experimental approach to entrepreneurship education, students not only learn about entrepreneurs – they become entrepreneurs.

Figure 6.5 illustrates the average performance of the US, Canadian and Danish universities in the area of educational set-up. It reveals that the Danish universities rank markedly lower compared to the United States and Canada.

US universities receive high marks in all but one of the areas of educational set-up. A limited number of US universities do not provide education training for teacher-entrepreneurs and there is little focus on providing students with an entrepreneurial way of thinking.

Canadian universities receive high marks in areas related to the practical approach to entrepreneurship, the use of role models, experimental approaches to teaching and developing student personalities.

Figure 6.5. Average ranking for the United States, Canada and Denmark – Educational set-up

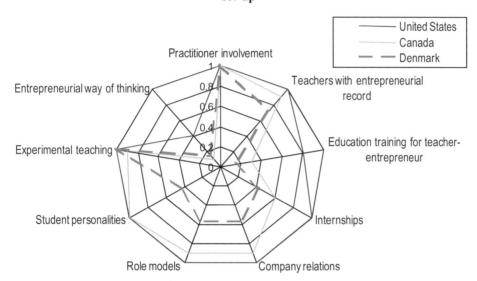

Source: EBST, 2004b.

Danish universities are among the best when it comes to guest lecturers and the use of experimental teaching. Approximately half of the universities interviewed offer internships, have ongoing relations with the business community, or involve role models. However, only a few are engaged in developing student personalities, education training of teacher-entrepreneurs, or embracing an entrepreneurial way of thinking.

The involvement of practitioners is one of the areas that have been approached differently in the United States. Guest teachers with practical experience often go through some kind of education prior to their involvement. The training helps the entrepreneurs to transform their "war stories" into "case studies". In Denmark practitioner education was nonexistent. Good-practice examples of training programmes for teacher-entrepreneurs were identified at Babson College and at the University of California at Berkeley.

Under the PriceBabson programme the effectiveness of teacher-entrepreneurs is enhanced by training them in teaching techniques. The aim is to provide training programmes that ensure the practical and intellectual collision between the academic and business worlds. Through the programmes, they are committed to helping colleges and universities develop creative and innovative entrepreneurship curricula, to increasing teaching effectiveness, and to developing the teaching skills of entrepreneurs who are interested in engaging in full- or part-time teaching.

Training programmes for teacher-entrepreneurs are also offered at the Lester Center at UC Berkeley. The Center is devoted to training teacher-entrepreneurs and maintains a strong focus on transforming war stories to case studies. Teacher-entrepreneurs are recruited from among former MBA entrepreneurship students or among Berkeley's extensive alumni network.

Institutional characteristics

The dimension of institutional characteristics deals with aspects of entrepreneurship education that may be influenced by teachers but that is ultimately set forth by institutions, faculties or the university itself. Thus the dimension determines whether entrepreneurship is a top priority for the relevant faculties and for the university as a whole. If the quality of institutional characteristics is sub-standard, teachers will find it difficult to address issues related to educational scope and educational set-up.

The dimension also covers the involvement of business and other faculties in the management of the entrepreneurship programme, network activities, interdisciplinary activities, study labs where students can exchange ideas, rules pertaining to transfer of credits, and the extent to which entrepreneurship is a part of the overall educational approach.

Figure 6.6 illustrates the average performance of the US, Canadian and Danish universities in the area of institutional characteristics.

Figure 6.6. Average ranking for the United States, Canada and Denmark – Institutional characteristics

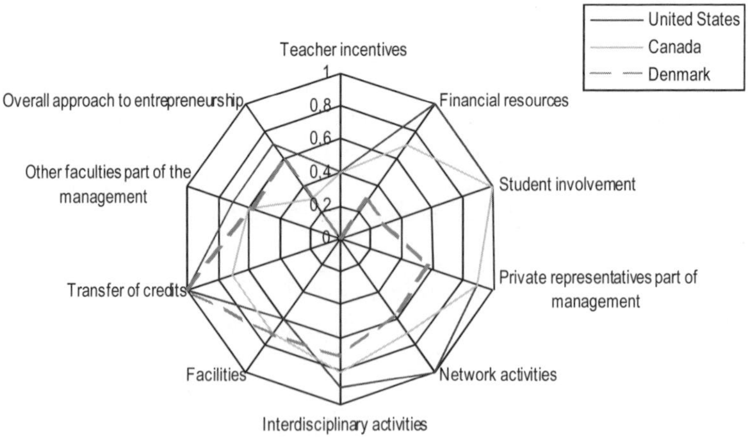

Source: EBST, 2004b.

While US universities received high marks in almost all areas of educational scope and education set-up, a greater variation in performance was detected within the area of institutional characteristics. Seen all together, the United States is the highest-scoring country and receives high marks in available funds, student involvement, networking activities and the inclusion of private business in the management of entrepreneurial programmes.

Canadian universities are on a level with their US colleagues when it comes to student involvement, the involvement of private business, teacher incentives and the accessibility of meeting places for entrepreneurial students. On the other hand, Canada's performance in embracing entrepreneurship as an integrated part of the university's approach, available resources for entrepreneurial activities, networking activities and rules pertaining to the transfer of credits are below the US level.

The performance of the Danish universities is well below average for all but one of the areas. In general, Denmark's ranking reflects the lack of prestige associated with entrepreneurship education. There are low scores for the presence of teacher incentives, available funds for new initiatives, student involvement and the overall approach to entrepreneurship. However, it should be emphasised that Danish entrepreneurship programmes are working hard to improve institutional characteristics, and new initiatives have surfaced recently.

Two areas within the dimension of institutional characteristics especially can serve as good-practice examples for policy makers, universities and other institutions: student involvement and network activities.

The Entrepreneur Association is the largest student organisation at the UCLA Anderson School of Management. Entrepreneur Association offers its 500+ members a wide range of entrepreneur-related activities, with the main emphasis on mentor networks and experience-based learning. More than 30 programmes are scheduled throughout the year to encourage and inspire students to start their own business, and to build an entrepreneurial mindset.

At Berkeley in the United States, the Entrepreneurship Association and the Entrepreneurs Forum actively work to develop and participate in networks typical in the San Francisco area. The activities of the Entrepreneurship Association include inviting entrepreneur and business leader guest speakers as well as facilitating internships for MBA students in start-up companies. The Entrepreneurs Forum meets monthly during the academic year. It works actively to facilitate the networking process and brings together investors, lawyers, accountants, students and researchers.

Outreach

Outreach deals with the prevalence of networks and the extent of co-operation with parties outside university boundaries that provide counsel and aid to entrepreneurial students. Specifically, outreach covers access to incubators, the extent to which incubators are a part of the university setting, vocational guidance (mentoring), venture capital or business angels, alumni networks, IPR support and business plan competitions.

Outreach is important, since the start-up of a knowledge-intensive company poses a number of complicated issues. Proper guidance and the availability of adequate venture capital are crucial elements in the successful launch of a business concept.

As Figure 6.7 illustrates, the United States heads the ranking, slightly ahead of Canada and Denmark.

Figure 6.7. Average ranking for the United States, Canada and Denmark – outreach

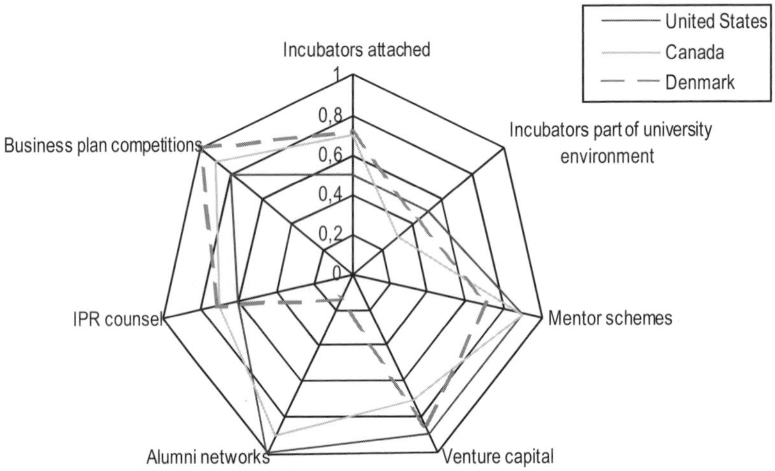

Source: EBST, 2004b.

US performance is solid in the areas of vocational training, alumni networks and venture capital but lower in IPR counsel, business plan competitions and access to incubators. Canada receives high marks in vocational training, alumni networks and business plan competitions. In the areas of access to incubators, venture capital and IPR counsel, the Canadian ranking is average. Denmark ranks at the top in the areas access to incubators, IPR counsel and business plan competitions. Apart from alumni networks Denmark is on a level with the United States in other areas related to outreach activities.

All US universities have alumni networks that help bring practitioners to the class room, promote the use of role models, supply internships, interact with private business, arrange for vocational training, establish relations with venture capitalist and business angels, and act as fundraisers. While attempts have been made to organise alumni activities in Denmark, much work needs to be done in matching the quality of US alumni networks.

A good-practice example of alumni networks can be found at Cornell University. The Cornell Entrepreneur Network (CEN) brings together Cornell alumni with the goal of "linking Cornellians to foster career success". CEN is the national network of Cornell alumni that combines regional events and virtual networks. Events include lectures, discussion groups, black-tie dinners and other networking activities.

The Babson Brain Trust is a select group of talented and experienced individuals who have agreed to actively mentor top student entrepreneurs. Members of the Brain Trust include entrepreneurs, CEOs, venture capitalists, business angels, business advisors and leaders from the Boston business community. The core purpose of the Brain Trust is to create networking opportunities with the world beyond Babson College. Mentors serve as sounding boards, offering advice and counsel and assisting students with the evolution of ideas, business models and strategies. Perhaps more importantly, the mentor serves as a connection to additional resources or individuals who can guide the student.

Evaluation

Evaluation covers university assessment of entrepreneurial activities, stakeholder influence on educational scope, monitoring of the career paths of entrepreneurship graduates, and the extent to which activities are being replicated by other institutions.

US universities receive high marks in the extent to which education is replicated, student and faculty evaluation, and stakeholder needs (Figure 6.8). The United States fails to match Denmark in questions related to the monitoring of student career paths.

Canadian scores are almost on a level with the US colleagues. Canada receives high marks in the extent to which education is replicated, student/faculty evaluation and stakeholder needs, but are ranked behind the United States and Denmark in monitoring effects of education on student career paths.

Figure 6.8. Average ranking for the United States, Canada and Denmark – Evaluation

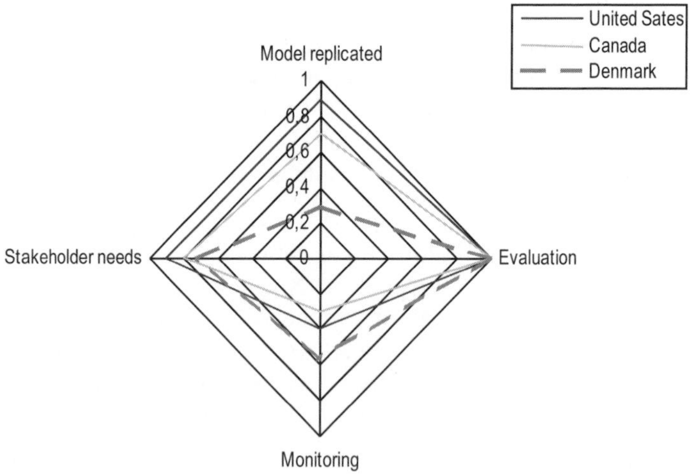

Source: EBST, 2004b.

Denmark is equal to Canada and the United States in three of the four areas. Danish universities are leaders in terms of evaluation and monitoring, and perform well in stakeholder involvement.

The difficulties in evaluating entrepreneurial activity among entrepreneurship graduates are substantial, since most graduates do not engage in a business start-up immediately following graduation. Most take regular jobs and later move to a smaller company or become entrepreneurs. The Graduate School of Business at Stanford has established a unit that monitors future career paths of all Stanford graduates. However, it is not possible to make a distinction between entrepreneurial and non-entrepreneurial students.

Insights and policy implications

The benchmark study points to significant shortcomings in entrepreneurship education at Danish universities relative to leading universities in the United States and Canada. In some areas, such as industry ties and student involvement, the low activity level is more evident than in other areas, such as the level of business plan development courses offered.

But what can Danish policy makers and universities learn from the US and Canadian experiences? What should be done differently in Denmark?

To answer these questions, it is important to understand the underlying factors behind the successful development of US and Canadian entrepreneurship programmes. Initiatives carried out in the best-practice countries may serve as inspiration to Danish universities. However, differences in the cultural and institutional framework imply that it is not desirable to simply "copy and paste" entrepreneurship programmes. The special characteristics of a given society and economy – as well as the culture and traditions of a specific university – have to be taken into consideration.

Approach to entrepreneurship education

A distinction was made earlier between the focused and the unified or university-wide model. That distinction provides valuable insight into how universities approach entrepreneurship education. The most common approach in the United States has been to offer courses and degrees through business schools. As the importance of entrepreneurship across multiple disciplines has been recognised, a new university-wide model has been developing.

Two models within the university-wide approach were also defined. These are the magnet model, where a single entity facilitates entrepreneurship classes offered to students from all departments, and the radiant model, where individual departments develop their own entrepreneurship faculty and course offerings (Streeter, Jaquette Jr. and Hovis, 2002).

The analysis here shows that very few students participate in entrepreneurship classes at Danish universities, and that entrepreneurship programmes are not very developed. The good news is that Denmark is now in a position to learn from successful programmes and evaluate models in order to choose the one most appropriate for its universities. To promote entrepreneurial thinking among students in general, it is important that Danish universities pursue one of the university-wide models: the magnet model or the radiant model. However, it is not possible to determine clearly one specific "best practice" model.

In some respects the magnet model seems appropriate. Given the problem of limited resources identified in the analysis, the magnet model will be the least resource-intensive approach to offer a wide variety of entrepreneurship classes to all students at a university. Furthermore, it is more effective to manage industry ties from a central office and to allow a greater pool of students to connect with a greater pool of private organisations. On the other hand, the magnet model has the disadvantage that students may not become aware of the classes offered, as they are offered outside their own department.

To develop entrepreneurial competences specific to the students' degree of specialisation, the *radiant model* has the advantage of having a specialised entrepreneurship faculty within the department. It may make it easier to promote classes among students, and furthermore obviate the location disadvantages of the magnet approach. The clear disadvantage is that the decentralised radiant approach means fewer resources and less outreach per programme, and most likely a smaller set of classes for students to choose from.

Universities could choose a combination of the two models – that is, have a centralised administration to manage industry ties and to facilitate one or more core entrepreneurship classes, which would be required for all students at the university. The individual departments could then provide specialised entrepreneurship electives within their field of study.

While it is difficult to determine clearly which model Danish universities should apply, it is very important that they choose one. It furthermore seems important that the model be adapted to the special characteristics of the Danish society and economy, as well as the culture and traditions of the Danish universities.

International entrepreneurship

Certain static circumstances must be taken into consideration when designing entrepreneurship education. Small countries have a smaller national market and a smaller set of successful entrepreneurs. As such, it is extremely important to look beyond the borders of the country, which in turn could become a significant advantage.

Consequently, the international dimension needs to be placed at the core of entrepreneurship education at Danish universities. One way to do that is to integrate entrepreneurship education with international business education at the universities. Within the discipline of international entrepreneurship, students need to learn how to think in terms of establishing international ventures and thereby develop competencies that are necessary in sustaining competitiveness in the global economy.

Alumni networks

Alumni networks are another central feature that should be established when Danish universities design their entrepreneurship educations. At US universities alumni networks constitute one of the main contributors of financial resources, human resources and industry ties for entrepreneurship education.

The United States is characterised by a strong entrepreneurial culture, and it is often successful entrepreneurs who help establish entrepreneurship programmes and endowed chairs in entrepreneurship. US universities are status symbols, and their graduates take great pride in promoting their alma mater. This leads to a culture where universities are ranked and where the alumni contribute significant amounts of money to sustain the university's brand name and future success. Successful entrepreneurs and executives are known to donate millions of dollars to the universities they have attended.

US universities are in some senses businesses themselves. Even public universities depend on revenues generated through tuition, as well as private donations. Some receive as little as 10% in public funding. Hence, alumni support is essential to their survival as it provides large proportions of the funding needed to sustain university operations.

Financial support from former students is not as important to Danish universities as it is to their American counterparts. Danish universities are fully supported through public funds, and operations will most likely never be contingent upon private donations from alumni networks. Even in the event a private university is established, they may receive as much as 80% through public funds.

Alumni networks in Denmark do, however, play a critical role as facilitators of industry ties. Danish universities do not involve entrepreneurs and hands-on experience in entrepreneurship education to the same degree as US universities. At the US universities included in the study, the knowledge and experience of practitioners and hands-on experience with entrepreneurial projects or internships are systematically integrated and considered essential elements in entrepreneurial education.

Alumni networks also provide universities with a source of mentors and internships. Former students will often be more than willing to share lessons learned and provide opportunities for students to get hands-on experience. Common to many entrepreneurial environments are multidisciplinary multi-tasking, long working hours, unpredicted situations and a profound sense of urgency that easily leads to stressful work under pressure. The ability to work and thrive in such environments is not something that can be taught in a classroom setting; rather, it is conveyed through hands-on experience with entrepreneurial projects or internships. It is an important part of teaching entrepreneurship, because anyone involved with early stage ventures – be it as entrepreneurs, employees or external advisors – will need to learn the different pace, higher level of expectations and working under pressure.

Even if it is a challenging task, Danish universities should develop alumni networks to create and maintain relations with former students.

Conclusion

The study has used a general benchmark method to show that entrepreneurial activity at Danish universities is significantly lower than that in the United States and Canada. The entrepreneurial spirit in the United States is highly evident at educational institutions, where entrepreneurship remains a reputable discipline. Establishing a comprehensive entrepreneurship programme covering all aspects involves a great deal of work and resources, but many universities in the United States have been successful in embracing entrepreneurship.

While overall approaches may differ, the study has illustrated that there are a number of common characteristics in programme design and activities at the US and Canadian universities that are not prevalent at Danish universities.

The study has highlighted that entrepreneurship education should be given a higher priority in Denmark and that action is needed in this area. Some steps have already been taken since the study was first published. The Danish government has initiated a number of measures to improve entrepreneurship education, among them an entrepreneurship academy. The academy, funded with approximately EUR 4 million, was established to develop entrepreneurship activities for Danish university students. However, more initiatives seem necessary.

Bibliography

Betts, J. and C. Lee (2004), "Universities as drivers of regional and national innovation: An assessment of the linkages from universities to innovation and economic growth"; paper prepared for the John Deutsch Institute conference on Higher education in Canada, Queen's University, Kingstone, Canada, 13-14 February 2004.

Charney, A. and G.D. Libecap (2000), *Impact of entrepreneurship education*, The Kauffman Centre for Entrepreneurial Education, The Ewing Marion Kauffman Foundation, Kansas City, MI.

DVCA (Danish Venture Capital Association) (2004), "Kortlægning af danske universiteters uddannelsestilbud indenfor entrepreneurship", (Mapping entrepreneurial education in Denmark), DVCA, Copenhagen.

EBST (The Danish National Agency for Enterprise and Construction) (2004a), *Entrepreneurship Index 2004 - Entrepreneurship conditions in Denmark*, EBST, Copenhagen, www.ebst.dk/publikationer/ivaerksaettere/entrepreneurship_index_2004/pdf/EBS_Ivaerk_GB_5k.pdf,

EBST (2004b), *Education at Universities: A Benchmark Study - Background Report for the Entrepreneurship Index 2004*, EBST, Copenhagen.

EBST (2004c), *Entrepreneurial Education in the Danish Educational System*, EBST, Copenhagen.

GEM (Global Entrepreneurship Monitor) (2003), *GEM Denmark 2003: The Danish Entrepreneurial Situation – The Growth of New Firms*, Børsens Forlag.

Kjeldsen, C., J. Rosted, and M.D. Bertelsen (2003), *"A benchmark study of entrepreneurship – What can Denmark learn?"*, FORA, July 2003 (in Danish).

Lundström, A. and L. Stevenson (2001), "On the road to entrepreneurship Policy", *Entrepreneurship for the Future Series*, Vol. 1, Swedish Foundation for Small Business Research, Stockholm.

Menzies, T. and Y. Gasse (1999), *Entrepreneurship and the Canadian universities: Report of a national study of entrepreneurship education*; St. Catharines, Ontario.

OECD (2004), "Fostering entrepreneurship and firm creation as a driver of growth in a global economy", background report for the 2nd OECD SME Ministerial Conference, Istanbul, 3-5 June 2004.

Streeter, D.H., J.P. Jaquette Jr. and K. Hovis (2002), "University-wide entrepreneurship education: Alternative models and current trends", working paper, Department of Applied Economics and Management, Cornell University, USA.

Chapter 7

Entrepreneurship Education for Central, Eastern and Southeastern Europe

by
Shaker Zahra
University of Minnesota, United States
Friederike Welter
Rhine-Westphalia Institute for Economic Research (RWI),
Germany

As the former Soviet Bloc countries transform their economies, significant cultural, legal, political and institutional forces continue to constrain entrepreneurship. This chapter examines the role that entrepreneurship education can play in creating momentum for change. It starts by examining entrepreneurship education in turn in the United States, in leading European OECD countries, and in Central and Eastern Europe, noting major differences in how these countries value entrepreneurship and entrepreneurs. The discussion then turns to an assessment of the impact of entrepreneurship education. Finally, lessons are drawn on how to improve entrepreneurship education in Central, east and south east European countries, including through introducing innovative curricula and interactive teaching methods.

ENTREPRENEURSHIP AND HIGHER EDUCATION – ISBN- 9789264044098 © OECD 2008

Introduction

For those who study and regularly interact with entrepreneurs and observe the birth and growth of their companies, the importance of entrepreneurial education is evident. This education refines and hones what entrepreneurs know and sharpens their creative skills. It inspires them to search more systematically for opportunities, select the appropriate form for their enterprises, and develop effective management teams that lead their companies as they go through various transitions (Fiet, 2001a; Honig, 2004). Entrepreneurship is a mindset that centres on the creative discovery and the pursuit of opportunities, even when resources are scarce. Education provides the intellectual tools and skills that allow "would be" entrepreneurs to visualise and evaluate opportunities (Fiet, 2001b). It also helps them conceive ways to overcome barriers while pursuing these opportunities. Understandably, the value of entrepreneurship education is widely recognised in the United States (Katz, 2003) and some other OECD countries (Welter, 2005). However, this is not always the case in other parts of the world – especially Central, Eastern and Southeastern European countries, where entrepreneurship education is still in its infancy. These are countries where the need for entrepreneurship is greatest but the supply of entrepreneurship teachers and role models is scarce.

This chapter examines the experiences of the United States and leading European OECD countries in promoting entrepreneurial education. In so doing it attempts to distil some lessons that can enrich the experiences of Central, Eastern and Southeastern European countries in fostering a willingness among their people to take the risks associated with new business creation. In these countries, the privatisation of state-owned monopolies has created opportunities for entrepreneurship in well-established companies as well as new ventures (Zahra, Ireland, Guitterz, & Hitt, 2000). Of course, there are major differences among the various countries that constitute the former Soviet bloc countries. History, geography, culture and ideology have shaped the experiences of these different countries as well as their transition to a market-based economy. Those differences have important implications for the interest in and support for entrepreneurship education. There are also differences in how the United States and European OECD countries view entrepreneurship, both as a profession and as an academic discipline. These differences are deep and wide, and have shaped the way entrepreneurship education has developed in these countries. Appreciating them can set the stage for an informed discussion of how Central, Eastern and Southeastern European countries might develop and promote their entrepreneurial educational systems.

The chapter begins with an overview of the current state of entrepreneurship education. It highlights a continental divide between the United States and other OECD countries in how they view the field and profession of entrepreneurship. Next, it analyses different levels of entrepreneurship education, contrasting graduate and undergraduate programmes. It also discusses postgraduate entrepreneurship education in the form of executive development and in-house corporate education. With this background in mind, the discussion turns to entrepreneurship education in selected Central, Eastern and Southeastern European countries, covering the strengths and weaknesses of existing programmes. It concludes by offering suggestions on how to best improve entrepreneurship education through innovative curricula and interactive teaching methods.

The United States vs. other OECD countries: A continental divide?

In the United States, entrepreneurship education is extensive and varied, from high school through to the doctoral training. Universities and specialised trade associations also offer courses and development programmes that foster entrepreneurial risk taking. The US Small Business Administration, through its university-affiliated institutes, also has a range of courses that keep small business owners abreast of developments in their industries and teach them to deal with the problems faced in managing and growing their companies (Solomon, Duffy and Tarabishy, 2002). In-house corporate executive programmes also offer a range of courses on entrepreneurship. This training is premised on the idea that entrepreneurship centres on discovering and exploiting opportunities to create wealth for the individual, firm, community, and society at large. Entrepreneurship training focuses on developing and honing *individual skills* in identifying, evaluating, and exploiting opportunities (Sexton, Bowman-Upton, Wacholtz and McDougall, 1997).

Most entrepreneurship education in the United States takes place at the graduate level. This growing demand has put serious pressures on faculty resources (Fiet, 2001b). Some universities have responded by changing teaching responsibilities, providing training opportunities for some faculty as they make the transition to teaching entrepreneurship (Katz, 2003). Programmes at Babson College, Case Western Reserve University and Syracuse University have sought to retrain interested faculty from other disciplines to teach entrepreneurship. Other universities have hired former government officials, managers and entrepreneurs to teach their entrepreneurship courses. Numerous universities have combined the skills of traditional academics with those of entrepreneurs by providing opportunities to co-teach specialised courses such as technology-based entrepreneurship or new venture financing. Several universities (*e.g.* Indiana University and the University of Washington) have also expanded their doctoral course offerings to train professors in entrepreneurship. However, as a recent review indicates much of the doctoral training in entrepreneurship in many US universities is done on an *ad hoc* basis (Brush *et al.*, 2003; Kuratko, 2003). The growing demand for faculty and entrepreneurship courses has prompted some universities (University of Louisville) to explore launching (Babson College and Clemson University) and/or actually offering doctoral programmes in entrepreneurship (University of Louisville).

The picture is different in a number of other OECD countries, where entrepreneurship is not seen simply as a way to make profit or create wealth. In these countries, entrepreneurship is often equated with the successful management of small businesses. Such is the case today in the German-speaking countries and in some of the new EU member states such as Poland or Slovenia. This orientation reflects a long-standing tradition of vocational education centred on increasing small business creation and ownership. As such, entrepreneurship training often emphasises nurturing the "functional" management skills, such as production, marketing and distribution that small business managers need (Welter, 2002). In these countries the training is carried out through professional organisations, specialised consulting companies and university outreach programmes. Other countries have created new entrepreneurship chairs, aiming to expedite and improve entrepreneurial education. Still, in European OECD countries, graduate and undergraduate entrepreneurship education remains limited in scope, partly because it only started in the late 1990s. The first chair for entrepreneurship in Germany, for example, was founded in 1998. Even today, there are fewer entrepreneurship educational activities in some of the Southern European countries such as Italy (Klandt, 2004; Koch, 2003a, 2003b).

Entrepreneurship education often has a more academic flavour in the European OECD countries than it has in the United States. Typically, this training is grounded in traditional disciplines such as economics, psychology, sociology, engineering, math, science and the like, though most undergraduate and postgraduate entrepreneurship education tends to be clustered at the faculties/colleges of economics and business administration (Schmude, 2001; Schmude and Uebelacker, 2002). The majority of entrepreneurship professors are traditional academics, reflecting long-standing recruitment policies and practices of not employing practitioners. Thus, universities have made little use of former entrepreneurs in teaching. This is markedly different from the experiences of some US business schools, where practitioners and former entrepreneurs are well represented in the classroom – as teachers, guest lecturers, or executives in residence who counsel the faculty, students, and the administration about entrepreneurship curricular issues. Increasingly however, the US model is being copied in OECD countries. More and more entrepreneurs and managers are being recruited to teach entrepreneurship in Europe, where university regulations permit. This trend reflects a growing recognition of the value of practical experience in teaching entrepreneurship; it also signals a serious shortage of qualified faculty who can teach entrepreneurship at undergraduate and graduate levels.

Undergraduate vs. graduate entrepreneurship education

The US experience

The first graduate course in entrepreneurship was offered at Harvard University in 1948 (Katz, 2003). Since then courses have proliferated, covering a wide range of topics: new venture creation, business planning, family business, entrepreneurial finance, technology-based entrepreneurship, international entrepreneurship, social entrepreneurship, corporate entrepreneurship, gender issues in entrepreneurship, franchising, and many others. Some universities have also sought to differentiate themselves by focusing on specific niches where they can build a distinctive advantage (Kuratko, 2003). Regardless, these programmes usually connect traditional business courses with those offered in the sciences (engineering and liberal arts). Indeed, the Kauffman Foundation recently provided grants to several US universities with the explicit goal of nurturing entrepreneurship throughout the universities/colleges, not only within their business schools. This has encouraged the introduction of a broad set of courses that creatively exploit the intellectual capital that exists across universities' research centres, institutes and academic units. Donations from the business community and successful entrepreneurs have contributed to the recent phenomenal growth in graduate courses in the United States.

US universities have also initiated entrepreneurship programmes for their undergraduate students, aiming to instil in them the ability and desire to create their own companies. Some of these programmes are "tracks" within established academic majors; others are academic "minors." Still other programmes confer certificates on their graduates. Overall, typical United States-based undergraduate entrepreneurship programmes aim to: (a) foster students' creativity and allow them to explore their potential as entrepreneurs; (b) provide the basic concepts and skills to define, evaluate, and pursue promising business opportunities; and (c) develop students' skills as owner-managers. Most undergraduate students receive their degrees in an established functional major (*e.g.* civil engineering, accounting, biology or computer science) and usually use their training in entrepreneurship to explore creating their own firms. Some graduates accept positions with start-ups or family businesses. Graduates also work for established corporations, gaining an opportunity to apply what they have learned and acquire new skills should they decide to venture on their own and start their own new companies.

The goals espoused by US undergraduate entrepreneurship programmes are achieved using several methods (Barry and Tagg, 1995). These methods include hands-on training in creativity techniques; lectures and case studies in the various aspects of business; training in communication; and providing opportunities for networking with entrepreneurs and venture capitalists to gain confidence in dealing with diverse stakeholders. Some universities also give students a chance to work in teams to develop and refine their business plans; universities usually provide faculty or executive coaching and feedback for these teams. With the help of faculty and entrepreneurs, students typically spend time analysing their teams' decision-making processes and their own decision-making styles, and develop effective strategies for improvement. Other universities introduce their students to the process of entrepreneurship and then require them to develop business plans for ventures of their own choosing. Students usually work with faculty advisors or entrepreneurs on refining their plans. Through role playing and presentations to peers and business people, students also sharpen their presentation skills. Given undergraduate students' limited education and experiences, US universities often rely heavily on guest speakers to inspire and motivate students, share their experiences, and offer feedback on student projects. The business plans that undergraduate students produce are often basic in nature, frequently favouring "lifestyle" new venture ideas.

Universities' graduate programmes focus more on making best use of students' prior education and business experience. Students are immersed quickly in various analytical techniques to give them an opportunity to learn by doing. Case studies are widely used to expose students to diverse types of new ventures, present situations they might encounter in managing a new business, and show them how to best use analytical tools to make important decisions. Some universities use consulting relationships with local entrepreneurial companies. Graduate students can thus hone their skills while serving local companies' needs – and these internships often lead to jobs. Many universities often hold business plan competitions, in which students submit and present their plans for evaluation and critical review; winning proposals receive some funding to bring their venture ideas to life. Other universities complement these awards with seed money to help with the initial start-up costs. Some universities have incubators that host budding ventures, supporting their transition from a conceptual idea to fully fledged entities.

Table 7.1 summarises the key differences over the years in graduate vs. undergraduate entrepreneurship training in the United States. These differences emanate from the nature of students being served, as well as their skills and career ambitions. This leads us to pose the question: Is there a quality distinction between graduate and non-graduate firms? It appears there are several qualitative differences. First, in the United States there is greater attention to graduate-level entrepreneurship, though more schools are focusing on undergraduates at the urging of companies, successful entrepreneurs and donors. Second, the graduate education curriculum in most schools is better developed and integrated into university goals than undergraduate programmes. This is likely to change, however, as more schools become more proficient in undergraduate entrepreneurial education. Third, in terms of outcomes, graduate students often start their businesses in more diverse fields, many of which are knowledge-based (social science and business administration) or more technology-based (natural science or engineering). Undergraduate students tend to emphasise "lifestyle" new venture ideas.

Table 7.1. Differences in goals, opportunities and challenges associated with undergraduate and graduate entrepreneurship programmes

Item	Undergraduate	Graduate (master's level)
Key premises	• Students are likely to work for other companies, both new and established. A small percentage of students will actually create their own businesses. • Most businesses created by undergraduates are likely to be related to lifestyles or hobbies.	• Students have some prior business experience. • Students are more likely than undergraduates to own and manage a professional practice. • If they work for a well-established company, graduates are more likely to engage in corporate venturing activities – formally or informally.
Objectives	• Developing awareness of the importance of entrepreneurship. • Helping students to recognise their potential as entrepreneurs by understanding their strengths and weaknesses. • Providing a framework for defining and evaluating business opportunities.	• Preparing students for a second career by honing the skills already learned in prior education and business. • Developing the skills needed to transform ideas into business. • Improving skills necessary to lead a new venture and assemble an effective

Item	Undergraduate	Graduate (master's level)
	• Developing basic business skills and competencies, especially planning. • Understanding the various challenges associated with the different stages of a company's evolution. • Improving students' networking skills.	management team.

Preferred teaching methods	• Undergraduate courses tend to be more applied, emphasising a variety of teaching approaches that include:
	  ▪ Case studies.
	  ▪ Business plan preparations.
	  ▪ Role playing.
	  ▪ Guest speakers in class.
	  ▪ Company visits.
	  ▪ Visits to trade shows and science parks.
	  ▪ Simulation.
		• Developing new cases.
		• Readings (that build theory).
		• Business plan competition.
		• Internships.
		• Consulting arrangements organised through the university.
		• Growing use of Internet technology to facilitate learning and sharing of experiences.

Opportunities	• Interdisciplinary collaboration. • Fundraising; entrepreneurs appear to identify most with undergraduate students whom they consider the future of their industries and nations.	• Specialization (e.g. tech entrepreneurship). • Careers as entrepreneurs and in established companies. • Opportunities for executive and in-house management development programmes.
Challenges	• Lack of realism because of lack of experience. • Focus on lifestyle or hobby ventures.	• Career tracks (where do graduates go and which skills could be bundled together in unique career paths). • Creating an effective balance between traditional MBA training and experiential learning.

The situation in European OECD countries

As indicated earlier, there are major differences between the experiences and focus of entrepreneurship educational programmes in the United States and other OECD countries. In the European OECD countries, there is a greater focus on the academic side of entrepreneurship without recognising it as a legitimate academic discipline. This academic focus has led some professional organisations such as chambers of commerce to offer short training courses and seminars for the basics of setting up a business, while universities concentrate on the "core" business. Universities' academic focus goes hand-in-hand with a strong reliance on teacher-centred pedagogical methods; there is infrequent use of practitioners in teaching except for guest lectures. However, case studies and the use of videos are gaining ground. Contrary to the academic focus of entrepreneurship courses, the success of newly founded entrepreneurship chairs is often measured by the number of businesses founded by university graduates and students, a factor that has promoted practical-oriented courses.

A more accurate picture entails consideration of the different academic traditions and training backgrounds that exist across the European OCED countries. For example, entrepreneurship education in the United Kingdom is based on a strong tradition of small business research and teaching. This might explain the predominance of SME chairs, most of which were established decades ago. In fact, the first entrepreneurship course in the United Kingdom was offered at the Manchester Business School in 1971. Today, nearly 86 out of 200 UK degree-awarding institutions "have got some form of entrepreneurship education in place for students" (Watkins, 2000, p. 54). SME chairs also have been a long-standing tradition in German-speaking OECD countries. For example, the Institute for SMEs at the University of St. Gallen in Switzerland has been training small business owners and teaching small business management to students for more than 50 years. The same is true in Germany, where only recently universities and universities of applied sciences have established entrepreneurship chairs. Most of these chairs have been endowed for a five-year period by the public SMEs and entrepreneurship bank (Kreditanstalt für Wiederaufbau – KfW) or by companies such as SAP, raising the question about their sustainability over a longer period. Entrepreneurship education in smaller European countries such as the Netherlands or Belgium remains limited in scope and outreach. It is primarily in modules in the economics or business administration programmes (Klandt, 2004; Koch, 2003a).

In the European OECD countries, entrepreneurship is often offered as an elective subject and mainly as stand-alone courses and seminars until the "critical mass" forms to integrate the topic into the curriculum (Wilson, 2004). Depending on the respective academic tradition and the academic unit where entrepreneurship education is located, courses are offered at both the undergraduate and graduate levels. Undergraduate courses or modules are few in number and usually focus on giving students an overview of entrepreneurship. At the graduate level, courses emphasise either analysing entrepreneurship from an academic and theoretical perspective or providing "hands on" experiences such as the specifics of business plans, procedures for creating a new business, and legal and tax information.

Increasingly, classroom instruction is supplemented by extracurricular activities such as business plan competitions, student consulting companies, and internships within new or small firms. There is also some support for venture creation from incubators, depending on the extent to which graduate entrepreneurship education is embedded into local and regional support networks. In those programmes where entrepreneurship education is offered by a few teachers, any extracurricular activities are sporadic and done on an *ad hoc* basis. Exceptions include, for example, the science parks installed in Sweden during the 1990s in 19 universities. These parks aim to foster the high-growth, knowledge-based and technology-oriented spin-offs of university graduates and university employees (Klofsten, 2000).

There are only a few doctoral programmes in entrepreneurship in OECD countries. One successful example is the "European Doctoral Programme (EDP) in Entrepreneurship and Small Business Management". EDP was developed by the European Council of Small Business and Entrepreneurship in 1990, and 165 participants from over 47 countries have attended since its inception (Box 7.1). The EDP is also one of the few organisations apart from universities that have created an alumni organisation, establishing a postgraduate network and drawing on the experiences and support of its graduates. European universities do not have a long tradition of creating alumni organisations; only recently have they begun to make use of this resource in recruiting practitioners to teach in their entrepreneurship programmes.

European universities use a variety of teaching methods in their programmes. Though the use of these methods varies from one country to the next, "traditional" lectures and seminars or group work continue to dominate classroom instruction. Interactive teaching methods such as role playing, case study discussions and simulations are used less frequently in teaching entrepreneurship (Gibb, 1996; Koch, 2003a). However, case-based teaching is gaining ground, especially across business schools and younger programmes. A lack of European-based cases and teaching material continues to hamper the use of case method teaching. Case writing and development is a fine art, and few European countries have devoted the resources necessary to develop entrepreneurship cases. Case teaching is also intensive, requiring great creativity, extensive mastery of the subject matter and flexibility. Training is also lacking for teachers interested in leading case discussions, making it difficult to move away from reliance on lectures.

Box 7.1. The European Doctoral Programme in Entrepreneurship and Small Business Management

The three main objectives of the European Doctoral Programme (EDP) are (1) to offer graduate students the opportunity to study in some detail three interrelated subjects, namely (i) Entrepreneurship and enterprise formation, (ii) Small business management and development, and (iii) SME in economic and regional development; (2) to promote and coach the participants' individual thesis work; (3) to strengthen the development of common research themes throughout the world in the general field of entrepreneurship and small business development. The programme has been initiated by the ECSB based on a concept developed by a committee of the Council, chaired by Professor Dr. Josep M. Veciana of the Universitat Autònoma de Barcelona (UAB). The ECSB has established a network of 15 European universities and business schools that support and contribute to the programme.

EDP was founded under ERASMUS/SOCRATES, which means that (1) it benefits from grants for the reciprocal exchange of students and teachers; and (2) it adopts a common curriculum designed to fill a gap in the study of entrepreneurship in Europe. The programme is also part of the European Doctoral Programmes Association in Management and Business Administration (EDAMBA), a forum for co-operation among doctoral programmes of leading European business schools.

Source: www.edp-site.net

The results of a recent survey on entrepreneurship education in European universities and business schools are revealing (Wilson, 2004). The survey, which was completed by 240 entrepreneurship teachers across Europe, illustrates the progress made to date as well as the problems these universities often encounter in designing their curricula, selecting teaching topics and choosing their teaching methods. Three key findings are evident from this survey.

First, entrepreneurship education is not well integrated into the university curriculum. Instead, frequently, entrepreneurship modules and courses are offered on an *ad hoc* or stand-alone basis. This is markedly different from US universities, where entrepreneurship courses build on other courses in the curriculum. The problem is compounded by the fact that in most European schools, only a few faculty members are engaged in teaching or researching entrepreneurship. Second, there is an almost exclusive focus on the start-up phase of the entrepreneurial process, as reflected in business plan writing. Respondents felt a need to follow the various stages of new venture growth and expansion. They also recognised the importance of fostering and developing the entrepreneurial skills associated with working in well-established companies. Third, course materials often are generated locally, possibly limiting the scope and depth of topics covered. There is also a strong and pressing need for training in interactive and innovative teaching methods.

Table 7.2 captures the key differences between the United States and other OECD countries in terms of entrepreneurial education. As stated earlier, however, there are important differences among European OECD countries in this regard, and Table 7.2 should be interpreted as simply identifying broad differences.

Table 7.2. Differences in goals, opportunities and challenges associated with undergraduate and graduate entrepreneurship programmes

Dimension	United States	European OECD
Entrepreneurship programmes are best described as	• Dominated by the view that entrepreneurship is risk taking in pursuit of opportunities to create wealth. • Paracademic (applied discipline), with a focus on experiential learning. • Having entrepreneurs and former executives involved in teaching and leading the programmes. • An important means of fund raising, providing opportunities for internships and potential jobs. • More diverse in their foci. • Placing increasing emphasis on "differentiation" through discipline specialisation (e.g. biosciences), stage of development (e.g. corporate entrepreneurship), or focus (e.g. international entrepreneurship). • Though the profit motive remains strong, there is growing attention to social issues in entrepreneurship.	• Tending to equate entrepreneurship with creating, managing and growing SMEs. • Academic (scholarly), with strong identification with theory building. • More analytically focused. • Usually housed in traditional academic departments, even though some universities have created entrepreneurship centres. • More focused and narrower in scope • Placing greater emphasis on studying family firms.

Entrepreneurship education in Central, Eastern and Southeastern Europe

Even after more than a decade of transition, entrepreneurs in post-Soviet countries continue to face enormous problems, though the problems differ significantly across countries and stage of economic transition (Smallbone and Welter, 2001). These countries vary markedly in various dimensions. For instance, they differ in the scale of privatisation of their economy. Countries such as Croatia, the Czech Republic, Hungary, the three Baltic States, Poland, the Slovak Republic and Slovenia have undergone massive privatisation. In contrast, the pace of privatisation in Belarus and Turkmenistan has been limited. In addition, former Soviet bloc countries vary in terms of price liberalisation. For instance, Hungary, Poland, Slovenia, Romania and Moldova have enacted aggressive policies to bring about market reforms and liberalise their economies. In Belarus, Turkmenistan and Uzbekistan, liberalisation policies have been more limited.

Differences in the scope of market reforms, combined with other economic, social and historical differences, limit generalisations across the countries that comprise Central, Eastern and Southeastern Europe and the former Soviet Union. Still, there is evidence that in the former Soviet republics (*e.g.* Russia, Belarus and Ukraine), many enterprises are set up, survive and even grow *despite* the stringent and sometimes dysfunctional government policies. Entrepreneurs in those countries have shown creativity in mobilising resources to pursue their business ideas, as well as great flexibility in adapting to hostile external environments (*e.g.* Peng, 2001; Smallbone and Welter, 2001). Still, the number of new firms founded in these countries remains small. New firms' contribution to job creation, innovation and external income generation is limited. Clearly, in these and similar countries, the desirable types of entrepreneurial activities, and the effective national strategies necessary to stimulate new firm creation, depend on political, ideological (Peng, 2001; Peng and Heath, 1996), and institutional realities (Welter, 2002).

Promoting entrepreneurship education in Central and Eastern Europe is becoming an important topic of discussion and debate (Schramm, 2004). In these countries, there is a growing recognition of the vital importance of rebuilding national economies, adopting new technologies and creating jobs. These countries need to develop their economies not only to meet the growing needs of their citizens, but also to rise to the international standards of competitiveness. Global competition is knowledge-based, centring on the accumulation and utilisation of well-developed and highly trained intellectual capital (Schramm, 2004). Assuming adequate incentives and effective organisation, knowledge capital is the cornerstone of innovation; it allows countries to modernise their economies and improve the quality of life of their citizens.

There is also a growing realisation that governments in Central and Eastern European countries do not appreciate the importance of systematic, formal entrepreneurship education. One possible reason is these governments' preoccupation with changing the legal frameworks and institutions that thrived under communism, and with aiming to encourage risk taking and new venture creation. Dismantling these institutions is only one of several steps needed to bring about an effective transition to a free market economy that encourages entrepreneurialism. For entrepreneurship education to become a legitimate part of universities' curricula, society at large should also value enterprise and entrepreneurship by respecting individual initiatives, maintaining an appropriate infrastructure, supporting new firm creation, and protecting ownership rights (Hayton, George and Zahra, 2002). When these values are embedded in the national culture, society begins to view entrepreneurship as an important, if not vital, profession. Such an appreciation of entrepreneurship is still lacking in some former Soviet bloc countries, especially where economic and political reforms have not progressed much – as in Belarus, Ukraine, Moldova and most Central Asian republics (Smallbone and Welter, 2001) – or where reforms have been set back through war, as happened in the former Yugoslavian republics in Southeastern Europe.

Entrepreneurs in Central and Eastern European countries, too, bear some responsibility. The uncertain political and economic environment has compelled some entrepreneurs to pay more attention to solving daily business problems, instead of strategically developing their businesses (Welter, 2005) or sharing what they have learned with others. Without training in modern production and marketing skills, and lacking effective role models, these entrepreneurs are "learning by doing" through trial and error. Corruption has also raised the cost of doing business in some of these countries, making it difficult for entrepreneurs to share their wealth with universities or research centres.

The picture is somewhat different in other Central, Eastern and Southeastern European countries where reforms have progressed well (*e.g.* new EU members or those in line for such membership). In these countries, entrepreneurship education is now offered through private foundations, business associations and universities. These educational programmes usually follow existing teaching traditions, with some initial input from either European or US institutions.

In some Southeastern European countries, there is a strong dominance of entrepreneurship education that is linked to management faculties. Entrepreneurship in these programmes, as noted above, is often equated with small business management. This is the case today in Romania, where the Academy of Economic Studies, the largest university (with 40 000 students), offers courses focusing on SME management, business development, and international comparative SMEs.

Estonia is one of the few countries that have introduced entrepreneurship education into its curriculum as early as the 1990s. This effort began when three public universities that provided economic education substituted their older curricula with new, market-based economy curricula. The goal of this change was to advance the knowledge about entrepreneurship and skills needed to create and manage new companies. At the same time, several new private universities and advanced schools were founded, adopting curricula oriented to business administration and entrepreneurship. Presently, there are more than 20 such universities and advanced schools teaching business administration and entrepreneurship. Along with its development in higher and applied education, entrepreneurship has been included in the curricula of vocational and general education schools. In fact, the curricula of all vocational education schools now contain a business administration or entrepreneurship course that provides basic knowledge on starting and managing a business.

Applied education in business administration and entrepreneurship is also provided in Estonia, in 16 advanced schools with 20 different programmes. Bachelor-level education is provided in nine advanced schools and universities (for a total of 14 programmes) and master-level education in five universities. Thirty-six different consulting and training firms and universities also have entrepreneurship-related training courses. The number of different training courses in Estonia is 237. These courses cover a wide range of topics that include: general management and administration (33%), marketing (11%), accounting and taxation (11%), quality management (5%), financial management and law (5% each), and communication training (4%), among others.

In the Baltic States and in large cities in Russia, entrepreneurship education is also offered through international business schools, such as the Stockholm School of Economics with its branches in Riga (Latvia) and St. Petersburg (Russia). Yet, training here relies heavily on international teachers. Though this initially might have expedited the introduction of entrepreneurship education into the curriculum, it could ultimately impede the development of local teaching expertise and materials, especially where no attempt is made to educate and train teachers.

In countries where the pace of economic and political reforms has been slow, most entrepreneurship education still exists outside higher educational institutions; it is usually carried out through business support centres and enterprise development agencies. This raises a question about the financial sustainability of such efforts, because these business agencies have been established with the financial support of various international donors (Bateman, 2000). Such foreign, donor-led initiatives are the major means of educating entrepreneurs in most of Southeastern Europe (OECD, 2003). Often they are supplemented by a strong vocational system – as is the case in Albania, where university-level courses are still lacking (OECD, 2005).

Some international donors have also initiated specific projects to train and educate potential entrepreneurs, mostly focused on general management issues. Here, the experience of the Ukraine is revealing. Two of the earliest efforts were the International Management Institutes in Kiev and Lviv, which have been launched by the International Management Institute in Switzerland. By 1999, around 60 certified private educational institutions were established, most with some donor funding (Isakova and Smallbone, 1999). This phenomenal growth in private institutions stems from local entrepreneurs (who often were previous university lecturers) recognising the opportunity to provide entrepreneurship and management education to meet the growing demands of the private sector and recently privatised companies. Moldova presents another interesting case in point regarding the development and evolution of entrepreneurship education (Box 7.2).

Box 7.2. Entrepreneurship education in Moldova

Several universities and colleges in Moldova offer short courses in business education. These mainly focus on how to start a small business, but they are not offered regularly as obligatory part of the curricula. The same applies to schools and lyceums. In 2000, a course titled "Applied Economics" was introduced into the national education programme as an elective course for lyceums, starting in the 10th class for 34 school hours. In practice, the course is seldom offered because of a lack of qualified entrepreneurship lecturers, and there is little demand from pupils. The same problems apply to universities.

International donors often support extracurricular entrepreneurship training activities. One example is a business plan competition for young people, which was initiated by the National Association of Young Managers of Moldova in collaboration with Canadian Business Incubators and the Academy of Economic Studies of Moldova in 2003 (www.antim.org). Officially, the Moldova government recognises the need to introduce and encourage entrepreneurship education – e.g. in the Law on Employment, the Strategy for the Youth and the State Programme on Small Business Support 2002-05. However, entrepreneurship training is still scarce, and available courses are expensive and lack a practical approach

Source: Information from Elena Aculai, Institute of Economy, Finance and Statistics of the Academy of Sciences of Moldova (IEFS).

Still, most private educational institutions as set up in the Ukraine and other Eastern European countries focus on training managers who work for large multinational companies (Isakova and Smallbone, 1999). This focus leaves a major void in existing educational programmes, which are not equipped to motivate students and graduates to pursue entrepreneurship in an environment that does not reward new venture creation. Ironically, this is where entrepreneurship education can make a major difference – in promoting a willingness to explore various opportunities for creating and growing companies. Entrepreneurship education can enhance an individual's self-efficacy (Shepherd, 2004) and encourage them to create new businesses, promoting "necessity entrepreneurship" that breaks the vicious cycle of underdevelopment. Barriers to such entrepreneurship are deeply embedded in national cultures, institutions and legal frameworks; these stifle a person's willingness to create new firms and instead reinforce dependence on government-sponsored business programmes. Therefore, a concerted effort by the private sectors, combined with a strong and sustained government commitment to changing existing educational systems, could encourage entrepreneurial risk taking.

There is also the need for a stronger focus on developing and promoting entrepreneurship topics and integrating them into existing university curricula. To gain legitimacy within universities' decision-making processes, entrepreneurship education should become part and parcel of the universities' intellectual life. Such legitimacy has two dimensions: research and teaching. Undertaking original and rigorous entrepreneurship research can help advocates of entrepreneurship become legitimate within academia. Improving teaching requires innovative curriculum development and delivery. A particularly interesting initiative aimed at developing new teaching materials, though not focused exclusively on entrepreneurship, is the "Regional Academic Partnership Scheme" (www.reapnet.ru). This is a bilateral initiative funded by the United Kingdom government and involves several Central and Eastern European countries. For example, the School of Business and Management of Technology at Belarus State University has developed, jointly with the Kingston Business School in the United Kingdom, modules for management education, including personal development.

Table 7.3 summarises some of the key opportunities and challenges for entrepreneurship education in Central, Eastern and Southeastern Europe. While the literature is replete with discussions of the challenges awaiting "would be" entrepreneurs, there are major opportunities for individual and corporate entrepreneurs to create new businesses, ensure their success, and see them grow. Therefore, Table 7.3 also outlines several entrepreneurial educational needs and corresponding skills.

Table 7.3. Opportunities and challenges to entrepreneurship education in Central, Eastern and Southeastern Europe

Implications for higher education institutions

Dimensions	Issue	Implications
Opportunities	• Young population: need for new venture creation (opportunity vs. need). • Need for catch-up technologically. • Economic progress: raising standard of living. • Excellent math and engineering background. • Flow of foreign investments.	• Start early, with foundation skills in creativity techniques. Courses in opportunity recognition and evaluation are also important. • Leverage contacts with business companies by bringing in guest speakers to share experiences. • In addition to new ventures in consumer goods, technology-based ventures would be an excellent focus.

Challenges	• Heritage of state ownership:
	  ▪ Privatisation creates opportunities.
	• Incentives are lacking.
	• Capital/funding.
	• Lack of teachers:
	  ▪ Retooling existing faculty.
	• Entrepreneurial culture is lacking:
	  ▪ Role models.
	• Academic institutions are theoretical / abstract.
	• How to get started.
	• Linking science / engineering with business programmes.
		• Education should target well-established companies and new ventures alike.
		• Key role of entrepreneurial education is to create momentum for change; development starts in small steps, as others follow and momentum grows.
		• Engage local entrepreneurs as role models and source of feedback and learning.
		• Create joint programmes between science / engineering and entrepreneurship. Joint appointments and faculty rotations might be important ways to achieve this.

Assessing the impact of entrepreneurship training in higher education

Stimulating and nurturing entrepreneurship at the national level demands attention to three key policy decisions: (1) Which groups can be influenced by entrepreneurship education in higher education institutions? (2) Are higher education institutions the right organisations to offer entrepreneurship education? and (3) What is the likely economic and social impact of entrepreneurship education? These three questions are discussed below.

Which groups can be influenced?

It is tempting to propose that all students attending colleges or universities would benefit from learning about entrepreneurship. Yet, these students are likely to differ greatly in their attitudes, aptitudes and career aspirations. Also, as already noted, teaching resources and qualified faculty who can train these students are in short supply. Therefore, it is important to consider the goals of entrepreneurship programmes. If the purpose is to excite and motivate students to explore their entrepreneurial potential and develop an awareness of entrepreneurship, then these programmes could be offered throughout the campus. That broad coverage could promote an appreciation of the role of entrepreneurship in economic development and wealth creation. Over time, this could change prevalent attitudes about the risks and rewards of creating and managing one's own business and ensuring its success and eventual growth.

Higher institutions could create programmes that provide assistance in starting a business. They could target those individuals who are already motivated to have careers as entrepreneurs and have ideas for businesses. The programmes can help these individuals think about the opportunity they wish to exploit, testing the potential market, developing the business model, creating the business plan, crafting the competitive strategy the firm will follow, delineating the firm's competitive advantage and its various sources, seeking and gaining funding, and building an appropriate and professional top management team.

Analysis of the population data of several of the former Soviet bloc countries reveals three viable target groups: science and engineering students; students from other disciplines on campus; and career professionals. These groups have different goals and different expectations from institutions of higher learning.

- *Science and Engineering* – Entrepreneurship programmes should venture beyond traditional business and economic schools on campus and target other disciplines. In particular, science and engineering students (undergraduates and graduates) would make an ideal target. With the growing emphasis on knowledge as the foundation of global competitiveness, it would be natural to focus on these graduates, stimulate their interest in entrepreneurship and support them as they explore business opportunities. With unemployment so high in some former Soviet bloc countries, training and education in the mechanics of new venture creation could stimulate "necessity entrepreneurships", defined as those efforts aimed at creating firms to overcome barriers to employment or access to opportunities. By targeting science and engineering students, institutions of higher education can unleash the creative energies of their graduates and build momentum for change.

- *Supportive Services and Industries* – Focusing on engineering and sciences in turn requires that higher institutions of education consider entrepreneurial activities that might exist in "supporting services and industries". Technological development requires the existence of a modern infrastructure that includes effective telecommunication, administrative and secretarial help, and supply-chain value-creating activities such as logistics, transportation, and warehousing. Start-ups might also need the services of temporary employees and business and financial consultants, as well as the guidance of legal experts. New ventures might need access to modern technologies imported from advanced Western countries, or the expertise of export companies and agencies. Universities and colleges could (and should) also target various students who might be interested in creating these varied activities. To achieve the goals just discussed, universities and colleges could target their existing students or offer short courses to train the interested general public. Types of programmes are needed. The first would focus on developing basic entrepreneurial skills; the second would focus more on the specifics of the issues involved with different activities, such as how to import or export.

- *Career professionals* – A third important group in planning entrepreneurship education is career professionals, those individuals who are already in the labour force and would like to change careers or simply create their own companies. This is an important but frequently neglected market, probably because some believe the skills these professionals have are outdated. That might be true, but many of them have a great appreciation for the dynamics of the markets and have connections to established institutions and power centres. Focused short courses could help this group to master key skills and better understand the vital role of entrepreneurship in their countries' changing economies. Trapped in the process of economic and political transition, some might find this training useful as they explore other career options in supporting industries, creating their own companies, or simply looking for jobs in newly created ventures.

Are higher education institutions the right organisations?

Institutions of higher learning are also undergoing massive transformation in their missions, foci and teaching methods. This transformation provides a golden opportunity to shape younger institutions to embody entrepreneurship as a source of their distinctive competence. Even in the United States and leading Western European economies, the integration of entrepreneurship education into existing university curricula has proved problematic. Many still view entrepreneurship as a subfield of strategy and continue to debate its value added as a separate field (Zahra, 2005). Entrepreneurship research is in its infancy and often lacks theoretical grounding and methodological rigor. It is no coincidence that most early efforts to institutionalise entrepreneurship in the United States have taken place in younger institutions and specialised academic programmes. This has changed over the past decade, with many leading research institutions creating major research centres in entrepreneurship.

There is no wish to export the US or Western European experience to former Soviet bloc countries. Rather, there is a need for a more comprehensive plan where both higher educational institutions and other groups work to fill different needs and niches. There is a need for organisations that teach the basics of business, economics and management. This could be best accomplished in universities and other institutions of higher learning. Those institutions can play a key role in instilling a desire for entrepreneurship in their students. They can be alliance partners, who work with others to offer specialised programmes to ease the transition of professionals into productive entrepreneurial careers. They could also work with local agencies or foreign universities to sponsor entrepreneurship programmes.

Other specialised organisations could also target younger populations. Institutions of higher learning could collaborate with chambers of commerce and civic organisations to reach high school and even younger students and introduce them to the joys and challenges of being entrepreneurs. Graduate and even undergraduate students could volunteer to work with younger students, hoping to stimulate interest in entrepreneurial careers.

As the discussion indicates, institutions of higher learning could be a key node in a network of agencies and organisations working to encourage and nurture entrepreneurship education. Given the high stakes involved in economic and political transitions and the shortage of qualified faculty members in the institutions of higher education in former Soviet bloc countries, it is imperative to engage other partners – domestic and foreign – in bringing about change through entrepreneurial education and training.

ENTREPRENEURSHIP AND HIGHER EDUCATION – ISBN- 9789264044098 © OECD 2008

What is the likely economic and social impact of entrepreneurship education?

Assessing the impact of entrepreneurial education is a challenging task because it often takes years to see its effects. In addition, even the most effective entrepreneurial training does not automatically translate into new business creation. Political, sociological and personality variables significantly influence the transition from classroom learning to actual entrepreneurial behaviour. In addition, some of the results of entrepreneurial education are direct (*e.g.* creating companies) whereas others are indirect (*e.g.* changing attitudes and developing awareness of the activities associated with creating and growing a business). As a result, multiple approaches are necessary to capture the direct and indirect contributions of entrepreneurial education.

Institutions of higher education should also track enrolment numbers in their various courses. This serves as a baseline to document changes over time, signalling shifts in student and participant interests. The mix of students enrolled in these programmes is another area to examine, because it could serve as an indicator of the locus of future business creation activities.

An important measure of successful entrepreneurial activities is the number of companies created by graduates and the fields in which these firms are started. Of course, care should be exercised in using this criterion to safeguard against premature conclusions; it might take years to see ideas and the learning gained from entrepreneurial education become business enterprises. It is also important to gather data on the numbers and types of the jobs created by these companies, their revenue and profitability. More long-term indicators of success would include the sophistication of the products and technologies generated by companies whose founders graduated from various entrepreneurship programmes; the types of customers and markets they serve at home and overseas; and their track records in gaining funding.

From a societal perspective, the efficacy of entrepreneurship training and education could also be measured by the number of jobs created, the representation of women and men in employment created by new firms, the tax revenues created, new goods and services offered, the wealth created, direct financial contributions to local communities by business owners, indirect contributions by these owners to their society (*e.g.* service as role models; providing internships to youth; serving as guest teachers in universities), and the general change in national attitudes about self-employment and new firm creation. The growth of a viable and vibrant middle class would also serve as an important signal of the success of entrepreneurial education. Finally, development economists traditionally have argued that there is only a limited supply of entrepreneurs in each country – a proposition that has ignited fierce discussion and debate (Smallbone and Welter, 2001). True, personality factors have their important role in entrepreneurship. However, as stated throughout this chapter, context matters even more; entrepreneurship is socially embedded and therefore influenced not only by individual personality variables but also by a society's overall institutional context. Therefore, a major indicator of successful entrepreneurial education is reduced fears associated with the risks normally surrounding entrepreneurship.

Lessons learned

What are the general problems in entrepreneurship education across Central, Eastern and Southeastern European countries? What are the key lessons these countries can learn from the experiences of the United States and European OECD countries as they seek to increase the potential impact of entrepreneurship education? The analyses here suggest four recommendations.

First, a major problem in Central and Eastern European as well as other transitional countries is the lack of qualified teachers. Educational programmes that train future entrepreneurs in the various stages of new venture creation are almost nonexistent. Further, though new management chairs have replaced the Marxism-Leninism chairs in some public education institutions, the same teachers and professors are often retained after switching to topics like general business management. Some of these professors do not fully appreciate the value of entrepreneurship and do not have first-hand experience in the mechanics of new firm creation and growth. There is also little systematic research on the unique obstacles that entrepreneurs face in these countries, making teaching entrepreneurship a complicated and challenging task. Training facilities that familiarise professors with recent research findings or teaching methods are also widely lacking. Further, in some countries, entrepreneurship education activities are frequently concentrated in and around the urban centres, depriving other regions from access to recent developments in the theory and practice of entrepreneurship. As long as governments do not recognise the need for systematic entrepreneurship education of younger as well as senior faculty members and students, the lack of qualified professors will continue to be a serious handicap for economic development and technological progress. Fortunately, some international donors have given attention to these issues and have begun to train local entrepreneurs and faculty. These international efforts to enhance entrepreneurial education and training remain limited and sporadic.

Second, entrepreneurial skills are learned in a variety of ways and methods. Some are best learned by doing and observing others. Of course, lecture-based education has its place in the curriculum, but the training of future entrepreneurs should also include interactive and action-oriented methods. Governments have an important role in this process, as public education systems in Central and Eastern Europe remain very rigid and inert. They rely on traditional and teacher-centred teaching methods, though curricula leave little or no room for introducing new topics and methods. Governments and educational institutions should recognise that entrepreneurship is not something a person is born with, but a set of skills that can be taught and learned.

The OECD might have an important role to play in promoting entrepreneurship education. An obvious area is faculty and professor exchanges. One option is to team up experienced entrepreneurship professors from the United States and other countries with local talent. Another option is to arrange for leading scholars and teachers to offer intensive courses on entrepreneurship research and teaching. The OECD can also develop an active network of educators in Central and Eastern Europe and connect them with leading experts in the United States and European OECD countries. The OECD could moreover help with training local professors and students and supplying necessary educational material.

Third, entrepreneurship education should not be limited to higher education institutions. Programmes targeting high school (or even younger) students could also help to change prevailing attitudes about the nature and value added of entrepreneurship. Other programmes could target business owners or employees (and professionals) in existing enterprises, especially where business support infrastructure is still lacking. These programmes could augment peoples' learning needs and introduce new concepts and practice to improve their operations. The programmes might also stimulate interest in entrepreneurship as a profession, thus increasing the potential supply of entrepreneurs.

Fourth, though the basic principles of establishing a new business are the same worldwide, entrepreneurship is deeply embedded in national cultures and draws upon the previous experiences of individuals and their societies. As stated earlier, entrepreneurs learn from the various role models they encounter in their lives and careers. Teaching materials should reflect the variety of starting points that entrepreneurs use to build their organisations. Entrepreneurial training should seek to overcome the psychological barriers that have evolved in national cultures over generations. These new educational materials and techniques should focus on improving potential entrepreneurs' self-efficacy by giving them the foundation to realistically assess and evaluate the risks associated with new venture creation.

Conclusion

When the authors began writing this article, they were overwhelmed with the repeated references in the literature to the challenges and barriers that limit entrepreneurship in Central, Eastern and Southeastern Europe. Even some of their long-term collaborators from those countries also questioned the wisdom of tackling this topic. Many have already given up in great disappointment at the slow pace of economic and ideological transitions; they have been disappointed with and frustrated by the lack of progress. Yet, as the authors reflected on what they saw and know about the rich heritage of these young democracies, their young and educated populations, and their stated national and individual aspirations, they could not abandon their work. Their own research tells (indeed, reminds) us that the winds of change are strong and there is no going back. Economic progress resides in individual initiatives that, when honed through entrepreneurial training and education, transform national dreams of progress into visible and sustained development that enhances a society's quality of life and its global competitiveness.

Bibliography

Barry, R.B. and J. Tagg, (1995), "From teaching to learning: A new paradigm for undergraduate education", *Change*, Vol. 27, No. 6, Heldref, pp. 12-25.

Bateman, M. (2000), "Business Support Centres in the transition economies – progress with the wrong model?", *Small Enterprise Development,* Vol. 11, No. 2, Practical Action, pp. 50-59.

Brush, C.G., *et al.* (2003), "Doctoral education in the field of entrepreneurship", *Journal of Management*, Vol. 29, No. 3, Sage, pp. 309-331.

Fiet, J.O. (2001a), "The theoretical side of teaching entrepreneurship", *Journal of Business Venturing*, Vol. 16, No. 2, Elsevier, pp. 1-24.

Fiet, J.O. (2001b), "The pedagogical side of entrepreneurship theory", *Journal of Business Venturing*, Vol. 16, No. 2, Elsevier, pp. 101-117.

Gibb, A. (1996), "Do we really teach (approach) small business in the way we should?", in H. Klandt, J. Mugler and D. Müller-Böling (eds.), *Internationalizing entrepreneurship education and training*, proceedings of the IntEnt93 Conference in Vienna, *FGF Entrepreneurship Research Monographien*, 6, Köln, Dortmund, pp. 3-20.

Hayton, J., G. George and S. Zahra (2002), "National Culture and Entrepreneurship: A Review of Behavioral Research", *Entrepreneurship: Theory & Practice*, Vol. 26, No. 4, Blackwell, pp. 33-52.

Honig, B. (2004), "Entrepreneurship education: Toward a model of contingency-based business planning", *Academy of Management Learning and Education*, Vol. 3, No. 3, Academy of Management, pp. 258-273.

Isakova, N. and D. Smallbone (1999), "The training needs of entrepreneurs in Ukraine", paper presented at the IntENT Conference, Sofia, Bulgaria, 14-16 June.

Katz, J.A. (2003), "The chronology and intellectual trajectory of American entrepreneurship education 1876-1999" *Journal of Business Venturing*, Vol. 18, No. 2, Elsevier, pp. 283-300.

Klandt, H. (2004), "Entrepreneurship education and research in German-speaking Europe" *Academy of Management Learning and Education*, Vol. 3 No. 3, Academy of Management, pp. 293-301.

Klofsten, M. (2000), "Teaching and training entrepreneurship in Sweden", in: BMBF (ed.), *Ausbildung zu unternehmerischer Selbständigkeit: Erfolgreiche Ansätze zur Integrierung unternehmerischer Selbständigkeit in unterschiedliche Ausbildungssysteme in Europa und den Vereinigten Staaten – ein Erfahrungsaustausch, Band 1*, BMBF Publik, Bonn, pp. 45-47.

Koch, L.T. (2003a), "Theory and practice of entrepreneurship education: A German view", *International Journal of Entrepreneurship Education*, Vol. 1, No. 4, Senate Hall, pp. 633-660.

Koch, L.T. (2003b), "Unternehmerausbildung an Hochschulen. Zeitschrift für Betriebswirtschaft", *ZfB-Ergänzungsheft*, supplement issue 2/2003, pp. 25-46.

Kuratko, D.F. (2003), "Entrepreneurship education: Emerging trends and challenges for the 21st century", *2003 Coleman Foundation White Paper Series for the US Association of Small Business and Entrepreneurship*, US-ASBE, Madison, WI.

OECD (2003), *South East Europe region. Enterprise policy performance: A regional assessment*, OECD, Paris.

OECD *et al.* (2005), *Enterprise policy performance assessment: Albania*, OECD, Paris.

Peng, M. (2001), "How entrepreneurs create wealth in transition economies", *Academy of Management Executive*, Vol. 15, No. 1, pp. 95-111.

Peng, M. and P. Heath (1996), "The Growth of the Firm in Planned Economies In Transition: Institutions, Organizations, and Strategic Choice" *Academy of Management Review*, Vol. 21, No. 2, pp. 492-529.

Schramm, C. (2004), "Building Entrepreneurial Economies", *Foreign Affairs*, Vol. 83, No. 4, Council on Foreign Relations, pp. 104-116.

Schmude, J. (2001), "Gründungsforschung und Unternehmerausbildung an Hochschulen" *Internationales Gewerbearchiv*, Vol. 49, No. 2, Schweizerisches Institut für gewerbliche Wirtschaft an der Universität St. Gallen, St Gallen, pp. 89-103.

Schmude, J. and S. Uebelacker (2002), *Gründungsausbildung in Deutschland und den USA: Eine Analyse zur Organisation und Ausrichtung von Entrepreneurship-Professuren*, DtA-Studie, Bonn.

Sexton, D.L., *et al.* (1997), "Learning needs of growth-oriented entrepreneurs", *Journal of Business Venturing*, Vol. 12, No. 1, Elsevier, pp. 1-8.

Shepherd, D.A. (2004), "Educating entrepreneurship students about emotion and learning from failure", *Academy of Management Learning and Education*, Vol. 3, No. 3, Aademy of Management, pp. 274-287.

Smallbone, D. and F. Welter (2001), "The role of government in SME development in transition countries", *International Small Business Journal*, Vol. 19, No. 4, Sage, pp. 63-77.

Solomon, G.T., S. Duffy and A. Tarabishy (2002), "The state of entrepreneurship education in the United States: A nation-wide survey and analysis", *International Journal of Entrepreneurship Education*, Vol. 1, No. 1, Senate Hall, pp. 1-22.

Watkins, D. (2000), "The history of entrepreneurship education in the U.K", in: BMBF (ed.), *Ausbildung zu unternehmerischer Selbständigkeit: Erfolgreiche Ansätze zur Integrierung unternehmerischer Selbständigkeit in unterschiedliche Ausbildungssysteme in Europa und den Vereinigten Staaten – ein Erfahrungsaustausch Band 1*, BMBF Publik, Bonn, pp. 52-54.

Welter, F. (2002), "Entrepreneurship-Förderung an Hochschulen", *RWI-Mitteilungen*, Vol. 53, No. 1-4, pp. 89-106.

Welter, F. (2005), "Entrepreneurial behavior in differing environments", in D. B. Audretsch, H. Grimm and C. W. Wessner (eds.), *Local Heroes in the Global Village. International Studies in Entrepreneurship*, Springer, New York, pp. 93-112.

Wilson, K. (2004), "Entrepreneurship education at European universities and business schools: Results of a joint pilot survey", www.efmd.org/attachments/ tmpl_1_art 050201rpku_att_050201igbl.pdf, accessed 8 March 2005.

Zahra, S. (2005), "Disciplinary Research and Entrepreneurship Scholarship", in S. Alvarez, R. Agarwal and O. Sorenson (eds.), *Disciplinary Research in Entrepreneurship*, Springer Science + Business Media, Inc., New York.

Zahra, S., *et al.* (2000), "Privatization and Entrepreneurial Transformation: A Review and Research Agenda", *Academy of Management Review*, Vol. 25, No. 3, Academy of Management, pp. 509-524.

Chapter 8

Developments in the Teaching of Entrepreneurship in European Transition Economies

by
Urmas Varblane, Tõnis Mets
University of Tartu, Estonia

Piero Formica
Jonkoping Univeristy, Sweden

The aim of this chapter is to map the current situation in the entrepreneurship education of 22 European transition economies and to develop a shared source of data on entrepreneurship education in the region. The analysis covers 774 higher education institutions from the region, of which 363 had entrepreneurship-oriented courses, modules or curricula. The creation of entrepreneurship profiles in the schools as well the level of teaching is analysed. The chapter also identifies examples of the best practice in entrepreneurship teaching from the three viewpoints: how the specialised units co-ordinating teaching and research of entrepreneurship are designed; the best examples of curricula; and the level of internationalisation of the programmes offered in these schools.

Introduction

During the past decade serious changes have taken place in the European system of higher education, and these have led to more attention being paid to entrepreneurial education at different levels. Research has been carried out to monitor trends in entrepreneurship teaching and training among the old European Union (EU) member states (Wilson, 2004). Unfortunately, there is no similar overview or understanding of the current status of entrepreneurship teaching in the new EU member states. What knowledge there is about this field of education in Russia, Ukraine and Southern European transition countries is very limited.

Consequently, current research has focused on entrepreneurship education at the universities and business schools of the European transition countries, with their country-specific factors facilitating or inhibiting the development of entrepreneurship education. The research objectives were: to obtain a general understanding about the coverage and level of entrepreneurship education in the new EU member states, the South European transition countries, and the European part of the Commonwealth of Independent States (CIS); to identify the best examples of entrepreneurship education in these countries; and to develop a shared source of data on entrepreneurship education in the region.

Following the introduction, the chapter gives background about the entrepreneurial activity in the region, and then provides both a short overview of earlier research and the methodology of the current research. Major statistical results concerning coverage of transition countries with entrepreneurship teaching are presented and discussed. The discussion then turns to best practices in the region, and concludes with some policy recommendations for improvements in the entrepreneurship education of the region.

Entrepreneurship in the European transition countries

The political, economic and social systems of the former command system countries have faced considerable changes since the late 1980s. Most countries in Eastern and Central Europe have gone down their own individual road of transition from a centrally planned system to a more or less liberalised market economy, and these different pathways of entrepreneurship development in the various post-communist countries have led to different results (Berkowitz and Jackson, 2006; Smallbone and Welter, 2001, 2003).

The group of transition countries can broadly be divided into four groups. Russia, Ukraine and the other former Soviet Union republics, excluding the three Baltic States, form the first group. In these countries, almost all private entrepreneurship activities were banned until late 1980s. The duration of extreme suppression of private entrepreneurship lasted 50-60 years, and this was reflected in the radical change in the mindset of population, which had lost the instinct for entrepreneurship.

Estonia, Latvia and Lithuania form the second group of countries, where private ownership was suppressed in a similar way but over a somewhat shorter period of 35 to 40 years. Private ownership was banned after occupation of the Baltic States in 1940s; yet, a social memory about the roots of entrepreneurship was still in the minds of people by the beginning of the transformation in the late 1980s. An additional positive role was played by the closeness of Scandinavia to Baltic countries. For example, the majority of the population in Northern Estonia regularly watched Finnish TV, which provided information about the roots of the market economy during the heaviest Soviet occupation. In addition, regular personal contacts with Finns helped to keep alive an internal willingness to reform business in Estonia. The knowledge inflow and personal contacts with Scandinavian business people helped in the late 1980s to initiate the rapid growth of entrepreneurship in Baltic countries.

The third group of countries comprises Poland, Hungary, the former Czechoslovakia, Romania, and Bulgaria, where private ownership was still allowed to a greater or lesser extent. Most notably, in Poland about 90% of farms were privately owned, while in Hungary small business in services was also partly private. In these countries the entrepreneurial spirit did not disappear completely; a kind of continuity existed in the society.

The fourth group of countries contains principally Slovenia and Croatia, as well as Serbia and the other republics of the former Yugoslavia. There, private ownership was allowed more widely and an entrepreneurial attitude was supported by the acceptance of employee ownership of companies. In this group the free movement of labour was allowed, which helped to transfer entrepreneurial spirit from the neighbouring western countries (Germany, Italy and Austria).

The above-mentioned historical background, combined with the socioeconomic and cultural differences, produced variety in the entrepreneurial activity among transition countries. The general attitude of the population toward entrepreneurship is an important aspect that should be taken into consideration in trying to evaluate current level of entrepreneurship education. To that end, data from the Global Entrepreneurship Monitor (GEM) were used. The GEM project enables researchers to measure the total entrepreneurial activity (TEA) Index, expressed as the ratio of the number of people per 100 adults (between 18 and 64 years of age) who are trying to start their own business or are owners of/managers in an active enterprise not older than 42 months. Figure 8.1 provides comparative evaluation about entrepreneurial activity in Central, Eastern and Southeastern Europe and other regions.

Figure 8.1. Entrepreneurial activity by global region, 2002

(Eastern Europe covers Russia, Poland, Slovenia, Croatia and Hungary)

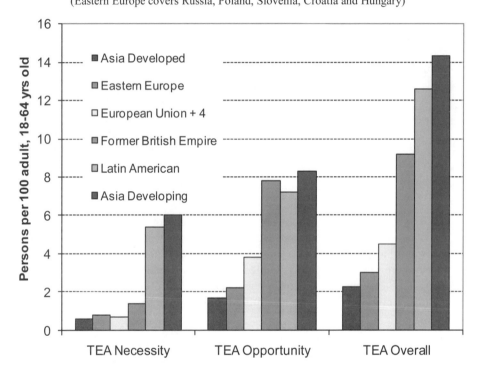

Source: Authors' drawing based on data from Reynolds et al., 2002; Frederick et al., 2002.

Unfortunately, only a limited number of transition countries were covered by GEM 2002, and the assessment of the TEA Index in Eastern European countries is not regular, even in the five-country group described in Figure 8.1 (Reynolds *et al.*, 2005). Since 2002, the entrepreneurial activity of the population has occasionally been measured in other post-Soviet countries; in Estonia for example, it was 5% (in 2004: Lepane and Kuum, 2004) and in Latvia it was 6.6% (in 2005: Dombrovsky, Chandler and Krēsliņš, 2005). In 2005 the TEA was also measured in Croatia at 6.1%, and in Slovenia where it was 4.4 % (Minniti, Bygrave and Autio, 2006), but not in other CEE countries. However, the TEA Index of those Central, Eastern European countries that are included is still low compared with the majority of other regions – the average in 2005 was 8.4% (Minniti, Bygrave and Autio, 2006), signalling the need to encourage entrepreneurship.

Previous analyses of the entrepreneurship education

Entrepreneurship education began to be an important subject for research relatively recently; and the first serious analyses were published in the early 1990s (an overview of the early research is in Hisrich and O'Cinneide, 1996, pp. 46-50). The major emphasis was on analysis of the US educational system, which already had remarkable traditions of teaching entrepreneurship. But first results of the research indicated that only one-third of US institutions of higher education provided one or more courses in entrepreneurship. Since the late 1990s, European entrepreneurship teaching has also become an object of investigation (Twaalfhoven, Suen and Prats, 2000, 2001; Twaalfhoven and Wilson, 2004). These works established a wide gap between the United States and Europe in the level of entrepreneurship teaching. Unfortunately we can find only some comparative papers about the teaching of economics and business in the European transition countries (Pleskovic, Åslund, Bader and Campell, 2000). Even more rare are studies of entrepreneurship education; only a few papers have been written. Mitra and Matlay (2004) gave a general overview of the situation in the region, based on information obtained from surveys among faculty members from the region. There are also some country-specific papers on entrepreneurship education (*e.g.* Leko-Simic and Oberman, 2004; Cepani and Haxhia, 2005).

The methodology for the current research was strongly affected by the size of the research object. As the aim of the research was to map entrepreneurship education in all the European transition countries, it was impossible to go into the underlying the programmes in depth. But from the descriptions of curricula and the lists of chairs, it was still possible to identify the focus of the institutions in terms of entrepreneurship education. As a methodological basis, a classification was also used (as proposed in Twaalfhoven, Suen and Prats, 2001) to distinguish three types of approach to entrepreneurship programme development. The first is the research-oriented model, which places the focus on academic research, the creation of new ideas about entrepreneurship practices and the development of new pedagogical tools. The second is the "consulting" model; here the focus is on establishing relationships with the local business community. Faculty – and often students too – provide services in consulting, offering practical courses in, *e.g.*, writing a business plan and managing a business. Finally there is the Teaching/Practice-Oriented Student Development model, with a wide range of courses for students, business plan competitions, internships, and strong connections to active businesspeople to encourage students to establish start-up firms.

The analyses consisted of two stages. In the first, analysis was carried out on the basis of secondary information – Web pages of schools, various research articles, previous reports and analyses of entrepreneurship education in other regions. In total, 774 Web pages were reviewed from HEIs in the Baltic States (Estonia, Latvia, Lithuania); the Central European group (Poland, Czech Republic, Slovakia, Hungary, Slovenia, Croatia); the Southern European group (Romania, Bulgaria, Serbia, Bosnia-Herzegovina, Macedonia, Albania); and CIS countries (Russia, Ukraine, Moldova). In the process of analysing the Web pages of schools, the limitations of the information in English became evident. Therefore, in order to gain a broader understanding of the situation in the schools, the native language homepages were also analysed as far as language limitations permitted (Russian, Ukrainian, Polish, Czech, Slovakian, Slovenian, Croatian, Bulgarian, Macedonian). After the selection process identified those schools offering at least some level of entrepreneurship teaching, the analysis covered 363 institutions from 22 transition countries. Clearly the research team was not able to cover the vast educational system of Russia or Poland as closely as small countries like Slovenia or Estonia, but the most important educational centres in European part of Russia were monitored. A database of entrepreneurship education in the HEIs of European transition countries was created; improvement of data there is an ongoing process.

In the second stage of research, a special questionnaire was prepared and sent to 36 schools identified during the first stage of research based on the Web page information. In total, 16 answers were received, which makes the return rate of surveys 44%. The questionnaire focused broadly on the entrepreneurship activities of the institution and the university-industry relationship. In addition, phone interviews were held with several experts from the transition countries.

Entrepreneurship-oriented teaching in Central and Eastern Europe

Table 8.1 gives a general overview of the entrepreneurship teaching in HEIs in the European transition countries. But the table also presents the number of schools that offer a full curriculum or separate courses in entrepreneurship, or provide training in entrepreneurship in various forms. It also gives the distribution of curricula between undergraduate (bachelor), graduate (master) and postgraduate (PhD, DBA) levels.

In the first column of the table, figures are given for the total number of institutions of higher education in each country, according to information from following international databases: Web Databases of World Universities (www.canadian-universities.net/World_Universities); the Higher Education Institution Registry (www.siu.no/heir); Universities Worldwide (http://univ.cc/world.php); and national databases. The total number of institutions of HEIs in each country is followed by the number of schools analysed by the research process. In total, 1 873 schools were listed and 774 institutions were analysed in depth; entrepreneurship was taught in 363 out of the 774 schools analysed. In general, entrepreneurship-oriented teaching in the region is relatively rarely offered; only in 47% of all the schools included in the analysis was it possible to identify at least one entrepreneurship-oriented course. In only 12% of schools was there at least one curriculum in entrepreneurship available. There were 65 curricula in entrepreneurship at bachelor's level, and 50 at master's. Only in six schools in Central Europe and 14 schools in Russia was it possible to take a PhD programme with specialisation in entrepreneurship.

Bachelor-level curricula in entrepreneurship existed in only 8.4% of schools, and various master-level curricula in 6.4%. The proportion of all schools with doctoral specialisation in entrepreneurship was 2.5%. These proportions are very similar to the results of recent research by Wilson into the situation of entrepreneurship education in Europe (2004).

The most widespread entrepreneurship-oriented teaching among the countries investigated was in Slovenia and Croatia. In these countries of relatively small size with a small number of institutions of higher education, the share of schools with entrepreneurship-oriented courses was almost 50% (Slovenia) and 45% (Croatia).

There was also relatively high coverage of schools with entrepreneurship-oriented courses in the Baltic States (Latvia 71%, Estonia 31%, Lithuania 38%). In Slovakia and the Czech Republic around one-third of schools had specific courses in entrepreneurship. Poland, with its huge educational system, was impossible for the research group to cover fully, and therefore the coverage rate of less than 40% could be an underestimate. Hungarian data may be understated due to language problems in analysing Web sources. Among the Southern European countries the supply of entrepreneurship teaching is generally much lower. Among this group of countries the coverage is better in Bulgaria, followed by Serbia-Montenegro; in Romania and Moldova the number of schools teaching entrepreneurship is very low. Among the countries of the Commonwealth of Independent States, the Russian situation is most diverse. Because of the enormous number of institutions of higher education in the country (1 142), a selective approach was implemented, and teaching of entrepreneurship was found in 363 schools. In Russia 38 schools offered a curriculum in entrepreneurship, including 14 PhD programmes that specialised in entrepreneurship.

Table 8.1. General overview of the teaching of entrepreneurship in HEIs of Central, Eastern and Southern Europe

Country	Total number of schools existing* / analysed	Schools teaching entrepreneurship		Number of schools with curriculum in entrepreneurship	Number of curricula in entrepreneurship (or with entrepreneurship specialisation)			Number of HEIs with entrepreneurship centres
		Total number of schools	Of which, with chair / depart. of entrepreneurship		Under-graduate (bachelor) level	Graduate (master level) or specialised MBA	Post-graduate (PhD or DBA) level	
Estonia	39/39	12	2	8	6	2	-	3
Latvia	34/34	24	1(+4**)	8	5	3	-	1
Lithuania	48/48	18	-	1	-	1	-	7
Poland	164/65	18	9	9	5	5	2	8
Czech R.	35/22	10	5	6	7	4		8(+1)
Slovakia	28 /11	6	2	3	2	2	2	4
Hungary	94/24	8	1	6	5	3	(1)	3
Slovenia	10/6	5	2	3	4	3	1	
Croatia	16/12	8		5	4	3		1
Romania	64/31	20		1				6
Bulgaria	41/30	10	2	2	1	4	-	4
Moldova	13/10	4			1			2
Serbia & Montenegro	21/10	6		1	2	1		3
Macedonia	9/3	2		1				
Albania	11/3	1(+5***)						(1)
Bosnia and Herzegovina	10/6	4						1
Ukraine	46/46	14	1	1	2			3
Russia	1142/353	185	26	38	21	18	14	31
Belarus	15/11	5						2
Azerbaijan	14/4	2						
Georgia	9/4	1		1		1		
Armenia	10/2							
TOTAL	1873/774	363(+5)	51(+4)	94	63	50	19(+1)	87(+2)

* The total number of schools was obtained from the Web databases of world universities (www.canadian-universities.net/World_Universities); the Higher Education Institution Registry (www.siu.no/heir); Universities Worldwide (http://univ.cc/world.php); MEO.RU (http://vuz.meo.ru/); FAK.RU (www.fak.ru/baza/); and other national databases. All other data are result of the analysis of authors.

** The data in brackets shows the number of subjects partly corresponding to the topic.

*** Cepani and Haxhia 2005

ENTREPRENEURSHIP AND HIGHER EDUCATION – ISBN- 9789264044098 © OECD 2008

Discussion of results

Discussion can open with analysis of the creation of the entrepreneurship profile in the schools. The results indicate that in general, entrepreneurship-oriented education is launched earlier and is better developed in the newly established institutions of higher education. The flexibility required to establish new institutions of higher education was extremely high in the transition countries in late 1980s and early 1990s, as this was the period when the old regulations did not function and the new rules were weakly developed. In the late 1980s, specifically entrepreneurship-oriented schools were founded: GEA College of Entrepreneurship opened in Slovenia in 1990; the Estonian Business School opened in 1988, etc. These were mostly private schools, with the clearly formulated target of offering an education that favours the entrepreneurial mindset.

Often when the new private business schools were established, the fundamental principles of the school were transferred from the Western experience. A typical example is the creation of Business School Ostrava in 1990. A group of university teachers went to the United Kingdom where they visited several business schools; after returning, their vision was to create a market-oriented faculty or school, offering professionally oriented education in the area of business and entrepreneurship. The main strategy for the execution of the vision was the acquisition and training of teachers who would have not only theoretical but (more importantly) practical skills. Furthermore, they decided to create an entrepreneurial clinic where both teachers and students could work on solving practical problems in business.

Another way of developing entrepreneurship-oriented courses, or even the whole curriculum, was to establish the school with the direct support of a foreign institution of higher education. For example, the Stockholm School of Economics was founded in Riga, Latvia in 1994. The activities of the school are strongly geared toward entrepreneurship, and it was launched with the direct help of the Stockholm School of Economics and Jönköping International Business School from Sweden. A similar experience was the founding of the International School of Management at the University of Management and Economics in Lithuania in 1999 by the Norwegian School of Management. They brought over expertise and opened several curricula, including an MSc in Business with the major in Innovation & Entrepreneurship. A notable feature of this greenfield method of founding schools was the transfer of the whole attitude toward the teaching process and the careful selection of teaching staff, who in many cases were originally taken from the mother schools and gradually replaced with local faculty. That made it possible to create an entrepreneurship-friendly climate and establish close links with businesses through different forms of entrepreneurship centre.

The early 1990s was also a period when new universities were established by combining several technology-oriented universities with business schools or economics faculties. The idea was to meet the growing demand of the market, but also to generate additional funding for the existing universities. This process also generated some very interesting entrepreneurship-oriented universities. A good example is Tomas Bata University in Zlín, in the Czech Republic.

Another important aspect of the analysis is the classification of schools by their level of teaching entrepreneurship (undergraduate, graduate, postgraduate). Among the 363 schools covered where a specific entrepreneurship-oriented course was identified, only 94 schools offered the full curriculum of entrepreneurship, or provided entrepreneurship as a major field of specialisation. There were in total 65 undergraduate and 50 master's-level full programmes available in the region. At doctoral level, specialisation in entrepreneurship was possible only in 20 universities.

At the undergraduate level

The typical duration of the programme is three years, but in several cases four-year programmes also exist (*e.g.* GEA College, Slovenia). The orientation of the undergraduate programmes was deduced according to the title and list of contents, which existed in many cases (although unfortunately in native languages, which sometimes created difficulties in comprehension). Unfortunately, in many cases the curriculum was titled as entrepreneurship but the list of courses was not targeted toward entrepreneurship. In those cases it was eliminated from the list.

At undergraduate level the whole sample of entrepreneurship-oriented curricula could be divided into five different groups.

The first group consists of bachelor programmes, where the title is BSc in Business Administration with specialisation in Entrepreneurship (Corvinus University in Budapest), or BSc in Economics with specialisation in Entrepreneurship (University of Veszprém, GEA College, Corvinus University).

The second group of undergraduate programmes are directly called Entrepreneurship (Maria Curie-Sklodowska University and **University of Łódź**, Poland); Economics of Entrepreneurship (VERN Higher College, Croatia); Entrepreneurship and Business Management (Riga Teacher Training and Educational Management Academy, Latvia); Enterprise

Economics and Management (Matej Bel University, Slovakia); Entrepreneurship and Management (Riga Technical University, Latvia).

The third group of schools has moved toward a curriculum that is associated with the small and medium-size businesses and is called Small Business (Kuressaare College of Tallinn University of Technology, Estonia), Management of Small Business (University of Split, Croatia) or Company Management (Jagiellonian University in Krakow, Poland).

A fourth group of undergraduate courses are put together as a combination of entrepreneurship with certain technologies or innovation. The representatives of this approach are the BSc in Economics with specialisation in Entrepreneurship and Innovations (Krakow University of Economics, Poland), and Production Engineering and Entrepreneurship (Virumaa College of Tallinn University of Technology, Estonia). In Tomas Bata University (Czech Republic), a three-year bachelor programme in Entrepreneurial Economics is available with four modules: Technology of Commodities, Entrepreneurial Economics I, Entrepreneurial Economics II, and Innovation Management.

The fifth group of programmes are designed to reflect specific aspects of entrepreneurship in various economic sectors. For example, the Ostrava Business School (Czech Rep.) offers a bachelor's programme in Entrepreneurship and Management in the Environment, and another in Entrepreneurship and Management in the Tourist Industry; Pärnu College of the University of Tartu (Estonia) offers a diploma course in Tourism and Hotel Management.

At the master's level

A total of 50 full programmes were identified in the region. The typical duration of the master's programme was two years or five years (*e.g.* in the **University of Łódź,** where a master's programme is available without any preceding bachelor's programme). In general, two broad approaches could be distinguished. The first and bigger group of schools has chosen the approach whereby entrepreneurship master's programmes are designed with academic orientation and awarded degrees as Master of Science in Entrepreneurship or MSc in Economics or Business Administration with the major in Entrepreneurship. A second group of schools are offering entrepreneurship as the field of specialisation inside the MBA programmes.

One example of a school that offers an MSc in Economics with specialisation in Entrepreneurship is Corvinus University in Budapest. Another version is the MSc in Entrepreneurship and Macroeconomic Management from the University of Rijeka, Croatia. In Poland a system of offering the master's programme as the Management of Small and Medium-sized Enterprises is widely used (University of Podlasie); the Nicolaus Copernicus University in Torun offers Entrepreneurship and Management of SMEs. In Slovakia and the Czech Republic the master's level study programmes are often called engineers' study programmes, and an entrepreneurship-oriented curriculum is typically called Enterprise Economics and Management Economics (Matej Bel University, Slovakia) or Entrepreneurial Economics (Tomas Bata University in Zlín, Czech Republic).

The next group of master's programmes are combinations of entrepreneurship with other disciplines. Most commonly, entrepreneurship and technology management or innovation management are connected – in the Crakow University of Economics, an MSc in Economics with specialisation in Entrepreneurship and Innovations is available. Since 2002 the University of Tartu, Estonia, has offered a master's programme in Entrepreneurship and Technology Management. Similarly, in the Lithuanian International School of Management in the University of Management and Economics, there is an MSc in Business with the major in Innovation & Entrepreneurship, while the University of Maribor (Slovenia) runs an MSc in Economics and Business Science with specialisation in Innovation Management.

In the area of combining entrepreneurial education with specific technology-based teaching, an excellent example is the Gdansk University of Technology. The Faculty of Management and Economics in there teaches an Economic Entrepreneurship module to all students of the five-year full time Master of Engineering programme. Another positive example is from the Technical University in Kosice. There, the Department of Management and Marketing teaches all students on the five-year engineering course in "Production Engineering" and the three-year postgraduate PhD study in "Engineering Technologies and Materials" courses in the Strategy and Management of Small and Medium Enterprises, Control of Manufacture in Small-scale and Medium-scale Enterprises, and Private Enterprises.

In the Faculty of Wood Sciences and Technology of the Technical University in Zvolen, Slovakia, a module in Entrepreneurial Management is compulsory for all students taking an MSc in Wood Technology. Courses in Enterprise Management are also compulsory for all other students obtaining an MSc degree. In addition, students should get practical experience in the School of Forest Enterprise.

Alongside schools offering entrepreneurship as a specialisation of the academic programme, there is also a group of schools where entrepreneurship is proposed as a full specialisation field in the MBA programme or as an important module. In this group are found the two-year course in Master of Business Administration in Technology Management at Krakow University of Economics; the seven-week module in Entrepreneurship in the MBA programme of the International Graduate Business School in Zagreb; and the two-year vocational diploma of higher education as an Entrepreneurial Manager at the University of Miskolc.

At the postgraduate level

Here, the situation is much weaker than at undergraduate or graduate levels. There are some positive examples of entrepreneurship offered as the field for specialisation in PhD studies, particularly in Poland and Russia. In the University of Łódź it is possible to specialise in entrepreneurship during PhD studies, while in the University of Szczecin specialisation during PhD studies in the Innovations in Enterprises, Quality Economics, or Economics and the Organisation of Enterprises is available. In Crakow University of Economics, the PhD in Economics includes also specialisation in Entrepreneurship and Innovations, and Comenius University in Bratislava has launched a PhD study specialisation in Entrepreneurship Management. Doctoral study in the field of Management and the Economics of Enterprises is available in Matej Bel University, Slovakia.

Best practices of entrepreneurship teaching in transition economies

The following section of the chapter is devoted to analysis of best practice from three viewpoints: how the specialised units co-ordinating teaching and research of entrepreneurship are designed; the best examples of curricula; and the level of internationalisation offered in the programmes.

General information about *the special institutional units that co-ordinate entrepreneurship education* is very hard to collect, as in many cases the name of an institution does not reflect the major field of its activities. Therefore, the only way to grasp the main essence of the work of an institution is to analyse its work thoroughly. The current analyses allowed a total of 51 institutional units to be distinguished (schools, institutes, departments, chairs); these were directly linked with entrepreneurship teaching at university level (see Table 8.1 above). The largest numbers of this type of unit were in Russia (26), Poland (9) and the Czech Republic (5).

There are several interesting schools where the institutional structure already reveals a systematic approach to entrepreneurship education. The best examples in this field are the Leon Kozminski Academy of Entrepreneurship and Management in Poland; the School of Entrepreneurship in the GEA College in Slovenia; the Faculty of Entrepreneurship and Management in the Higher School of Business of the

National Louis University of Nowy Sacz in Poland; the Institute for Entrepreneurship and Innovation Management in the University of Maribor (Slovenia) ; the Department of Small Business in the Warsaw School of Economics; and the Department of Entrepreneurial Economics in Tomas Bata University in Zlín.

One of the most sophisticated research centres in the area of entrepreneurship is the Leon Kozminski Academy of Entrepreneurship and Management in Warsaw. The school is doing extensive research into entrepreneurship, with special emphasis on intellectual entrepreneurship. Applying the classification of Twaalfhoven, Suen and Prats (2001), the school has reached for the research-oriented model of entrepreneurship programme development. Another important centre of research in the field of entrepreneurship is the Department of Entrepreneurship and Industrial Policy in the University of Łódź, Poland, with its Centre of Excellence in the Knowledge-based Economy (KNOWBASE). It is a virtual research structure set up on the basis of the Faculty of Management, the Faculty of Economics and Sociology, and the Faculty of International and Political Studies. The co-ordinator for KNOWBASE is the Department of Entrepreneurship and Industrial Policy.

Applying the classification of Twaalfhoven, Suen and Prats (2001), Ostrava Business School in the Czech Republic is an example of the successful implementation of the consulting-oriented model of development for entrepreneurship education. Ostrava Business School is a new private school, where the structure of the school reflects the importance of an entrepreneurial attitude toward the study process. The school contains four departments, all of which are entrepreneurship-oriented: Entrepreneurship and Management in the Environment; Entrepreneurship; Entrepreneurship and Business Management; and Information and the Internet in Entrepreneurship. They together co-ordinate the teaching of the courses for the Bachelor in Entrepreneurship, Bachelor in Entrepreneurship and Management in the Environment, and Bachelor in Entrepreneurship and Management in the Tourism Industry. The whole study process is connected to the practical training by the help of the entrepreneurial clinic, created in the school in order to offer teachers and students the opportunity to solve practical problems in business. The especially strong entrepreneurship orientation of teaching is expressed by the Graduate Profile, which also covers the following topics of entrepreneurship: personal characteristics important for doing business – creativity, independence, flexibility; theoretical principles of entrepreneurship and enterprise; entrepreneurial skills; and the independent entrepreneur in SMEs.

The Higher School VERN in Croatia is also a new private school. It was founded in 1990 as a private language school, but since 1996 it has also been offering an entrepreneurship-oriented vocational programme, "Business Entrepreneurship". In 1999 VERN started a two-year professional course of business studies under the name Economics of Entrepreneurship, and in 2001 it expanded this into a three-year course of professional studies. The school has grown rapidly, from 50 students in 1996 to 750 students currently, and the total number of faculty members is around 100. The school is innovative in using modern teaching methodology. Lectures are combined with true-to-life simulations of business situations in small study groups. Students are trained to work effectively in dynamic teams; role playing is widely used. The study programme is very much entrepreneurship-oriented, consisting of general courses on entrepreneurship (Essentials of Entrepreneurship; Entrepreneurship I and II; The Entrepreneurial Business Plan), special courses on entrepreneurship in different sectors (Entrepreneurship in Sports; Entrepreneurship in Tourism; Entrepreneurship in International Trade) and some methodological courses (Quantitative Methods in Entrepreneurship Economics; Dynamic Entrepreneurship).

Josip Juraj Strossmayer University of Osijek is an old university in Croatia, where the teaching of entrepreneurship is carried out at undergraduate and graduate levels. The whole programme is designed with the aim of building an entrepreneurial mindset in students. The methodology of teaching is highly innovative; role playing learning is used, as are case studies, business plan development, etc. The list of courses reflects the overwhelming entrepreneurship orientation of the programme: Entrepreneurial Marketing; Creation of Entrepreneurial Creativity and Innovativeness; Entrepreneurial Accounting; Entrepreneurial Information Systems; Entrepreneurial Management; Consulting for Small and Medium Business.

Internationalisation of entrepreneurship education in the transition economies is developing, but the proportion of the entrepreneurship curriculum taught in English is still very low in general. English as a teaching language in entrepreneurship-oriented education is most widespread in Slovenia. In the Bled School of Management 70% of students are now from outside Slovenia. In the GEA College of Entrepreneurship many courses were available in English already in 2001-04 and as of the 2005/06 academic year it launched a three-year International Bachelor Study of Entrepreneurship. The universities of Maribor and Ljubljana offer a wide range of English courses in entrepreneurship. In the Baltic States, English as the study language predominates in those schools that have strong links with foreign institutions like the Stockholm School of Economics in Riga or International School of Management in Lithuania. In the University of Tartu one-third of the master's programme in entrepreneurship and technology management is taught in English. In Poland, Hungary and the Czech Republic, countries with relatively big domestic educational markets, the majority of education in entrepreneurship is still in the native language; it is predominant in the Hungarian and Polish universities. In these countries English is used as the study language in the major universities, which have extensive contacts with foreign universities. It allows them to import whole curricula; for example, the Warsaw School of Economics offers online access to the MBA in Entrepreneurship of Jones International University. Use of foreign partners has also supported the opening of programmes teaching business and entrepreneurship in French and German, particularly in Hungary, the Czech Republic and Poland.

Conclusion

The present research focused on mapping entrepreneurship education in 774 higher education institutions from the 22 European transition countries. Analysis of information obtained from Web-based sources and a questionnaire identified 363 institutions in the region offering entrepreneurship-oriented courses, modules or curricula. There were 65 curricula in entrepreneurship at bachelor's level and 50 at master's. In only six schools in Central Europe and 14 schools in Russia was it possible to follow a PhD programme with a specialisation in entrepreneurship.

The best coverage of entrepreneurship-oriented teaching among countries in the region was in Slovenia and Croatia, followed by the Baltic States, the Czech Republic and Slovakia. Among the Southern European countries the coverage of entrepreneurship teaching was much lower. Among the countries of the Commonwealth of Independent States the Russian situation is most diverse; there are good examples, but the general level is low.

The results of the analyses indicate that in general, entrepreneurship-oriented education is much better developed in private schools and in those public universities established since the mid-1990s. An entrepreneurship orientation is stronger in smaller institutions. This could be explained by the higher flexibility of private and smaller new public institutions of higher education, which allowed them to introduce a clearly formulated movement towards education that favours the entrepreneurial mindset.

On the basis of the analyses, the following major barriers and problems in entrepreneurship teaching can be outlined:

- The relative weight of entrepreneurship-oriented curricula in the total curricula is still too small.

- Teaching in native languages dominates and the development of skills in foreign languages is rare.

- In a majority of schools the methodology is to teach about entrepreneurship and provide very little training in entrepreneurship. Many courses are titled as small business-oriented courses, which are taught using passive teaching methods (as reflected in the descriptions of the courses).

- Seldom do curricula contain courses about the building of the entrepreneurial attitude (creation of entrepreneurial creativity and innovativeness, entrepreneurial psychology, entrepreneurial dynamics etc.).

- Insufficient use of real entrepreneurs in the teaching programmes reflects the strict regulations in the transition economies about the permission to teach – formal requirements predominate and preclude the use of real experts.

- There is an inadequate link between schools of business administration and technological education, a fact reflected in the low number of technical universities offering entrepreneurial modules.

- The current number of university centres of entrepreneurship in the region is small and clearly insufficient. Corporate professorship is a unique phenomenon of the region.

- Research into entrepreneurship in the region is in an embryonic stage, with only 3-5 schools using a research-oriented model for entrepreneurship teaching.

With that list of problems and barriers in mind, the following recommendations could be made with the aim of encouraging the teaching of entrepreneurship:

- The list of schools offering entrepreneurship as a compulsory or elective topic should be enlarged. This is especially necessary in Southeastern European countries, but also in the region as a whole. Entrepreneurship as a specialisation field for doctoral studies should be accepted more broadly in the European transition countries.

- In order to promote good-quality entrepreneurship teaching, it is important to facilitate the sharing of good practice in entrepreneurship education among the transition countries themselves. For example, the experience of the GEA College of Entrepreneurship in Slovenia, Josip Juraj Strossmayer University of Osijek in Croatia, Tomas Bata

University in Zlín, and Ostrava Business School should be learned and disseminated.

- Specialised entrepreneurship-oriented curricula should be enriched with courses aimed at building the entrepreneurial attitude (creation of entrepreneurial creativity and innovativeness, entrepreneurial psychology, entrepreneurial dynamics etc.).

- The governments of the transition economies should revise their current strict regulations about permission to teach. Instead, what should be encouraged is the opening of entrepreneurship professorships that will be filled with the staff with previous experience in entrepreneurship. This is an improvement tool that would facilitate the link with the real entrepreneurial world and wider use of the real entrepreneurs in the teaching process.

- In the regions where several technology - or natural science-oriented universities are located, it is necessary to establish schools that serve these higher education institutions with the basics of entrepreneurship as a compulsory subject. In this respect, positive experiences from the Stockholm School of Entrepreneurship (www.sses.se/public/frameset.asp) could prove helpful, as could those from the Gdansk University of Technology or Technical University in Kosice.

- In addition to technology management- or innovation management-oriented programmes, it is necessary to launch specific curricula to prepare "technopreneurs" who have learned specific aspects of starting and doing business in the specialised field of technology they have studied.

- In the context of transition countries, which are generally small and open economies, stronger attention should be given to designing global entrepreneurship curricula, and preparing people with the skills to generate international teams. The teaching of global entrepreneurs requires co-operation between students from different universities as they elaborate joint business plans.

Bibliography

Berkowitz, D. and J. Jackson (2006), "Entrepreneurship and the Evolution of Income Distributions in Poland and Russia", *Journal of Comparative Economics,* Vol. 34, No. 2, Elsevier, pp. 338-356.

Business School Ostrava (2005), www.vsp.cz/old_vsp/fr_hlavni_studium.htm.

Cepani, A. and G. Haxhia (2005), "Entrepreneurship Education and Training: The Albanian Story", paper presented at the International Conference of OECD: Fostering Entrepreneurship: The Role of Higher Education, Trento, Italy, 23-24 June.

Dombrovsky, V., M. Chandler and K. Krēsliņš (2005), *Global Entrepreneurship Monitor 2005-Latvia Report,* www.gemconsortium.org/download/1212748955158/GEM%20Latvia% 202005%20EN.pdf

Frederick, H., et al. (2002), Bartercard New Zealand Global Entrepreneurial Monitor 2002, UNITEC Institute of Technology, Auckland.

Hisrich, R.D. and B. O'Cinneide (1996), "Entrepreneurial activities in Europe-oriented institutions", *Journal of Managerial Psychology,* Vol. 11, No.2, Emerald, pp. 45-64.

Leko-Simic, M. and S. Oberman (2004), "Business Education in Croatia: The Transitional Challenge", paper presented on the 14th Annual IntEnt Conference, University of Napoli Federico II, Napoli, Italy, 4-7 July.

Lepane, L. and L. Kuum (2004), *Enterprise of Estonian Population,* Estonian Institute of Economic Research, Tallinn. (in Estonian).

Minniti, M., W. D. Bygrave and E. Autio (2006), *Global Entrepreneurship Monitor 2005-Executive Report,* Babson College and London Business School, www.gemconsortium.org./download/1212749560908/GEM_2005_Repor t.pdf.

Mitra, J. and H. Matlay (2004), "Entrepreneurial and vocational education and training: Lessons from Eastern and Central Europe", *Industry and Higher Education,* Vol. 18, No. 1, IP Publishing, pp. 53-61.

Pleskovic, B., *et al.* (2000), "State of the Art in Education and Research in Transition Economies", *Comparative Economic Studies,* Vol. 42, No. 2, Palgrave Macmillan, pp. 65-108.

Reynolds, P.D., *et al.* (2002), *Global Entrepreneurship Monitor 2002-Executive Report,* Ewing Marion Kauffman Foundation, Kansas City, Missouri,
www.gemconsortium.org/download/1212749903252/WebGlobalGEMReport11.12_1.pdf

Smallbone, D. and F. Welter (2001), "The Distinctiveness of Entrepreneurship in Transition Economies", *Small Business Economics,* Vol. 16, No. 4, Springer US, pp. 249-262.

Smallbone, D. and F. Welter (2003), "Institutional Development and Entrepreneurship in Transition Economies", paper presented at ICSB 48th World Conference - Advancing, Entrepreneurship and Small Business, Belfast (Northern Ireland), 15-18 June.

Stockholm School of Entrepreneurship (2005), www.sses.se

The Higher School VERN (2005), www.vern.hr

The Higher Education Institution Registry (2005), www.siu.no/heir

Twaalfhoven, B., W.W. Suen and J. Prats (2000), *Entrepreneurship education and its funding: A comparison between Europe and the United States,* European Foundation for Entrepreneurial Research (EFER), Hilversum, Netherlands.

Twaalfhoven, B., W.W. Suen and J. Prats (2001), *Developing Entrepreneurship Programmes in MBA Schools: A Contrast in Approaches-Survey of 7 Business Schools,* European Foundation for Entrepreneurial Research (EFER), Hilversum, Netherlands.

Twaalfhoven, B. and K.Wilson (2004), *Breeding More Gazelles: The Role of European Universities,* European Foundation for Entrepreneurial Research (EFER), Hilversum, Netherlands.

Universities Worldwide (2005), http://univ.cc/world.php

Wilson, K. (2004), *Entrepreneurship Education at European Universities and Business Schools – Results of a Joint Pilot Survey,* European Foundation for Entrepreneurial Research (EFER), Hilversum, Netherlands.

World Universities (2005), www.canadian-universities.net/World_Universities

Chapter 9

Higher Education, Knowledge Transfer Mechanisms and the Promotion of SME Innovation

by
Edward J. Malecki
Ohio State University, United States

This chapter addresses the question: How can higher education institutions (HEIs) promote innovation in the small and medium-size enterprises (SMEs) in their region? It assesses what we know from previous research about various mechanisms involved in the promotion of SME innovation by higher education institutions. A variety of mechanisms exist, including technology consultancy, technology transfer offices, contract research, science parks, incubators, technology centres, shared research equipment, education-industry labour mobility, and technology training. However, existing linkages between higher education institutions and regional SMEs tend to work best when they are informal rather than formal, and thus the extent to which they are actually used is not precisely known. Recommendations for policy development in advanced (OECD) economies are suggested.

Introduction

Higher education institutions (HEIs) have been associated traditionally with a primary role in basic research. The linear model of innovation generally assumed that universities were among the few performers of basic research; the others are government research institutes and the small number of industrial laboratories doing basic research. The other components – research and development (R&D), applied research and product and process development – were the province of industrial firms (Marquis, 1988). In several respects, HEIs still fulfil this role, but they have added a second role: to facilitate entrepreneurial commercial success, generally through spin-off of scientific knowledge into new enterprises. The experience of, first, the electronics industry in Silicon Valley and, later, the proliferation of biotechnology firms in several locations suggested to many that HEIs are central players in several dimensions of "academic capitalism", extending beyond technology transfer and high-tech spin-offs to include entrepreneurship (Slaughter and Rhoades, 2004; Tornatzky, Waugaman and Gray, 2002). Colleges and universities are part of the "triple helix" of university-industry-government as well as the trilateral networks and hybrid organisations created in the overlap of the three, with technology transfer a major part of each (Etzkowitz, 2003; Etzkowitz and Leydesdorff, 2000).

Spin-offs from university research are a common goal, if only in the context of imitating the Silicon Valley experience (Castells and Hall, 1994; Rosenberg, 2002). The experience of MIT is a somewhat more appropriate model, studied systematically over several decades (Roberts, 1991; Etzkowitz, 2002; Shane, 2004). Despite 134 spin-offs from 1980 to 1996, outside perception of the entrepreneurial spirit of MIT and the Boston area has suffered from the severe criticism of Saxenian's (1994) comparison of Boston and Silicon Valley, in which she characterised Boston as far less supportive of new firms. However, the relative decline of Silicon Valley after the dot.com bust of 2001 and the success of the Boston area in biotechnology have shifted the two regions toward an equal footing once again. Despite their prominence, these two models are difficult for other regions to imitate, since the numbers of spin-off firms from top research institutions are not possible to match in other settings (Degroof and Roberts, 2004).

Shane (2004, pp. 152-154) categorises university spin-offs into three types: inventor-entrepreneurs, technology licensing office shoppers, and investors, with about one-third in each category. Inventor-led spin-offs tend to be more common in industries where patent protection tends to be weak and when the knowledge on which it is based is tacit. They also are more likely to be established near the university that generated them, with the (perhaps part-time) entrepreneur retaining his or her academic employment. Inventor-led spin-offs occur earlier in the life of university technologies than the other types, which generally wait until patent applications are filed. By contrast, external entrepreneur-led spin-offs are more common at universities that generate high numbers of spin-offs as opposed to those where they are less common. Both investor- and external entrepreneur-led spin-offs are more common in major cities and technology centres, where investors and technology managers are abundant.

Others find that technology licensing offices are perhaps excessively oriented toward making money – because they must "break even" financially – and far less toward supporting spin-offs (Markman *et al.*, 2005). Shane (2004) also found that creating spin-offs is more profitable than licensing to established companies. Perhaps this is an inevitable consequence of the proliferation of patenting from the era prior to 1980, when only a handful of HEIs were active in patenting. Mowery and Ziedonis (2002) find that, since 1980, patents are indeed less important and less general than earlier patents.

Licensing of HEI technology tends to go to large firms, which have become accustomed to seeking out new knowledge produced elsewhere and are even more accustomed to appropriating that knowledge via intellectual property rights. In countries and regions outside the successful places, spin-offs from HEIs are important intermediating entities between academic research and the commercial world. For this reason, spin-offs should be encouraged (Fontes, 2005). Less common are more traditional forms of technology transfer from HEIs to small and medium-size enterprises (SMEs). It is not entirely clear why this is the case. Helping SMEs may be considered too time-consuming, or perhaps it is viewed as less interesting or less rewarding than alliances and linkages with large firms.

Universities bring many long-term and often subtle benefits to a region (Etzkowitz and Leydesdorff, 2000). HEIs have become more entrepreneurial, seeking to both make money explicitly and generate economic growth (*i.e.* jobs) in the local region. Before 1980, HEI-industry collaboration was often informal, whereas today it is typically much more formalised; at the same time, the view has become dominant that HEIs are important drivers of economic growth and development and central actors in a web of knowledge producers. This view has two important consequences. First, HEIs are no longer dominant among knowledge producers; instead, they are only one among many, such as private research centres, R&D performing firms, and consultancy agencies. Second, and as a result this shift, HEIs have to adapt to their "new" position by becoming team players (Rutten, Boekema and Kuijpers, 2003).

Knowledge flows from HEIs to SMEs tend to be largely unplanned and informal in nature. Unlike alliances and linkages with large firms – which tend to bring prestige, revenue, and contacts for students – connections with SMEs are less attractive for technology transfer offices. Therefore, informal interaction between HEIs and SMEs often avoids formal procedures and those who administer them (Rappert, Webster and Charles, 1999). Studies of formal links and collaborations miss many – perhaps most – of the links between the two. Technology embodied in professors, staff members or research students ebbs and flows, as specific projects require some links and later projects do not (Löfsten and Lindelöf, 2005). The benefits to SMEs may be larger from long-term, iterative relationships with academics, rather than from formal commercialisation activities (Benneworth, 2001). Moreover, local systems of governance vary, suggesting that "triple helix" relationships are not the same in all places (Lawton Smith, 2007).

At their best, spillovers from HEIs create a general local culture of interaction, which translates into a culture of innovation. Several labels have been applied to innovation-rich regions characterised by a high level of local interaction: associational economies (Cooke and Morgan, 1998), innovative milieus (Maillat, 1998), local and regional systems of innovation (Cooke, 2004), clusters (Rocha, 2004), local ecosystems of technical entrepreneurship (Bahrami and Evans, 1995), learning regions (Florida, 1995), and knowledge economies (Cooke, 2002). Moulaert and Sekia (2003) note that these "territorial innovation models" developed from different origins but, from a policy perspective, they have become similar targets to emulate. In any of these local systems, any university or, even more so, any of its departments or schools is but one player or part of the local innovation system. To the degree to which there are a number of overlapping and intersecting webs of interactions, the local system will have a stronger local culture of interaction (Smilor and Feeser, 1991).

Cooke (2002, p. 147) believes that "[t]he cluster is the organizational form best suited to smaller firm development and growth", a conclusion that resonates in the detailed research of Rocha and Sternberg (2005), who found that entrepreneurship is enhanced by location in a cluster, but not in a mere industrial agglomeration.

Less commonly addressed is the importance of agglomeration effects of HEIs: if several HEIs are in the region, there is not only a greater cumulative quantity of knowledge and possibilities for interaction; there also is the opportunity – and obligation – for specialisation and division of labour among them. Rosenfeld (2000), for example, suggests that community colleges (*i.e.* teaching-oriented institutions in which little or no R&D takes place) are better suited for training than are research universities.

Higher education institutions as infrastructure

HEIs now are seen as "an important element in a region's knowledge infrastructure, and the knowledge infrastructure, to a large extent, decides the success of a region in today's knowledge-based economy" (Rutten, Boekema and Kuijpers, 2003, p. 4). The goal of regions today is to become learning regions. HEIs also have increasingly been looked to as partners in their regional setting, with an obligation to contribute to regional prosperity through multi-product production (Goddard and Chatterton, 1999; Luger and Goldstein, 1997). However, HEIs do not just produce "products" – whether intellectual property to which they can claim title and intellectual property rights, or graduates who carry skills and knowledge learned at the institution in their heads. HEIs are a central piece of the regional infrastructure of a learning region (Keane and Allison, 1999). However, while universities are involved in knowledge transfer, unintended, informal knowledge spillovers from them are largely ignored (Howells, 2002).

In the paradigmatic HEI today, research takes place "not in an ivory tower, but in a complex network of relationships among universities, hospitals, other affiliated institutions, corporations and entrepreneurs" (Appleseed, 2003, p. 49). The eight universities in the Boston area, for example, are considered major parts of the intellectual infrastructure that supports the innovation-driven economy of the region, and as "sources of scientific research, technical skills and entrepreneurial initiative" (Appleseed, 2003, p. 18).

In Boston, as in relatively few other places, formal and explicit effects of HEIs are documented: development of new Boston-area businesses, several incubators and investments, faculty involvement in new business development, and university graduates as entrepreneurs (Appleseed, 2003). Few institutions have kept track of firms founded by graduates – unlike MIT, which has claimed a large share of Silicon Valley start-ups as initiated by MIT graduates (BankBoston, 1997). Yet, Pirnay, Surlemont and Nlemvo (2003) classify university spin-offs into two types: student spin-offs and researcher spin-offs. Entrepreneurial universities are most interested in spin-offs founded by university researchers, based on a codified technology that can be sold or licensed for revenue.

Small and medium-sized enterprises

Despite the growing web of university-industry relationships, the "new industrial ecology" (Coombes and Georghiou, 2002) and "Mode 2" connections between HEIs and industrial firms (Gibbons, 2003) represent a growing web of connections in which HEIs operate. The number of interconnections is accelerating, but they move with the problem context (scientific field or policy priority) and survive only as long as they are useful.

It remains the case, however, that SMEs rarely look to HEIs as a primary source of information or technology. This poses serious challenges for knowledge transfer. The greatest challenge is that SMEs are diverse and many, perhaps most, do not behave in the optimal manner assumed by policy vehicles. Specifically, SMEs are not privy to perfect information; instead, (sometimes severe) information asymmetries operate.

Research on the economics of knowledge stresses several important dimensions that bear on this problem. First, knowledge is not homogeneous. Some knowledge is tacit; other knowledge is codified. Codified knowledge is in databases or other written, retrievable forms. Tacit knowledge is difficult to communicate except in person, frequently because it is not well understood except in the specific context in which it was first learned. The sharing of knowledge among people within a group or organisation demands significant effort; sharing among organisations generally requires even more effort.

Tacit knowledge typically is embodied in people, rather than in written form or in objects, and can be acquired through hiring, R&D, and interpersonal networking (Faulkner, Senker and Velho, 1995; Nonaka and Takeuchi, 1995). It is rarely easy to transfer complex knowledge from one person to another. On-the-job training, on-site engineering, and other means of learning technologies have been central to the process of technology transfer, but few attempts have been made to translate these mechanisms to more general situations. In an important contribution, Nonaka and Konno (1998) propose the Japanese concept of *ba*, or shared space, as the key to relationships of knowledge creation. Knowledge is created through a spiralling process of interactions between explicit (or codified) and tacit knowledge: socialisation (sharing tacit knowledge), externalisation (expression of tacit knowledge to transmit to others), combination (conversion of explicit knowledge into more complex explicit knowledge), and internalisation (conversion of newly created knowledge into the organisation's tacit knowledge). There are four types of shared space or *ba:* face-to-face, peer-to-peer, group-to-group, and on-site. The need to shift from individual knowledge to knowledge understood by a group, and vice versa, seems to be the central feature the *ba* concept and the spiralling process. Group and individual knowledge generally are distinct in accounts of tacit knowledge.

The significance of Nonaka and Konno's spiralling process of interactions is twofold. First, it explicitly recognises knowledge creation and learning as continual, ongoing processes. Moreover, there is no quick one-way path for knowledge or transfer. Second, several different "shared spaces" are involved in knowledge creation. Some of these are internal to the firm; others are external. Some can be local; others rely on organisational rather than geographic proximity (Rallet and Torre, 1998).

Knowledge transfer is varied and complex. It may be transferred through formal mechanisms, informally in casual network contacts, or somewhere in between (which can be thought of as semi-formally). The SMEs most likely to develop informal links with other firms and organisations are extroverted firms (Fuellhart and Glasmeier, 2003; Kingsley and Malecki, 2004; Malecki and Poehling, 1999). They are the ones who seek out resources – managerial, financial, technical – which they do not have within the start-up firm. Informal technology transfer typically is done by faculty through personal relationships, by students in internships or class projects, or as extension or service activity (Rappert *et al.*, 1999). Rarely are all of these activities reported or catalogued, and even when they are, it is even more rare to track longitudinally the actual effects of the knowledge transfers on the performance of firms. In fact, it is likely that no single technology transfer incident significantly affected firm performance, and more likely that it was part of a process of learning by smart and extroverted firms (Malecki and Poehling, 1999; Woolgar *et al.*, 1998). Informal collaborations between firms and professors to enhance class experiences are rarely reported, since they fall between the standard categories of research, teaching, and service.

Tacit knowledge flows primarily through interpersonal, informal relationships and are likely to be omitted from tallies of official collaborations of HEIs (Goddard and Chatterton, 1999). Knowledge flows take place in conferences and symposia, informal talks, and events organised by universities. Discussion and idea exchange, both formal and informal, are central to the development of ideas and to the innovativeness of SMEs.

Policies for higher education institutions

Entrepreneurial universities might not be right for all countries, yet our understanding of the new production of knowledge (Gibbons *et al.*, 1994) and of the "triple helix" (Etzkowitz, 2003) are far from complete. The new production of knowledge is much more widely cited in Western Europe, the United States and Canada, whereas the impact of the triple helix is broader in Latin America, Asia and Africa (Shinn, 2002).

Science parks, along with incubators, are types of *premises* (Potter, 2005). For large firms in particular, science parks allow collaborative links to be established with a recognised academic "centre of excellence" in a field, and to take advantage of an agglomeration of researchers and new graduates. Successful parks are located in major urban regions and are affiliated with a world-class research university. The "prestige" associated with proximity to a centre of excellence attracts large firms, but does not necessarily indicate any linkage or interaction with the local universities – or with one another (Johannisson *et al.*, 1994; Joseph, 1989). Science parks may attract some firms, but parks themselves do not increase the propensity for new firms to form. They may, however, enhance the formation of linkages with local universities (Löftsten and Lindelöf, 2002). And science parks with an incubator role may attract entrepreneurs with higher levels of educational and prior working experience, thereby resulting in firms that show higher growth rates, adoption of advanced technologies, participation in international R&D programs, and establishment of collaborative arrangements, especially with universities (Colombo and Delmastro, 2002; Monck *et al.*, 1988). Given the "right" conditions, then, science parks can add measurably to regional economic development (Luger and Goldstein, 1991), but they alone may not provide the impact on high-tech employment desired by local officials (Shearmur and Doloreux, 2000).

Simply building a science park does not create the synergy necessary for a self-sustaining area. The synergy is found in an active local or regional *ecosystem*, a "constellation of specialised enterprises" with which large firms can link (Bahrami and Evans, 1995). A similar idea is expressed in the Austin "technopolis wheel" which includes venture capital, a service infrastructure, a talent pool, and an entrepreneurial culture (Smilor and Feeser, 1991). A region with "institutional thickness" provides much more than can be provided by a science park alone.

According to Macdonald and Deng (2004, p. 3), "what little evidence there is does not conclude that science parks offer the optimum location for high technology firms. Indeed, it would seem that the science park offers little advantage at all". They remind us that the most successful regions, Silicon Valley and Boston's Route 128, were the product of serendipity rather than of planning – but a serendipity grounded in the benefits of agglomeration economies, externalities, networking, and clustering, with most information flow occurring informally.

Business incubators have been around for many years, and fall into several categories. Bøllingtoft and Ulhøi (2005), in an excellent state-of-the-art review of business incubators, strongly recommend what they call networked incubators, which facilitate the formation of relationships of entrepreneurs into both internal and external networks. In this sense, the networked incubator can be a broker-led network that benefits from agglomeration advantages because firms are housed in the same facility. Shared facilities and opportunities for informal interaction with other entrepreneurs are the benefits, rather than capital investment or provision of professional business services. The premises and shared facilities may be subsidised or not, depending on the needs of tenants. Indeed, it is difficult to construct an incubator that addresses the needs of firms at different stages in the lives of their ventures and with different sets of needs (Chan and Lau, 2005). Moreover, HEIs may attempt to create incubators for spin-off firms but be unable to create the appropriate conditions for them, being deficient either in resources or in competence (Clarysse *et al.,* 2005).

It may be impossible to imitate the famous examples of regional incubators, such as Boston, California, and Cambridge (United Kingdom), where the incubator is, in effect, the region – in each case a networked learning region, rather than a sole HEI. Of the 50 early-stage start-up companies in the Boston area that attracted the most outside investment in 2001-02, 25 – including seven of the top ten – had connections to one or more of the region's eight universities. That is, they were engaged in the commercialisation of technology first developed at one of the universities, were founded by a faculty member or graduate, started life in a university incubator, or had a CEO who had graduated from one of the eight (Appleseed, 2003).

Little research has distinguished clearly the services typical of any incubator (shared office services such as photocopiers, telephones and conference rooms, subsidised rent, business networks, business assistance and access to capital) from those that are associated with a university. The latter include a range of formal and informal links to university people and facilities: faculty consultants, student employees, library services, labs and workshops, computers, employee education and training, and awareness of related R&D (Mian, 1996).

Most importantly, interaction does not necessarily take place despite geographical proximity (Massey, Quintas and Wield, 1992; Johannisson *et al.*, 1994). That also is the finding of Hansson, Husted and Vestergaard (2005), who endorse a social capital role for science parks – in effect providing networking opportunities across the campus, rather than only on the premises of the science park. They term this "second generation" science park thinking. It is likely that active policies for networking are most needed in smaller cities and towns, where the lower density of firms makes networking require more effort than in large agglomerations. In rural and backward areas, only extroverted firms seem able to thrive (Vaessen and Keeble, 1995; Kingsley and Malecki, 2004). Introverted firms need policy intervention.

Policies for small and medium-sized enterprises

Policies to support SMEs do not involve a large number of links between HEIs and SMEs. Storey (2003) lists several areas of concern to SMEs and to governments for assisting SMEs and enhancing entrepreneurship (loan finance, equity capital, managed workspace, etc.). Of these, only science parks are clearly a province of HEIs.

There are three ways in which policy can address the needs of small firms (Chabbal, 1995). The first is to channel government resources in the right direction and to provide technology and demand forecasts, fiscal incentives, performance-orientated standards and regulatory measures that stimulate rather than impede innovation. The second route is to subsidise intermediaries, who then provide services and information for small firms. The third set of policy measures directly funds ways to increase the absorption capacity of firms by sharing risk, employing technical staff, and hiring consultants. These traditional sorts of programmes all involve in some way the transfer of information to small firms (Estimé, Drilhon and Julien, 1993, pp. 69-76). The weakness of most programmes is that they fail to fall within the existing information network of small firms, and therefore are often not tailored to the needs of those firms (Estimé, Drilhon and Julien, 1993).

Work in the OECD (OECD, 2003) suggests a range of policies: development of business networks, networks of business angels (investors in new firms), referral systems for professional advice (both pre-founding and post-founding), business incubators, enhanced usage of information and communications technology (ICT), and encouraging the creation of team-based firms (rather than solo entrepreneurs). Perhaps the most important recommendation of the OECD approach is the focus on local, rather than national, initiatives, and on incorporating new objectives into existing institutions rather than creating new organisations (Potter, 2005). Local initiatives are able to match the opportunities and constraints found in the local environment (Lichtenstein and Lyons, 1996). At the same time, co-ordinated compilation of local experiences and creation of opportunities for local entities to learn from the experiences elsewhere are important responsibilities of higher levels of government (regional, national, supranational) (Huggins, 2000).

Given the reality that most small firms will not seek out information from HEIs, the number of SMEs is so great that policy measures are unlikely to reach them all. Again, it is the extroverted firms that are most amenable to forging more and stronger links to HEIs. At the same time, we cannot assume that all HEIs are alike: regions vary tremendously in the degree to which a local "knowledge economy" has developed, with local

HEIs as central players and knowledge hubs. To the degree that their geographical context might be manipulable, regions that approach the "innovative milieu" and are characterised by extroverted firms will have strongly performing, innovative firms. Other, less supportive regions have fewer firms, and their lower density means that they provide less support for one another. Extroverted firms in less supportive regions are able to overcome this lack of support in their environment (Malecki and Poehling, 1999; Vaessen and Keeble, 1995).

Policies for technology transfer and knowledge transfer

It is not clear how the division of labour or specialisation among HEIs should be determined. While universities are perhaps not best for training in routine or widely applicable technologies, training in cutting-edge technologies might comprise an opportunity for some SMEs to have a major impact.

Technology transfer offices (TTOs) increasingly look to commercialisation of the technology originating in their HEI as a source of recurring revenue. The focus on a revenue stream from intellectual property might not be a viable option unless there is a critical mass of technologies to justify a technology transfer office (Degroof and Roberts, 2004).

Science parks and incubators need not be successful; their existence is able to generate a great deal of political capital or goodwill as more or less "expected" economic development activity. Overall, political goodwill and a revenue stream from licensing produce lower financial returns than taking equity in start-ups in accordance with the level of risk (Markman *et al.*, 2005).

Lagendijk and Rutten (2003) point out that there are several dilemmas in the creation of strategies to regional support organisations for regional innovation and technology transfer, including a tendency for policies that utilise a network model to fail to include regional HEIs. Universities tend to be involved in policies through top-down or hierarchical models, reminiscent of the linear model of technology. Personnel in HEIs are already in networks of firms, but only informally, so they are difficult to find when larger networks are developed.

Gatekeepers

All organisations need gatekeepers; they usually play a role on the demand side, both seeking out information from appropriate sources and filtering it for use by others in the receiving organisation (Macdonald and

Williams, 1995). Few SMEs can have, or can afford to have, a full-time gatekeeper, as may be the case in large firms. The knowledge that must be filtered includes – increasingly – knowledge found on Web sites. That is, SMEs need to have capabilities in both hard and soft networks: hard networks referring to information available on Internet sources, and soft networks referring to contacts made via social interaction (Malecki, 2002).

This is where there is a role for policy. Whether based on geographic or organisational proximity, time, space and infrastructure must be available for seeking, generating and exchanging knowledge (Prusak and Cohen, 1998). Often, this is best done by urban institutions that can provide the shared space for many different groups, generally supporting the network of actors and their *ba* in the region (Crevoisier, 1999; Kostiainen, 2002; Lester and Piore, 2004; Maillat, 1998). Whether in shared spaces or elsewhere, firms' innovativeness – their ability to introduce products new to the market – is enhanced when they are able to form interactions with HEIs. This interaction is most effective if it is based on informal bridges or boundary-crossing activities rather than being co-ordinated through technology transfer offices, which are relatively ineffective (Kaufmann and Tödtling, 2001). University-based incubators may form part of this intermediating middle ground between business and university cultures (Grimaldi and Grandi, 2005).

Universities are core institutions within knowledge-based regions, because they are "centrally involved in knowledge transfer, intended and unintended, formal and informal" (Howells, 2002, p. 877). Because knowledge transfer is neither predictable nor automatic, it must rely on people with the ability to serve as bridges across boundaries. Knowledge brokers who have credibility and understanding in both academic and commercial cultures are key catalysts in knowledge regions (Reichert, 2006).

The issue of demographic diversity also arises. Pages (2005) suggests that agencies responsible for technology transfer and liaison with SMEs are often unable to earn the trust of SMEs headed by women and minorities. Indeed, Hanson (2003) demonstrates that women entrepreneurs are far more likely to communicate with, and to have received help from, other women.

Conclusion

Fontes and Coombs (2001) strongly endorse the encouragement of new technology-based firms (NTBFs). The main contribution of NTBFs is their "technological dynamism", which gives them two major roles: a challenging role, whereby they break with the inertia of existing organisations; and a more long-standing technology transfer role, acting as a source of new technologies by linking to research at home and abroad. These roles can be especially important in less advanced economies, strengthening indigenous capabilities. However, intermediate economies such as Portugal presented NTBFs with some problems: a limited number of knowledgeable users, and difficulty reaching other clients, suggesting a need for demand-oriented policies.

Designing policies to "weave" a network where interaction is not the norm is not a simple matter (Bianchi and Bellini, 1991; Malecki and Tootle, 1996). In designing policies to assist SMEs, local institutions themselves must be entrepreneurial in nature, responding flexibly to the differentiated needs of local environments (Gibb, 1993). In particular, it is difficult to blend a productive mix of private- and public-sector involvement and interaction; it may be best to place the entrepreneurial institutional network in a non-governmental organisation, such as a flexible manufacturing network, that has the respect of actors in both private firms and government agencies. Such a policy relies on the characteristics and personality of a local community entrepreneur or *animateur*, who brings experience and external contacts to an area.

A common missing piece in most economies, this role of *animateur* or social entrepreneur can be played collectively by an institution or organisation (Bellini, 2000; Morgan, 1997). The regional *animateur* works to facilitate inward investment, upgrade local firms, and to effect technology transfer. Reichert (2006) believes that intermediary institutions, led by knowledge brokers trusted by all parties, must be established and supported to forge new links between universities and knowledge-based businesses. "The importance of these intermediary institutions cannot be overestimated". They "identify promising areas of co-operation" and "create the climate and mutual understanding on which sustainable partnerships can be built" (p. 38).

The expectations placed on HEIs continue to grow as a knowledge-based economy becomes a high priority in more places. The expectations for HEIs – in education, research, and regional responsiveness – continue to grow. Connection with SMEs in their regions can easily be neglected in the quest for higher-visibility activities. Building and maintaining support for the informal links on which SMEs rely will in the long term have a large impact on knowledge transfer and innovation.

Bibliography

Appleseed (2003), *Engines of Economic Growth: The Impact of Boston's Eight Research Universities on the Metropolitan Boston Area,* Appleseed, New York www.masscolleges.org/files/downloads/economicimpact/EconomicRepo rt_Full%20Report_FINAL.pdf

Bahrami, H. and S. Evans (1995), "Flexible Re-Cycling and High-Technology Entrepreneurship", *California Management Review,* Vol. 37, No. 3, Haas School of Business, University of California, Berkley, pp. 62-89.

BankBoston (1997), *MIT: The Impact of Innovation*, BankBoston, Boston. http://web.mit.edu/newsoffice/founders/Founders2.pdf

Bellini, N. (2000), "Planning the learning region: the Italian approach", in F. Boekema, *et al.* (eds.) *Knowledge, Innovation and Economic Growth: The Theory and Practice of Learning Regions*, Edward Elgar, Cheltenham.

Benneworth, P. (2001), "Academic entrepreneurship and long-term business relationships: understanding 'commercialization' activities", *Enterprise and Innovation Management Studies,* Vol. 2, No. 3, Routledge, pp. 225-237.

Bianchi, P. and N. Bellini (1991), "Public policies for local networks of innovators", *Research Policy,* Vol. 20, No. 5, Elsevier, pp. 487-497.

Bøllingtoft, A. and J.P. Ulhøi (2005), "The networked business incubator – leveraging entrepreneurial agency?", *Journal of Business Venturing,* Vol. 20, No. 2, Elsevier, pp. 265-290.

Castells, M. and P. Hall (1994), *Technopoles of the World: The Making of 21st Century Industrial Complexes*, Routledge, London.

Chabbal, R. (1995), "Characteristics of innovation policies, namely for SMEs", *STI Review,* Vol. 16, OECD, Paris, pp. 103-140.

Chan, K.F. and T. Lau (2005), "Assessing technology incubator programs in the science park: the good, the bad and the ugly", *Technovation,* Vol. 25, No. 10, Elsevier, pp. 1215-1228.

Clarysse, B., *et al.* (2005), "Spinning out new ventures: a typology of incubation strategies from European research institutions", *Journal of Business Venturing,* Vol. 20, No. 2, Elsevier, pp. 183-216.

Colombo, M.G. and M. Delmastro (2002), "How effective are technology incubators? Evidence from Italy", *Research Policy,* Vol. 31, No. 7, Elsevier, pp. 1103-1122.

Cooke, P. (2002), *Knowledge Economies: Clusters, Learning and Cooperative Advantage,* Routledge, London.

Cooke, P. (2004), "Introduction: regional innovations systems – an evolutionary approach", in Cooke, P., M. Heidenreich and H.-J. Braczyk (eds.), *Regional Innovation Systems*, Routledge, London.

Cooke, P. and K. Morgan (1998), *The Associational Economy: Firms, Regions, and Innovation*, Oxford University Press, Oxford.

Coombs, R. and L. Georghiou (2002), "A new 'industrial ecology'", *Science,* Vol. 296, No. 5567, American Association for the Advancement of Science, pp. 471.

Crevoisier, O. (1999), "Innovation and the city", in E.J. Malecki and P. Oinas (eds.), *Making Connections: Technological Learning and Regional Economic Change*, Ashgate, Aldershot.

Degroof, J.-J. and E.B. Roberts (2004), "Overcoming weak entrepreneurial infrastructures for academic spin-off ventures", *Journal of Technology Transfer,* Vol. 29, No. 3-4, Springer Netherlands, pp. 327-352.

Estimé, M.-F., G. Drilhon and P.-A Julien (1993), *Small and Medium-sized Enterprises: Technology and Competitiveness*, OECD, Paris.

Etzkowitz, H. (2002), *MIT and the Rise of Entrepreneurial Science*, Routledge, London.

Etzkowitz, H. (2003), "Innovation in innovation: the triple helix of university-industry-government relations", *Social Science Information,* Vol. 42, No. 3, Sage, pp. 293-337.

Etzkowitz, H. and L. Leydesdorff (2000), "The dynamics of innovation: from national systems and "mode 2" to a triple helix of university-industry-government relations", *Research Policy,* Vol. 29, No. 2, Elsevier, pp. 109-123.

Faulkner, W., J. Senker and L. Velho (1995), *Knowledge Frontiers: Public Sector Research and Industrial Innovation in Biotechnology, Engineering Ceramics, and Parallel Computing*, Clarendon Press, Oxford.

Florida, R. (1995), "Toward the Learning Region", *Futures,* Vol. 27, No. 2, Elsevier, pp. 527-536.

Fontes, M. (2005), "The process of transformation of scientific and technological knowledge into economic value conducted by biotechnology spin-offs", *Technovation,* Vol. 25, No. 4, Elsevier, pp. 339-347.

Fontes, M. and R. Coombs (2001), "Contribution of new technology-based firms to the strengthening of technological capabilities in intermediate economies", *Research Policy,* Vol. 30, No. 1, Elsevier, pp. 79-97.

Fuellhart, K.G. and A.K. Glasmeier (2003), "Acquisition, assessment and use of business information by small- and medium-sized businesses: a demand perspective", *Entrepreneurship and Regional Development,* Vol. 15, No. 3, Taylor and Francis, pp. 229-252.

Gibb, A.A. (1993), "Small business development in Central and Eastern Europe – opportunity for a rethink?", *Journal of Business Venturing,* Vol. 8, No. 6, Elsevier, pp. 461-486.

Gibbons, M. (2003), "A new mode of knowledge production", in R. Rutten, F. Boekema and E. Kuijpers (eds.), *Economic Geography of Higher Education: Knowledge Infrastructure and Learning Regions*, Routledge, London.

Gibbons, M., *et al.* (1994), *The New Production of Knowledge*, Sage, London.

Goddard, J.B. and P. Chatterton (1999), "Regional development agencies and the knowledge economy: harnessing the potential of universities", *Environment and Planning C: Government and Policy,* Vol. 17, No. 6, Pion, pp. 685-699.

Grandi, A. and R. Grimaldi (2003), "Exploring the networking characteristics of new venture founding teams", *Small Business Economics,* Vol. 21, No. 4, Springer Netherlands, pp. 329-341.

Grimaldi, R. and A. Grandi (2005), "Business incubators and new venture creation: an assessment of incubating models", *Technovation,* Vol. 25, No. 2, Elsevier, pp. 111-121.

Hanson, S. (2003), "Geographical and feminist perspectives on entrepreneurship", *Geographische Zeitschrift,* Vol. 91, No. 1, pp. 1-23.

Hansson, F., K. Husted and J. Vestergaard (2005), "Second generation science parks: from structural holes jockeys to social capital catalysts of the knowledge society", *Technovation,* Vol. 25, No. 9, Elsevier, pp. 1039-1049.

Howells, J.R.L. (2002), "Tacit knowledge, innovation and economic geography", *Urban Studies,* Vol. 39, No. 5-6, Sage, pp. 871-884.

Huggins, R. (2000), *The Business of Networks: Inter-firm Interaction, Institutional Policy and the TEC Experiment*, Ashgate, Aldershot.

Johannisson, B., *et al.* (1994), "Beyond anarchy and organization: entrepreneurs in contextual networks", *Entrepreneurship and Regional Development*, Vol. 6, No. 4, Taylor and Francis, pp. 329-356.

Joseph R.A. (1989), "Technology parks and their contribution to the development of technology-oriented complexes in Australia", *Environment and Planning C: Government and Policy*, Vol. 7, No. 2, Pion, pp. 173-192.

Kaufmann, A. and F. Tödtling (2001), "Science-industry interaction in the process of innovation: the importance of boundary-crossing between systems", *Research Policy*, Vol. 30, No. 5, Elsevier, pp. 791-804.

Keane, J. and J. Allison (1999), "The intersection of the learning region and local and regional economic development: analysing the role of higher education", *Regional Studies*, Vol. 33, No. 9, Taylor and Francis, pp. 896-902.

Kingsley, G. and E.J. Malecki (2004), "Networking for competitiveness: the role of informal linkages for small firms", *Small Business Economics*, Vol. 23, No. 1, Springer Netherlands, pp. 71-84.

Kostiainen, J. (2002), "Learning and the 'Ba' in the development network of an urban region", *European Planning Studies*, Vol. 10, No. 5, Taylor and Francis, pp. 613-631.

Lagendijk, A. and R. Rutten (2003), "Associational dilemmas in regional innovation strategy development: regional innovation support organisations and the RIS/RITTS programmes", in R. Rutten, F. Boekema and E. Kuijpers (eds.), *Economic Geography of Higher Education: Knowledge Infrastructure and Learning Regions*, Routledge, London.

Lawton Smith, H. (2007), "Universities, innovation, and territorial development: a review of the evidence", *Environment and Planning C: Government and Policy*, Vol. 25, No .1, Pion, pp. 98-114.

Lester, R.K. and M.J. Piore (2004), *Innovation: The Missing Dimension*, Harvard University Press, Cambridge, MA.

Lichtenstein, G.A. and T.S. Lyons (1996), *Incubating New Enterprises: A Guide to Successful Practice*, Aspen Institute, Washington, DC.

Löftsten, H. and P. Lindelöf (2002), "Science parks and the growth of new technology-based firms – academic-industry links, innovation and markets", *Research Policy*, Vol. 31, No. 6, Elsevier, pp. 859-876.

Löfsten, H. and P. Lindelöf (2005), "R&D networks and product innovation patterns – academic and non-academic new technology-based firms on Science Parks", *Technovation,* Vol. 25, No. 9, Elsevier, pp. 1025-1037.

Luger, M.I. and H.A. Goldstein (1991), *Science in the Garden: Research Parks and Regional Economic Development,* University of North Carolina Press, Chapel Hill.

Luger, M.I. and H.A. Goldstein (1997), "What is the role of public universities in regional economic development?", in R.D. Bingham and R. Mier (eds.), *Dilemmas of Urban Economic Development: Issues in Theory and Practice,* Sage, Thousand Oaks, CA.

Macdonald, S. and Y. Deng (2004), "Science parks in China: a cautionary exploration", *International Journal of Technology Intelligence and Planning,* Vol. 1, No. 1, Inderscience, pp. 1-14.

Macdonald, S. and C. Williams (1993), "Beyond the boundary: an information perspective on the role of the gatekeeper in the organization", *Journal of Product Innovation Management,* Vol. 10, No. 5, Blackwell, pp. 417-427.

Maillat, D. (1998), "Interactions between urban systems and localized productive systems: an approach to endogenous regional development in terms of innovative milieu", *European Planning Studies,* Vol. 6, No. 2, Taylor and Francis, pp. 117-129.

Malecki, E.J. (2002), "Hard and soft networks for urban competitiveness", *Urban Studies,* Vol. 39, No. 5-6, Sage, pp. 929-945.

Malecki, E.J. and R.M. Poehling (1999), "Extroverts and introverts: small manufacturers and their information sources", *Entrepreneurship and Regional Development,* Vol. 11, No. 3, Taylor and Francis, pp. 247-268.

Malecki, E.J. and D.M. Tootle (1996), "The role of networks in small firm competitiveness", *International Journal of Technology Management,* Vol. 11, No. 1-2, Inderscience, pp. 43-57.

Markman, G.D., *et al.* (2005), "Entrepreneurship and university-based technology transfer", *Journal of Business Venturing,* Vol. 20, No. 2, Elsevier, pp. 241-263.

Massey, D., P. Quintas and D. Wield (1992), *High Tech Fantasies: Science Parks in Society, Science and Space,* Routledge, London.

Marquis, D.G. (1988), "The anatomy of successful innovations", in M.L. Tushman and W.L. Moore (eds.), *Readings in the Management of Innovation,* Ballinger, Cambridge, MA.

Mian, S.P. (1996), "Assessing value-added contributions of university technology business incubators to tenant firms", *Research Policy,* Vol. 25, No. 3, Elsevier, pp. 325-335.

Monck, C.S.P., *et al.* (1988), *Science Parks and the Growth of High Technology Firms*, Croom Helm, London.

Morgan, K. (1997), "The learning region: institutions, innovation and regional renewal", *Regional Studies,* Vol. 31, No. 5, Taylor and Francis, pp. 491-503.

Moulaert, F. and F. Sekia (2003), "Territorial innovation models: a critical survey", *Regional Studies,* Vol. 37, No. 3, Taylor and Francis, pp. 289-302.

Mowery, D.C. and A.A. Ziedonis (2002), "Academic patent quality and quantity before and after the Bayh-Dole act in the United States", *Research Policy,* Vol. 31, No. 3, Elsevier, pp. 399-418.

Nonaka, I. and N. Konno (1998), "The concept of 'Ba': building a foundation for knowledge creation", *California Management Review,* Vol. 40, No. 3, Haas School of Business, University of California, Berkley, pp. 40-54.

Nonaka, I. and H. Takeuchi (1995), *The Knowledge-Creating Company*, Oxford University Press, New York.

OECD (2003), *Entrepreneurship and Local Economic Development: Programme and Policy Recommendations*, OECD, Paris.

Pages, E. (2005), "The changing demography of entrepreneurship", *Local Economy,* Vol. 20, No. 1, Taylor and Francis, pp. 93-97.

Pirnay, F., B. Surlemont and F. Nlemvo (2003), "Toward a typology of university spin-offs", *Small Business Economics,* Vol. 21, No. 4, Springer Netherlands, pp. 355-369.

Potter, J. (2005), "Entrepreneurship policy at local level: rationale, design and delivery", *Local Economy,* Vol. 20, No. 1, Taylor and Francis, pp. 104-110.

Prusak, L. and D. Cohen(1998), "Knowledge buyers, sellers, and brokers: the political economy of knowledge", in D. Neef, G.A. Siesfeld, and J. Cefola (eds.), *The Economic Impact of Knowledge*, Butterworth Heinemann, Boston.

Rallet, A. and A. Torre (1998), "On geography and technology: proximity relations in localised innovation networks", in M. Steiner (ed.), *Clusters and Regional Specialisation*, Pion, London.

Rappert, B., A. Webster, and D. Charles (1999), "Making sense of diversity and reluctance: academic-industrial relations and intellectual property", *Research Policy,* Vol. 28, No. 8, Elsevier, pp. 873-890.

Reichert, S. (2006), *The Rise of Knowledge Regions: Emerging Opportunities and Challenges for Universities,* European University Association, Brussels.

Roberts, E.B. (1991), *Entrepreneurs in High Technology: Lessons from MIT and Beyond,* Oxford University Press, New York.

Rocha, H.O. (2004), "Entrepreneurship and development: the role of clusters", *Small Business Economics,* Vol. 23, No. 5, Springer Netherlands, pp. 363-400.

Rocha, H.O. and R. Sternberg (2005), "Entrepreneurship: the role of clusters theoretical perspectives and empirical evidence from Germany", *Small Business Economics,* Vol. 24, No. 3, Springer Netherlands, pp. 267-292.

Rosenfeld, S.A. (2000), "Community college/cluster connections: specialization and competitiveness in the United States and Europe", *Economic Development Quarterly,* Vol. 14, No. 1, Sage, pp. 51-62.

Rosenberg, D. (2002), *Cloning Silicon Valley: The Next Generation High-Tech Hotspots,* Reuters, London.

Rutten, R., F. Boekema and E. Kuijpers (2003), "Economic geography of higher education: setting the stage", in R. Rutten, F. Boekema and E. Kuijpers (eds.), *Economic Geography of Higher Education: Knowledge Infrastructure and Learning Regions,* Routledge, London.

Saxenian, A. (1994), *Regional Advantage: Culture and Competition in Silicon Valley and Route 128,* Harvard University Press, Cambridge, MA.

Shane, S. (2004), *Academic Entrepreneurship: University Spinoffs and Wealth Creation,* Edward Elgar, Cheltenham.

Shearmur, R. and D. Doloreux (2000), "Science parks: actors or reactors? Canadian science parks in their urban context", *Environment and Planning A,* Vol. 32, No. 6, Pion, pp. 1065-1082.

Shinn, T. (2002), "The triple helix and new production of knowledge: Prepackaged thinking on science and technology", *Social Studies of Science,* Vol. 32, No. 4, Sage, pp. 599-614.

Slaughter, S. and G. Rhoades (2004), *Academic Capitalism and the New Economy: Markets, State, and Higher Education,* Johns Hopkins University Press, Baltimore.

Smilor, R.W. and H.R. Feeser (1991), "Chaos and the entrepreneurial process: patterns and policy implications for technology entrepreneurship", *Journal of Business Venturing*, Vol. 6, No. 3, Elsevier, pp. 165-172.

Storey, D.J. (2003), "Entrepreneurship, small and medium sized enterprises and public policies", in Z.J. Acs and D.B. Audretsch (eds.), *Handbook of Entrepreneurship Research*, Kluwer, Boston.

Tornatzky, L.G., P.G. Waugaman and D.O. Gray (2002), *Innovation U.: New University Roles in a Knowledge Economy*, Southern Growth Policies Board, Research Triangle Park, NC. www.southern.org/pubs/pubs_pdfs/iu_report.pdf

Vaessen, P. and D. Keeble (1995), "Growth-oriented SMEs in unfavorable regional environments", *Regional Studies,* Vol. 29, No. 6, Taylor and Francis, pp. 489-505.

Woolgar, S., *et al.* (1998), "Abilities and competencies required, particularly by small firms, to identify and acquire new technology", *Technovation,* Vol. 18, No. 8-9, Elsevier, pp. 575-584.

Chapter 10

University Knowledge Transfer and the Role of Academic Spin-offs

by
Åsa Lindholm Dahlstrand
Halmstad University, Sweden

There are several reasons for the growing interest in knowledge transfer and academic spin-offs. First, it has been noticed that science and technology have become increasingly important for economic growth. Second, many studies confirm that new and expanding entrepreneurial firms are creating a high share of net new jobs. This points to "science and technology-based entrepreneurship" as a phenomenon of high importance for industrial renewal and, again, economic growth. Third, since earlier research has established that universities and existing companies are the two main sources of new technology-based firms, it is not surprising that academic spin-off has been considered an important mechanism for the transfer and commercialisation of university research. This chapter provides some findings on how academic spin-offs are created, how frequent they are, and what impact they have on economic growth. Two examples – the United States and Sweden – are included to illustrate the mechanisms of licensing and spin-off firm creation.

Introduction

Universities are often seen as a resource of technology development that is important for economic growth (Rosenberg and Nelson, 1994; Mowery *et al.*, 2001). This resource has historically not had a strong focus on commercialisation, and thus it is sometimes considered to be an unexploited reservoir of commercialisable knowledge and ideas. Stimulated by such perceived potential, universities have been rapidly escalating their involvement in technology transfer. In recent years, the enthusiasm has grown for the more risky ways of forming academic spin-off companies around a university-developed technology, and licensing to small private firms rather than through the traditional commercialisation route with large public companies (Powers and McDougall, 2005).

This chapter focuses on the role of academic spin-offs in university knowledge transfer processes. These spin-offs can be considered a special category of knowledge/technology-based entrepreneurial firms. Such firms, it is believed, play an especially critical role in the development of high technology industries, and give rise to novel fields and markets (Callan, 2001). Universities and policy makers throughout the industrial world are currently extremely interested in fostering the creation of spin-offs from the public research base. Taking these considerations together, it is easy to jump to the conclusion that technology-intensive entrepreneurial firms – and especially academic spin-offs – ought to have a key role for economic growth. That might not, however, be the case. Analysis of the situation would require, for example, some knowledge of how frequent the phenomenon is, and to what extent the firms tend to grow. The chapter will help do so by providing some insights on how academic spin-offs are created, how frequent they are, and what impact they might have on economic growth.

Scope and coverage

The chapter offers an overview of mechanisms for transfer and commercialisation of university research. Existing research on the role of academic spin-offs is presented, as are findings about their frequency, growth and innovativeness. Moreover, their potential indirect effects for knowledge transfer, as "innovation providers", and regional development are discussed.

After outlining the current policy issues and state of existing research, two very different examples are discussed. One is taken from Sweden, and illustrates what is called the "spin-off route"; the other summarises some earlier findings from the United States, to illustrate what is called the "licensing route".

The final section focuses on implications. There are a number of challenges for policy makers wanting to increase the frequency of university spin-offs, as well as for increasing the economic effects of academic entrepreneurship and commercialisation of university research. Policy makers have many tools to help them succeed with that commercialisation. While some of these can be beneficial for economic development, others could instead be damaging in the long run. As always, there is a need for further research and studies before a complete picture and solid conclusions can be established. Sometimes it is wise for policy makers to await further studies before implementing new strategies and tools.

Current policy issues

Universities are increasingly expected to show tangible returns to society for the public research grants they receive. Academic research is made useful to society through many mechanisms; the traditional ones of publishing and of teaching are the most well known. Recently the commercialisation of university research through mechanisms like the development of products, patents and academic spin-offs has gained in importance. Today many universities view themselves as catalysts of new venture formation and regional development.

Even though the academic spin-off is not a new phenomenon – indeed it has existed ever since academia was first established – it is increasing in frequency and importance. The last two decades have witnessed a growing interest among researchers, practitioners and policy makers. The rise in frequency of new academic spin-offs seems to have happened in parallel with the adoption of national, regional, and even institutional policies in support of seed capital funds, researcher mobility, and services for new firm creation (Callan, 2001). However, since this awakened interest is still relatively young, there is as yet no common consensus on the critical ingredients of a well-functioning spin-off policy. Government policies are only now being formulated, and put into place at different levels (Mustar, 2001). A spin-off policy must include considerations at the university level, the regional level, the national level, and sometimes (as with the European Union and the United States) the supranational level as well.

Much of the interest in technology-based entrepreneurship and academic spin-offs has its roots in their development in the United States. For example, already in the early 1950s, the first US science parks were created in order to increase the possibilities and profitability of commercialising university research (Mian, 1994; Kung, 1995). In Europe, it took almost an additional twenty years until – often inspired by American success stories – the first science parks were established. Also, early research on technology-based entrepreneurship was mainly conducted in the United States. In Europe the subject has gained in importance during the past twenty years. Both there and in other parts of the world, the number of new technology-based firms (NTBFs) has increased drastically in recent years (Autio, 1997; Keeble *et al.*, 1998). There has been a build-up of local, technologically dynamic and export-oriented clusters of specialised NTBFs in several places. The most famous of these are still the Silicon Valley and Route 128 in the United States, but there are also well known clusters in places like Cambridge (United Kingdom), Munich, Bangalore, Tel Aviv and the "Third Italy". Many policy makers around the world dream of creating a similar "high tech" cluster.

Licensing and spin-off companies

Reporting on a 1999 OECD survey on the formation of high technology spin-offs from public sector research institutions, Callan (2001) argued that "The number of spin-offs generated in an economy is understood as an indicator of the public sector's ability to develop commercially relevant knowledge, of its entrepreneurial capacity, and of the depth of knowledge transfer between the public and private sectors" (p. 14). There are, however, many various *mechanisms* through which academic research is made socially useful. These include of course the traditional mechanisms of publishing and of teaching (undergraduates as well as graduates) and the development of products, patents and firms by academics, but roles are also played by various types of networks, meeting places and markets for the sharing of information and knowledge. There are many types of benefits accruing from academic research; these go far beyond providing new information of a public good nature or the direct growth effects of a spin-off.

Studies on university entrepreneurship, however, usually focus on the mechanisms for development of products, patents and academic spin-offs. There seems to be two major routes for entrepreneurial commercialisation of university research: (I) the licensing route and (II) the spin-off route (Figure 10.1).

As a starting point, to have commercial value, a technology transfer possibility needs both a business/market opportunity (sometimes labelled a "market pull") and some university research results (sometimes labelled a "technology push"). A formal technology transfer function may exist in some universities, while in others this function might be informal or intangible. Usually a formal Technology Transfer Office (TTO) is responsible for undertaking the licensing of university patents. Where universities own the IP rights of university research and formal TTOs are set up, it is usual that academic spin-offs are set up as a combination of the licensing and the spin-off routes, *e.g.* spin-offs have to acquire a license for the intellectual property. In countries where the IP rights belong to the individual researcher (*e.g.* Sweden, Italy, Estonia and, until 2005, Finland), academic spin-offs are set up without licensing. In addition, the licensing route is not an option where IP is not protected by patents. Moreover, many university patents are without commercial value if they are not accompanied by the knowledge of the academic researchers themselves (*e.g.* Jensen and Thursby, 2001; Lööf, 2005); thus, TTOs might not want to use the option of patenting. An additional path in Figure 10.1 is where the transfer possibilities are not being commercialised at all, or put to "rest" for a while. As will be illustrated in the Swedish example below, it is not unusual that former members of faculty make use of university IP after being employed for a period in private industry.

Figure 10.1. Commercialisation of university research

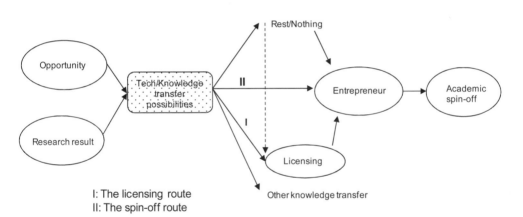

Much of the American literature has focused on the licensing route and the commercialisation of patents, while European studies instead have been more interested in the creation of entrepreneurial academic spin-off firms. To some extent this is mirrored by the greater European focus on regional development, in which academic spin-offs are considered to have a critical role. One example of the difference between the US and the European focus can be found in a paper by Goldfarb and Henrekson (2003). In the paper the authors compare the "bottom-up" versus "top-down" strategy of US and Swedish policy makers (respectively), and find that "the Swedish data inform us of all technology transfer in which the mechanism of transfer is a new firm, regardless of the existence of legally protected intellectual property. However, in US studies that use data from TLOs, the unit of observation is usually the invention" (p. 649). Unfortunately, the authors are not able to present any data on academic spin-offs in any of the two countries. No doubt both the licensing route and the spin-off route exist in both, but the balance and the focus of policy makers and universities might differ.

The Swedish situation is not a rare exception. In many OECD countries inventions have traditionally been the property of individual university researchers, and there are often no obligations – or incentives – for universities themselves to monitor the commercialisation activities among academic researchers (Callan, 2001). In the United States, the Bayh-Dole Act of 1980 provides incentives for universities to focus resources on the commercial exploitation of their technology.

Direct and indirect economic effects

Few OECD countries record the creation or development of academic spin-offs. In addition, the definitions used vary between countries. Much of the information that exists is gathered by external consultants on an irregular basis (Callan, 2001). As a result, there is little definitional consistency and international comparisons are difficult. Callan only reports national or aggregate data for eight OECD countries: Australia, Belgium, Canada, Finland, France, Germany, Norway and the United States. And, according to her, only Canada, France, Finland and Norway sponsor regular nationwide studies.

The conclusion of the OECD study was that academic spin-offs accounts for no more than 2% of new firm creations in any OECD country (Callan, 2001). Callan reports that in a medium-sized OECD country, all public institutions taken together usually generate no more than a few dozen spin-offs per year. There is however a clear difference in spin-off formation rates between different OECD countries. According to Callan, the United States seems to have one of the highest rates, with the creation of, on average, two new firms per research institution and year. Data from Belgium and Finland suggested only one new spin-off per research institution every second year, while Canadian data suggest one spin-off per year and institution (Callan, 2001).

Very few studies have focused on growth within academic spin-offs. Instead, the success of commercialising university research is usually measured in terms of patents licensed or number of spin-offs created. Most prior US work focusing on the link between universities and spin-offs has largely overlooked the employment argument (Clarysse *et al.*, 2005).

European studies have instead often focused on unemployment and job creation in a regional setting.

Callan (2001) concludes that even if public spin-offs have high survival rates, they tend to have slow growth rates and remain small. In Canada, France, Germany and Australia the spin-offs are very small firms, with the great majority of existing firms having fewer than 50 employees. In addition, Callan claims that in many countries spin-offs rarely grow larger than 20 employees. Unfortunately, she provides no information about the age of these small and slow-growing firms. As will be discussed in the Swedish case below, the size and growth of academic spin-offs vary with the age of the firm. Mansfield (1998) has shown that the mean time interval between the academic research result and the first commercial introduction of the product is between six and seven years. Not surprisingly then, and in line with Callan's finding, newly established spin-offs grow more slowly than other technology-based new firms. But, as we shall see, many of the Swedish academic spin-offs improve their growth later in life. At the age of ten years, 87.5% of the Swedish university spin-offs employed less than 25 persons. Five years later, at the age of 15, as many as 50% of the firms had over 25 employees. That is to say, the growth rate of the Swedish spin-offs increased considerably after the initial ten years of operations. One reason might be that innovation and product development are complex and take considerable time in academic spin-offs.

University spin-offs are not – on average – high-growth firms. Even if they do create jobs, and mainly high-skilled jobs, growth in the number of employees might not be the most important criterion for assessing their value to the economy. For example, in Sweden it was found that, in relation to their size, university spin-offs (USOs) had a significantly higher degree of innovativeness than other new technology-based firms (Lindholm Dahlstrand, 2001). The impact of these firms are likely to be indirect, in addition to direct, in that USOs often contribute knowledge to firms that are their customers. Both the form of production and the innovation process has changed in recent years (Autio, 1997). Firms are becoming more dependent on external knowledge and technology sources (Granstrand and Sjölander, 1990; Lindholm Dahlstrand, 1996; Chesbrough, 2003), and the need for sourcing technology makes firms participate in innovation networks. Academic spin-offs are important in these networks as they provide specialised and often science-based inputs. Several studies, partly originating from Marshall's concept of the industrial district, have stressed the regional aspects of these networks (Storper, 1995, Cooke, 1996, Garnsey, 1996, Sternberg, 1996, Pavitt, 1998, Audretsch and Feldman, 1996). Olofsson and Wahlbin (1993) found that the main part of technology traded came from university spin-offs. Lööf (2005) found that about a quarter of Sweden's established innovative companies co-operate with Swedish universities, and that this had a significant impact on their innovativeness. University researchers working as consultants in industry are often more important than the purchasing of patents and licences (Lööf, 2005) and in Sweden, university researchers working as consultants are mostly found in university spin-off firms. Thus, the university spin-offs may have a significant but indirect impact on industrial transformation, regionally or nationally. Although academic entrepreneurship and the associated issues of patenting, incubators and seed funding related to the "entrepreneurial university" (see *e.g.* Etzkowitz *et al.,* 2000) have been the focus of public debate for some time, we have little knowledge of the strength of this particular mechanism. This refers not only to the direct impact on growth, but – more importantly – to the indirect effects.

The spin-off route: The Swedish example

Sweden is a country with a relatively strong technology focus and resources invested in R&D. Three-quarters of Swedish R&D are carried out in the private industry. As in many other countries, public research funding overwhelmingly supports university research, and government bodies try to encourage commercialisation and exploitation of university research as an economic development tool. The government has stipulated a so-called "third task" for universities: responsibility for transferring the results of university research into the private business and production sector. Despite this, the dominant belief in Sweden is that science policy has failed to achieve a high utilisation of the fruits of academic research. The latest Science Policy Proposition (Regeringen, 2005, p. 140) wrote that: "The investments in research give…insufficient results in the form of economic growth…knowledge transfer to industry and commercialisation of research results need to be increased". One of the main funders of academic research, VINNOVA, also suggests that: "…the knowledge and results from research are not efficiently transformed into firm formation and growth" (VINNOVA, 2002, p. 1).

Particular attention has been given to academic entrepreneurship as a central, but underutilised, mechanism for exploiting the results of academic research. In the Swedish context, this mechanism began to receive attention in the early 1990s. A great deal of concern has been raised over an allegedly poor propensity to spin off firms from academia and over the poor growth, and associated little direct impact on the economy, of those that have been spun off (*e.g.* Jacobsson and Rickne, 1997; Goldfarb and Henrekson, 2003; Delmar and Wiklund, 2003). Consequently, many policy initiatives have centred on promoting academic entrepreneurship. The more prominent among these are the Innovationbridge (*Innovationsbron,* founded in 2005) and its predecessors – the VINNOVA Incubator programme and seven Teknikbro-organisations (bridging organisations) that have both had a clear focus on increasing the number and (direct) growth of academic spin-offs, *e.g.* by providing seed funding. The ambition of the *Innovationsbron* is to "help researchers, innovators and entrepreneurs with business development and commercialisation, and to increase knowledge transfer and sharing between industry and university" (www.innovationsbron.se). When introducing this new organisation, the Swedish Minister of Industry wrote that "During a ten year period, Innovationsbron AB will spend 1.8 billion SEK to enhance the conditions for commercialising research results and ideas in industry" (DN, 2005). Hence, both the predecessor and the new *Innovationsbron* focus on academic entrepreneurship (and on seed funding).

As was argued in the introduction to this chapter, in order to assess the importance of academic spin-offs there is a need to know how frequent the phenomenon is, and to what extent – and which – firms tend to grow. In a study of some 350 Swedish NTBFs, Lindholm Dahlstrand (2004) found that almost half of the firms were spin-offs from established private firms, and that an additional sixth were either directly or indirectly spun off from universities (Figure 10.2). The remaining third had originated either from the founders' own idea, or were based on an externally acquired ideas.

Figure 10.2. Where do the NTBFs originate?

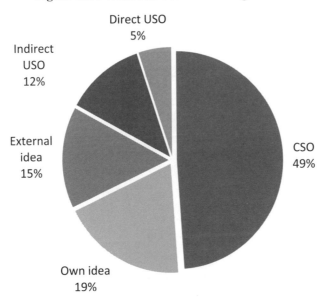

Source: Lindholm Dahlstrand, 2004.

ENTREPRENEURSHIP AND HIGHER EDUCATION – ISBN- 9789264044098 © OECD 2008

Sweden has a relatively high share of new firms created in knowledge-intensive and manufacturing industries (c. 35% and 15%, respectively – ITPS, 2006). International estimations in the *Global Entrepreneurship Monitor* suggest that in general less than 10% of the new firms can be classified as "Science, Technology and High Potential" (Reynolds *et al.*, 2002). This (presumably too low) figure suggests that approximately 5% of the new firms in Sweden are corporate spin-offs, and a corresponding 0.5% direct university spin-offs. Slightly over 1% can be considered indirect university spin-offs – that is, they are based on an idea originating in a university, but not established until the founder(s) have been working an additional period in private industry. In addition, among the start-ups based on an external idea, approximately one-fifth of these ideas had been developed in universities. That is, 3% of the NTBFs (and less than 0.5% of all new firms) were set up by external entrepreneurs acquiring rights to university research.

Figure 10.3 illustrates the academic spin-offs in the Swedish case. Here, 24% of the spin-offs are direct university spin-offs (USOs), with faculty members establishing the new firm. Most of the academic spin-offs, 62%, are indirect university spin-offs. In these firms the IP or ideas have "rested" while the entrepreneur was working in private industry. The third category, 14% of the academic spin-offs, consists of cases where an external entrepreneur – not a faculty member – acquires the university research (with or without a licence).

Figure 10.3. Academic spin-offs and spin-outs in the Swedish case

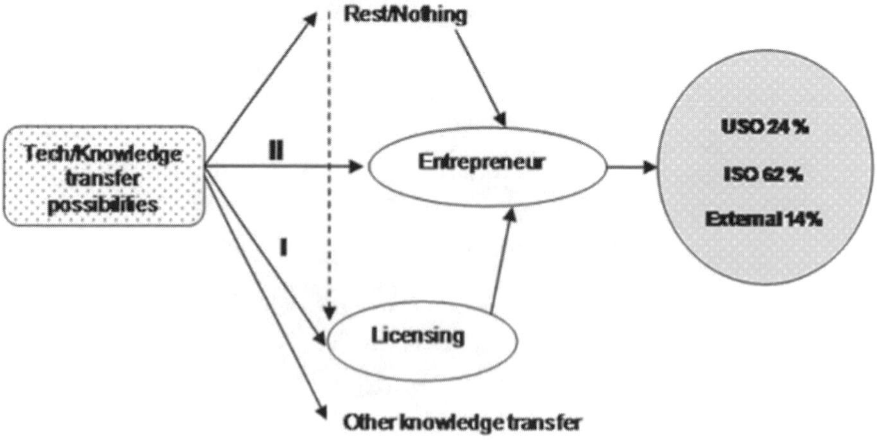

Thus, taken together, the share of academic spin-offs in Sweden is approximately 2% of all new firms. This figure is in line with the findings reported for several other countries in the OECD (Callan, 2001).

In an earlier paper on Swedish NTBFs, Lindholm Dahlstrand (2001) found that corporate spin-offs (CSOs) are outperforming other spin-offs in terms of economic growth. However, in comparison to direct USOs, the indirect university spin-offs (ISOs) were able to generate higher growth. Possibly, the founders of ISOs have been able to complement their knowledge to compensate for some of the growth disadvantages of direct USOs. Moreover, in the same study, in relation to their size, the USOs were found to have a significantly higher degree of innovativeness. Because of this, the USOs' innovations are often exploited outside the firm itself, and the economic potential of that exploitation may indirectly benefit the economy. It is also possible that the USOs may be especially important for radical innovations/industrial change, but this is a question for further studies to more fully explore.

Interestingly, the new firms set up by external entrepreneurs commercialising university ideas are demonstrating the highest growth of all Swedish NTBFs. They are growing faster than both the ISOs and the CSOs. The firms are not set up by entrepreneurs previously employed as university researchers, and it might be that the founders are able to combine the "best of two worlds", *i.e.* both commercial knowledge and advanced technical research. Possibly, these European firms are able to demonstrate the same high growth rates that have been found in US studies. Moreover, it might be that this category of academic spin-offs is more common in the United States as compared to Europe. Available data do not answer this; the question is one for future studies.

One final comment on the growth of Swedish academic spin-offs is that it takes considerable time for these firms to start to grow. While the direct university spin-offs had very limited growth during their first ten years of operations, they managed to improve significantly after this. At the age of ten years, the average size of the direct spin-offs was 15.5 employees. Five years later the mean has grown to an average number of 33 employees, *i.e.* an annual increase of 16.3%. This means that at the age of 15, half of the firms had over 25 employees. However, the corresponding figure for the indirect spin-offs is about the same, *i.e.* an annual increase of 17.6%. At the age of 15, the average number of employees in the indirect spin-offs was 44. Thus, in both direct and indirect university spin-offs, the growth rates increased considerably after the initial ten years of operations. This suggests that innovation and product development is complex and takes considerable time in academic spin-offs.

The licensing route: The US example

In the United States, the Bayh-Dole Act, which was passed in 1980, permits universities and small business to obtain title to inventions funded by the federal government so as to license inventions (Bozeman, 2000). It has led to a significant increase in patenting, and to an interest among US universities in commercialising research and appropriating private returns from the inventions. Universities already active in patenting for many decades before the Bayh-Dole Act have increased the emphasis on commercialisation; other universities began to patent only after the passage of the act. The Association of University Technology Managers, AUTM, annually surveys the commercial use of university research. From 1991 to 1997, university licence revenues increased over 315%. Markman *et al.* (2005) argue that the numbers of start-up and mature firms that utilise technologies developed by university faculty, staff, and students have skyrocketed since the early 1990s. For example, in 2000 AUTM reports over 4 000 new licences and options, out of which 626 went to 454 start-up companies specifically created to develop and commercialise the results of academic research (Powers and McDougall, 2005).

However, previous research has found that the Bayh-Dole Act in itself had little effect on the increase in academic entrepreneurial activity that has occurred in the United States since the 1980s. Colyvas *et al.* (2002) argue that the range of research results (for example in biotech) that are patentable has increased since the introduction of the Act. Also, much of the increase has been driven by contemporaneous shifts in intellectual property laws and regimes for funding academic research (Henderson, Jaffe and Trajtenberg, 1998). Shane (2004) argues that the Bayh-Dole Act has led to an increase of university patenting in those fields in which licensing is an effective mechanism for knowledge transfer.

There are three potential licensees of federally sponsored technology – existing companies, start-up entities and third-party licensing organisations. Traditionally, the mechanism by which US universities have developed and commercialised research has been the licensing route to large, established corporations. A growing trend among US universities, however, is to pursue riskier paths through the creation of academic spin-offs or the licensing to young and newly created firms. Powers and McDougall (2005) conclude that slack resources provide universities with greater flexibility to choose the more risky spin-off route to commercialisation rather than the traditional large firm-licensing path. Doing so, they argue, appears to result in greater awards and more successful licensing to firms that go public in an IPO (Initial Public Offering). Also Massing (2001) argues that, in general, the start-up companies hold the greatest potential for spurring economic growth.

Even so, the AUTM survey reports that the majority of US university licences are sold to existing corporations. Only around 10% of new licences are sold to start-up companies (Massing, 2001). When it happens, some of the spin-offs have to pay a royalty to the university; others are set up without costs for the researcher.

Major US universities have relatively recently started investing in their own spin-offs. Usually this is done by taking a minority equity post in the academic spin-off. Powers and McDougall (2005) found that licences with equity are becoming much more common, due to the belief that the returns of a few successful firms could be enormous. Licensing for cash is almost invariably paired with IP-based technologies at the prototype stage, for which a market has been identified. Instead, new ventures are the primary licensing targets of technologies at the proof of concept stage (Markman *et al.*, 2005).

Several earlier studies have pointed to the growing sophistication of technology transfer activities at US universities (Matkin, 2001; Powers and McDougall, 2005). One example of this is the increasing use of equity investments in new academic spin-offs. By licensing –for equity, major US universities have recently started investing in their own spin-offs. In a study of 128 US universities, Markman *et al.* (2005) found that this licensing-for-equity strategy is positively related to new venture formation, and that while the licensing-for-cash strategy is the most prevalent transfer strategy, it is least correlated with new venture formation. In the past, they argue, universities have passively licensed their technologies, while today many research universities actively search for ways to spawn new companies.

Small, marginally capitalised spin-offs are often the only customers for university-owned intellectual property, so the universities must either take an equity stake or issue no licence at all (Matkin, 2001). In spin-offs where the university holds an equity stake, this is often accompanied by universities providing space, support and financing – for example in an incubator – to the new firms. This is a costly strategy, but might have long-turn financial returns.

Markman *et al.* (2005) conclude that those US universities most interested in generating short-term cash flows from their IP licensing strategies are least positioned to create long-term wealth through venture creation. Patenting imposes a cost that, from an economic perspective, is worth incurring only if the royalties from licensing those patents exceed the average cost of patenting. If licensing is not effective in an industry, *e.g.* because knowledge is mainly tacit and not easily codifiable, the willingness of firms to license university technology is low; the ability of universities to successfully license those patents is limited; and the royalties that universities can charge are small (Shane, 2004). Jensen and Thursby (2001) found that in around two-thirds of university patents, commercialisation was difficult without the tacit knowledge of the researchers that had contributed to the patent. The commercialisation of such patents may require either an academic spin-off, or the engagement of the academic researchers as consultants, in order to have economic value. Thus, a high share of university patents might never be commercially exploited if universities focus too narrowly on the licensing route. A combination of the licensing and the spin-off route may be an option.

A related issue is that of exclusive and non-exclusive licences. It is sometimes argued that an exclusive licence is needed in order to have a new venture created. However, Colyvas *et al.* (2002) are not in favour of exclusive licenses. They argue that it was almost never clear in advance just which firm would show the initiative and have the capability to do the additional work needed successfully. Their conclusion is that "while for embryonic technologies some exclusivity may be necessary to induce development, it is precisely for these types of technologies that the costs of strong exclusivity are greatest" (p. 66). In line with this, Shane (2000) argues that different people will discover different opportunities. At any given time only some people, and not others, will know about particular customer problems, market characteristics, or the ways to create particular products or services (Venkataraman, 1997). Shane (2000) argues that no university officer or government officer will be able to identify all entrepreneurial opportunities, and thus by granting an exclusive licence, a university precludes the possibility that a future entrepreneur will exploit a more valuable use for the technology.

Conclusion

In the university sector, creating and exploiting new commercial ideas are not part of the traditional core operations. At the same time, radically new ideas often have a university origin, and in the period following World War Two there has been an increased emphasis on different ways of exploiting and commercialising such inventions. This interest of policy makers is also reflected in a large number of earlier studies focusing on academic entrepreneurship and university spin-offs (see for example Roberts and Wainer, 1968; Roberts, 1991; Klofsten and Jones-Evans, 1996; Callan, 2001).

Some of the critical questions for policy makers were asked by Callan already in 2001: "Are there policies that can accelerate firm growth? Should policies distinguish between spin-offs which are essentially consulting firms or research boutiques, and spin-offs which aspire to rapid growth and product development?" (p. 37). These are still very important unanswered questions. A key question for governments and policy makers must be whether a policy should focus on helping the formation of a high number of academic spin-offs, or if it should help the formation of a few high-growing academic spin-offs. These policies, and the programmes necessary to accomplish them, ought to be quite different. If policies focus solely on the "gazelles" (*i.e.* the few highest-growing spin-offs), there is a risk of losing sight of the importance of the phenomenon (Mustar, 2001). Policy must be aware that it takes considerable time to create successful spin-offs out of university research. Transferring science and academic research into commercial products and firms often takes many years. The Swedish data presented in this chapter demonstrate that it takes considerable time, often over ten years, for academic spin-off firms to create substantial growth. This is confirmed by Powers and McDougall (2005), who concluded that the success of academic spin-offs improves over time. They argue that the learning that takes place within Technology Transfer Offices influence the performance. Before designing spin-off programmes, policy makers need to decide what they want to accomplish, and to tailor the policy in accordance to this. Programmes effective for creating both a high number of academic spin-offs and, at the same time, a high number of high-growth firms are not very likely – at least not without high costs.

Several regions (*e.g.* in Germany, Finland and Sweden) with low entrepreneurial activity are able to demonstrate high levels of academic spin-offs. Regions like this are often well aware of their weak entrepreneurial community and have designed policies to encourage the creation and development of academic spin-offs. Clarysse *et al.* (2005) label this a "technology push" strategy, where policies focus on offering support to venture creation and development in the spin-off process. The support has often been offered in incubators and science parks with links to the universities. In Sweden, such policies have been strongly influenced by a general belief that utilisation of the results of academic R&D have been poor. Since academic spin-offs are considered a central mechanism for transferring research results into the Swedish society, and the growth of academic spin-offs is considered a key indicator of their impact, this has led to the general conclusion that Swedish academic spin-offs are not very successful. The basis for this conclusion is, however, weak. There are, for example, no studies analysing the indirect effects of the mechanism; also, systematic international comparisons are missing. A successful shift away from a general encouragement of a high number of academic spin-offs toward a policy targeting future high-growth firms prove very expensive.

Even if the spin-offs are able to generate some employment opportunities themselves, and there are a handful of highly successful firms

(Mustar, 2001), this is not very likely to have a huge direct impact on economic growth and job generation in many countries: they are far too few. Instead, it might be that other indirect effects of academic spin-offs have more to do with economic growth. A major aspect is the role of mediator between universities and private industry. Another, perhaps even more important, is the behaviour of some spin-offs as research boutiques. Many academic spin-offs do not focus on commercialising innovations; instead, they sell their innovations to other firms which, in turn, might be better equipped to commercialise them. The author, however, knows of no serious attempt to analyse this aspect – future studies would be welcome and highly recommended. There is a need to know more about the role played by academic spin-offs in society, and about both the direct and the indirect effects.

Finally, and perhaps most important, a spin-off policy "leaves no room for half measures" (Mustar, 2001, p. 169). Earlier research suggests that a well-functioning spin-off policy should be either a) encouraging entrepreneurship in general, or b) a comprehensive, and costly, system focusing on the creation of high-growth firms. For example, Clarysse *et al.* (2005) found that incubators trying to support academic spin-offs, but not having the required resources, were the most unsuccessful; those with a (less costly) entrepreneurial enhancing policy were much better off. Thus, a spin-off policy should be very clear on whether it tries to encourage the creation of a high number of small entrepreneurial academic spin-offs, or if it is designed to facilitate the creation of a smaller number of highly growing firms. An intelligent spin-off policy also needs to both include a long time perspective and incorporate the nature of indirect economic effects. Before there is a better understanding of these mechanisms there is only limited value in designing programmes for spin-off financing, support services, business networks and so on.

Bibliography

Audretsch, D.B, and M.P. Feldman (1996), "R&D spill-overs and geography of innovation and production", *American Economic Review*, Vol. 86, No. 3, ABI/INFORM Global, pp. 630-640.

Autio, E. (1997), "New, technology-based firms in innovation networks: symplectic and generative impacts", *Research Policy*, Vol. 26, No. 3, Elsevier, pp. 263-281.

Bozeman, B. (2000), "Technology transfer and public policy: A review of research and theory", *Research Policy*, Vol. 29, No. 4-5, Elsevier, pp. 627-655.

Callan, B. (2001), "Generating spin-offs: Evidence from across the OECD", *STI Review*, Vol. 2000, No. 26, Organisation for Economic Co-operation and Development, pp. 14-54.

Chesbrough, H. (2003), Open Innovation: The New Imperative for Creating and Profiting from Technology, Harvard Business School Press.

Clarysse, B., *et al.* (2005), "Spinning out new ventures: A typology of incubation strategies from European research institutions", *Journal of Business Venturing*, Vol. 20, No. 2, Elsevier, pp. 183-216.

Colyvas, J., *et al.* (2002), "How Do University Inventions Get Into Practice?" *Management Science*, Vol. 48, No. 1, Institute for Operations Research and the Management Sciences, pp. 61-72.

Cooke, P. (1996), "The new wave of regional innovation networks: analysis, characteristics and strategy", *Small Business Economics*, Vol. 8, No. 2, Springer Netherlands, pp. 159-171.

DN (2005), "Två miljarder kronor satsas för att stärka innovationer", *Dagens Nyheter*, published February 18 (in Swedish).

Delmar, F, and J. Wiklund (2003), *The involvement in self-employment among the Swedish science and technology labour force between 1990 and 2000*, ITPS – Swedish Institute for Growth Policy Studies, Östersund.

Etzkowitz, H., *et al.* (2000), "The future of the university and the university of the future: evolution of ivory tower to entrepreneurial paradigm", *Research Policy*, Vol. 29, No. 2, Elsevier, pp. 313-330.

Garnsey, E. (1996), *Location of the High Technology Milieu - A Systems Approach*, working paper No. 6, Judge Institute of Management Studies and Department of Engineering, Cambridge University, UK.

Goldfarb, B. and M. Henrekson (2003), "Bottom-up versus top-down policies towards the commercialization of university intellectual property", *Research Policy*, Vol. 32, No. 4, Elsevier, pp. 639-658.

Granstrand, O. and S. Sjölander (1990), "The acquisition of technology and small firms by large firms", *Journal of Economic Behaviour and Organization*, Vol. 13, No. 3, Elsevier, pp. 367-386.

Henderson, R., A. Jaffe and M. Trajtenberg (1998), "Universities as a source of commercial technology: a detailed analysis of university patenting, 1965-1988", *The Review of Economics and Statistics*, Vol. 80, No. 1, MIT Press, pp. 119-127.

ITPS (2006), *Newly-started enterprises in Sweden 2004 and 2005*, ITPS – Swedish Institute for Growth Policy Studies, Östersund (in Swedish).

Jacobsson, S. and A. Rickne (1997), "New Technology Based Firms in Sweden - a study of their direct impact on industrial renewal", *Economics of Innovation and New Technology*, Vol. 8, No. 3, Routledge, pp.197-223.

Jensen, R. and M. Thursby (2001), "Proofs and Prototypes for sale: The tale of university licensing", *American Economic Review*, Vol. 91, No. 1, American Economic Association, pp. 240-259.

Keeble, D., *et al.* (1998), *Collective Learning Processes and Inter-Firm Networking in Innovative High-Technology Regions*, working paper No. 86, ESRC Centre for Business Research, University of Cambridge, Cambridge.

Klofsten, M. and D. Jones-Evans (1996), "Stimulation of Technology-based Small Firms – A Case Study of University-Industry Co-Operation", *Technovation*, Vol. 16, No. 4, Elsevier, pp. 187-193.

Kung, S.-F. (1995), "The role of science parks in the development of high technology industries, with special reference to Taiwan", PhD dissertation, St. Catherine's College, Cambridge University.

Lindholm Dahlstrand, Å. (1996), *Acquisition and Growth of Technology-Based Firms*, working paper No. 47, ESRC Centre for Business Research, University of Cambridge.

Lindholm Dahlstrand, Å. (2001) "Entrepreneurial Origin and Spin-Off Performance: A Comparison between Corporate and University Spin-offs", in P. Moncada-Paternò-Castello *et al.* (eds.) *Corporate and Research-based Spin-offs: Drivers for Knowledge-based Innovation and Entrepreneurship*, IPTS Technical Report Series, European Commission, Brussels.

Lindholm Dahlstrand, Å. (2004), *Teknikbaserat nyföretagande, tillväxt och affärsutveckling*, Studentlitteratur, Lund (in Swedish).

Lööf, H. (2005), *Vad ger samarbetet mellan universitet och näringsliv, Tillväxtpolitisk utblick*, ITPS – Swedish Institute for Growth Policy Studies, Östersund (in Swedish).

Mansfield, E. (1998), "Academic research and industrial innovation: An update of empirical findings", *Research Policy,* Vol. 26, No. 7-8, Elsevier, pp. 773-776.

Markman, G., *et al.* (2005), "Entrepreneurship and university-based technology transfer", *Journal of Business Venturing*, Vol. 20, No. 2, Elsevier, pp. 241-263.

Massing, D. (2001), "The AUTM Survey; Its development and use in monitoring commercialisation in North America", *STI Review*, Vol. 2000, No. 26, OECD, Paris, pp. 57- 73.

Matkin, G.W. (2001), "Spinning off in the United States: Why and how?", *STI Review*, Vol. 2000, No, 26, OECD, Paris, pp. 97-119.

Mian, S.A, (1994), "US university-sponsored technology incubators: An overview of management and performance", *Technovation,* Vol. 14, No. 8, Elsevier, pp. 515-528.

Mowery, D., *et al.* (2001), "The growth of patenting and licensing by US universities: An assessment of the effects of the Bayh-Dole act of 1980", *Research Policy*, Vol. 30, No. 1, Elsevier, pp. 99-119.

Mustar, P. (2001), "Spin-offs from public research: Trends and outlook", *STI Review*, Vol. 2000, No. 26, OECD, Paris, pp. 165-172.

Olofsson, C., and C. Wahlbin (1993), *Teknikbaserade företag från högskolan*, Slutrapport till näringsdepartementet, IMIT (in Swedish).

Pavitt, K. (1998), "The social shaping of the national science base", *Research Policy,* Vol. 27, No. 8, Elsevier, pp. 793-805.

Powers, J. and P. McDougall (2005), "University start-up formation and technology licensing with firms that go public: A resource-based view of academic entrepreneurship", *Journal of Business Venturing*, Vol. 20, No. 3, Elsevier, pp. 291-311.

Regeringen (2005), "Regeringens proposition 2004/05:80 Forskning för ett bättre liv", Utbildnings och kulturdepartementet, Stockholm (in Swedish).

Reynolds, P., *et al.* (2002), *General Entrepreneurship Monitor 2002,* GEM, Kaufmann Foundation, Kansas City, MI.

Roberts, E.B. (1991), *Entrepreneurs in high technology,* Oxford University Press Inc., New York.

Roberts, E.B. and H.A. Wainer (1968), "New enterprises on Route 128", *Science Journal*, Vol. 4, No. 12, pp. 78-83.

Rosenberg, N. and R. Nelson (1994), "American universities and technical advance in industry", *Research Policy*, Vol. 23, No. 3, Elsevier, pp. 323-348.

Shane, S. (2000), "Prior Knowledge and the Discovery of Entrepreneurial Opportunities", *Organization Science*, Vol. 11, No 4, pp 448-469.

Shane, S. (2004), "Encouraging university entrepreneurship? The effect of the Bayh-Dole Act on university patenting in the United States", *Journal of Business Venturing*, Vol. 19, No. 1, Elsevier, pp. 127-151.

Sternberg, R. (1996), "Technology Policies and Growth of Regions: Evidence from Four Countries", *Small Business Economics*, Vol. 8, No. 2, Springer Netherlands, pp. 75-86.

Storper, M. (1995), "The Resurgence of Regional Economies, Ten Years Later: The Region as a Nexus of Untraded Interdependencies", *European Urban and Regional Studies,* Vol. 2, No. 3, Sage, pp. 191-221.

Venkataraman, S. (1997), "The distinctive domain of entrepreneurship research: An editor's perspective", in J. Katz and R. Brockhaus (eds.), *Advances in Entrepreneurship, Firm Emergence, and Growth*, JAI Press, Greenwich, Connecticut.

VINNOVA (2002), VINNOVAs Verksamhetsplanering 2003-2007, VINNOVA Policy VP 2002:03, www.vinnova.se/upload/EPiStorePDF/vp-02-03.pdf, (in Swedish).

Chapter 11

Technology Commercialisation and Universities in Canada

by
Rod B. McNaughton
University of Waterloo, Canada

This chapter describes the institutional arrangements and policy structure of the Canadian university sector as they relate to transferring technology to industry and promoting entrepreneurship among students and the community. In addition to teaching and research, Canadian universities are increasingly expected to be agents of economic development and to commercialise the outcomes of research. Universities experience tension in trying to fulfil this expectation. They are keen to diversify revenue, but debate the fit of commercialisation with their mandate. Further, traditional systems of collegial governance and tenure-based incentives can inhibit commercialisation. The University of Waterloo's successful record of spinning out companies and interacting closely with its community serves as an example of good practice. There is increased interest in entrepreneurship-related courses, and substantial growth in the number and diversity of offerings. The Master of Business, Entrepreneurship and Technology programme introduced by the University of Waterloo serves as an example. Finally, the policy implications of the Canadian experience are discussed.

ENTREPRENEURSHIP AND HIGHER EDUCATION – ISBN- 9789264044098 © OECD 2008

Introduction

In November 2002 the Association of Universities and Colleges of Canada (AUCC) signed an historic memorandum of agreement with the government of Canada on the federal funding of university research. In the agreement, the AUCC pledged that its 93 member institutions would collectively double the research they perform, triple their commercialisation performance by 2010, increase graduate training, and contribute to the economic and social development of their communities. In return, the government promised to provide "…the necessary levels of investment in university research to achieve these aims, including ongoing contributions to the indirect costs of research" (AUCC, 2002, p. 1).

The agreement is a unique expression of partnership between universities and government to advance the emerging mandate for commercialisation of the intellectual property created within publicly funded universities. Reimbursement for the indirect costs of conducting research funded by the three major federal granting councils was a long-term lobbying objective for universities. From the government point of view, the agreement is part of a national Innovation Strategy, launched in February 2002 with the vision of Canada "…becoming one of the most innovative countries in the world and among the five most research intensive nations of the world" (AUCC, 2002, p. 1).

The importance of commercialising university research for the sake of both the economy and university finances is a frequent theme in discussions among Canadian university administrators, communities, business, and government. All universities engage to some extent in commercialisation activities, but many are renewing and expanding their commitment. Their initiatives include helping to foster entrepreneurial attitudes and skills in faculty and staff; identifying sources of funds for applied research and prototype development; bringing together technology and business resources in incubators; and offering innovative new entrepreneurship degrees. These developments are in part spurred by government policy and in part by the need to develop additional sources of revenue to support university operations. This chapter provides an overview of the context of the Canadian university sector, university technology transfer, and degree programmes designed to increase the level of innovation in Canada.

The context of Canadian universities

Canada offers diverse higher education options at its universities and university colleges. Universities range from small campuses with a liberal arts focus to large metropolitan universities with comprehensive and professional programmes. There are 92 universities located across the country, with at least one in each province, and 29 in Ontario – the most populous province.

Education, including the tertiary sector, is primarily the responsibility of the provinces and territories. There is no federal ministry of education or formal accreditation system. Instead, membership in the Association of Universities and Colleges of Canada, coupled with the university's provincial government charter, is generally deemed the equivalent. Canadian degrees are globally recognised and considered equivalent to those from institutions in the United States and Commonwealth universities.

Canadian universities rely heavily on government funding for their operating budgets. The proportion of the budget coming from tuition fees varies by province and programme. In most cases students pay at least 25% of programme costs, and the trend is to increase this proportion. For example, the total expendable funds for Ontario universities in 2002-03 was CAD 6.7 billion, of which 35% came from provincial grants, 11% from the federal government, 30% from tuition fees, 18% from sales and donations, and 4% from investments (Rae, 2005).

There is considerable variability among provinces on tuition policy. For example, British Columbia recently rescinded a tuition freeze and universities are rapidly escalating their fees, while a recent budget in Ontario extended the tuition freeze in that province for another two years.

Canadian universities, and especially those in Ontario, are not well funded compared to comparator jurisdictions in the United States. Total provincial expenditures on post-secondary education, when measured on a per capita and constant dollar basis, are below the level of the early 1990s. Among the provinces, government expenditures on post-secondary education in 2002-03 were highest in Manitoba (CAD 509), Quebec (CAD 504), Newfoundland (CAD 480) and Saskatchewan (CAD 472) (CAUT, 2004). Expenditures were lowest in Ontario (CAD 324) and Alberta (CAD 354). Federal cash transfers to the provinces to assist in funding post-secondary education, when adjusted for inflation and population growth, are 50% lower than at the beginning of the 1990s (CAUT, 2004).

Funding of university research, science and technology

Federal involvement with universities is primarily through transfers to the provinces, and the direct provision of research funding. There are three principal federal granting agencies: the Natural Sciences and Engineering Research Council, the Social Sciences and Humanities Research Council and the Canadian Institute for Health Research. Funds are distributed through a competitive peer review system. In 1997, the federal government created the Canada Foundation for Innovation (CFI). The CFI is an arm's-length independent corporation mandated to rebuild and reinvest in research labs, installations and facilities in universities and teaching hospitals across the country. The Canada Research Chairs programme provides support for 2 000 positions for top university-based researchers (at a cost of CAD 900 million). The federal government also committed CAD 300 million to Genome Canada for the creation of five research centres across the country. Each of these centres brings together industry, governments, universities, hospitals, research institutes and the public to build a genomics research infrastructure, and to provide leadership in ethical, environmental, legal and social issues related to genomics.

In both the December 2001 and the February 2003 federal budgets, the annual budgets of Canada's university research granting agencies were increased. Specifically in 2001, the budgets of the Natural Sciences and Engineering Research Council (NSERC) and of the Social Sciences and Humanities Research Council (SSHRC) were increased by 7% each, resulting in an additional CAD 36.5 million per year for NSERC and CAD 9.5 million per year for SSHRC. The 2001 Budget also provided a CAD 75 million per year increase to the annual budget of the Canadian Institutes of Health Research (CIHR). In February 2003, the government further increased its support for the three granting councils – NSERC, SSHRC and CIHR – by CAD 125 million per year. The combined annual budget of these councils was CAD 1.3 billion in 2002-03.

Provincial governments also invest in university research. In contrast to the Research Councils, provincial programmes often target specific industries, and try to engage universities and businesses in partnership. Ontario, for example, invests through its "Centres of Excellence" programme, which promotes economic development through research, commercialisation and graduate training. The Centres operate by creating and managing relationships between industry and universities from research through to the market. Recently merged into a single organisational structure, the Centres consist of: Communications and Information Technology Ontario, the Centre for Research in Earth and Space Technology, Materials and Manufacturing Ontario, Photonics Research Ontario, and Centre for Energy. The Centres have invested more than CAD 70 million and involve 2 400 researchers and 800 firms in projects. Outcomes include 47 technology licences granted to industry, 126 technology licences "in-force", and 19 new companies created (OCE, 2005).

The "new" mandate of universities: Technology commercialisation

Canadian universities were traditionally viewed as an independent forum for debate and criticism; there was little consideration of their economic impact (CAUT, 1999a). This view is changing and universities are increasingly expected to take a leading role in fostering commercialisation and economic development (Advisory Council on Science and Technology, 1999; AUCC, 1995, 1998, 2001). This shift in public expectations is accompanied by a similar shift in funding requirements. Funding is scarcer, often project-specific, and frequently comes with the expectation that commercialised technology will result (AUCC, 2001).

There is increased public identification of the need to commercialise university knowledge (AUCC, 2001; Industry Canada Innovation and Policy Branch, 1999). For example, a number of Industry Canada reports recommend that grants and other funding be tied to the commercialisation potential of research activities (Industry Canada Innovation and Policy Branch, 1999; Advisory Council on Science and Technology, 1999).

Many universities address their funding gap through increases in student enrolment and tuition fees (CAUT, 1999a). However, universities have also responded with a range of other actions, for example, business incubator activities, patenting and licensing, and university-based business consulting. Studies looking at these initiatives find that universities are able to generate increased revenues from new venture spin-offs (Bray and Lee, 2000) as well as from patenting and licensing (Mowery, Nelson, and Sampat, 2001). Furthermore, university contacts with industry open doors for consulting (Rainsford, 1992; Stocker, 1996), which in turn enriches and supplements university course work (Mallick and Chaudhury, 2000; Badawy, 1998).

Of the approximate CAD 22 billion of R&D performed in Canada in 2003, about 35% is conducted in universities (Thompson, 2004). The Survey of Electronic Commerce and Technology 2003 (SECT) identified about 3 000 firms that acquired technology from a Canadian university. It estimates that 1 400 firms licensed technologies from universities over the preceding three years, and 1 350 firms considered themselves as spin-offs from Canadian universities. According to SECT, about 25% of university spin-offs were healthcare and social assistance firms, followed by firms in other services (except public administration), waste management and remediation services, and professional, scientific and technical services.

The Association of University Technology Managers (AUTM) conducts an annual survey of technology commercialisation by US and Canadian universities. The latest survey (FY 2004) shows that Canadian research institutions experienced considerable growth in research expenditures since

FY 2002 (18.8%). Technology transfer activity (products brought to market) increased 11.5%, invention disclosures increased 9.1%, new licences and options increased 23.8%, and licence income increased 20.7% compared to FY 2002. Fifty-one companies were founded in 2004 to commercialise university research. Overall, the latest survey concludes that on a per-research expenditure basis, Canadian technology transfer is more people-intensive, selective, cost-effective, and creates more start-ups than in the United States (AUTM, 2004).

Clayman (2000), having analysed AUTM surveys and the case studies of four university technology transfer organisations, concluded that there is a linear relationship between the amount of technology that is measurably transferred from universities and research expenditures. He also found that local conditions, especially provision of resources and support for staff dedicated to technology transfer, are a major determinant of the effectiveness of technology transfer. However, he also concluded that there is no evidence of ownership of intellectual property by universities resulting in more or better technology transfer. In fact, the universities that claim ownership of IP have an inferior record of commercialisation activity.

Case Study: University technology transfer in Canada's Technology Triangle

Canada's Technology Triangle (CTT) consists of the cities of Waterloo, Kitchener and Cambridge, co-located in southwestern Ontario. The region has a population of over 450 000 and an annual economic output of over CAD 12 billion in 2001 (PricewaterhouseCoopers Canada, 2001). This area has a high concentration of technology businesses. Among more than 12 000 incorporated businesses in Waterloo Region, 958 either produce or facilitate technologies. Forty-five per cent of total area growth in employment is in the technology sector (PricewaterhouseCoopers Canada, 2001).

Universities and research institutions have an outstanding impact on the economic and technology development in this region. The Waterloo Region embraces more than 150 research centres and institutions affiliated with three world renowned universities – the University of Waterloo (UW), Wilfrid Laurier University (WLU), and the University of Guelph (UG). The province's highest-ranked college, Conestoga College, is also located in the region. With over CAD 6 billion in revenue, the high-tech sector is a major component of the local economy – much of it emanating from, and encouraged by, the local universities.

UW and UG act as knowledge generators for the CTT cluster. UW and UG were founded in 1957 and 1964 respectively. Since 1973, the University of Waterloo has spun off 59 high technology firms, 28% of the total number of high technology firms born within the cluster. The two universities in total have generated more than one third (36%) of the cluster's firms during the past 45 years.

Supporting, encouraging and teaching entrepreneurship at universities

Universities like UW that are heavily involved in technology transfer have a comprehensive set of activities to foster entrepreneurship among faculty and students. They provide education dealing with entrepreneurship and the commercialisation process; manage the technology transfer process; and incubate spin-out companies. Almost all universities have a technology transfer unit; its size and importance vary with the size of the university, the relative strength of faculties, and the university intellectual property policy. Intellectual property (IP) policy is an important influence on the incentive to commercialise university research, and the manner in which commercialisation is pursued (*e.g.* start-up versus licensing). In Canada, ownership of university research is largely determined by institutional policy. These policies range from inventor ownership to institutional ownership, with both extremes being rare. Most universities have policies that allocate ownership between the institution, the creator, and the department in which the research was conducted. Some funding agencies and industrial contracts include negotiation of IP rights as part of the funding process.

In addition to the technology transfer office, universities may also have investments in research parks, incubators, or "pre-incubators" that provide support for the very-early-stage commercial ideas of faculty, students and alumni. A small number of universities, most notably the University of British Columbia (UBC), have venture funds. Another model, represented by the University of Guelph, is to raise money for commercialisation by listing the university's intellectual property portfolio on the stock market. (The company called GUARD Inc. was delisted in 2002.) Other activities include entrepreneurship boot camps, mentoring programmes, entrepreneurship resource centres, and various short courses targeted at alumni and local small business owners. A final category of activity is student societies. A variety of student groups interested in entrepreneurship and business operate on Canadian university campuses. The group with the most substantial national presence (on 47 campuses) is Advancing Canadian Entrepreneurship (ACE).

Universities also include entrepreneurship and innovation within their curriculum in the form of credit courses and degree programmes. There are approximately 21 undergraduate entrepreneurship degree programmes in Canada. Teressa Menzies, a faculty member at Brock University, conducts a periodic survey of entrepreneurship courses and related activities at Canadian universities. Her 2004 survey found that entrepreneurship courses are growing in popularity, and every university in Canada offers at least one entrepreneurship course. The province of Quebec particularly stands out as having the largest number of entrepreneurship enrolments, the most variety in entrepreneurship courses, and the highest average number of undergraduate entrepreneurship courses (6.5 undergraduate courses per university, compared with 4.3 in Ontario, 4.1 in the Eastern provinces, and 3.0 in the West). Across Canada, the most common undergraduate course is "Introduction to Entrepreneurship", followed by "New Venture Creation" and "Technological Entrepreneurship".

The majority of undergraduate entrepreneurship courses – 84% – are offered by faculties of business, 12% by faculties of engineering, and the remainder by a range of other faculties. This situation is supported by 60% of the deans surveyed, with only 16% expressing the view that every faculty should offer entrepreneurship courses. One implication is that the majority of entrepreneurship courses are taken by students in business programmes, and relatively few courses are available to students in disciplines where there is a higher potential for technology-based start-ups.

A number of recent reports identify weakness in Canada's record of managing and mobilising entrepreneurial and technological opportunities into commercially viable products (Canadian Manufacturers and Exporters Association, 2001; Conference Board of Canada, 2001; Porter and Martin, 2001). A common theme in these reports is that Canadian business leaders and managers have not adequately shifted their thinking toward entrepreneurial activities and, when they do, they lack the managerial, marketing and financing skills to bring innovations to commercial success. For example, Nixon (quoted by Little, 2005) argued, "Canadian business leaders – in small, medium and large companies - lack the culture of innovation to take their companies to the next level".

A survey by the Financial Post and Compass (2001) of leaders of small, medium and large corporations and executives of the local and national chambers of commerce indicated dissatisfaction with MBA programmes and the skills of their graduates. The report argued that universities should consider offering new, niche degrees differentiated from an MBA. An associated article questioned the need for 39 MBA programmes in Canada and argued that (1) the high number of MBA programmes explains the trend toward mediocrity and replication in business education, and (2) there is a need to move away from the MBA model. These observations by Canadian business and media leaders echo the questions raised about MBA education in general by respected business academics Mintzberg (2004) and Pfeffer and Fong (2002).

Case Study: Master of Business, Entrepreneurship and Technology programme

In response to demand for business education focused on developing leaders of innovation and commercialisation, Canadian universities are designing and launching new niche degrees that provide specialised graduate business experiences. An example is the Master of Business, Entrepreneurship and Technology degree (MBET) launched by the University of Waterloo in 2003. The curricula were developed during a series of retreats with faculty and members of an advisory council consisting of successful entrepreneurs, and aspects of the programme were trialled with focus groups of potential students.

The outcome is a unique "education adventure" that is differentiated from existing graduate business opportunities, in Canada and internationally. The programme adopted a new venture life cycle model to structure the curriculum into ten courses that each extend over twelve months, and deliver knowledge "just in time" during seed/concept, product development and market expansion stages (Figure 11.1). The goal is to provide exceptional people who have a technology background along with the business knowledge, soft skills and networks they need to commercialise their ideas. Other innovative features include:

- A commercialisation practicum in which students start to develop their business, or help an existing business commercialise a new technology-based product or service.

- Integration among disciplinary areas in the curriculum, including an online integrated case each term that is specially written about a new technology developed at UW.

- Student attendance at seminars and networking events offered by Communitech (the technology industry association in the Waterloo Region).

The MBET programme simulates the entrepreneurial process – concept/seed, product and market development – and introduces subject matter, not in a traditional discipline-centric or term-by-term fashion, but as it is required for a particular phase in the entrepreneurial process. There is heavy emphasis on the "doing" element. Material in each subject area is presented in modules that support the actual entrepreneurial effort. The primary purpose of class work is to support outside study and further the development of ideas.

In their final two terms, students work with real technologies and have the opportunity to produce assessments and plans for bringing new technologies to market. This commercialisation practicum involves working with company sponsors and industry advisors in southwestern Ontario. Each team's final project – which may include market research, a design for a product, profiles of desired management teams, licensing plans, technology or market assessment, and/or a business plan – is submitted to the institution that originated the technology. The practicum gives students insights and experience in the early stages of entrepreneurial technology commercialisation, various aspects of company formation and finance, and technology licensing and intellectual property issues.

Figure 11.1. Model of MBET curriculum

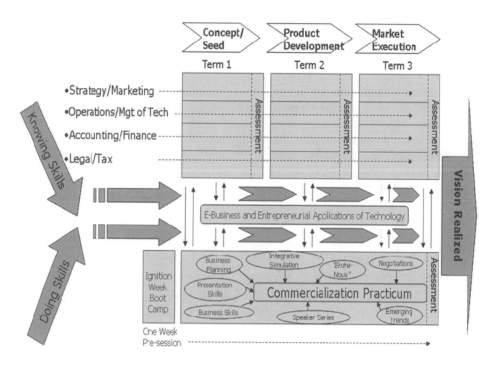

University technology transfer challenges in Canada

The federal government's agreement with the AUCC to triple commercialisation outcomes provides impetus for the expansion of such activities. However, the vision of economic development through greatly increased transfers of knowledge from universities to the private sector faces challenges:

- It is difficult to create and implement national strategies for university technology transfer, as the provinces are primarily responsible for universities. The federal government made the environment more attractive for university research by expanding the budgets of the research councils, creating new programmes like the Canada Research Chairs, and targeting a few areas like genomics for special funding. There is no easy way to create a consistent commercialisation framework for university research, nor to co-ordinate, rationalise or otherwise strategically direct the technology transfer process. One result is a proliferation of programmes at federal, provincial and local levels to assist university-industry collaboration and technology transfer. A report prepared for the Innovation Strategy found over 150 programmes whose objective was to increase innovation.

- The environment does not have absorptive capacity. The Canadian economy is relatively small, with approximately 32 million people. There are relatively few large firms, and even fewer in the technology-based sectors. Many firms are branches or subsidiaries of US companies and do not have an R&D mandate. The SECT 2003 survey found that only 8% of firms had ever licensed a technology. The most common way of acquiring technology was purchasing an off-the-shelf solution. Universities typically transfer technology through licences to large firms, or start-ups associated with the creator of the technology.

- Little attention is paid to changing the internal structure and incentives for commercialisation within universities. Canada retains a tenure-based system in which commercialisation activities are given little weight. Pressures to publish create problems for protecting IP, and there are few systematic processes for managing IP. Some universities make it difficult for faculty to take leaves or make flexible arrangements to spend time transferring intangible knowledge to industry, or to devote periods to establishing their own businesses. In addition, many faculty members do not support the notion of commercialisation as a university mandate, and vocally express their concern that this threatens the independence of universities and the notion of collegial governance.

- Universities are looking to commercialisation as a new source of revenue to offset declining government grants for degree programmes. The emphasis on revenue instead of investment means that universities often overvalue their technologies, and demand upfront payment on licences. Further, as ancillary services, technology transfer offices rarely receive budgets commensurate with their revenue generating potential, and staff does not have participatory incentive schemes. Some universities claim significant ownership of IP, reducing the incentive for faculty to disclose their inventions and creating equity dilution problems for spin-outs.

- Entrepreneurship education is not a priority and is largely captured within business faculties where business students take it as an elective. There is no concerted effort to introduce entrepreneurship across the curriculum (as there is with internationalisation, for example). In particular, it would be useful to expose science and technology students to the processes of commercialisation, and help them to develop skills for dealing with industry and making the process of transferring technology smoother and faster.

Conclusion

Despite the challenges, the Canadian experience does illustrate some unique approaches to supporting and providing incentives for university-industry collaboration and technology transfer. The first of these is the notion of a national Innovation Strategy, with clear objectives and negotiated buy-in from the university sector. A second lesson is that commercialisation of university research is a public good, and public investment is needed to encourage the process and underwrite some of the risk. Third, it is difficult to change universities from the outside. None of the approaches tried so far in Canada is aimed at changing the organisational structure of universities, their governance system or faculty incentives to make universities more entrepreneurially oriented. Finally, the potential role of entrepreneurship education needs to be emphasised to educate the next generation of scientists and technologists about the technology-industry interface and the commercialisation process.

Bibliography

AUCC (Association of Universities and Colleges of Canada) (1995), "A Primer on Performance Indicators", *Research File, Vol.* 1, No. 2, Association of Universities and Colleges of Canada, Ottawa.

AUCC (1998), "The Economic Impact of University Research", *Research File*, Vol. 2, No. 3, Association of Universities and Colleges of Canada, Ottawa.

AUCC (2001), *Background Report on the Facilities and Institutional Support Costs Incurred by Canadian Universities in conducting Federally Sponsored Research*, Association of Universities and Colleges of Canada, Ottawa.

AUCC (2001), *Commercialization of University Research*, Association of Universities and Colleges, Ottawa.

AUCC (2002), *Framework of agreed principles on federally funded university research between the government of Canada and the association of universities and colleges of Canada*, Association of Universities and Colleges of Canada, Ottawa.

Advisory Council on Science and Technology (1999), *Public Investments in University Research: Reaping the Benefits*, report of the Expert Panel on the Commercialization of University Research, Industry Canada, Ottawa.

AUTM (Association of University Technology Managers) (n.d.), *AUTM Licensing Survey: Fiscal years 1999-2004*, Association of University Technology Managers, Deerfield, Illinois.

Badawy, M. (1998), "Technology Management Education: Alternative Models", *California Management Review*, Vol. 40, No. 3, Haas School of Business, University of California, Berkley, pp. 94-116.

Bordt, M. and L. Earl (2004), *Public Sector technology transfer in Canada, 2003*, Science, Innovation and Electronic Information Division Working Papers, No. 18, Statistics Canada – Canada's National Statistical Agency, Ottawa.

Bray, M. J., and J.N. Lee (2000), "University Revenues from Technology Transfer: Licensing Fees vs. Equity Positions", *Journal of Business Venturing*, Vol. 15, No. 5-6, Elsevier, pp.385-392.

Canadian Manufacturers and Exporters (2001), *The Business Case for Innovation*, www.cme-mec.ca/national/documents/caseforinnovation.pdf

CAUT (Canadian Association of University Teachers) (1999a), *CAUT Commentary on the Final Report of the Expert Panel on the Commercialization of University Research,* Canadian Association of University Teachers, Ottawa.

CAUT (1999b), "Commercialization Report Trivializes University Research", *CAUT Now,* Vol. 1, No. 4, Canadian Association of University Teachers, Ottawa.

CAUT (2004), "The Funding Shortfall: government expenditures on post-secondary education, 2002/03", *CAUT Education Review,* Vol. 6, No. 1, Canadian Association of University Teachers, pp. 1-5.

Clayman, B. (2000), *Technology transfer at Canadian universities*, a report for the Canadian Foundation for Innovation, Ottawa.

Conference Board of Canada (2001), *Investing In Innovation: 3rd Annual Innovation Report*, Conference Board of Canada, Ottawa.

COMPAS Inc (2001), "M.B.A.s, Business Schools, and their Marketing Challenges", *Financial Post*, December 21, http://www.compas.ca/polls/011221-BLMBA-PB.htm.

Gault, F. and S. McDaniel (2004), *Summary: joint Statistics Canada-University of Windsor Workshop on Intellectual Property Commercialization Indicators,* Science, Innovation and Electronic Information Division Working Papers, No. 6, Statistics Canada – Canada's National Statistical Agency, Ottawa.

Government of Canada (2001), *Achieving Excellence, Investing in People, Knowledge and Opportunity: Canada's Innovation Strategy,* Industry Canada, Ottawa.

Industry Canada Innovation and Policy Branch (1999), *The Commercialization of University Research in Canada: A Discussion Paper*, The Canadian Institute for Advanced Research, Toronto.

Little, B. (2005), "RBC's Nixon takes aim at Corporate Canada's competitive failures", *Globe & Mail*, published May 9, Toronto.

Mallick, D.N., and A. Chaudhury (2000), "Technology Management Education in MBA Programs: a Comparative Study of Knowledge and Skill Requirements", *Journal of Engineering and Technology Management*, Vol. 17, No. 2, Elsevier, pp. 153-173.

Martin, R. L. and M. E. Porter (2000), *Canadian Competitiveness; Nine Years after the Crossroads,* Rotman School of Business, Toronto.

Menzies, T. (2004), *Entrepreneurship and the Canadian Universities: Report of a National Study of Entrepreneurship Education*, Brock University, St. Catharines, Ontario.

Mintzberg, H. (2004), *Managers not MBA's: A Hard Look at the Soft Practice of Managing and Management Development*, Berrett and Koehler Publishers, San Francisco.

Mowery, D.C., R.R. Nelson, and B.N. Sampat (2001), "The Growth of Patenting and Licensing by U.S. Universities: An assessment of the effects of the Boyh-Dole Act of 1980", *Research Policy,* Vol. 30, No. 1, Elsevier, pp. 99-119.

OCE (2005), Ontario Centres of Excellence, www.oce-ontario.org.

Pfeffer, J., and C. T. Fong (2002), "The end of business schools? Less success than meets the eye", *Academy of Management Learning & Education*, Vol. 1, No. 1, Academy of Management, pp. 78-95.

PricewaterhouseCoopers Canada (2001), *University of Waterloo: Regional Economic Benefits Study,* University of Waterloo.

Rae, B. (2005), *Ontario – a leader in learning*: *Report and Recommendations*, Ministry of Education, Ontario.

Rainsford, P. (1992), "The Small Business Institute: Hands-On Learning", *Cornell Hotel and Restaurant Administration Quarterly,* Vol. 33, No. 4, Sage, pp. 73-76.

Read, C. (2003), *Survey of intellectual property commercialization in the higher education sector, 2001*, Science, Innovation and Electronic Information Division Working Papers, No. 12, Statistics Canada – Canada's National Statistical Agency, Ottawa.

Statistics Canada (2004), "What's up, docs?", Innovation *Analysis Bulletin*, Vol. 6, No. 3 (October), Statistics Canada – Canada's National Statistical Agency, Ottawa.

Stocker, S. (1996), "Training future consultants", *Journal of Management Consulting*, Vol. 9, No. 1, pp. 39-44.

Thompson, J. (2004), *Estimates of Canadian research and development expenditures (GERD) Canada 1992-2003, and by province 1992-2001*, Science, Innovation and Electronic Information Division Working Papers, No. 3, Statistics Canada – Canada's National Statistical Agency, Ottawa.

Zieminski, J. and J. Warda (1999), *Paths to commercialization of university research – collaborative research*, Conference Board of Canada, Ottawa.

Chapter 12

Promoting Innovation in Slovenia Through Knowledge Transfer to SMEs

by
Will Bartlett
University of Bristol, United Kingdom

Vladimir Bukvič
CIMOS d.d. avtomobilska industrija, Slovenia

Slovenia has sustained a relatively high level of public expenditure on research and development and a relatively large proportion of employees and value added in high technology manufacturing compared to the EU average. However, innovation among SMEs is relatively low compared to the average in EU member states. This chapter reviews the Slovenian government's innovation policy framework and the extensive programme to promote knowledge transfer from institutions of higher education and research to the business sector. The review covers policies towards SME incubators, technology parks, technology centres, technology networks, industrial clusters, financial subsidies for high technology SMEs, and the mobility programme for young researchers. The research is based on documentary evidence and interviews, and presents case studies of an innovative university-based incubator and a successful industrial cluster in the automotive industry. It concludes with a number of suggestions for policy measures to improve the transfer of knowledge from HEIs to SMEs.

Introduction

Under the socialist system in the former Yugoslavia, Slovenia had a strong research capacity within large self-managed enterprises. Following the break-up of Yugoslavia and the collapse of the self-management system, many of the research teams that had been employed in the business sector were dispersed. Fortunately, the science capacity of public research institutes and universities was preserved and Slovenia managed to maintain a greater research capability in its public research sector than most other accession states in Eastern Europe. Slovenia currently has a relatively high rate of public investment in research and development (R&D), equal to the EU average (EC, 2004a). However, the bulk of research personnel are still employed in the public sector. In 2001 only one-quarter of Slovenian researchers were employed in R&D units in private manufacturing and service industries (MoE, 2003), and R&D expenditure by the private sector is relatively low compared to the average in the EU (EC, 2004a). Innovation surveys have shown that although one-fifth of enterprises are innovation-active, SMEs are less innovative than large companies (SORS, 2004; EC, 2004a). Slovenia also has a poor record in patenting and the commercialisation of research activity (EC, 2004b).

The public science research sector consists of two established universities at Ljubljana and Maribor, which host 39 research institutes, laboratories and clinics, and a third university established at Koper in 2003. There are a further 56 state-owned research institutes that employ more than 3 000 R&D personnel. The largest of these are the Chemical Institute and the Jozef Stefan Institute (covering natural and technical sciences, technology and engineering), both located in Ljubljana. Various studies have pointed to the wide gap between the public research sector and the business community, and low level of co-operation and knowledge transfer between universities and the business sector (Bučar, 2004; EC, 2004a). What co-operation exists between research institutes and the business sector is mainly directed towards larger firms rather than towards SMEs; universities are more likely to co-operate with public administration institutions than with the business sector. Only 5% of innovation-active firms reported that they consider universities to be an important source of information, while research institutes are even less important (Koschatzky, 2002). A significant obstacle to knowledge transfer from higher education institutions (HEIs) to industry has been the focus on publications in academic journals as an indicator for promotion, rather than involvement in HEI-industry links. According to a recent influential report, "universities are still primarily teaching rather than research institutions…What matters for career progress are publications and citations rather than practical applicability of research accomplishments" (GEM Monitor, 2002, p. 26).

This chapter reviews the Slovenian government's innovation policy framework and the extensive programme to promote the transfer of knowledge from institutions of higher education and research to the business sector. It concludes with a number of suggestions for policy measures to improve knowledge transfer from HEIs to SMEs.

The policy framework for knowledge transfer

Slovenia has developed a clear framework to support the design and implementation of science and technology policy. The National Science and Technology Council is the leading policy-making body. It has six members each from the research community, the Ministry of Economy and the business sector and one representative each from civil society and the researchers' union; it is chaired by the Prime Minister. Following widespread consultations, it reports to the Ministry of Education, Science and Technology, on the basis of which the ministry adopts the National Research and Development Programme (NRDP). The current NRDP specifies that research institutes are required to demonstrate the financial participation of business partners in new research projects. This is intended to enhance co-operation between research institutes and the business sector.

In the 1990s the technology field was under the responsibility of the Ministry of Science and Technology, which established a Technology Development Fund to provide venture capital to high technology small enterprises. (The Fund was later merged within the Slovenian Development Corporation.) Two technology parks were established in 1995 backed by research institutions, companies and the ministry. In 2000 a new Ministry of Education, Science and Sport was established and responsibility for technology was transferred to the Ministry of Economy, which introduced several measures to support knowledge transfer, entrepreneurship and competitiveness. The Programme of Measures to Promote Entrepreneurship and Competitiveness 2002-2006, adopted in 2002, established three basic sub-programmes focused on the stimulation of innovation, investments in knowledge, and technological development. These sub-programmes supported the creation of business incubators at universities, the development of technology networks and technology parks, joint research projects between HEIs and business enterprises, and support for the development of industrial clusters and networks of enterprises, universities and research institutions.

The Knowledge for Development sub-programme aimed to improve knowledge transfer from universities and research institutions to the business sector. It included measures to promote the establishment of business incubators in universities and research institutes; to support research infrastructure by co-financing enterprises for equipment used in R&D projects with research institutes; and to promote the entry of young university researchers into industry. The overall aim was to further co-operation between HEIs and the business sector, and to speed up the transfer and commercialisation of knowledge.

The second sub-programme on Improving Enterprises' Competitive Capacity supported the creation of industrial clusters involving both research institutes and businesses, and the establishment of technology centres and technology networks to develop new technologies and widen access to existing technologies.

The third sub-programme on Promoting Entrepreneurship included a number of measures specifically geared towards promoting knowledge transfer to SMEs. One measure provided financial incentives for SMEs involved in incubators and technology parks, while another was designed to promote the creation and growth of innovative enterprises through subsidised loans and investment guarantees.

Additional support for incubators, technology parks, technology centres and technology transfer offices was provided under a law on The Support Environment for Entrepreneurship, adopted in January 2004 to finance the pre-start-up phase of new businesses. It provides small grants to university academics in order to stimulate the development of new ideas.

A National Agency for Technology Development was established in February 2004 under R&D law. The aim of the Agency is to offer financial support to development programmes of companies and especially to promote their co-operation with science institutions in projects that would result in the transfer of knowledge. An Agency for Scientific Research had already been established in November 2003, while the European Regional Development Fund provides funding for technology parks and new services and infrastructure to support R&D activities.

The coalition government elected in 2004 reorganised the ministries and created a new Ministry of Higher Education, Science and Technology. There was some concern among Slovenian policy experts that some of the old problems were likely to re-emerge under this new structure, and that the new measures recently introduced would not be implemented. However, the Slovenian Strategy for Development 2006-2013 launched by the government in July 2004 emphasised the importance of innovation and of support for applied research.

Outcomes of knowledge transfer policies

The policy framework for knowledge transfer between HEIs and the business sector was designed to establish an active programme of support for spin-offs from HEIs to university-based incubators and technology parks, for technology centres, for high technology business clusters and for technology networks. This section reviews the main outcomes of these policies, and identifies a number of weaknesses as well as strengths in the implementation of the various programmes. The evidence presented suggests that policy for the development of business clusters and networks has had greater success than the policies designed to promote university spin-offs through incubators and technology parks. Thus, it casts doubt on the extent to which these programmes have succeeded in fostering knowledge transfer between HEIs and the SME sector. These issues and the policy adjustments that would be needed to overcome them are taken up for further analysis in the concluding section.

Incubators and spin-offs

Several business incubators have been established with state support within universities and research institutes to provide infrastructure and joint consultancy services for new start-ups. The Knowledge for Development Programme co-finances the costs of project preparation and the premises, staff and running costs of the business incubators. Under the specific measures for SMEs – Promoting Entrepreneurship – the Ministry of Economy co-finances 50% of the costs of consultancy services to enterprises in the initial phase of project start-up within an incubator, and up to 25% of the costs of equipment, land, and buildings used for the R&D activities of an incubator.

Currently, three business incubators have been established in Ljubljana, Maribor, and Koper, supported by the government programme. The incubator in Ljubljana is based at the university while the incubator in Maribor is based outside the university, supported by the local city council. These incubators provide assistance to new companies for the development of their business plans and provide other early-stage support. Once the business plan has been developed within an incubator the new companies are supposed to transfer to a technology park.

Up to now the officially supported incubators have not been very successful. For example, in 2003 the Slovenian Enterprise Fund announced a competition for subsidised long-term loans for companies spun off from universities through incubators, but no applications were received. In response to the weak performance of the officially supported incubators, personnel from the university Faculty of Economics and Business in Maribor established an unofficial incubator known as the "Venture Factory". This case study, reported below, shows how a group of entrepreneurial academics have been able to work around some of the restrictive institutional arrangements that prevent the state-run universities from fulfilling their potential for knowledge-transfer to the SME sector. Through the imaginative development of new institutions based on non-profit principles, they have initiated a process that has created new, more flexible institutional arrangements based on interaction with the local business community, and have stimulated interest in science-industry collaboration through practical collaborative activities.

Box 12.1. Case Study: The Venture Factory

In 2000 a small group of enthusiastic academics within the Faculty of Business and Economics at the University of Maribor established an unofficial incubator known as the Venture Factory. It was set up as a non-profit Foundation on through funds from an EU-Phare project. Although the Venture Factory is formally a project of the university, the university is only a passive partner; the incubator depends on the energy and enthusiasm of the individual founders. Currently the incubator is housed within an office space in the university equipped with some computers. The Venture Factory provides hands-on advice through a network of experts and partner companies that can provide specialised assistance to new start-ups. It is essentially an awareness-building organisation that focuses strictly on the provision of business services. It organises a business plan competition, advertises entrepreneurship throughout the university, and holds one-day and one-week seminars. Overall, it assists start-up companies from within the university to commercialise innovations.

The Venture Factory has proposed the idea of a Technology Transfer Office (TTO) to take care of property rights and licensing of new ideas and innovation arising from within its walls. While intellectual property rights from research conducted within the university belong to the university, the TTO would be able to license an innovation to the business sector, or sell it on behalf of the university. The TTO would set out a schedule for sharing the royalties from the licensing of university intellectual property, or for equity shares in spin-off companies. It is expected that the university will establish the TTO as a limited liability company.

A private institute called the Institute for Entrepreneurship Research (IER) has been established alongside the Venture Factory. It has been set up as a non-profit association/foundation that has the advantage that it can employ people. It runs annual conferences on innovation and a joint project with the Austrian Institute for Small Businesses called Industry Monitor. An agreement has been reached to establish a Technology Centre in Maribor called "Inceptum". The Centre is owned jointly by IER, the university and a private company "Prevent" with a 60% equity stake. It employs research workers and will eventually become a research institute aiming to attract top-class Slovene researchers who have left the country to work abroad.

Overall, the policies to develop incubators and to promote academic spin-offs in Slovenia have not fulfilled their expectations. As in other countries, spin-off activity in Slovenia has been held back by the lack of managerial expertise and the difficulty in attracting risk capital. Even in advanced countries within the EU, spin-off policies have worked best where the approach has been highly selective, and where support has been targeted on a small number of spin-offs with high growth potential (Druilhe and Garnsey, 2004; Degroof and Roberts, 2004). The example of the Maribor Venture Factory described in Box 12.1 indicates the direction that policy makers could follow to overcome some of these difficulties.

Technology parks

A technology park is a special form of incubator aimed at enterprises with high technology requirements that facilitates the commercialisation of academic research activities. There are three technology parks – in Ljubljana, Maribor and Nova Gorica – funded partly by the Ministry of Economy and partly through rents earned from their tenant companies. The basic aim of the parks is to provide a favourable environment for SMEs to commercialise innovations from HEIs. The Ljubljana Technology Park is considered to be the most successful, while the Maribor Technology Park is less technology-based. The Nova Gorica Technology Park is still in an early stage of development. The government provides some support for the activities of companies based in the parks. The funding measures under the Promoting Entrepreneurship programme are the same as for the incubators: the Ministry of Economy co-finances one-half of the costs of consultancy services to enterprises in their initial start-up phase within a technology park, and for up to one-quarter of the costs of equipment land and buildings used for R&D activities.

The Ljubljana Technology Park (LTP) supports the creation and growth of new enterprises spun off from research carried out within universities and research institutes. LTP aims to develop the entrepreneurial spirit among science students and staff from the various Faculties and research institutes in Ljubljana, and to encourage them to set up small high technology companies. Its purpose is to create an environment in which innovation, finance and production interact to accelerate the development of innovative products. In addition to the Institute Jozef Stefan, the LTP has extended its collaboration to other HEIs such as the Faculty of Informatics and other institutions in the field of natural sciences. While collaboration with the science research institutes is strong, the collaboration with the University of Ljubljana is much weaker, partly as a result of the entrenched division between pure science and technology in Slovenia.

The Jozef Stefan Institute established the precursor of the LTP in 1992; that pilot project had already enabled the creation of nine high technology spin-off companies. Three years later, in 1995, the LTP was founded as a non-profit limited liability company. Its founder-owners were the Jozef Stefan Institute, which owned 54% of the shares; the Institute for Biology; the Institute of Chemistry; some private companies (IskraTEL, Helios, LEK, SKB Bank); and a state body, the Technology Development Fund. More recently, the Municipality of Ljubljana has become a majority owner, with 60% of the shares. LTP has a staff of three – a director, a business secretary and a project manager. It owns its premises, which cover an area of 4 725 square metres. It provides professional and educational courses to its tenants, organises the participation of tenant companies in international trade fairs, and provides consultations on development strategies, financing, participation in foreign markets and the placement of products.

Table 12.1. Evolution of membership of the Ljubljana Technology Park

Number of...	1995	1996	1997	1998	1999	2000	2001	2002	2003
Companies*	9	15	17	19	25	39	45	51	54
Companies in incubation**	9	16	17	22	19	24	28	28	25
Start-ups	9	10	12	17	22	31	33	39	40
Spin-offs	9	10	10	11	15	24	26	30	32
Employees in companies	75	114	120	154	181	224	241	256	299

Notes: *These figures include both, regular companies (being incubated) and affiliated companies; ** the companies in incubation are considered only those that are regular members (the affiliated members are not included).

By 2004, the LTP hosted 55 active companies of which 44 were new start-ups, and of these 34 were spin-off companies from universities and the research institutes. Spin-off companies had been established in the fields of information systems, energetics, automation, biotechnology, opto-electronics and environmental protection. A few companies had graduated from the park and had established their premises elsewhere. The 55 active companies based in the park had 317 employees, of whom two-thirds had at least two years of higher education.

The management and professional staff of the Ljubljana Technology Park have experienced a number of problems. Chief among these are the lack of financial support for the early stages of SME development; problems concerning the protection of intellectual property; difficulties posed by very restrictive and rigid legislation and bureaucracy; and the isolation of high technology companies, which generally expect more support than is available. Although the official period of tenure of companies in LTP is four years, it is clear that in practice most companies are able to renew their tenure and remain within the protective environment of the park for a longer time. The number of companies in the park, as well as the number of spin-offs, has increased consistently over the years. There was a peak of new company establishment in 2000; since then the number of new annual registrations has declined.

Technology centres

A law on technology centres was passed in 1999. In contrast to technology parks, the technology centres – which are financed by the Ministry of Economy – focus on a specific industrial branch or region. By the end of 2001, 31 sectoral technology centres and four regional technology centres had been established. The centres provide participating companies with assistance in marketing, legal and technical information, and links with R&D facilities in research institutes. One such centre is TECOS – a technology centre for the machine tools sector – which provides services such as computer testing and CAD simulation analyses. The centre receives funding from infrastructure subsidies, the Young Researchers programme, and through funding for applied research projects. Public funding through these different programmes accounts for about 40% of running costs. Other funding comes from membership and service fees. Technology centres are supported by a specific measure within the 2002 Programme of Measures, which aims to ensure the long-term linkage between the enterprises and the research and development sphere. Under the measure, the Ministry of Economy co-finances the costs of introducing new services and support activities, and the costs of R&D projects.

As in the case of university spin-offs, the technology parks and technology centres have performed below expectations. Technology parks have seen declining entry in recent years and technology centres rely heavily on state funding. Isolation and lack of funds for growth hinder the development of the high technology firms within the parks, and many remain too long in that protective environment. It appears that the proclaimed advantages of technology parks and technology centres to promote knowledge transfer and spillover from interaction among tenant firms have not been realised to the extent expected.

Industrial clusters

One of the most successful knowledge transfer programmes has been the development of industrial clusters and networks involving both companies and research institutes. These began with a pilot activity in 2000-03; one of the aims has been to promote knowledge transfer from HEIs to the companies that are members of the cluster. The programme co-finances the costs incurred in creating clusters and in preparing joint development strategies, as well as all costs incurred during the first two years of operations. The first three pilot clusters were established in the automotive industry, in transport and logistics, and in tool making. Following a second call for projects, further clusters were formed in wood processing, plastics, information and telecommunication technologies, air conditioning and high-tech equipment for services in the tourist sector. Although clusters include small companies, the leading companies are normally medium-sized or large.

A precondition for forming a cluster is that at least one-third of the members must be HEIs, including research institutes. At least ten companies and three HEIs must be involved in order to obtain financial support. The cluster must provide its own co-finance, and be established through a legal contract. A cluster is developed in three phases: (i) in the first year the ministry provides 100% finance for the pilot stage – to create an atmosphere and to build trust; (ii) in the second stage a non-profit interest association is established with 40% co-financing from the ministry to establish an office and a management team; (iii) in the third phase the cluster is internationalised. The clusters are linked through the Cluster Network of Slovenia, based at the Chamber of Commerce. According to the Chamber, new spin-offs within the cluster programme have come about mainly as a result of networking activity between the established clusters.

By 2004, 36 clusters were supported by the ministry; 19 of these were considered to be successful, and operated on an international level. Eighteen cluster offices were active, and 29 cluster projects were supported, including the three pilot cluster initiatives, 13 early-stage clusters and 13 developed clusters. They involved 350 companies and 40 HEIs, including the Universities of Ljubljana and Maribor. Knowledge and technology transfer has taken place between members of the clusters, including knowledge transfer from HEIs to SMEs, and spin-off companies have been established through the activities of clusters in plastics and engineering. The transfer of knowledge has also gone in the opposite direction – clusters have stimulated the development of new technology courses in the universities and polytechnics. An evaluation report considered that the cluster programme represented good practice (Jaklič, Cotic-Svetina and Zagorsek, 2004).

The members of the clusters have co-operated mainly in the field of joint promotion, joint R&D projects, and joint education events. Co-operation in setting up the joint infrastructure of the cluster and in lobbying for common interests has also been an important knowledge transfer activity. This reflects the current initial development stage of the Slovenian clusters, during which the infrastructure for joint operation is established, and after which the cluster members should begin to co-operate in fields in which they are not direct competitors; only later do they begin to work on more demanding co-operative projects.

A recent evaluation of the cluster measures (Jaklič, Cotic-Svetina and Zagorsek, 2004) indicated that the main reasons for entering a cluster are (a) the financial subsidy from the state, (b) the commercial pressure for a higher degree of linkage and co-operation between companies and (c) improved access to information resources and knowledge transfer through joint projects.

Box 12.2. Case Study: The Slovenian Automotive Cluster

An example of a successful cluster can be found in the automotive industry. In 2004 the automotive cluster was in its third phase – a stage of growth and deep co-operation among its members. The cluster had established strong co-operation in the field of innovation activities among companies and other institutions involved in the development and diffusion of knowledge. It had been aiming for some time to create a polycentric technology centre as a regional innovation system. This orientation was supported by the Ministry of Economy, which provided financial support for a "Polytechnic Technology Centre" project within the public invitation for tenders of the European Regional Development Fund (ERDF). The Polytechnic Technology Centre (PTC) is an international innovation system which incorporates companies, institutions of higher education and research, and the government (Verhovnik, 2005). The realisation of the project should enable a qualitative development of the Slovenian automobile producers at the local, regional, state and international levels. The polycentric development of R&D activities will be a base for joint projects and for the further development and improvement of the competitiveness of the companies.

The vision of the PTC is to become a reliable development-intensive network of suppliers for the global automobile industry in selected areas, based around complex products with high value added. Among the joint projects carried out within the PTC are development evaluation for new materials and products, an innovative development of parts and technologies for the automotive industry, and the development of mechanotronic joints. Several key goals have been set out for the PTC in the period to 2008. It is expected that PTC will establish one technology centre and three R&D centres, create almost 300 new jobs, and produce some new innovative materials and technologies, including 30 new high technology products. It is also expected that about 40 joint projects will be undertaken with institutions of higher education and research, and that jobs will be created for around 40 new researchers.

According to the study, interviewed companies reported positive effects of clustering, but two-thirds expected that it would take about six years for the benefits in terms of increased sales to exceed the costs of forming and administering the cluster. Both value added and exports were expected to increase due to the positive effects on competitiveness of joint projects undertaken within a cluster. The report emphasised the benefits of improved communication, faster knowledge transfer among the actors in the cluster, and the possibility of offering more complex products. Key success factors include the creation of trust among the members, effective leadership of the cluster, and the effective support of top management. Interviews with the representatives of the clusters revealed that lack of trust is the main barrier to effectiveness at the early stage of cluster development. Overall, the study found that the government programme triggered off a process that would otherwise never have occurred.

Technology networks

In addition to clusters, the government has also supported the development of less localised technology networks. The 2002 Programme of Measures included a measure on promoting the development of technology networks. It provides co-financing for the costs incurred in establishing the organisation and initial operation of technology networks, and the costs of preparing long-term research and development projects. The purpose of technology networks is to identify and support investments in new technologies in sectors where a critical mass of knowledge exists and where there is a high level of interest in the application of this knowledge. They are also intended to widen access to new technologies by involving SMEs, large firms and HEIs. One of the most successful has been the ICT technology network led by IskraTEL from Kranj. Other successful technology networks have been established in the fields of process control, biotechnology, and advanced materials. An additional programme to develop networks of small enterprises employing up to 50 workers in defined geographical areas that supported several successful networks in the construction industry has been assisted by the Small Business Development Centre of the Ministry of Economy. By 2003 the small business networks involved more than 550 companies and 50 HEIs. Among the institutions involved are faculties within the Universities of Ljubljana and Maribor, private colleges and business schools, R&D institutes, technology centres, and the Ljubljana Institute of Economics (EC, 2003).

As mentioned at the beginning of this section on outcomes, industrial clusters and technology networks appear to have had more success than the policies to promote university spin-offs through incubators and technology parks. Although the clusters and networks are mainly focused on the needs of larger firms, business networks can be an especially powerful policy tool for the development of SMEs in transition economies supporting mutual learning and knowledge transfer among members of the network (Franičević and Bartlett, 2001). In Slovenia, the programme to support the development of technology networks specifically oriented toward SMEs appears to have had some success and has involved a large number of SMEs in combination with research institutes. However, issues of sustainability, bottom-up development, and internationalisation have yet to be fully addressed.

Young Researchers programme

The universities have contributed to the science base in Slovenia by increasing the number of master's and doctoral degree holders in the R&D sector, which reached 32% by 2001 (MoE, 2003). However, relatively few researchers were employed in the business sector, where highly educated personnel accounted for just 12% of R&D employees. The Young Researchers programme aims to address this deficiency. It was introduced in 1985 in order to support the employment of younger researchers in research institutions, and to support their transfer from these institutes to employment in industry. The programme did not succeed however, as the best researchers stayed with the research institutions. Therefore, since 2002 the Ministry of Economy has given more attention to the mobility aspects of the programme. The Young Researchers measure now focuses on promoting the entry of young researchers from the universities into industry by co-financing the continuing education of junior researchers employed by enterprises or technology centres for the duration of their studies. Under the programme, the government also pays part of the salary of newly employed postgraduate students. According to a recent report, the proportion of researchers in industry now exceeds the proportion employed in the research institutions. According to government data, some 200-300 new researchers pass through the programme each year (MoE, 2003).

Financial support for high technology SMEs

Difficulty in accessing finance has been a persistent problem facing the development of SMEs in Slovenia (Bartlett and Bukvič, 2001, 2003). To redress this barrier to growth, the Ministry of Economy supports new high technology enterprises through subsidised loans, investment guarantees and direct credits with co-ownership of risk capital funds, through the sub-programme on Promoting Entrepreneurship. Subsidised loans are provided through the Slovene Enterprise Fund for various categories of high technology SMEs, including new companies co-owned by private venture capital funds and SMEs in information technology and information services. They should be companies which are manufacturing products or services developed on the basis of their own research and development or joint R&D with universities and research institutes, and which can display evidence of the marketability of the product. The loans were available with a subsidised interest rate with a four-year grace period and a ten-year payback period.

Applicants should provide at least 30% of the total finance from their own funds. In 2003, the Fund received 23 applications under this heading, of which 21 were based on university-business collaboration. After evaluation, seven applications were approved for subsidised loans. The average size of the successful companies was 10.7 employees; there are plans to increase employment to an average size of 14.7 employees. One-half of the value of loans to successful applicants was for companies operating in the manufacturing sector, and 24% for companies in the real estate sector.

Conclusion

This chapter has shown that the institutional framework to support knowledge transfer from HEIs to the business sector has been powerfully developed in Slovenia. The Programme of Measures to Promote Entrepreneurship and Competitiveness 2002-2006 contained a proliferation of policy initiatives to support the knowledge transfer process. These included support for the creation of business incubators and technology parks, the development of technology centres and technology networks, the development of industrial clusters involving collaboration between industry and HEIs, a Young Researchers programme to promote the mobility of junior researchers from R&D institutions to the business sector, and financial support for high technology SMEs.

This policy framework has succeeded in establishing an active programme of knowledge transfer. Yet, there remain doubts as to the extent to which these programmes are really succeeding in fostering knowledge transfer between HEIs and the SME sector. Many of the programmes involve support for innovation within the large-company sector and do not specifically target SMEs. While medium-sized firms may benefit to some extent, there are reasons to doubt that small firms are benefiting much from the measures that have so far been implemented. Recent reports from the Global Entrepreneurship Monitor research programme (Rebernik, Tominc and Pušnik, 2004) have voiced similar concerns and suggest that linkages between academic institutions and the business sector are weak, the performance of the science parks and business incubators is poor, and government programmes are often introduced without sufficient preparation and lack sufficient finance for effective implementation. The problem appears also to be deeper in regard to SMEs compared to large firms. For example, as identified above, no applications were made for financial support provided by the programme for new start-ups in incubators. The programme of subsidies for small high technology firms appears to have disproportionately benefited firms in the real estate sector, and has not reached the target group of companies in high technology manufacturing. Moreover, SMEs have not been sufficiently involved in industrial clusters.

On the other hand, the SME network programme has been relatively successful.

The available evidence indicates that despite the supportive policy framework, there has been relatively little knowledge transfer from HEIs to SMEs in Slovenia. The Slovenian Innovation Survey has shown that HEIs are minor providers of information to SMEs compared to other sources of information (clients and customers, fairs and exhibitions and even their own competitors). A significant minority of SMEs reported that a lack of qualified personnel is a barrier to innovation. The consequence has been that Slovenia has fewer innovative SMEs than many other EU member states. Slovenian SMEs rank sixteenth in terms of in-house innovation activity among the EU-25, and seventeenth in innovation expenditure. The authors' review of the outcomes of knowledge transfer policies in Slovenia suggests that a range of policies and actions are required to boost the extent of knowledge transfer from HEIs to SMEs in Slovenia.

Drawing on Slovenian experience, a number of different measures can be identified that could address these deficiencies in the policy framework. For example, the National Agency for Technology Development should increase support for the HEI-SME knowledge transfer process in order to increase the proportion of innovative SMEs in Slovenia. It should assist HEIs, technology centres, technology networks and technology parks in accessing EC funds to support innovation and knowledge transfer. The government should establish a joint venture capital fund within the universities to back their academic spin-offs with equity capital. Technology parks should be encouraged to promote networking between their tenants, and end the reported isolation of high technology companies on their premises. Technology parks should enforce limited tenure for resident companies and promote their dispersal to a normal commercial environment, to make space for new high technology start-ups. Industrial clusters should be encouraged to move rapidly to the stage of internationalisation, to develop an outward exporting orientation and link up with international systems of innovation. The business sector also needs a more skilled labour force; the HEI sector has an important role to play in fostering the skills of young people in science and technology.

The universities also have a critical role to play in improving the environment for knowledge transfer to SMEs, through spin-offs and improved relationships with the business sector. Universities should be given greater autonomy to commercialise innovations and to react to opportunities to transfer knowledge to the private sector through the development of industrial clusters. They should boost their business incubators in order to provide more support to researchers for commercialising their inventions through the creation of new spin-off enterprises. They should develop co-operation between their incubators and share best practice. Universities and research institutes should join together to establish a joint venture capital fund to co-finance spin-offs from the HEI sector. Universities should assist and facilitate their academic staff to establish non-profit associations and foundations that will operate as vehicles for knowledge transfer and commercialisation of innovation. Here, they could learn from the experience of the Venture Factory in Maribor. They should establish Technology Transfer Offices to handle property rights issues and the licensing of inventions and innovations created in university laboratories, and to encourage patenting and licensing of technology to SMEs.

Intellectual property regulation and protection for researchers in HEIs should be reformed, and the Agency for Technology should support patent applications by HEIs. Since spin-offs typically lack managerial expertise, university spin-off SMEs should be encouraged to form joint ventures with established companies. Universities should include applied research activities and a record of collaboration with SMEs in their staff promotion criteria. Finally, they should permit researchers to take sabbaticals to create spin-off companies with a guaranteed right to return to their previous post. In general there is a need for academic researchers to become much more involved in commercial R&D projects in Slovenian businesses, in order to establish a more comprehensive process of knowledge transfer that would improve the competitive position of Slovenian companies.

Bibliography

Bartlett, W. and V. Bukvič (2003), "Financial barriers to SME growth in Slovenia", *Economic and Business Review for Central and Southeastern Europe,* Vol. 5, No. 3, pp. 161-182.

Bartlett, W. and V. Bukvič (2001), "Barriers to SME growth in Slovenia", *MOT-MOST: Economic Policy in Transition Economies*, Vol. 11, No. 2, Springer Netherlands, pp. 177-195.

Bučar, M. (2004), "Slovenia's potential for knowledge-based economy with focus on R&D and innovation policy", in J. Švarc, *et al.* (eds.), *Transition Countries in the Knowledge Society*, Institute of Social Sciences, Zagreb.

Degroof, J-J. and E.B. Roberts (2004), "Overcoming weak entrepreneurial infrastructures for academic spin-off ventures", *The Journal of Technology Transfer*, Vol. 29, No. 3-4, Springer Netherlands, pp. 327-352.

Druilhe, C. and E. Garnsey (2004), "Do academic spin-outs differ and does it matter?", *The Journal of Technology Transfer*, Vol. 29, No. 3-4, Springer Netherlands, pp. 269-285.

EC (European Commission) (2003), *European Trend Chart on Innovation: Theme Specific Country Report Slovenia*, Innovation/SMEs Programme March 2003, Enterprise and Industry Directorate General, Brussels.

EC (2004a), *European Trend Chart on Innovation: Annual Innovation Policy for Slovenia Covering Period: September 2003-August 2004*, Innovation/SMEs Programme, Enterprise and Industry Directorate General, Brussels.

EC (2004b), *Trendchart: Innovation Policy in Europe 2004*, Enterprise and Industry Directorate General, Brussels.

Franičević, V. and W. Bartlett (2001), "Small firm networking and economies in transition: an overview of theories, issues, policies", *Zagreb International Review of Economics and Business,* Vol. 4, No. 1, Faculty of Economics and Business, University of Zagreb, pp. 63-89.

Jaklič, M., A. Cotic-Svetina and H. Zagorsek (2004), *Evaluation of the Measures for fostering of the cluster development in Slovenia in 2001-2003*, Final Report, Faculty of Economics, Institute for Competition and Co-operation, Ljubljana.

Koschatzky, K. (2002), "Networking and knowledge transfer between research and industry in transition countries: empirical evidence from the

Slovenian innovation system", *The Journal of Technology Transfer*, Vol. 27, No. 1, Springer Netherlands, pp. 27-38.

MoE (Ministry of the Economy) (2003), *Benchmarking Slovenia 2003: An Evaluation of Slovenia's Competitiveness, Strengths and Weaknesses*, Republic of Slovenia, Ministry of the Economy, Ljubljana.

Rebernik, M., P. Tominc and K. Pušnik (2004), *Podjetništvo na prehodu*, Institute for Entrepreneurship and Small Business Management, Maribor.

SORS (Statistical office of the Republic of Slovenia) (2004), "Innovation activity in manufacturing and selected services, Slovenia, 2001-2002", *Research and Development, Science and Technology - Rapid Report*, No. 370, Statistical Office of the Republic of Slovenia, Ljubljana.

Verhovnik, V. (2005), "Co-operation of the Academic, Economic and Government Spheres in Slovenia with Aid of the Model of a Triple Spiral", master's dissertation, Economic Business Faculty of Maribor, University of Maribor.

Chapter 13

Knowledge Transfer Mechanisms in the European Transition Economies

by
Piero Formica,
Jonkoping University, Sweden

Tõnis Mets and Urmas Varblane
University of Tartu, Estonia

There are a variety of definitions of knowledge transfer, and differing viewpoints as to the extent to which it is possible to establish a difference between knowledge transfer and technology transfer. By tapping into the positions taken by parties into the knowledge transfer debate, this chapter examines the main characteristics of these two different, albeit related, concepts. It goes on to propose a theoretical model in conjunction with the results of a preliminary field survey (details of which follow). This model is a contribution to extensive empirical work that has to be undertaken in order to assess the impact of university-industry interactions, especially in the Central, eastern and south eastern European countries (CESE) countries. The chapter then offers policy recommendations aimed at forging even closer ties between HEIs and regional small and medium-sized enterprises in European transition economies.

Introduction

The sustained phase of transition experienced by economies has been characterised by considerable – and sometimes revolutionary – advances in science, technology and related industries. Coupled with the subsequent profound changes in both the economy and society, this transition has increased the importance of the knowledge-intensive phases of production for value creation. Accordingly, policy makers in a growing number of countries have become increasingly concerned with management of the entire knowledge chain: from creation to the diffusion, conversion and entrepreneurial exploitation of scientific and technological knowledge. The knowledge chain also has profound implications for universities and business schools. To be successful, higher education institutions (HEIs) need to help companies create knowledge and become part of knowledge streams.

This chapter considers the existing and potential channels for knowledge transfer from HEIs in Central, Eastern and Southeastern European (CESE) countries. A preliminary field survey examines the appropriateness of existing links between HEIs and regional small and medium-sized enterprises (SMEs) in those countries, and the role of university spin-offs. A supportive environment is needed to improve the current interaction between academia and business; the chapter therefore sets out proposals to give policy makers a proper role in their attempt, together with university and industry, to establish new avenues for knowledge transfer and innovate within existing channels for the purpose of pursuing a process of knowledge interchange. The resulting exploitation of scientific and technological knowledge could lead to higher productivity, greater economic growth and increased entrepreneurial activity.

Closer co-operation between academia and business underpins growth in a knowledge economy. First and foremost in the United States – as an OECD report submits – "stronger interactions between science and industry have characterised the innovation-led economic growth of the past decade and are currently helping the country to secure a lead in science-based industries ranging from IT and biotechnology to the new field of nanotechnologies" (OECD, 2002). Other large advanced economies, such as Japan, Germany and France, are responding – the same report highlights – with reforms "aimed at removing regulatory barriers to closer industry-science relations, while creating incentives for public research to join forces with business".

When compared to the most advanced economies and the core 15 EU countries, the Czech Republic, Estonia, Latvia, Lithuania, Hungary, Poland, Slovakia, Slovenia and other emerging market economies in Central and

Southeastern Europe are lagging behind in bringing academia and business close together (Box 13.1). Paradoxically, the ability to harness the right conditions for mutually reinforcing research and commercialisation goals that can feed cutting-edge entrepreneurial opportunities is one among few available alternatives for the emerging market economies to boost their economic activity.

Box 13.1. Knowledge flow: The Latvian case

The lack of knowledge flow between universities (public research institutions) and enterprises is one of the major problems. On the one hand, there is the low innovation literacy level of business, which cannot formulate its own ideas or find sophisticated partners, and is not open to co-operation. On the other hand, one has to recognise the unsatisfactory business literacy level of academic society, with its accompanying inability and unwillingness to offer co-operation. The result is not only small industry investment in R&D, but also the far more destructive lack of outcome: neither universities nor enterprises make much of a contribution to knowledge, technology-intensive industries and products, the GDP or the national budget. The necessary positive economic feedback does not exist.

Source: Karnitis, 2005.

Defining knowledge and technology transfer

Knowledge transfer is the process that puts knowledge into action. It relies on the flow by which largely tacit knowledge, not technology *per se*, is transmitted among people: from one unit (the source: a single person, group or organisation) to another (the recipient), with all kinds of feedback loops. The process is in fact complex and non-linear with a large number of interactions. It is not simply a matter of knowledge that passes down a production line linking academic researchers upstream and their business counterparts downstream.

Knowledge transfer is concerned with the subsequent absorption through which the recipient is affected by the experience of the source. How to transfer knowledge that exists in a given unit to another unit is more than a communication problem that information technology (IT) tools can fully solve.

Technology transfer is a related but different subject. Technology transfer places importance on information and efficiency rather than knowledge and effectiveness. If implemented with efficiency and speed, an information- and data-oriented approach helps develop practical applications that solve practical problems in the products and processes of an individuated industry.

In the academic context, knowledge transfer covers the processes of transferring research, skills, experience, and ideas within universities, and from universities to the greater community of users – including the business sector – for the purpose of increasing economic returns from this investment and achieving cultural, educational and social benefits for society (Box 13.2) (HMSO, 2003, p. 39). This definition embraces the forms of knowledge transfer and technology transfer.

Box 13.2. Knowledge transfer activities from an academic perspective

Knowledge transfer activities from an academic perspective include:

- Exchange of knowledge through teaching, training, research or industrial partnerships involving faculty members and students.

- Application of knowledge to social and political issues of the day through participation in advisory boards, government consultations, advice to interest groups, public commentary and other forms of community service.

- Codification of knowledge through written articles, conference presentations or patent applications.

- Commercialisation of knowledge through the development, exploitation and marketing of products for the domestic and international marketplace.

Source : Trends in Higher Education, 2002, page 78; Natural Environment Research Council (NERC), United Kingdom, www.nerc.ac.uk/using/ktcall.shtml.

Theoretical foundations of the field survey

The knowledge transfer process from CESE universities and other HEIs to the SME sector, particularly with firms in the same region or locality as the HEI, is the subject of the field survey.

Knowledge transfer can occur via various routes. Processes of integration, collaboration, communication, and commercialisation of knowledge are associated either with the softer side of the transfer process, such as sponsored students, contract and collaborative research, or with the harder side, such as intellectual property, licensing and spin-off companies (HMSO, 2003, p. 39).

This section provides a description of these processes.

Knowledge integration process

The rationale that sustains this process is that economies are shifting from information to knowledge integration. This requires an integrated approach to respond to the new economic and social needs.

The field survey examines the knowledge integration process from two angles. One perspective looks at the interdependency between academic institutions and SMEs, taking into account the number of research partnerships between the HEIs surveyed with SMEs embedded in its environment (from now on, local business enterprises).

The second perspective reveals two basic types of relationship for knowledge transfer:

- *Type A: Transfer of inputs ("supply push")* – A type of relationship that concerns contract research, consultancy and other university outreach initiatives to business, such as transfer of research, skills, management strategies, and knowledge capital in general. This relationship emphasises the supply of input (of a "knowledge package"), lending relatively little weight to the interaction with the end-users. The crucial consequence of a linear approach to knowledge transfer is that organisational and behavioural characteristics of local business enterprises and their capacity to absorb the input–transferred are neglected.

- *Type B: Knowledge transfer designed in a demand-led way ("demand pull")* – This is a coupling type of relationship that holds two properties. One property makes the relationship dependent on the needs of business; therefore, its primarily objective is that of fitting the cognitive characteristics of the recipient actors (Garavelli, Gorgoglione and Albino, n.d., Part 1). A second property is that the relationship is driven by the interplay between the supplier and the receiver of knowledge. The better the interchange, the higher the value of knowledge transfer and the more intense the iterative process, as trial and error produces new knowledge at every stage.

Knowledge collaboration

Knowledge collaboration describes an open process of value creation in which contributing members make every effort to capture all the relevant

294 – CHAPTER THIRTEEN

pieces of knowledge across functions, businesses and even nations (Amidon, Formica and Laurent-Mercier, 2005).

Different tools are used to create meaningful venues for collaboration. They show two facets: one is that of a controlled situation (closer to the concept of a contrived consultation) in which each party involved solicits a demand or a response from the other component(s). The other is that of an unstructured, unpredictable and spontaneous interaction which promotes cross-fertilisation of ideas for prosperous innovation.

Traineeships/internships

In this organisational form, knowledge transfer occurs by means of interaction between the knowledge provider ("teacher") and the recipient individual ("learner"). The training process enables the learner to use, in a well-defined context, the knowledge transferred by the source. The provider knows *a priori* the solution to a specific problem that the recipient has to solve (Garavelli, Gorgoglione and Albino, n.d.).

Knowledge practice includes both project-based placements of students in a company and company employees in an academic lab for the realisation of a specific project.

Continuing professional development

Continuing professional development (CPD) is an important form of knowledge transfer, which an increasing number of universities are providing to business employees. Through continuing professional development, "[b]usinesses can raise the skill levels of their workforce and learn about the latest academic ideas, while universities gain access to the latest developments in professional practice" (HMSO, 2003, p. 122).

Collaborative research

The collaborative research form of knowledge transfer aims at promoting a context where academic researchers work alongside company employees for the purpose of creating, developing and testing a prototype based on their reciprocal ideas.

Collaborative research can be carried out in a "collaboratory" – an appropriate lab-type infrastructure that links teams of people from university and companies with disparate cultures, different cognitive systems and skills (Box 13.3). In a "collaboratory", research is focused on specific company problems, and scientific research is carried out through the interactions between corporate researchers and university researchers willing to put their scientific results to practical use.

Box 13.3. "Collaboratories": the programme to establish a co-operative research centre in Hungary

One of the objectives of the Hungarian R&D and innovation policy is the promotion of R&D in enterprises and their collaboration with universities. This aims to promote joint R&D actions undertaken by universities and enterprises and the appropriate transfer, which may lead to new processes or products.

Objectives: To create, or to strengthen the operation of, research centres allowing the formation of integral ties between the institutions of Hungarian college and university (higher) education, other non-profit research institutions and the enterprise-business innovation sector. The strategic integration of education, research and development, knowledge and technological transfer can thereby be realised.

Hungarian universities and colleges can submit bids, individually or jointly, or in a consortium form with enterprises in the capacity of Co-operative Research Centre (CRC) recipients. The leading institution of the consortium may only be an establishment accredited by the Hungarian Accreditation Committee for PhD training. CRC proposals shall be submitted exclusively with the participation of business partners. The centre to be established can be an independent legal entity or a separately financed, economically independent unit – within the organisation of an HEI.

The proposal shall detail a strategy for long-term (minimum three, but preferably six to nine years) research, training, plus knowledge and technological transfer, developed jointly by the participating partners and supplemented by the business plan required for the operation of the centre.

Source: http://europa.eu.int/comm/enterprise/enterprise_policy/enlargement/cc-best.

Knowledge communication

The extent to which knowledge communication is built on the principle of participation, by being evocative and not only informative, is a sign of how powerful it could be in shifting the current emphasis on information in favour of imaginative ideas to be converted into sound commercial ventures.

The much-vaunted university channel of knowledge communication is at the intersection of disciplines, both technical and business, and capable of melding the worlds of science and industry. Funding interdisciplinary chairs that focus on both technical and business topics is the first step toward giving fresh weight to the question of how universities can contribute to effective knowledge communication.

Knowledge commercialisation

The conversion of knowledge creation into economic knowledge that can constitute a business opportunity is the aim of an increasing number of academic institutions.

One-stop centres

There are universities that have set up one-stop centres to guide faculty inventions and scientific research through the commercialisation process. These centres are focused on:

- How to assess the commercial applications of the results of a research project.

- How to effectively formalise them into a business plan.

- How to identify the best way (product, service, technology) to commercialise research project results.

UK universities, for instance, have established science enterprise centres whose aims are "to foster the commercialisation of research and new ideas; to stimulate scientific entrepreneurialism; to incorporate the teaching of enterprise into the science and engineering curricula; to act as centres of excellence for the transfer and exploitation of scientific knowledge and expertise" (European Commission, 2004).

Incubation of research-based start-ups

Universities and other higher education institutions that put in motion processes of knowledge transfer are often also interested in embarking on a process of incubation of ventures through which knowledge-based opportunities flow across conventional intellectual and business borders. In doing so, they support ventures that originate from scientific research.

Scientists, academic researchers and talented students who perceive practical implications from their findings often lack the strategic vision and profit-seeking approach that a would-be entrepreneur should possess. The incubation process brings together into a single organisation ("incubator") these entrepreneurial scientists, researchers and students, and enhances their ability to interface knowledge and innovation. Research findings and novel technologies, which are the result of their curiosity-driven research projects, are redirected toward business concepts that can be converted into viable commercial products and services.

Spin-in

Developing spin-off firms based on sharing university potential is not the sole role of the incubation process. The same process can also "spin in" creative ideas from local businesses and help to form partnerships for new venture creation with the pool of knowledge-rich scientific and technical personnel and talented students, backed by the incubator infrastructure and its support staff (Powell, Harloe and Goldsmith, 2000, p. 11).

Licensing

A good number of university spin-offs that have the status of a joint closed stock partially or fully owned by both an academic institute (committed to the exploitation of its research results) and one or more scientific entrepreneurs (entrepreneurial scientists included) may not prove sustainable. Rather, this enhances the likelihood that something negative will occur, and therefore the propensity of universities to shift the emphasis from developing commercially viable academic spin-offs to being much more focused on licensing.

MIT, a leading institution in the transfer process, has been a pioneer of policy efforts designed to tackle the issue of licensing. A licensing policy opens up opportunities for incentives that motivate inventor-academics to patent as a means of maintaining control over future research (Strandburg, 2005).

Case studies of university-business linkages

This section presents the results of a preliminary field survey concerning knowledge transfer mechanisms from universities and other HEIs to the SME sector. The survey is part of broader research targeted to identify the main features of entrepreneurship teaching and links between entrepreneurship-oriented academia and the business community in the new EU member states, Southern European transition countries and Russia.

Non-probability convenience sampling as illustrated by Formica and Varblane (2005) was employed for sampling purposes. A specific section of the questionnaire (Formica and Varblane, 2005), covering university-industry relationships for knowledge transfer was sent to 35 selected schools. In total, 15 of the 35 questionnaires distributed were returned, resulting in a response rate of 43%. In addition, phone interviews were conducted with specialists.

Kaunas University of Technology

Kaunas University of Technology, Lithuania, has been teaching entrepreneurship as a special component in bachelor and master's programmes since 2000.

Links with the business community

University-industry joint teams and ten joint laboratories are operative in the following fields: commercialisation of research results; solving technology problems raised by industry; and organisational and business development. The University also has its own structural unit to commercialise faculty inventions.

Multidisciplinary chairs that focus on both technical and business topics, and synchronise educational resources with the requirements of local business, help to develop faculty members' and students' awareness of university-industry knowledge transfer.

Students and academics have created approximately 20 spin-off companies. Students play a pertinent role in the founding spin-offs, as they act as catalysts for new cluster formations and agents of innovation within the value chain of local businesses.

The University has one incubator, established in 1998, with 64 tenants.

University of Tartu

University of Tartu (UT), Estonia, started teaching "Basics of Enterprise Creation and Activities" as the special course in their BBA programme in 1997. Entrepreneurship and Technology Management (ETM), a new Masters curriculum, started in 2002.

Links with the business community

The University established the Institute of Technology (TUIT) in 2002 for the purposes of applying scientific research results and commercialising faculty inventions.

A Centre for Entrepreneurship (CFE), which has three permanently involved faculty members, was launched in 2003 as a faculty unit. Since April 2005, the CFE has been transferred into an interdisciplinary centre; it is now committed to developing international co-operation for knowledge transfer, creating new practices, fostering entrepreneurship research and training, advising university members and founders of new ventures nurtured in the incubators, and participating in regional development networks.

Since 1990, students and academics, mainly in the field of biotechnology and IT, have created approximately fifteen spin-off companies.

In 2004, students and graduates of ETM Masters programmes established their own association *House of Ideas* (Chamber for Entrepreneurship and Technology Development).

Jagiellonian University in Krakow

Jagiellonian University in Krakow, Poland, teaches "Entrepreneurship and Innovation" to business students at the bachelor level (45 students/year) and the master's level (60).

Links with the business community

A Centre of Innovation, Technology Transfer and University Development (CITTRU) was created as a unit of the Jagiellonian University aimed at promoting entrepreneurship among the scientific staff and encouraging academic researchers to create businesses within the University. CITTRU provides active support to technology transfer, contacting the business environment and promoting scientific projects eligible for commercialisation. At present CITTRU is working on the commercialisation of and offering business support to scientific projects, mainly in the field of biotechnology. In practice, CITTRU evaluates every project presented by the potential academic entrepreneur and eventually selects the one that stands the best chance of commercial success. CITTRU prepares a business plan for the project and takes care of all formalities related to the creation and operation of the company. If needed, CITTRU will search for a partner who will co-finance the project.

The University also owns the Jagiellonian Innovation Centre, whose aim is the creation of a technology incubator to assist the development of entrepreneurship based on the scientific potential of the University. Modern technical infrastructure, low operating costs and professional services give the academic entrepreneurs from the incubator the possibility to successfully compete on the market of advanced technologies.

A third centre, the Academic Science and Technology Centre (AKCENT), is committed to effectively transferring and commercialising new technologies developed by Krakow universities: the Krakow Technical University, the Krakow Agricultural University, the Academy of Metallurgy and Mining and the Jagiellonian University. The Centre has been legally formed as a consortium co-ordinated by the Jagiellonian University and represented by the CITTRU.

University of Miskolc

University of Miskolc (UM), Hungary, began teaching entrepreneurship as independent bachelor and master's programmes in 1990. Entrepreneurship curricula have been established in collaboration with local and foreign business partners.

Links with the business community

Three centres lead knowledge transfer:

- The Innovation and Technology Transfer Centre, whose main activities are: technology transfer, promotion of innovation, PR activities and services, expert and consultancy service, patenting, and services for innovative entrepreneurs (www.uni-miskolc.hu/ittc).

- The Co-operation Research Centre in Mechatronics and Material Science (established in 2001) (www.meakkk.uni-miskolc.hu).

- The Innovation Management Co-operation Research Centre, which conducts research in the field of innovation strategy, innovative organisation and marketing innovation.

A university-industry joint team with Borsodi Brewery Corp. provides organisational and business development.

In the UM there are approximately 35 joint university-industry laboratories. Academics and students have created five spin-off companies.

Budapest Corvinus University

Budapest Corvinus University (BCU) is an internationally recognised institution for both education and research. Entrepreneurship is currently presented as a major in the Faculties of Business Administration and Social Sciences. The coverage of students with fundamental entrepreneurship knowledge is widespread, and the University has set up three university-industry joint laboratories.

Links with the business community

A strong link with the business community is the Chair System of Corporate Professorships, under which the companies sponsor particular research areas and the professors represent them for a period of five years. This system of sponsorship is the first of its kind in Hungary and unique in the region. It enables stable, long-term, mutually beneficial co-operation between the sponsors and the University.

Another interesting institution is the IKU – Innovation Research Centre, established in May 1991 in the postgraduate school of the Budapest University of Economics. The aim of the Centre is to shape innovation policy through research and education and, within this, to improve international competitiveness. Research in science and technology policies, measurement of R&D and innovation and scrutiny of the strengths and weaknesses of the national/local innovation system are the main activities carried out in the Innovation Research Centre. The Centre also plays a vital part in education.

IKU attaches great importance to the dissemination of scientific research findings between academic, business-economic and government decision makers in Hungary and abroad.

Matej Bel University

Matej Bel University, Slovakia, began teaching entrepreneurship as an independent curriculum at the bachelor level with an emphasis on SME management. Effective from 1993, a master's curriculum in entrepreneurship has been in place.

Links with the business community

Over the past five years or so, fourteen faculty members have developed best practices in entrepreneurship and business. A Centre for Research and Development has been established at the Faculty of Economics for the purpose of applying and developing faculty competencies in education, consultancy and research. Nine of the faculty members are involved in the Centre.

Approximately 200 students participate in internship programmes as a component of their studies, over a period of 1.5 months per year. Sixty employees of local business enterprises take part in exchange programmes with academic labs, totalling 70 months per year. Students and academics in partnership with local business enterprises have created five spin-off companies.

The University of West Bohemi

The University of West Bohemi in Pilsen, Czech Republic was established by the decree of the Czech National Council in 1991, when the Institute of Technology in Pilsen and the College of Education merged.

Students of the technical faculties are invited to apply for the Annual Emil Skoda Award in various categories by submitting a diploma or PhD dissertation. This award is part of a contractual collaboration between the University of West Bohemia and Skoda Holding, A.S.

Links with the business community

Instrumental in forging links with the business community is the New Technologies Research Centre in West Bohemian Region, in collaboration with the Pilsen Business Innovation Centre and the Science and Technology Park. This forms a joint project between the Business Innovation Centre in Pilsen, University of West Bohemia and the City of Pilsen.

The Business Innovation Centre is focused primarily on the development of small and medium-sized enterprises. It has been providing its services since 1992.

As a result of an agreement on co-operation between the University and the Business Innovation Centre, a Science Park was established in Pilsen in 1996, in an attempt to facilitate and speed up the technology transfer processes.

The Science and Technology Park provides support for the:

- Formation of new innovative businesses.

- Creation of new (skilled labour) jobs.

- Transfer of R&D to innovative firms.

- Growth of innovative companies.

The first phase of the STP Pilsen project was the business incubator for innovative start-ups. The second phase set the stage for the creation of the Technology Centre for the purpose of addressing the needs of well-established high-tech and R&D companies.

The University of National and World Economy – Sofia

At the University of National and World Economy in Sofia, Bulgaria, approximately 2 000 students (80 foreigners) in all fields are enrolled in entrepreneurship courses.

Links with the business community

The University has established an Entrepreneurship Development Centre, where ten academics are employed. The Centre's main activities are:

- Training – designing and organizing specialised courses.

- Consulting – in business plan development, enterprises privatisation, restructuring and recovering, and the establishment and development of joint ventures and other kinds of strategic alliances.

- Research – local and international research projects in the field of entrepreneurship, small and medium-sized businesses, and large-scale enterprises.

- Publishing – books and teaching materials in the area of entrepreneurship and management, giving prominence to the distinctive traits of Bulgarian and Eastern European economies.

Three researchers, for a total amount of twelve man-months per year, are exchanged with local business enterprises.

Knowledge transfer processes have as constituent elements the transfer of research results, training in the field of SME strategic management, export management, growth management, and the creation of East-West joint ventures.

Approximately 200 students take part in internship programmes as a component of their studies, for the duration of one month per year.

University-industry joint teams are involved in organisation and business development processes in areas such as business evaluation and appraisal, and privatisation and restructuring strategies.

Strengths and weaknesses in knowledge transfer activities

Overall, universities of Central, Eastern and South European Countries appear to be connected with a variety of knowledge transfer processes, which gives strength to their initiatives for the promotion of business links. However, two points of weakness are worth noting. First, additional efforts must be made to capture all the relevant processes of knowledge transfer, embracing those related in a demand-led way ("demand pull"), continuing professional development, spin-in and licensing, which are not fully ingrained in the practices of the institutions surveyed. Secondly, the incubation process of academic, research-based start-ups is during the early stages of development. Further development of these actions will entice universities in CESE countries to integrate research-based start-ups as an essential step in knowledge transfer strategies.

Policy implications

Knowledge transfer is an increasingly pertinent area of public policy, one that poses a challenge to policy makers in the process enhancing the economic potential of a country or region through developing stronger mutual interaction between higher education and business.

CESE countries must shape a comprehensive system for increasing the flow of new ideas into and out of both academia and business.

This section suggests measures to influence existing patterns in knowledge transfer. The programme for action proposed encompasses:

- *Mobility* – that is, human interaction through the movement of between universities and industry that sets the stage for knowledge creation and business creation.

- *Knowledge transfer partnership* – that is, a project-oriented collaboration between a source of knowledge and its business user.

- *Incentives to entrepreneurial scientists* – that is, awards and other forms of incentives that can encourage academic investigators to change their current status of potential science-based entrepreneurs into either active founders of start-up ventures emerging from their research activity, or employees who perform an entrepreneurial function ("sub-entrepreneur") inside existing firms.

- *Relationship promoters* – that is, persons or *ad hoc* organisations that facilitate the communication between academia and business by reducing the barriers between research and the business communities.

- *Knowledge transfer funds* that support different forms of knowledge transfer.

- *"Start on Campus"* and *"Incubators of Entrepreneurial Ideas"* – that is, pilot actions for the promotion of university-based start-ups and university-embedded incubators that host academic spin-off firms.

- *A code of governance* for universities that improves the knowledge transfer relevance of research undertakings.

Mobility

Geographical mobility between EU countries – in particular, making knowledge transfer successful between the Eastern European countries and Western Europe, has become crucial, and inter-sectoral mobility between academia and business is necessary to achieve the transfer of scientific tacit knowledge.

Cross-border knowledge transfer initiatives such as the "Mobility Strategy for the European Research Area" (ERA) – which has given rise to the European Network of Mobility Centres (ERA-MORE) and the European

Researcher's Mobility Portal (European RMP) – are measures that should allow CESE countries to set up their own national Mobility Centres and Researcher's Mobility Portals. Latvia has already achieved this by the creation of the Latvian Researcher's Mobility Centre (Latvian RMC) and the Latvian Researcher's Mobility Portal (Latvian RMP - www.eracareers.lv) as a part of the ERA-MORE network and its Internet portal (Kokorevics, 2005).

Knowledge Transfer Partnerships

If experience is any guide, CESE countries can formulate a good transfer policy by looking to learn the lessons of the Knowledge Transfer Partnerships, formerly known as the Teaching Company Scheme (TCS), in the United Kingdom. It is argued in the *Lambert Review* that:

> *[this mode of transfer] is one example of a successful scheme that has promoted knowledge transfer between universities and business. At the heart of each partnership [there is] a high-calibre graduate who is recruited to work in a business on a project that is central to its strategic development. (HMSO, 2003, p. 35)*

Knowledge Transfer Partnerships also entail the migration of scientists, researchers and engineers from academic research to the private sector. As to how the knowledge transfer actually occurs, setting up new entrepreneurial ventures by those individuals in collaboration with business persons, or becoming employees or guest employees in someone else's entrepreneurial business, are possible organisational models (Witt and Zellner, 2005).

CESE countries still strikingly fail in this respect. Their policy makers must do more to put partnerships at the heart of their knowledge transfer policy.

Incentives to entrepreneurial scientists

The role of government-sponsored programmes in encouraging professors to found companies based on their research appears to be growing in importance. The US experience shows that the availability of awards and direct grants to university researchers encourages applications from academics who would not otherwise be likely to directly commercialise their own technologies. These incentives also serve to urge those researchers who do not actually have a firm for working with entrepreneurs to see common business opportunities in new scientific knowledge (Wessner, 2005; Lupke, 2005).

Incentives must also serve the purpose of facilitating professional career options inside the small business for academic scientists and researchers, so as they can contribute to creating a cognitive absorptive capacity in mid-size and smaller local enterprises.

Thus, CESE policy makers should anticipate actions that favour incentives whereby entrepreneurial scientists can compete in "market contests" for entrepreneurial business conceptions.

Relationship promoters

Relationship promoters, be they professionals imbued with talent for communication or *ad hoc* organisations, can bring both academic and business parties together. Their challenge consists of defining a common knowledge context by revealing the real needs of the migrating scientists as well as their entrepreneurial counterparts.

Relationship promoters would have to be given the power to organise a "gathering place" where knowledge could be shared, imparted and disseminated, by means of their skills as facilitators. From this standpoint, relationship promoters have to rely on policy-triggered regional and national initiatives through which they can draw on a sound pattern of university and private sector involvement and commitment.

Knowledge transfer funds

A knowledge-based funding policy in CESE countries should be developed by which more stress would be laid on the creation of knowledge transfer funds available to competitively awarded collaborative projects between academia and business.

A special fund should be set up for the specific purpose of improving the performance of the university transfer offices. It should channel resources, on the one hand, into the knowledge transfer training of academics and university administrators involved in the delivery mechanism and, on the other hand, into the recruitment process of people with substantial industry experience and proved skills in negotiation and deal-making.

"Start on Campus" and "Incubators of Entrepreneurial Ideas"

CESE universities should develop models that permit university-based new business ventures to start and remain on the university campus, while receiving support during their initial start-up phase.

A point of interest to both CESE policy makers and universities is the Baden-Württemberg state government's "Start-up Initiative", which has put the "Start on Campus" model project into action (Box 13.4).

Box 13.4. Baden-Württemberg state government's "Start-up Initiative"

The aim of the "Start on Campus" project is:

- To create a positive entrepreneurial spirit at the university.

- To select the business starters to be supported.

- To offer and arrange the consulting and training of business starters.

- To arrange access to resources and experts.

- To establish a network of entrepreneurs, researchers and support organisations.

- To develop pilot action for the promotion of university-based start-ups that can in turn be the base for further support schemes.

Source: Diegelmann, 2005.

In light of evidence that the spontaneous phenomenon of new venture creation does not appear adequate to configure a dense fabric of knowledge-based spin-offs ensuing from universities in the CESE countries, a second approach to be adopted is the establishment of incubators of entrepreneurial ideas.

In some respects, a situation not unlike those countries may be found in the Mezzogiorno in Southern Italy. In the case of the University of Sannio in Benevento (Campania region), an "incubator of entrepreneurial ideas" was established to sustain the growth of entrepreneurial ideas and thereby increase incrementally the number of academic spin-offs (Corti and Bianca, 2004).

A code of governance for universities

In transition countries, nascent entrepreneurs are negatively affected by a higher uncertainty and ambiguity of the external regulatory environment. Universities are part of that environment, and broad calls to "reform" them must aim to improve the relevance of research for knowledge transfer. In this respect, the CESE university sector should develop a code of governance adept at:

- Modifying the institutional culture and career incentives for researchers.

- Encouraging researchers to bring their research to the market.

- Identifying the market signals between employers and students.

- Stimulating industry interaction through contract research and mobility of students and researchers.

- Designing, implementing and communicating a policy that clearly establishes the ownership of intellectual property in research collaborations.

What lies inside the policy makers' scope is the introduction of a range of reforms that have much to do with:

- Greater autonomy for universities.

- A risk-based approach to the regulation of universities.

- New legislation that makes knowledge transfer an explicit mission of universities.

- The removal of obstacles to co-operation between universities and industry (for example, the Slovak Republic has taken steps aimed at smoothing the path between the country's science base and the business community).

Conclusion

The economic potential that SMEs in the CESE countries can harness through developing collaboration with universities is worthy of consideration. By this measure, there is a need in the CESE region to increase the flow of knowledge between higher education institutions and firms.

The fragile environment of countries in transition calls for action to take place in order to consolidate university-industry links. University and industry working hand-in-hand is a result of targeted and controlled governmental strategy that supports university departments undertaking work that industry values. Interested universities and firms all over the country must implement this strategy.

This chapter has described knowledge transfer modes and policy instruments that are required to initiate and sustain effectively concerted and persistent interactions between the intellectual resources of universities and the SME sector. In particular, because human interaction is the most effective form of knowledge transfer, the discussion has placed importance on university staff skilled in knowledge transfer and staff transfer between universities and firms, as a gateway for businesses wanting to access expertise and facilities available at the university.

To secure a better future for knowledge flow between universities and firms, knowledge transfer needs trustful and outward-looking knowledge brokers with excellent interpersonal skills, commercial awareness and contractual experience. Trust is a critical component of the business formula for those who build the necessary bridges in a field so subtle and ambiguous as that of transferring know-how, know-what, know-why, know-whom and know-when.

For the foreseeable future, knowledge transfer advancements would not be imperilled; arrangements for knowledge transfer are likely to be made within a frame of reference that fits with the enterprising role of knowledge intermediaries organised in trust-promoting groups. These groups could play a greater role in building sustainable relationships between the academic community and the business sector, with an emphasis on SMEs.

Bibliography

Amidon, D., P. Formica and E. Mercier-Laurent (2005), *Knowledge Economics: Emerging Principles, Practices and Policies*, Vol. 1, Tartu University Press, Tartu.

Andre van Stel, A., M. Carree and R. Thurik (2005), "The effect of entrepreneurial activity on national economic growth", *Discussion Papers on Entrepreneurship, Growth and Public Policy*, Max Planck Institute for Research into Economic Systems, Group for Entrepreneurship, Growth and Public Policy, Jena.

Corti, E. and M. Bianca (2004), "The Incubator of Entrepreneurial Ideas for Knowledge-based Spin-offs: The case of the Regional Centres of Competences in Campania region", revised version of the paper presented at the International Entrepreneurship School "Entrepreneurship in Europe: Best Practices and Regional Development", Paris, 27 June - 2 July 2003.

Diegelmann, C. (2005), "Start on Campus - Support for University-based Start-ups", in P. Formica and J. Stabulnieks, *Knowledge Based Entrepreneurship*, EffeElle Editori, Cento, Ferrara.

European Commission (2004), *Helping to Create an Entrepreneurial Culture: A guide on good practices in promoting entrepreneurial attitude and skills through education*, Directorate-General for Enterprise, Brussels.

Formica, P. (2004), *Strengthening the Knowledge Economy. Essays on Knowledge Policy and International Entrepreneurship*, EffeElle Editori, Cento, Ferrara.

Formica, P. and U. Varblane (2005), "Report About the Current Developments in the Teaching of Entrepreneurship in the European Transition Economies", paper presented at the OECD, LEED Programme International Conference on Local Development and Governance in Central, East And South-East Europe, OECD LEED Trento Center for Local Development, Trento, 23-24 June.

Garavelli, A. C., M. Gorgoglione and V. Albino (n.d.), *Strategies for Knowledge Transfer: Transmission and Acquisition*, Mimeo, Politecnico di Bari.

Harvie, C. and B. C. Lee (2003), *Public Policy and SME Development*, Economics Working Paper Series, WP 03-18, University of Wollongong.

HMSO (2003), *Lambert Review of Business-University Collaboration: Final Report*, HMSO, London

Karnitis. E. (2005), "A Small Country's Innovative Economy: Latvia's Case", in P. Formica and J. Stabulnieks (eds.), *Knowledge Based Entrepreneurship*, EffeElle Editori, Cento, Ferrara.

Kokorevics, A. (2005), "Researchers Mobility within the European Research Area – New Facilities for Innovations and RTD. Mobility Support and Promoting", in P. Formica and J. Stabulnieks (eds.), *Knowledge Based Entrepreneurship*, EffeElle Editori, Cento, Ferrara.

Leonard, D. A., (1997), "Mining Knowledge Assets for Innovation", *Knowledge Management*, Vol. 1, No.1, August-September.

Lupke, D. (2005), "Financing Entrepreneurship in the United States", in P. Formica and J. Stabulnieks (eds.), *Knowledge Based Entrepreneurship*, EffeElle Editori, Cento, Ferrara.

OECD (2002), *Benchmarking Industry-Science Relationships*, Directorate for Science, Technology and Industry, OECD, Paris.

OECD/Government of Canada (2003), *The Opportunity and Challenge of Diversity: A Role for Social Capital? Synthesis Report*, paper presented at the International Conference, Montreal, Québec, 23-25 November.

Powell, J., M. Harloe and M. Goldsmith (2000), "Achieving Cultural Change: Embedding Academic Enterprise", paper presented to the IMHE Conference *Beyond the Entrepreneurial University? Global Challenges and Institutional Responses*, OECD, Paris, 11-13 September.

Strandburg, K. J. (2005), "Curiosity-Driven Research and University Technology Transfer", paper presented at the Colloquium on Entrepreneurship Education and Technology Transfer, Tucson, Arizona, 13 January.

Wessner, C. W. (2005), "The US Small Business Innovation Research Program: A Model for Europe?", in P. Formica and J. Stabulnieks (eds.), *Knowledge Based Entrepreneurship*, EffeElle Editori, Cento, Ferrara.

Witt, U. and C. Zellner (2005), "Knowledge-based Entrepreneurship: The Organizational Side of Technology Commercialization", *Discussion Papers on Economics and Evolution*, Max Planck Institute of Economics, Evolutionary Economics Group, Jena.

Chapter 14

Entrepreneurship and Higher Education: Future Policy Directions

by
Jonathan Potter
LEED Programme, Organisation for Economic Co-operation and Development (OECD)

This chapter sets out some key conclusions and recommendations on fostering entrepreneurship for governments, development agencies and Higher Education Institutions (HEIs). The introduction draws out some major messages. Discussion then turns to the case for broadening HEI missions to incorporate entrepreneurship promotion and the rationale and role for policy intervention. The next section highlights the main approaches that leading HEIs are taking to promote entrepreneurship and the challenges in developing these approaches. Finally, a number of detailed recommendations are made.

Introduction

Following the discussions in earlier chapters, a number of major messages can be offered to those involved in developing Higher Education Institutions (HEI) engagement with entrepreneurship. These messages are highlighted below:

- *HEIs play an important role in fostering entrepreneurship.*

  Universities and other HEIs foster entrepreneurship through generating and diffusing innovations and supplying entrepreneurial workforces to business. Furthermore, the importance of this role is growing as we shift to a globalising knowledge economy. In this new environment, success in meeting economic and social challenges is strongly associated with the capacities of firms to generate and exploit new products, services and operating methods, and HEIs play an important supporting function.

- *HEIs should expand their activities to foster entrepreneurship.*

  Because of the traditions from which existing HEI activities have emerged, universities as a body are not engaging as strongly in entrepreneurship teaching and research commercialisation activities as they should. There is much untapped potential both to stimulate public benefits and to generate new sources of revenue for HEIs from these activities. In adapting to their changing environments, universities and other HEIs should therefore develop strategies to expand their entrepreneurship engagement and public authorities should support them in these efforts.

- *Certain countries and establishments are leading the way.*

  Entrepreneurship education and knowledge transfer activities have developed faster in leading establishments, concentrated in the USA, Canada and European OECD countries. These establishments offer a relatively large number and variety of entrepreneurship engagement activities and are demonstrating greater innovation in their teaching and commercialisation methods. They offer potential models for other countries and establishments seeking to expand their own activities.

- *There is strong scope for learning about good practices from other establishments.*

  There is a wide variety of entrepreneurship teaching and knowledge transfer approaches and as the field matures there should be a movement towards the most effective strategies. This requires assessments and learning from the experiences of others. As well as learning from the leaders, such as the most advanced establishments in the USA, it is also useful to exchange good practice with HEIs located in similar regions, with similar objectives and closer contexts in terms of the approaches required.

- *Entrepreneurship can be facilitated through teaching.*

It is sometimes argued that entrepreneurship cannot be taught because entrepreneurial behaviour is rooted in the innate character of the entrepreneur and because entrepreneurial success owes much to chance. But while it may not be possible or desirable to turn all students into entrepreneurs, there is a widespread view that entrepreneurship can be better facilitated. Thus through appropriate entrepreneurship teaching budding entrepreneurial behaviours can be encouraged and potential entrepreneurs assisted to avoid predictable pitfalls.

- *Entrepreneurship is best taught through interactive and experiential methods.*

Entrepreneurship teaching is best undertaken not through classroom lectures on their own, as has been the case in many early entrepreneurship courses, but through a series of more interactive, reality-based and experiential approaches. Such approaches may include virtual or real business creations, business plan competitions, strategy games and discussions with entrepreneurs. These methods are better placed than classroom lectures to support the development of key entrepreneurial behaviours such as creativity, innovation, teamwork, understanding of the external environment, networking and so on.

- *Entrepreneurship teaching should be offered across a wide range of university disciplines.*

Entrepreneurs can come from a variety of disciplines and entrepreneurship teaching should therefore be available across those subjects and not confined to its existing core in science and business. New interdisciplinary programmes should be developed or specialist programmes offered in subjects with sufficient demand. Indeed, rather than offering pure entrepreneurship degrees it is usually better to integrate entrepreneurship teaching within the teaching of traditional subjects.

- *The mix of knowledge transfer mechanisms employed by HEIs may not be optimal.*

Past practice has tended to favour knowledge transfer through technology licensing to established firms, reflecting relatively easy administration, early returns and low risks for the HEI. But in some cases the creation of a portfolio of spin-off companies, in which the university has equity and/or licensing stakes, may provide greater returns. In other cases techniques such as research contracting and consultancy may be more effective. Indeed, the optimal mix of knowledge transfer mechanisms is likely to vary according to the nature of the university concerned. What is important is for each HEI to assess the alternatives and pursue an appropriate strategy rather than simply reflect past practices or the practices of other institutions.

- *Innovation may be encouraged through collective learning networks.*

Innovation regularly comes about through exchange of ideas among linked actors, rather than solely within individual actors working in isolation. Various types of networks support this collective learning. However, given the externalities involved, public initiatives may be required to support the development of networks incorporating HEIs and firms. In doing so, the tacit nature of much knowledge transfer should be recognised and frequent and informal inter-personal interactions encouraged alongside more formal network programmes, for example through shared spaces and facilities and through linking key representatives of innovating firms into broader campus activities.

- *SME innovation absorption capacities should be increased.*

An important barrier to knowledge transfers from HEIs to industry is a lack of motivation and capacity on the part of SMEs to collaborate, despite the benefits that can often be demonstrated. Measures are therefore needed to complement knowledge transfer initiatives targeted at HEIs with measures to increase the innovation absorption capacity of SMEs, for example using skills development or innovation purchasing initiatives. It may prove most effective to focus these efforts on a small target group of dynamic and 'extroverted' SMEs that are most likely to engage and innovate in collaboration with HEIs.

- *The outcomes of university entrepreneurship engagement are likely to vary with local context.*

Although a wide range of HEIs can engage with entrepreneurship, the outcomes of such efforts are likely to vary with the nature of the HEI and the local economy in which it is embedded. The entrepreneurship experiences of some high profile universities and their regions are commonly used as inspiration for other areas, such as Boston, California and Ontario in North America, or Cambridge, Grenoble, Copenhagen and Vienna in Europe. However, the same results cannot be expected from places with weaker universities and local innovation systems. This suggests that the degree of spending and the methods of entrepreneurship engagement used should be adapted to the nature of the establishment concerned. Larger, forefront programmes may be justified in those places with the greatest potential. However, increased efforts to stimulate entrepreneurship from HEIs are justified even in less promising environments.

- *HEI incentive structures need to be revised.*

The regulatory and institutional environments that govern HEI behaviour were largely created for a previous era in which the focus was on basic research and academic teaching. These institutional and governance structures now need to be adapted to enable universities and university agents to build new forms of engagement with entrepreneurship. For example, there are often inappropriate constraints the involvement of university staff in entrepreneurship teaching, working in spin-off companies or collaborating with new and small firms and to the participation of entrepreneurs in entrepreneurship teaching programmes. HEI missions must be rethought in the light of the public importance of promoting entrepreneurship and innovation and some shift effected to an expanded agenda in which contributions to entrepreneurship and innovation are more highly valued.

- *HEI entrepreneurship engagement should be focused on promoting new and growing enterprises.*

Entrepreneurship can be seen as a process of innovating for firm creation and growth rather than as a simple question of operating existing SMEs. It is this function that gives entrepreneurship its principal economic and social value. The emphasis of entrepreneurship teaching should therefore be on promoting the skills to grow businesses and exploit new opportunities, targeting those motivated to follow such careers. Similarly, knowledge transfer efforts should focus on firms ready to make significant innovations and grow.

- *Evaluation of HEI entrepreneurship engagement will support learning and improvement.*

Evaluation of the impact of entrepreneurship teaching and knowledge transfers from HEIs is important to determine the right scale of effort and to identify the most effective forms of action. However, there is currently little evaluation evidence available in this field. For example, information on the impact of entrepreneurship teaching on firm start up or survival rates and the impact of HEI knowledge transfers on SME productivity and competitiveness would help better target public resources in given contexts. This requires greater evaluation than has taken place to date. In particular, there is a need for more control or comparison group studies on the impact of entrepreneurship education.

- *Initiatives to increase HEI entrepreneurship engagement should be integrated within wider entrepreneurship strategies.*

A range of initiatives can be taken by HEIs and their public partners in the areas of entrepreneurship teaching and knowledge transfer to enterprises. However, these initiatives are likely to be more successful when they are linked to existing entrepreneurship and innovation programmes offered by national, regional and local governments, development agencies, chambers of commerce and so on. In this way, those targeted by university entrepreneurship teaching and knowledge transfer support can also benefit from related services. It is therefore important to link together HEI initiatives with the range of other initiatives and actors concerned and to promote collaborations among the education, government and business sectors. Moreover, the success of university entrepreneurship initiatives will depend not just on the quality of these initiatives but also on the vitality of the broader national, regional and local entrepreneurial and innovative environment in which universities operate. This suggests a need to integrate university entrepreneurship engagement within clear and comprehensive strategies to improve entrepreneurial and innovative environments at national, regional and local levels.

HEI missions and public policy

There are at least three major developments behind the drive to rethink HEI missions and increase their role in fostering entrepreneurship that provides the logic for this book:

1. *The increasing importance of knowledge in economic growth.* As globalisation increases the pace of technological and market change and the competitive pressures faced by firms, opportunities for profits and wage growth are increasingly tied to the ability of firms to differentiate their products and services and develop more efficient production methods. In other words, firms are increasingly seeking to compete through the exploitation of knowledge through the vectors of entrepreneurship and innovation, implying greater benefits from working with HEIs than was the case in the past. Governments too are seeking to harness the potential of HEIs to contribute to entrepreneurship and innovation by generating and diffusing knowledge and building entrepreneurial human capital.

2. *New forms of innovation.* Until recently, innovation was commonly seen as a linear process, leading from basic research by universities to exploitation in established firms. Whilst this may still be true in certain sectors, successful innovation now tends to be seen as involving interactions among many actors – customers, suppliers, basic researchers, applied researchers, investors and others – summed up in the notion of collective learning. HEIs are now seen as a key player in these interactions.

3. *Increasing HEI competition for resources.* Although governments have ambitious objectives for higher education, they often find it difficult to expand the relevant budgets. HEIs are therefore increasingly looking to new sources of revenue for their expansion. Engagement with industry is one way of securing new revenue, for example from research contracts and commercialisation of research results. Engagement with business can also bring other benefits to HEIs, such as ideas for teaching and research, shared equipment and facilities, and increased attractiveness to entrepreneurially-minded students, teachers and researchers.

There is therefore a clear call from governments, HEIs and business to promote greater HEI engagement with entrepreneurship. This requires a re-interpretation of HEI missions by their key stakeholders to explicitly recognise their role in generating entrepreneurial skills and transferring knowledge to business. It must also be backed up with appropriate governance frameworks and institutional incentives that encourage these activities.

It is nonetheless pertinent to ask two questions concerning such a shift in mission: What is the rationale for public sector intervention to support entrepreneurship engagement by HEIs? What should be the public sector role?

The rationale for intervention appears clear. There are strong social benefits from entrepreneurship promotion by HEIs, linked to entrepreneurship's contribution to raising employment, productivity and economic growth, but because of important market and institutional failures in the field, public intervention is required to fully realise these benefits.

Clearly, there are strong public good and externality issues involved in university knowledge transfer and entrepreneurship education activities. They have public benefits, but because it is difficult for universities to appropriate their full value, the activities will be under-produced without public support. This of course is the fundamental logic for having largely publicly-funded higher education systems. It might be countered that some of the value from their entrepreneurship activities can indeed be captured by universities. For example, students pay fees for education and would probably be willing to pay for entrepreneurship education. However, the students may not capture the full social value from the increased entrepreneurship that results from their education and may not be sure of its value to them. Similarly, whilst firms are unlikely to pay for basic research, they may pay for applied research that they can appropriate and commercialise. Here again, however, the commercial benefits may not be clear to the firms at the outset and may not easily be appropriated by a single actor whilst there are also potential co-ordination failures and missing markets in applied research and knowledge transfer. All this implies the need for public support to HEI entrepreneurship activities.

Thus it is really the appropriate scale and form of relationships between HEIs and entrepreneurship that is in question. This can be framed as an issue of institutional failure. The university sector receives public subsidy for education and research in order to produce social benefits. However, the importance of entrepreneurship in public policy agendas is relatively new, and this may explain why institutional incentives have not yet emerged to properly support it in the university sector. Thus, the historical development of the incentives faced by universities may have led them to produce too little entrepreneurship for their current environment. The problem is that current institutional incentives faced by universities, university departments and university staff members appear to be too strongly focused on basic research and academic teaching and not sufficiently rewarding of entrepreneurship education and research commercialisation.

There seems to be potential then to achieve greater returns from public investment in higher education by adjusting institutional and governance arrangements and providing targeted public financial support to steer HIEs more strongly towards these activities. With relatively little diversion of effort, it would appear that the addition of entrepreneurship courses to university curriculums could encourage more graduates to consider entrepreneurship as a career option and improve the quality of their entrepreneurial ventures and translate a greater proportion of the knowledge produced in universities into economic value through commercialisation activities.

Helpful policy intervention can be envisaged in a number of areas:

- Using existing and new public funding streams to fine-tune HEI activities and stimulate greater entrepreneurship teaching and research collaboration with enterprises.

- Fostering new partnerships among government policy makers, entrepreneurs and educational leaders to develop joint entrepreneurship activities.

- Encouraging adaptation in HEI governance systems to facilitate entrepreneurship activities, such as in the regulations that govern access to funding and the criteria for the employment and promotion of university staff.

- Working on the demand side to influence the motivations and capacities of people and firms to absorb the entrepreneurial knowledge and skills offered by HEIs and to increase their information on these opportunities.

- Supporting the evaluation of what works and where in HIE entrepreneurship engagement, together with benchmarking and dissemination of best practices.

- Creating supportive national, regional and local entrepreneurial environments that will increase the results from HEI entrepreneurship engagement.

Forms of HEI entrepreneurship engagement

HEI entrepreneurship education aims to help those students with the motivation to start and grow a business to develop and improve the skills they will need. HEI knowledge transfer activities aim to increase entrepreneurship and innovation by commercialising the results of HEI research activities and knowledge from other sources.

Leading universities and colleges have developed a range of new and innovative approaches in these areas. A variety of hands-on teaching methods for entrepreneurship education have been adopted, greater support is being provided for commercialising the results of university research and there is a growing body of initiatives to support knowledge transfer to new and small firms.

The challenge now is for these practices to be extended to other institutions and faculties and for the experimentation and adaptation to continue. Inspiration can be drawn from the range of experiences presented in the previous chapters of this publication. Some of the most interesting developments and future challenges are summarised in the paragraphs below, focusing firstly on entrepreneurship teaching and then on knowledge transfers to enterprises.

Teaching entrepreneurship

Entrepreneurship teaching in HEIs has expanded in recent years, with an increasing number of institutions offering entrepreneurship courses and a greater number of students attending them both in North America and Europe. There has also been innovation in the teaching methods used, which increasingly emphasise experiential activities, the use of cases, the development of business strategy and the use of interactive computer technologies.

There are nonetheless important geographical differences in the state of the field, with United States institutions clearly leading the way. Key strengths of the United States approach include: the greater number of courses offered and higher proportion of students participating in them; their focus on developing growth-oriented ventures rather than on small business management; an HEI rather than public policy spurred drive for entrepreneurship teaching; the use of more experiential rather than classroom based teaching methods; more inter-disciplinary entrepreneurship courses; a greater use of experienced entrepreneurs in the delivery of teaching programmes; and greater assistance to entrepreneurship teachers in developing their teaching methods.

European OECD Members, whilst starting later and building from a smaller core of institutions, are nonetheless quickly expanding their entrepreneurship teaching offer. Traditional classroom teaching still dominates, but the use of case studies, simulations, role models, and the emphasis on growth entrepreneurship and inter-disciplinary approaches is increasing. Ironically, many Central and Eastern European countries are lagging behind both North America and the leading western European countries, despite the need to develop more entrepreneurial cultures in these countries following the end of their command economies. In these countries there is evidence of a relative dearth of university entrepreneurship courses, a lack of entrepreneurship teachers and continued dominance of passive and academic rather than action-oriented and practical approaches to entrepreneurship teaching, although there are some significant differences in the extent and quality of entrepreneurship teaching within the region.

Given these trends and geographical differences there is an opportunity to learn from experiences elsewhere. Table 14.1 summarises some of the main approaches being used and key associated challenges with the aim of providing inspiration for further programme development by interested HEIs.

Table 14.1. Types of entrepreneurship teaching approaches

Type of approach	Main activities	Challenges
Classroom lectures	Lectures on themes such as market analysis, venture creation, new product development, project management, financing, strategy development etc.	Classroom lectures need to be combined with more experiential approaches to learning. Theory needs to be combined with practice. Lectures must be made relevant to real-world entrepreneurship problems.
Business plans	Preparing business plans individually or in teams. Competitions and prizes for the best business plans.	Business plans must be made realistic. Ways are required to test business plans against market conditions and potential shocks. Teaching must also look at turning business plan ideas into real practice.
Case studies	Presentations and discussions of real company/entrepreneur experiences of business creation, growth, adaptation and failure.	Significant resources are required to develop case studies. Case studies must focus on problems potential entrepreneurs will actually face.
Entrepreneurs as guest speakers	Entrepreneurs invited to present their experiences in lectures and discussions, in the classroom or in their enterprise.	HEIs must find ways of attracting entrepreneurs to teaching programmes. They must also support entrepreneurs in their teaching practice, notably in drawing out the learning from their experiences.
Student business start-ups	Students start real or virtual businesses individually or in teams.	Funds will be required to create start-ups and to develop virtual firm technologies. Rules must be established for sharing rewards from successful starts.
Business games	Computer-simulated or other business games.	The requirements for developing or purchasing the technology should not be underestimated. Efforts are needed to integrate games with other teaching. Teachers need training to provide a framework for learning from the games.
Student entrepreneur clubs and networks	Student societies and networks to discuss entrepreneurship issues, create entrepreneurial teams, obtain mutual support and increase confidence.	Nurturing is required to make networks successful. Activities must be found to animate the networks. Networks should be expanded to include experienced entrepreneurs, investors, consultants etc.
Placements with small firms	Short-term assignments with small firms to assist with business development projects such as market or technology development.	Firms must be found to provide good quality placements. University staff must support the student during the placement.

Type of approach	Main activities	Challenges
Feasibility studies	Exploring the feasibility of business ideas with environmental scans, market potential investigations, competitor analysis etc.	It can be difficult to assess how well feasibility studies have been undertaken compared with real conditions on the ground.
Communication training	Presentation techniques, inter-personal communication.	Communication skills need to be developed under pressured and real-world conditions.
Consulting for SMEs	Student participation in consulting projects for new and small firms with the support of university staff.	It is necessary to find suitable companies and consulting opportunities. Although academics will often be expected to lead, ways must be found of involving students in the projects.
Support for graduate student start-ups following the course	Seed money, mentoring, incubation, consultancy etc.	Sufficient funds must be generated for the support. Decisions must be made about the right amount and duration of support. Where possible links should be made with existing support providers outside of the HEI.
University-wide entrepreneurship education	Spreading entrepreneurship teaching out to faculties beyond the business school.	The right point must be found in a trade-off between the benefits of proximity and tailoring to subject specificities through separate courses for each department and the benefits of economies of scale and greater experience through centralised and inter-disciplinary courses.
Specialist entrepreneurship degrees	Undergraduate or post-graduate degrees majoring in entrepreneurship.	It can be difficult to obtain academic rigour from purely entrepreneurship degrees. It can also be difficult to attract students to these degrees. Practical entrepreneurship outcomes are not guaranteed.
Distance education programmes	Use of electronic media including web-based programmes, interactive DVDs and electronic discussion groups.	Student learning rhythm must be maintained and student isolation avoided.
External partnerships	Creation of entrepreneurship centres with financial support from business and public agencies. Advisory boards with external experts.	It is necessary to maintain academic rigour and HEI independence whilst adapting to the concerns of other stakeholders.
Courses for entrepreneurship teachers	Courses for prospective teachers of entrepreneurship to understand the entrepreneur's environment and behaviour and to develop their teaching approaches.	Ways are required to develop insights on the world of the entrepreneur for teachers who have no entrepreneurship experience and to develop teaching abilities in existing or former entrepreneurs.

Transferring knowledge to enterprises

There has also been a significant expansion in HEI knowledge transfer activities in recent years together with an increasing sophistication in the techniques used, driven by an increasing emphasis on generating commercialisation revenues from university research. HEIs are increasingly monitoring their intellectual property, seeking to license it through technology transfer offices and brokers, filing patents when publishing scientific research, taking stakes in university spin-off companies, hosting university spin-offs and other companies on science parks and business incubators, seeking research contracts with enterprises and facilitating the movement of researchers in and out of industry. Within these developments a key trend has been a move away from essentially passive licensing of technologies to established firms towards greater encouragement of spin-offs, involving universities in combinations of licensing agreements and equity stakes with new enterprises. The greatest efforts in these areas tend to be found in a key group of United States research universities, but advanced knowledge transfer activities are quickly spreading to other places.

Table 14.2 sets out some of the main approaches being used in HEI knowledge transfers to enterprises and some associated challenges that HEIs and policy makers need to consider when seeking to apply these approaches.

Table 14.2. Types of knowledge transfer approaches

Type of approach	Main activities	Challenges
Licensing	Selling of licenses by university agents to use university-owned patents, copyrights and other intellectual property.	Alternative commercialisation options should also be considered that may provide greater revenues and economic development benefits. Other routes are required for intellectual property that cannot be legally protected. Other strategies will be needed where there is important tacit knowledge attached to an innovation. Incentives for commercialisation are likely to be greater for inventor than institutional ownership of intellectual property, potentially requiring changes in regulations.
Spin-offs	Creation of new firms based on knowledge acquired in the university, by university staff, students or external investors.	Numbers of spin-offs are generally low and concentrated in a few establishments, suggesting limits to the scope for spin-off programmes. Taking stakes in spin-off enterprises is more risky than licensing. A choice may have to be

Type of approach	Main activities	Challenges
		made between targeting resources on a few potential high-growth spin-offs and providing smaller scale support to a larger number. Successful spin-off activity requires building entrepreneurial skills in university staff and graduates.
Technology transfer offices	Offices that manage the process of selling university patents and other intellectual property, usually through licenses.	Offices need to be well connected to and respected by academics. Competencies and reward systems need to be set up so that a range of commercialisation routes are considered. Connections should be established beyond the traditional core of established large firm customers. Offices are likely to be justified only in universities with a large pool of exploitable intellectual property to manage.
Technology brokers	People and agencies to facilitate relationships among academics, entrepreneurs and support institutions that will help identify commercialisation opportunities and create exploitation partnerships.	Brokers need to audit and monitor intellectual property within the HEI and build relationships going beyond the obvious departments and individuals. Brokers need professional profiles with credibility for both academics and business.
Science parks	Real estate for firms located on or near a university or group of universities.	Channels for interaction with university staff, graduates and facilities must be built because co-location does not necessarily generate knowledge transfers. There may not be sufficient knowledge transfer opportunities to attract firms to science parks in smaller universities.
Incubators	Premises and support services such as consultancy for new firms created by university staff and graduates, with close access to the university.	Because spin-off numbers can be very low and variable it is important not to invest too heavily in physical incubators that may not be fully taken up. To keep focused on the objective of providing start-up support, it is important to develop a policy for moving firms to commercial premises as soon as they are ready.
Support for graduate entrepreneurship	Provision of mentoring, networking, financial support and other assistance to graduate students who wish to start firms.	Although many academics with exploitable knowledge may not wish to start an enterprise themselves the provision of suitable incentives and structures may encourage them to support start-ups by their students.

Type of approach	Main activities	Challenges
Research contracts and consultancy	Contractually defined interactions with clients that lead to tailored research results and strategic information for the client.	Recruitment and promotion structures based on publications performance and traditional university attitudes and cultures can discourage research contracting and consultancy. Better rewards for these activities may need to be introduced.
Collaborative research	Joint teams of academic and company researchers working on pre-competitive product development research.	Appropriate mechanisms must be created to share the intellectual property resulting from the collaboration. Cultural barriers may need to be overcome to joint working, potentially through co-location of the teams.
External training	Short courses for company employees in fields such as technology and business strategy development.	Demand needs to be built amongst a group of local small firms. Courses must be held at times appropriate to the firms.
Mobility programmes for research staff	Programmes or contractual arrangements that help university staff to spend time working in enterprises and company employees to work in universities.	Tenure-based employment policies, rigid employment practices and pressures to publish can make mobility between university and industry difficult.
Student placements in enterprises	Research and innovation projects undertaken in firms as part of the university research or degree programmes of students.	Policy measures may be required to increase the innovation absorption capacity of SMEs so that they demand and benefit from placements.
Technology centres	Centres set up within universities to assist staff to assess their commercialisation opportunities and support them in commercialisation, e.g. with advice and consultancy.	Centres need professional and credible staff to obtain buy-in from academics and the funding to provide useful services. University cultures need to shift to develop entrepreneurially-motivated carriers of technology.
Technology networks	Formal networks linking university staff or graduates to potential collaborators and exploitation partners.	Networks must be focused on specific technologies and actions. HEIs must monitor and build relationships with their alumni. It may be more productive to network with more distant rather than local firms. Tacit knowledge exchange must be facilitated by more informal interactions. Traditionally independent university cultures need to change.
Venture capital funds	Funds to invest in spin-off firms from individual universities or groups of universities.	Smaller universities may not generate the deal flow required for successful venture capital funds of their own.

Type of approach	Main activities	Challenges
Cluster initiatives	Building of mass and linkages in geographically concentrated sector clusters facilitating knowledge transfers and other externalities.	Cluster initiatives will not be appropriate in regions or sectors without critical mass. Where critical mass exists or can be built common sector strategies and collaborative activities such as joint research and training should be encouraged, including the participation of HEIs.

Policy recommendations

This final section draws out some more detailed policy recommendations for HEIs, national, regional and local governments and development agencies. The recommendations cover entrepreneurship education, knowledge transfers and institutions and governance arrangements.

Entrepreneurship education

Scale up

- Increase the number of courses in entrepreneurship and the number of students participating in them, particularly in lagging countries and institutions.

- Extend teaching across the HEI to address a wider range of potential entrepreneurs, moving beyond the traditional nucleus of entrepreneurship courses in university business schools. Offer courses to potential entrepreneurs in creative industries, science and technology and other fields and to both postgraduates and undergraduates.

- Integrate entrepreneurship teaching with subject-specific degree content in order to draw on the business ideas and expertise that emerge from the subject interests of students (medicine, biology, creative industries etc).

- Consider using inter-disciplinary entrepreneurship programmes to reach a wider range of students and obtain cross-fertilisation benefits from the mixing of students from different disciplines in the same courses and project teams, whilst retaining economies of scale.

- Expand the pool of entrepreneurship teachers. Provide training, encouragement and support for staff embarking on entrepreneurship teaching activities. Facilitating teaching activities by existing and former entrepreneurs by relaxing regulations constraining their involvement and training entrepreneurs in teaching techniques.

Focus on growth-oriented entrepreneurship

- Shift from traditional entrepreneurship teaching focused on business management to courses aimed at stimulating growth-oriented entrepreneurship. Focus courses on key growth challenges, including finance and internationalisation.

- Teach the skills that will be required for enterprise growth including opportunity identification, risk-taking, strategy making, leadership, negotiation, networking, building strategic alliances and intellectual property protection.

Introduce interactive and experiential teaching methods

- Encourage learning-by-doing in contrast to more traditional forms of academic learning.

- Increase the use of Internet and computer technologies.

- Introduce cross-functional problem-solving approaches that replicate the bundle of activities and functions that need to be applied in entrepreneurship situations, rather than breaking up teaching into separate business functions as in traditional management courses.

- Involve entrepreneurs in the design and teaching of entrepreneurship courses.

- Expose students to entrepreneur role models, for example by using entrepreneurs as mentors, speakers and interview subjects.

- Provide students with opportunities for working in existing SMEs and adding value to these firms through placements and consulting projects.

- Expand the use of case study teaching. Provide resources to develop cases tailored to the environment that students will face. Provide training to support teachers to use this approach.

Link into wider networks

- Tap into the resources of alumni networks to help fund and support entrepreneurship programmes, for example by providing teachers and links to companies for placements, mentors and so on. Monitor and build relationships with alumni to this end.

- Facilitate access to common materials and sharing of good practice by favouring networking among institutions and teachers and providing support for the inter-institution mobility of entrepreneurship teachers.

Knowledge transfers

Scale up

- Increase knowledge transfer activities from HEIs to enterprise. Build new channels and invest more strongly in existing channels.

- Create technology transfer offices, technology brokers and/or technology centres to help identify and commercialise knowledge. They should examine the range of available commercialisation channels and not over-concentrate on licensing.

- Develop incubators to promote and nurture university spin-offs. They should be open to both student spin-offs and researcher spin-offs.

- Develop science parks to promote knowledge transfer between HEIs and existing firms.

- Provide entrepreneurship training, mentoring and advice to staff and students wishing to create spin-offs.

- Venture capital and seed funds should be developed only where there is sufficient deal flow.

Adjust the mix of knowledge transfer approaches used

- Consider the costs and benefits of all the alternative forms of knowledge transfer and favour the use of more than one channel. Licensing tends to be the most common knowledge transfer mechanism, however less fashionable forms of knowledge transfer, such as consultancy, labour mobility and so on, may provide greater economic development benefits and returns to HEIs.

- Promote university spin-off enterprises. Although spin-offs represent only a small proportion of all start-ups they have strong innovation performance and can be used to exploit intellectual property that cannot easily be licensed. They can offer greater returns to HEIs than licenses, although risks are higher.

- Select a knowledge transfer strategy that suits the nature of the HEI concerned. In smaller and less science-based HEIs, encourage the development of non-traditional knowledge transfer mechanisms including provision of external training, student placements and graduate entrepreneurship. Put less emphasis in these establishments in major programmes such as venture capital funds, spin-off programmes, science parks and incubators and technology transfer offices with potentially low levels of demand.

- Invest for the long term. Commercialisation activities are seen as a source of new revenue by universities subject to funding pressures, but with this may come a desire to realise revenues as soon as possible. The revenues from knowledge transfer are instead likely to come over the long term, requiring patient investment from HEIs and economic development agencies.

- Do not over-invest in incubator facilities. Because spin-off numbers tend to be low and variable it is important not to invest too heavily in physical incubators that may not be fully taken up. Proper feasibility work is needed first to establish whether projected demand merits the physical space. Limits to the tenure of firms on subsidised space should also be established so that viable firms can move on to commercial premises or pay commercial rates, freeing up space or resources for new entrants.

Build networks and interactions

- In order to contribute to and gain from collective learning processes, HEIs need to adapt their behaviours to insert themselves in formal and informal networks of firms, research organisations, investors and other players, rather than seeking to work alone.

- New and small firms should be an important part of HEI networks since they have a potentially strong role in exploiting university research. The emphasis on connecting with these types of firms should be increased.

- Work is needed to strengthen SME demand for knowledge transfer. Information should be provided to SMEs on sources of knowledge in HEIs and their value and assistance given in making connections between SMEs and HEIs. Measures may also be taken to increase the innovation absorption capacity of SMEs, for example by supporting the use of consultants, placements of university students and staff and participation in collaborative research projects.

- Create informal networking spaces to stimulate the frequent, repeated and boundary-crossing linkages between HEIs and enterprises that favour tacit knowledge transfer, rather than seeking to channel all contacts through formal programmes and processes. Such spaces may include science parks and incubators, joint seminars and social networks.

- HEIs should monitor and build relationships with their alumni and incorporate them as important players in support networks for entrepreneurship activities. In particular, universities should monitor the companies their graduates and staff create and involve company founders in entrepreneurship programmes.

- Incubator and science park initiatives should focus more strongly on creating linkages between firms and host universities in order to facilitate continued knowledge transfer to and from spin-offs. For example, tenants should be given access to university facilities such as libraries, laboratories and canteens, research collaborations and seminars, HEI consultants and student recruits, and HEI training for their employees. Facilities should not be focused on provision of the physical space alone.

- Networking initiatives should facilitate both local and global linkages. Policy should not necessarily favour local linkages. Stronger universities with national and international roles may benefit more from linkages with more distant firms. Similarly, firms in weaker regions may wish to link to stronger universities rather than with their local HEI.

- Technology brokers can facilitate connections across boundaries. They may identify create relationship, identify potential areas of co-operation and broker agreements to work together. Brokers need experience in both industry and research and skills in identifying commercialisation opportunities and building collaborations to realise them. Brokers may usefully be placed within in semi-public or non-profit network organisations with public funding support but agendas should be driven by their members.

- Mobility of labour between universities and industries should be encouraged as a means of promoting knowledge transfer. This may involve firm researchers working in universities, university researchers working in firms or students undertaking placements in firms, potentially as part of supervised innovation and business development projects.

Institutions and governance

Show leadership

- HEI heads need to show leadership in promoting the development of entrepreneurship courses, knowledge exchanges with enterprise. They need to call for and instil a culture shift in their institutions to encourage greater awareness of the forms and value of entrepreneurship by staff and students.

- Public authorities should define and increase awareness of an explicit 'third mission' of HEIs to promote entrepreneurship and provide corresponding public funding to back up this mission.

Alter incentive structures

- Funding for entrepreneurship courses and knowledge transfer programmes should be given higher priority within HEI funding negotiations.

- Appropriate incentives should be introduced for teaching entrepreneurship.

- To encourage participation in entrepreneurship programmes, students should be enabled to obtain credit for degrees from participating in entrepreneurship courses and placements, consultancy and research for enterprises.

- Greater weight should be given to entrepreneurship teaching and knowledge transfer activities in hiring, promotion and tenure decisions. In particular, involvement in industrial partnerships and commercialisation of research should be taken into account in promotion criteria for university staff, in addition to scientific publications. Barriers to entrepreneurs joining teaching staff should be relaxed.

- Entrepreneurship teaching and knowledge transfer activities can also be promoted by the provision of public awards, grants and competitions.

- More flexible arrangements should be developed for mobility between universities and industry, including leaves of absence and sabbaticals with the right to return to the original university post during a given period.

- In countries with centralised HEI funding and regulation systems, reforms should be considered to provide greater autonomy to universities to promote entrepreneurial engagement in the ways most appropriate to their context.

Link with broader entrepreneurship support structures and strategies

- Support to entrepreneurship should not be confined to the HEI, but should make the most of wider support available for entrepreneurship more generally. A range of outside services may assist staff and students wishing to start businesses or transfer knowledge, including advice and consultancy, premises support, finance support and so on. Linkages should be created from HEI programmes to this support.

- HEI efforts to engage with entrepreneurship will be more successful in a context of a positive entrepreneurial culture and strong ties amongst innovation agents. Broader programmes are therefore needed to build favourable entrepreneurship environments. Cluster and local innovation system policies can be important in this respect.

- Whilst in smaller or less research-intensive HEIs there may not be enough demand to create individual initiatives such as a university venture fund, technology transfer office, science park or incubator, it may often be viable to create such initiatives by joining together with other HEIs, particularly where they are located close together.

Create variety in the HEI system

- HEIs should not all seek to introduce the same approach but should adopt distinct entrepreneurship engagement strategies reflecting their own contexts.

- HEI funding arrangements should also avoid the trap of seeking to impose uniform provision. An effective HEI system needs to provide for both basic and applied research and for teaching both academic knowledge and entrepreneurial skills and it may be beneficial for some establishments to build specialised roles. Variety in the system will also encourage experimentation and innovation in provision.

Evaluate the impacts of HEI entrepreneurship engagement

- It is important to evaluate the effectiveness of public interventions to promote entrepreneurship through HEIs to better understand the appropriate scale and form of interventions and support policy learning in this field.

- Evaluations should assess the outcomes of various forms of entrepreneurship teaching and knowledge transfer activities as well as monitor inputs, for example on start-up, growth and survival rates and on firm productivity and growth.

- Evaluation methodologies must be capable of addressing some difficult evaluation issues. For example, graduates may not start enterprises for some time after leaving university. Graduate behaviour therefore needs to be monitored over time. Similarly, the impacts of increased informal linkages are hard to track. Methods are required to pick up these impacts.

- In particular, there is a need to introduce more sophisticated evaluation techniques capable of establishing impacts relative to a counterfactual position, of the type recommended in the recent OECD Framework for the Evaluation of SME and Entrepreneurship Policies and Programmes.

OECD PUBLICATIONS, 2, rue André-Pascal, 75775 PARIS CEDEX 16
PRINTED IN FRANCE
(84 2008 03 1 P) ISBN-978-92-64-04409-8 – No. 56435 2008